D0781308

A Survivor's Guide to R

Los Angeles | London | New Delhi
Singapore | Washington DC

FOR INFORMATION:

SAGE Publications, Inc.
2455 Teller Road
Thousand Oaks, California 91320
E-mail: order@sagepub.com

SAGE Publications Ltd.
1 Oliver's Yard
55 City Road
London, EC1Y 1SP
United Kingdom

SAGE Publications India Pvt. Ltd.
B 1/I 1 Mohan Cooperative Industrial Area
Mathura Road, New Delhi 110 044
India

SAGE Publications Asia-Pacific Pte. Ltd.
3 Church Street
#10-04 Samsung Hub
Singapore 049483

Acquisitions Editor: Vicki Knight
Assistant Editor: Katie Guarino
Editorial Assistant: Yvonne McDuffee
Production Editors: Kelly DeRosa, Stephanie Palermini
Copy Editor: QuADS Prepress (P) Ltd.
Typesetter: C&M Digitals (P) Ltd.
Proofreader: Wendy Jo Dymond
Indexer: Kurt Taylor Gaubatz
Cover Designer: Anupama Krishnan
Marketing Manager: Nicole Elliott

Copyright © 2015 by SAGE Publications, Inc.

Printed in the United States of America

Library of Congress Cataloging-in-Publication Data

Gaubatz, Kurt Taylor, author.
A survivor's guide to R : an introduction for the uninitiated and the unnerved / Kurt Taylor Gaubatz.

pages cm
Includes bibliographical references and index.

ISBN 978-1-4833-4673-1 (pbk. : acid-free paper)
ISBN 978-1-4833-4688-5 (web PDF)

1. Statistics—Data processing. 2. R (Computer program language)   I. Title.

QA276.45.R3G38 2015
005.26'2—dc23   2013045399

This book is printed on acid-free paper.

14 15 16 17 18 10 9 8 7 6 5 4 3 2 1

BRIEF CONTENTS

Detailed Contents

LIST OF TABLES

LIST OF FIGURES

ABOUT THE AUTHOR

Kurt Taylor Gaubatz is an associate professor in the Department of Political Science and Geography and in the Graduate Program in International Studies at Old Dominion University (ODU). He teaches a range of courses in international relations, international law, and research methods. Before coming to ODU in 2000, he was the Visiting John G. Winant Lecturer in American Foreign Policy at Oxford University (Nuffield College) and was on the political science and international relations faculty at Stanford University. He has served as the Susan Louise Dyer Peace Fellow in the National Fellows program at the Hoover Institution and was a Pew Faculty Fellow in International Affairs with the Kennedy School of Government at Harvard University. He did his undergraduate work in economics at the University of California, Berkeley. He holds master's degrees in international law from the Fletcher School of Law and Diplomacy and in theology from Princeton Theological Seminary. He earned his PhD in political science from Stanford University. He is the author of *Elections and War* (Stanford University Press, 1999) as well as a number of prominent articles mostly focused on international law and on the relationship between domestic politics and international relations. More information can be found at www .sagepub.com/gaubatz.

PREFACE

few years ago, I was at a conference chatting with one of the most distinguished and technologically capable political scientists I know. This is someone who came to political science with an undergraduate degree in math from Caltech and is the author of a major text on game theory as well as a number of prominent articles using sophisticated statistical analysis. He recounted the experience of sitting in on an advanced seminar on Bayesian statistics. The statistics were pretty straightforward, he said. The real challenge was coming to grips with R for the first time. When I mentioned that I intended to switch to R for one of my introductory statistics classes, he shuddered.

This story might come as a revelation to many in the community of advanced R users, who view R syntax as essentially second nature. Having worked with R on a daily basis for many years, they have little trouble making it sit, lie down, and roll over. They are somewhat surprised when others think that the only trick R knows is playing dead.

I did start using R for teaching, and I, and every one of the students in those classes, survived. At its core, this book is a step-by-step guide to how we did that. In fact, although R does have a steep learning curve—on first encounter, it is often intimidating and unnerving—it has proven to have a number of significant advantages for teaching and learning statistics.

R is powerful and inexpensive (free!). It is rapidly becoming the package of choice for advanced statistical analysis across a number of fields. Moreover, it has probably been assigned to you, so you just have to buckle down and learn it. The purpose of this book is to help you survive and even to thrive in that process. The approach I take is to focus primarily on the challenges of using R to manage, manipulate, and visualize your data, rather than the usual approach of jumping right into conducting statistical analysis with R.

I take this alternative approach for three reasons. In the first place, data management is the foundation for all statistical analysis. Getting your data into the right form for analysis is a critical skill. Yet data management issues are rarely taught in statistics classes, where appropriate and well-groomed data sets appear to float down directly from heaven. This book provides the opportunity to get a handle on some of those essential background skills. Second, once you have learned the basic structure and rules of R in this context, you will find it much easier to follow up with learning the statistical procedures, which you will most likely do in the context of a statistics class and text. Finally, separating the statistics from the teaching of R allows the book to serve both as a tutorial and as a reference in which you can quickly find the commands and procedures that otherwise are mixed in and hidden among the statistical content of traditional texts.

Moreover, while this book starts with the very basics of installing R and getting it to run simple procedures, it ultimately covers R at a significantly greater depth than you are likely to encounter in a statistics class. This book is designed to carry you beyond the classroom, giving you the opportunity to gain and maintain the kind of facility with R that can make it a functional real-world skill in your analytical toolbox.

Because this book separates the mechanics of working with R from the teaching of statistics, it will be helpful in a wide range of contexts. It is designed to help tackle data problems that arise across a wide range of fields and at different levels of statistical sophistication. Whether you are tackling R in an introductory statistics class or an advanced graduate seminar or are just transitioning to R from another statistics program, you will find this a helpful guide along the way.

For users at the introductory level, Chapter 2 and Appendix B run through most of the procedures that might be encountered in an introductory statistics class. Chapter 3 offers a straightforward approach to understanding object types and their critical role in R. Chapter 5 goes over the basics for summarizing and reviewing data. Chapter 12 is an introduction to R's broad variety of built-in plots.

For those beginning to work on collecting and managing their own data, Chapter 4 goes over the process of getting data into R from a wide range of sources. Chapters 6 and 7 cover sorting, selecting, and transforming data. Chapter 10 teaches the critical skills for merging and aggregating data. Chapter 11 confronts the real-world challenge of dealing with missing data.

For more advanced users, the end of Chapter 7 gets into R programming techniques, including the powerful use of dynamic coding to incorporate variable- and data-driven elements into your R scripts. Chapter 8 deals with the particular issues of textual data and includes a tutorial on the use of regular expressions in R. Chapter 9 does the same thing for the sometimes surprisingly treacherous world of date and time data.

For users at all levels, some of the biggest rewards will come in Chapters 12 to 15, in which I provide a thorough but accessible guide to R's powerful graphics facility. At any level of statistical sophistication, the ability to produce and customize high-quality data visualizations will be a critical 21st-century skill.

There is a book website (http://www.sagepub.com/gaubatz), where I have posted a file with all the R code used in the book. You can go there to see exactly how the code works and to cut and paste for your own projects. You will also find there the example data sets, color versions of many of the plots, and a gallery of additional graphics examples, with the attendant R scripts.

It is likely that you have not chosen to learn R simply for the fun of it. For one reason or another, you have arrived in this somewhat scary place and now have to deal with it. My purpose is to make that as painless as possible. You can survive this. And, at the end of the day, you might just find that it is a little bit fun as well.

ACKNOWLEDGMENTS

I need to start by acknowledging my debt for the extraordinary wealth of materials that the R community has created. The developers of R have done an exceptional job creating a cutting-edge software package that has, in turn, engendered a community of users who are constantly moving R forward. I am occasionally critical in this book of the difficulties new users face in mastering the basics of R and of the difficulties that R experts sometimes have in appreciating the frustrations of new users. But this should not be viewed in any way as diminishing the enormous respect I have for the extraordinary services the R community provides. I have learned much from poring over the archives of the R Help list. It never ceases to amaze me how often it is the giants of the R development team that take time out to answer even the simplest questions from users.

I also need to thank the students in my statistics seminars who gamely served as guinea pigs for this project. Their trail breaking will help spare some of this pain for others who follow in their footsteps. If you find this book of help, you share with me a particularly significant debt of gratitude to several members of the first cohort to use R with me: Melodee Baines, Bill Eliason, Huhe Narisong, Andrew Townsend, and Christopher White. Cody Zimmerman and Scott Duryea also helped move the project forward with their excellent service as research assistants.

Vicki Knight and the editorial team at SAGE Publications have been terrific. Their enthusiasm helped move this project through its final stages. Shamila Swamy (with her team at QuADS Prepress), in particular, applied a careful eye and deft touch to the copyediting. The SAGE process included a very helpful review from a wide range of fields, and I am indebted to Jim Albert, Bowling Green State University; Woody Carter, University of Chicago; Ole J. Forsberg, Oklahoma State University; David Han, University of Texas at San Antonio; Yulan Liang, University of Maryland, Baltimore; A. Dean Monroe, Angelo State University; Charlotte Tate, San Francisco State University; and Toshiyuki Yuasa, University of Houston for their careful comments and insightful suggestions for making this a better and more useful book.

I would also like to thank Kevin Sweeney, who got me started on this whole thing by giving me the opportunity to be involved in some projects that required taking the R plunge.

Finally, of course, there is Kathy, whose constant love and support have been critical even for a sometimes opaque and mysterious project on statistical computing.

CHAPTER 1

GETTING STARTED

Across a broad range of fields, the accelerating revolution in computing power and digitization has created a world of vastly more data. A functional knowledge of statistics is an increasingly essential tool for those working in the many arenas that put a premium on the use of information. Alas, as if learning statistics wasn't stressful enough for many people, this data revolution increasingly requires learning some computer techniques for managing data, conducting statistical analysis, and producing effective visualizations for describing data and communicating statistical results.

This is where R, an open-source package for doing statistical computing, enters the picture. Its four most salient characteristics are as follows:

1. It's free (you can't beat that).

2. It is gaining rapidly in popularity.

3. It is an open platform, which has led to the development of thousands of add-on packages that facilitate more advanced data management and statistical operations.

4. It is more than a little intimidating to learn.

R facilitates all kinds of both traditional and really cutting-edge statistical analysis. It is a terrific tool for doing professional graphs and charts. However painful it may seem at first, using R for these tasks is a lot easier than doing them by hand, or through customized operations with traditional computer languages. Nonetheless, few would deny that R has a steep learning curve. Add that to the challenge of also learning statistics, and the unpleasant reality is that most of those who set out to learn R in the context of a statistics class face a series of late nights and the likelihood of some deeply frustrating experiences.

The purpose of this book is to lessen that pain. It does so by serving as a supplement to the more common textbooks that combine the teaching of statistics and R. It focuses instead on the essentials of using R and on helping you through the places where R is most likely to confound. In particular, this means a focus more on the challenges of managing and manipulating data than on the conduct of statistical analysis. In taking this approach, this book not only helps take some of the mystery and frustration out of learning R but also aspires to cover two significant gaps in the curriculum of many statistics classes.

◊   THINGS YOUR STATISTICS CLASS PROBABLY WON'T TEACH YOU

Once you've finished a statistics course or two, you will no doubt feel ready and anxious to take on the world with your newly acquired powers of quantitative analysis. One of the first things you will discover, however, is that in the real world, data rarely come to you in the form of nicely scrubbed-up files ready to be downloaded from a professor's website. Once you have a bit of statistics under your belt, running a simple regression or generating a chi-square statistic is relatively straightforward. The real challenge in many projects is finding appropriate data and maneuvering them into a useable form. Data often come from a variety of sources and are organized in ways that aren't necessarily optimal for your particular project. The skills necessary to pull together and prepare disparate data for analysis are rarely taught in statistics classes.

In fact, setting up and managing a data set are the essential foundation of all statistical analysis. Many analysts will lose more sleep over these untaught procedures than on the actual implementation of statistical procedures. As the authors of the official R guide for importing and exporting data point out, "Reading data into a statistical system for analysis and exporting the results to some other system for report writing can be frustrating tasks that can take far more time than the statistical analysis itself" (Ripley, Brian, & R Core Team, 2013). Students have largely had to acquire these skills on their own. This isn't such a stretch for statisticians with strong computer-programming backgrounds. But for those who come from other disciplines and have not had occasion to confront these kinds of problems, it can be a significant barrier to the effective use of statistical methods.

A second important area that often gets short shrift in traditional statistics courses is the creation of effective graphics. R is a powerful tool for data visualization. It goes far beyond the rather primitive and constrained graphics produced by a program like Microsoft Excel. For example, R is the tool used to produce many of the excellent data visualizations in the *New York Times*. This book devotes considerable space to working step-by-step through the procedures for basic default graphics, as well as showing you how to produce extensively customized R visualizations.

The Survivor's Guide distills the essential R skills into a logically structured and accessible instruction book. It covers a wide range of R issues, from the basics to quite advanced R programming and graphics customization. It is, however, consistently set at a level to provide clear guidance even for those who are new to the challenges of learning statistics and this form of computer programming.

WHY R?

R, sometimes affectionately referred to as "ARRGH!" by new users, has become a favored statistics program for a wide range of power users. These users possess an intimate understanding of the intricacies and idiosyncrasies of R, which may leave them somewhat deaf to the frustrations of the new user who has spent all night trying to open and apply a few simple transformations to a data set.

There are a number of other computer programs that have been developed to facilitate statistical analysis. It is likely that these other programs are powerful enough for your needs and are also widely used in the corporate and academic worlds. In significant contrast to R, most of them provide a graphical user interface, or GUI, that allows you to point and click your way through a wide range of statistical analysis, significantly flattening their learning curves. R experts are dismissive of this difference. The author of several prominent introductory computational statistics and R texts, Michael Crawley (2002, p. 11), dismisses the graphical user interface as a "waste of time" on the grounds that typing in commands is so much faster (5–10 times!). This, of course, assumes that you know the command and its parameters, type it correctly the first time, and don't require a bunch of esoteric options. If you have to type it three times and search through the help function twice to get it right, it's not really so quick.

Nonetheless, the R priesthood has a point. In addition to the great merit of being free, and the likelihood that you have been required to use it, the very fact that R is *not* point-and-click is really a very significant advantage. In a nutshell, this approach gives you more control over and encourages a more effective understanding of what the computer is doing, and also more easily creates a record of what has been done. This is exceedingly important for the learning process; beyond that, it is essential in a world that increasingly demands clear reproducibility of results.

Using R for your statistics and data management has the important advantage of providing a record of both your statistical analysis and any data manipulations and transformations. The advent of the Internet and the low price of computer storage have made the replication and sharing of data an important and widespread practice. Because R relies on a command line input—admittedly a source of frustration for new users who have become accustomed to the point-and-click world—it is straightforward to maintain a step-by-step record showing exactly how you moved from the source data to the final analytical results.

In addition to facilitating reproducibility, this record also helps in the learning process. It is much easier for you to retrace your steps to figure out what went wrong or what worked out correctly. Others helping you learn statistics can also more quickly see where your analysis might have gone awry.

For all these reasons, this is the path we now must take. My goal is to help you acquire functional R skills that will make it easier to get through a statistics class and also equip you for work in the real world beyond that. My approach is to organize this process around a systematic focus on learning R, rather than presenting R as a secondary issue within a textbook organized around the teaching of statistics. Nonetheless, our first step down this road is to think a little about the basic statistical context that is, after all, our motivation for learning R.

STATISTICAL MODELING

All statistics are a form of modeling the world. We use statistical models to simplify complex real-world phenomena by identifying and characterizing the relationships between the elements that are identified by theory as the most critical. The essential logic of statistical analysis is to ask how likely it is that our collected data would look the way they do if our model, and the theory from which it is derived, is an appropriate representation of the real world. If that is found to be too unlikely, then we have to reject the model, or its underlying theory.

The essential starting point for this effort is almost always the determination of an appropriate structure for the data. This particularly involves identifying the two fundamental dimensions of the data: the unit of observation and the variables.

The unit of observation is how we distinguish the comparisons that we are trying to make. If we are studying educational outcomes, the unit of observation might be schools, classes, or individual students. But for any given analysis, it will be only one of those things.[1] A data set is built by collecting information about individual observations. That can't be done if the unit of observation hasn't been carefully specified.

The second dimension is the identification of the relevant variables. For each observation, what are the concepts in which you are interested? How do they vary? How is that variation measured? These are theoretical and operational questions that will be answered according to the precepts of your particular discipline and the kinds of problems that interest you. The important thing for our purpose is understanding the body of knowledge in terms of discrete-variable concepts: How big is it? How long did it take? Is it male or female? Is it a graduate student or an undergraduate? How old is it? What voltage was applied? What was the manufacturing lot?

When we combine these two dimensions, variables and units of observation, we get a data set made up of individual data points. If our data are in a spreadsheet, as in Table 1.1, by convention we think of the observations as being the row dimension, while the variables are represented in the columns.

Table 1.1   A Simple Data Table

Observation	ID	V1	V2	V3	V4	V5
1						
2						
3						
4						

---

1. There are more complex hierarchical data structures, but they are still based on a minimum unit of observation. I'll cover hierarchical data in Chapters 4 and 7.

Each cell in the data set will be filled with some content representing the value of that variable for that unit of observation. These values will be either categorical or continuous. As the name implies, categorical variables apportion the observations into a fixed number of discrete categories. At the simplest level, categorical variables take on binary values: yes/no, on/off, democracy/nondemocracy, male/female, organic/inorganic. More complex categorical variables might include many discrete categories: grade in school, type of star, country of origin, brand, occupation, species. Categorical variables might be entered either as text ("Ford" "Chrysler" "Toyota" . . . "Ferrari") or as numbers (1 = "Ford" 2 = "Chrysler" 3 = "Toyota" . . . 78 = "Ferrari"). Continuous variables can be represented directly by numerical values: age, distance from the sun, number of legs, literacy rate, shots on goal.

Understanding the basic notion of observations and variables is critical for statistical analysis. For working with R, it is also critical to understand the character of the data. I will have much more to say about that in Chapter 3. For now, let's spend a little time on the basic principles of working with R.

A Few R Basics

The instructions for installing R are included in Appendix A. If you haven't done that yet, now would probably be a good time. Once R is installed, you will start it up by using either the R Console or an integrated development environment (IDE). I strongly recommend the latter and, in Appendix A, suggest at least starting out with RStudio (2013). If you have RStudio installed along with R, you just need to click on the RStudio icon to get R up and running.

Running R and Inputting Commands

For better or worse, R is a command-line processor. The "for worse" part is that there are no friendly drop-down menus or pick boxes to navigate with your mouse. You will need to learn a minimum set of commands and figure out where to get the other information when you need it. The "for better" part is that this makes it much more likely that you will produce clearly reproducible results. It does not guarantee that those results will be correct or that you will correctly interpret them. But for the learning process, it will be easier to reconstruct your work and figure out where things might have gone wrong.

R can be run entirely from its console screen, which is shown in Figure 1.1. R calls this a graphical user interface (GUI), but that is a rather pathetic misrepresentation. This is really just a window for entering your commands with a couple of shortcut buttons at the top. When the R Console needs something from you, it gives you the greater-than sign (>) to be sure you know your relative place in the R universe. After you type a command and press the Enter key, R consults its internals to determine whether to do what you have asked, request more input, or pop out some cryptic and unhelpful error message.

If the computer senses that you are new at R, it will most likely choose the error message. If you should be so fortunate that the problem is just an obvious typo, you can reenter previous commands by using the up-arrow key. R will take you back through the most recent commands, which can be edited using the arrow keys and the backspace/delete keys. When you've got it the way you want it, hit Enter to go back into the error message lottery.

As I have suggested, an alternative and superior way to interact with R is to use RStudio or one of the other available command editors. With RStudio, you write your commands in a dedicated editing window and then just push a button to send your commands from the editor to the R Console. My suspicion is that this makes it harder for the computer to sense your inexperience. In any case, this approach has the significant advantage of allowing you to easily maintain an R script file with all of the commands that have gone into your analysis. You can include thorough comments to

Figure 1.1   The R console

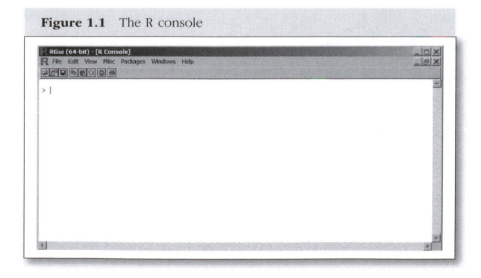

help you remember what you have done and why. Building up a library of these files will give you a head start on any project, for which many bits of code might be reused with only modest alterations.

In addition to providing a development environment for writing R code, RStudio also maintains a list of active objects (something I'll discuss a lot more in Chapter 3) and has a nice interface for R graphics and the R Help facility. It works basically the same way on Windows, Mac, and Linux computers. Figure 1.2 shows the RStudio interface. The top-left quadrant is the editor, where you will compose your R commands. On the bottom left is the R Console window. This is where the code gets executed and the output is produced. You send code from the editor to the console by highlighting it and hitting the Run button or the Ctrl-Enter key combination. You can send a single line at a time by just hitting Run when nothing is highlighted. RStudio will send whatever line the cursor is on. There may be occasions when you want to type commands directly into the console window, just to experiment, or to do something else that isn't saved as part of your R script in the editor window. Typing directly into the RStudio R Console window works just fine for that purpose. The top-right quadrant shows the R workspace, which holds the data and other objects you have created in the current R session. The bottom-right quadrant is a window for graphics output, but it also has tabs to manage your file directories, R packages, and the R Help facility.

Figure 1.2   The RStudio Interface

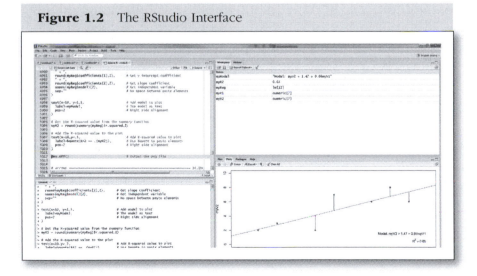

A whole file of R commands can also be run directly. In RStudio, you do this with the Source button on the top right of the editor window. To run an R script file from the R Console command line, use the command **`source()`**. If your command file is named **`myProgram.r`**, for example, then you would run it with the command **`source("myProgram.r")`**.[2]

Figure 1.3 shows what some R code might look like in the editor window of RStudio. The text following the hashtags (#) are comments. The actual commands are on lines 8, 10, and 12. These commands set values for a couple of variables (**myX** and **myX2**). **myX** is just the single value 7, while **myX2** is a set of values. In R-speak, **myX2** is a "vector." The instructions on line 12 tell R to find the mean of the values in **myX2**. (Don't worry, we'll talk details about how these commands work later on.)

Figure 1.3 An R Script in RStudio

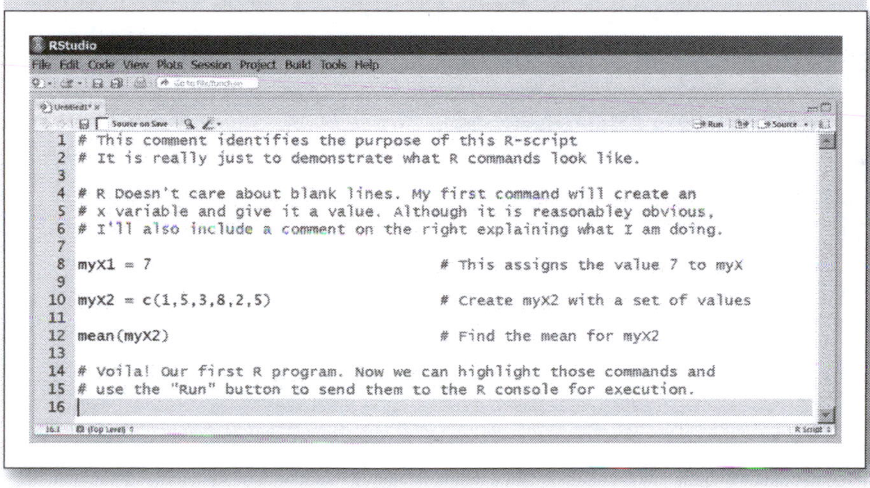
RStudio
File Edit Code View Plots Session Project Build Tools Help
Source on Save
Run
Source
1 # This comment identifies the purpose of this R-script
2 # It is really just to demonstrate what R commands look like.
3
4 # R Doesn't care about blank lines. My first command will create an
5 # x variable and give it a value. Although it is reasonabley obvious,
6 # I'll also include a comment on the right explaining what I am doing.
7
8 myX1 = 7 # This assigns the value 7 to myX
9
10 myX2 = c(1,5,3,8,2,5) # Create myX2 with a set of values
11
12 mean(myX2) # Find the mean for myX2
13
14 # Voila! Our first R program. Now we can highlight those commands and
15 # use the "Run" button to send them to the R console for execution.
16
R Script

To actually get R to pay attention to the instructions we have written in the editor window, we need to send them from the editor window to the R Console window in the lower-left quadrant. We do that by highlighting the three lines with the commands and hitting the Run button you can see in the upper right of Figure 1.3. (We could also send the comment lines to R, but it will ignore them, as well it should.) You can send a single line to the R Console by hitting the Run button with the cursor on the line you want to send. Rstudio will then step through the lines sequentially if you

2. You will need to be careful to be sure that you have set the location of your command file as the working directory. You can learn how to do this in Chapter 4.

keep pushing the Run button. If you highlight just part of a line, Rstudio will just send the highlighted piece when you hit the R button. Figure 1.4 shows the executed commands in the RStudio R Console window (the lower-left quadrant in RStudio).

You can see in Figure 1.4 that each of the commands has been entered into R following a ">" sign. The first two commands are just putting things into R's memory, telling it the values for **myX1** and **myX2**. The third command, **mean(myX2)**, tells R to get the mean of the values in **myX2**. The result of that operation, **4**, is indicated by the **[1]** at the left. Then, the next ">" sign indicates that R is ready for more commands.

Figure 1.4 Executed Commands in the RStudio R Console Window

```
Console ~/
> myX1 = 7                    # This assigns the value 7 to myX
> myX2 = c(1,5,3,8,2,5)       # Create myX2 with a set of values
> mean(myX2)                  # Find the mean for myX2
[1] 4
>
```

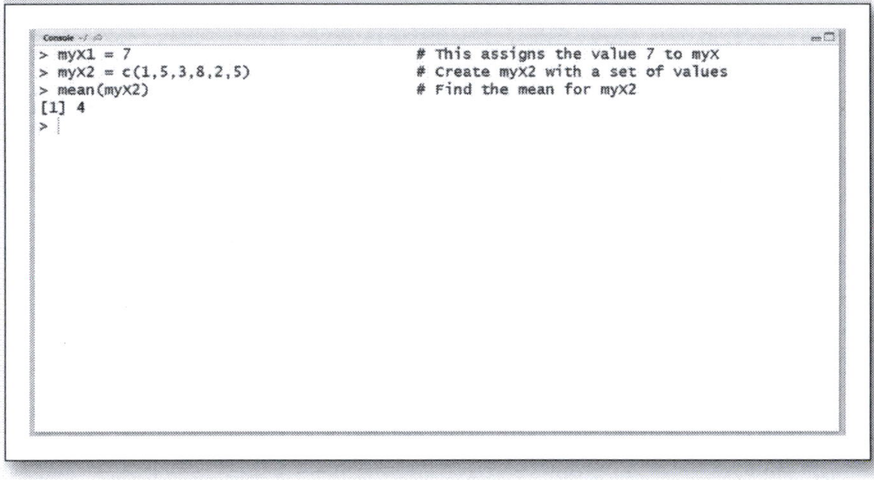

Whichever method you are using to input your R commands, it will be helpful to know that when your command goes longer than 128 characters—as it will if you are building complex models or assembling interesting plots with lots of esoteric options selected—you can put your command on multiple lines. If you are putting commands directly into the R Console, just hit the Enter key, and R will add a "+" to the beginning of the next line to indicate that the end of the command hasn't been seen yet. You can, in fact, hit the Enter key at almost any point in a command line and R will recognize that it is waiting for more.[3] I consistently take the approach of dividing a command over many lines. You will see that it allows for writing clearer

_____

3. A normal line is 80 characters in 12-point Courier, so this is a pretty good general rule for a breaking point.

code, with a single function per line and plenty of room for copious comments. You do have to be careful to remember the commas between function options that often come at the end of a line. Conversely, if you want to pack more commands onto a single line, you can do so by separating them with a semicolon. This I do not recommend.

If things are going really wrong—R seems hung up on some programming instructions—you can hit the Escape key to stop program execution. I'm pleased to report that this is not a problem you are likely to have, unless you get into programming loops, as discussed in Chapter 7.

Comments

I discuss some programming style issues more generally in Appendix D, but it is worth a little detour here to say a bit about comments. Comments are things in your written program that R ignores. Comments are indicated by the hash mark sign (#). Anything that goes between hash signs or that comes after a hash sign at the end of a line is skipped when R is reading your instructions. You can put whatever you want in the comments, and R, for all its vaunted powers, *will be unable to see it!* Comments are an important weapon in the battle for R mastery.

Traditional programming style manuals recommend a certain judiciousness toward comments (see, e.g., Kernighan & Plauger, 1974). For normal programming, it is considered bad form to include comments that simply explain what is obvious. I say forget about that. Normal programming is meant for normal programmers. If that's you, great! But for most of us, especially those first learning R, very little of what R is up to is obvious.

R makes it easy to maintain a record of what you are doing. New projects can build on the programming you developed for a previous project. Copious comments make it easier to reuse code. This is particularly true for those who only use R intermittently and thus need to relearn parts of it over and over again. In many disciplines, it is not uncommon to take a statistics class early in your educational program and then leave it aside until a thesis or research project a year or two later. Picking up your old R work will be much easier if you have kept detailed comments to remind you why you did things the way you did.

Command Conventions

As you enter the world of R coding, there are a few universal syntax principles that are critical to keep in mind.

First, you will notice that most R commands end with a set of parentheses. These are usually used for providing variables for the command to work on or for setting options. But even those commands that have no options and don't need any data input to work on will usually have the parentheses to tell R that they are commands. For example, there is nothing that can go in the parentheses of the **getwd()** command.

Here are some examples of commands at work. In each case, I provide a comment on the right side after the hash mark to explain what the command is supposed to do. The commands come after the greater-than sign. Where R has a response, it is provided after the number in brackets. In all of these examples, the number in brackets is **[1]**, because there is only one element in each response.

```
> myVar = c(1, 2, 4, NA, 7)          # Create a variable w/some data

> mean(myVar, na.rm = T)             # Mean of myVar w/o missing values
[1] 3.5

> length(myVar)                      # Num of observations in myVar
[1] 5

> ls()                               # List all objects
[1] "myVar"
```

This example shows the inputted R commands following the ">" signs and then the R output. On the right side of each line, I have included a brief comment indicating what the command is supposed to do.

R commands usually have a relatively simple form that assumes default values for a range of optional parameters. In this book, I usually try to start with that form, but I also discuss some of the more relevant options you may want to include. Once you start getting the hang of R, you can start looking up the complete command syntax to find the specialized options that may apply to unusual or particularly complex situations.

Command options, which are also called "arguments," can be included either by memorizing their order and then just separating them by commas (not usually a very good idea, especially when you are just learning) or by using the option names and an equal sign to set the option values. The first approach works well for functions with just a few intuitive options, while the second is clearly better for something like the **par()** command, which has (at last count) 72 different options. Using the option names allows the options to be set in any order and, especially when you are new to R, makes it easier to see what you have done. Throughout this book, I usually indicate a command option by connecting it directly to an equals sign: **length=**, **data=**, **x=**, **type=**, etc.

Here are some examples of the different approaches. Each of these commands does the same thing: generating a single random number from a normal distribution with a mean of 0 and a standard deviation of 1.

```
myRandNum = rnorm(1)              # A single random number from a
                                  #   normal dist assuming defaults
myRandNum = rnorm(1, 0, 1)        # The same thing showing defaults

myRandNum = rnorm(1,              # A random number from normal dist
   mean = 0,                      #   with mean 0
   sd = 1)                        #   and std dev 1

myRandNum = rnorm(n = 1,          # A random number from normal dist
   sd = 1,                        #   with std dev 1
   mean = 0)                      #   and mean 0
```

All four of these commands create a variable called myRandNum and give it a value from a random normal distribution with a mean of 0 and a standard deviation of 1.

Arguments (the things you pass to commands and functions in the parentheses) can be abbreviated down to their minimum uncommon starting letters. If, for example, one of the arguments tells the command what data to use with a **data=** statement, and there is no other option starting with *d*, the **data=** statement can be abbreviated to **d=**. You'll get the hang of some of these abbreviations right away. For others, you'll have to wait until you have memorized the entire corpus of R commands, functions, and objects to recognize how many letters of each you will need to type. In the following example, all of the commands do exactly the same thing.

```
xtabs(formula = ~x + y, data = MyData1)
xtabs(form = ~x + y, dat = MyData1)
xtabs(for = ~x + y, da = MyData1)
xtabs(f = ~x + y, d = MyData1)
```

It is essential to figure out early on in your R experience that R is case sensitive. **Variable1** is not the same as **variable1** or **VARIABLE1**. Most R commands and options are lowercase, but capital letters pop in here and there to distinguish words in multiword commands or for no readily apparent reason at all (**FUN=** being my favorite of these) (Table 1.2).

Table 1.2   Examples of R Capitalization

TRUE
%Y
%y
readClipboard
readLines
stringsAsFactors=FALSE
MARGIN=
NA
POSIXct
Sys.time()
as.Date()
x=
X=

Another important principle to learn is the use of quotation marks to distinguish text from object names. R objects—data frames, vectors, matrices—are not put within quotation marks. When the value that you want an R object to take is made up of textual characters, you need to enclose it in quotation marks. This is pretty easy to understand when you are assigning a value to a variable.

```
state = "Kansas"
studentName = "Michael"
crop = "wheat"
excuse = "The dog ate it"
```

It takes a bit more effort to see that this also applies to other arguments that pass to functions. For example, computer files or path names are strings of text characters that you want to pass to the program.

```
myData = read.csv("c:/data/proj7/mydata.csv")
setwd("c:/statsclass/homeworks")
```

It gets more complex still on those occasions when you may be uncertain about what is and isn't an object and what kind of object it is. In Chapter 3, I'll tour you around the world of R objects, and then in Chapter 8, I'll go into much more detail on dealing with characters and the use of quotation marks.

Parentheses ( ), Brackets [ ], and Braces { }

We have already seen the critical role of parentheses in demarcating functions. It is important to note that parentheses can still play their traditional role of grouping numeric operations together. **3 * (x + y)** is different from **3 * x + y**.[4]

Brackets, **[ ]**, are for indexing vectors and matrices. The fifth element of the vector **myVector** is notated **myVector[5]**. In Chapter 3, we'll also look at the use of double brackets, which are used with list objects to extract the things within a list element rather than just the element itself.

---

4. Mathematical operations have a hierarchy, so if there are no parentheses for guidance, R will do the multiplication first and then the addition. Using parentheses is a safe way to be sure of the order of operations.

Braces, { }, are for grouping sets of commands. You would use these commonly in **for()** loops, **if()** constructions, functions, or anywhere else where you need to package a set of commands together. It is traditional to put the closing brace on a line of its own to make these structures clear.

```
for(i in 1:10){
  x[i] = model1[i, 3] + 15
  y[i] = model1[i, 5] * 10
}

if(x == 3){
  x1 = 15
  x2 = 11
  x3 = 6
}
```

Comparison Operators

R works with the usual complement of symbols for making comparisons:

<   Less than

>   Greater than

<= Less than or equal to

>= Greater than or equal to

== Exactly equal to

!=   Not equal to

The two unusual symbols to note here are the not-equal comparator and the equality comparator. The not-equal sign is simply an exclamation point followed by an equals sign (**!=**). In the case of the equality test, R uses the double equals sign (**==**). This importantly distinguishes the comparison process from the assignment process, which uses only one equals sign (**=**). The assignment process, the single equals sign, tells R to make the object on the left side of the equation equal to the expression on the right side of the equation. The double equals sign (**==**) tells R to check whether what is on the left side of the double equals sign is the same thing as what is on the right side.

Despite its long provenance in the worlds of mathematics and computer science,[5] the equals sign is a relatively new innovation in R. Most serious R aficionados use the symbol combination **<-** as the assignment operator. The argument for this is both philosophical, that there is a distinction between assignment and comparison, and practical, that there is a little less chance of confusing the assignment operator (**=**) with the comparison operator (**==**). This is a very dangerous confusion because when you think you are comparing something and mistakenly use the single equals sign, you unwittingly change its value. Still, my own view is that this advantage is outweighed by the requirement to repeatedly type two symbols instead of one.[6] There is also the danger of confusing the dash in the **<-** assignment operator with a minus sign: **x<-7** has a different meaning from **x < -7**. Since R does recognize the equals sign for assigning values, its mistaken use in a comparison is still going to change the value, regardless of your choice of assignment symbol.

I grew up using the equals sign as an assignment operator, so I have continued that habit into my R work. Someday when I get really good at R, I may switch. You can do it whichever way you like (or, perhaps, whichever way the person grading your assignments likes).

It is also worth mentioning here that if you use **==** to compare two vectors, R will return a vector of **TRUE/FALSE** values for each vector element. To find out if two vectors are the same, use the **identical(vector1, vector2)** function.

SAVING YOUR WORK

As you work in an R session, you will build up a set of data and other objects. You can save these for future work by using the **save()** command. The arguments passed to this command are the names of the things you want to save and the file name. If you do not provide the full path

---

5. The invention of the equals sign is attributed to the Welsh mathematician Robert Recorde in 1557. Many computer scientists have bemoaned the general use of the equals sign as an assignment operator, but its use is widespread in most of the major languages.

6. RStudio uses the Alt– (Alt and minus sign) key combination to insert a "**<-**" combination, so that is a pretty quick alternative.

name, the file will be saved in the current working directory. The procedures for setting the working directory are outlined in Chapter 4.

```
save(x, y, dataset3, file = "my-rstuff.Rdata")
```

Note: Dashes aren't allowed in R names, but this is the name of a file, so it only needs to abide by the file-naming rules of the operating system.

You can then reload these objects with the load command.

```
load("my-rstuff.Rdata")
```

To save everything in your current workspace, use the **save.image()** command. Then, all you need to do is provide the file name, along with any path information if you want to save it somewhere other than the current working directory. Alternatively, in RStudio you can hit the little Save button in the workspace quadrant (it looks like a little blue floppy disk, if you remember what those used to look like). Saving your workspace can be an effective way of keeping together a variety of things that you are working with on a particular project. My own predilection on this is that it is often preferable to maintain things in their native format in order to keep everything clear and to set up your R workspace by rerunning a saved file of R commands.

Saving the workspace does not save your R script. Save your R script with the little blue floppy disk button in the top-left corner of the RStudio editor window. The workspace can then be re-created from the original data simply by rerunning the R script. Which approach is best will depend on the complexity of your situation and your personal preference. The bottom line is to be sure to save your work in some reusable form.

 R PACKAGES

The R program is built up from a set of packages. These are modular programs that contain sets of commands. A core set of packages is launched every time you start R. In addition, there are literally thousands of add-on packages you can install to do more specialized analysis or even to make some regular tasks a little easier. I discuss the installation and management of these add-on packages in Appendix A and list some of the most popular add-ons in Appendix C.

Beyond that, I do not spend much time on the add-on packages in this book. That is not to say that they are not an important part of the power of R. But the add-on packages tend to be something of a moving target. When you learn to work with core R, you will be able to transition relatively smoothly to the specialized packages as needed.

HELP WITH R HELP

R, you will be glad to learn, has an extensive help facility. Alas, in my experience, most new users tend to find R's official help pages inaccessible and cryptic. Do not despair. The challenge of the official R Help pages is that they do not really become very useful until you have sufficient familiarity with R to correctly and effectively interpret them. Once you get to that exalted state, you will find these pages much more meaningful and really quite indispensible.

RStudio and the RGui Console both give you direct access to the R Help pages. You can open the R Help server from the RGui interface by choosing the Help menu and then selecting "Html help." The same thing can be accomplished from RStudio by clicking on the Help home icon (the little house under the Help menu). If you want RStudio to open Help in a new browser window, click on the "Show in new window" icon to the right of the little Help house button. Alternatively, you can just use the command **help.start()**. All of these approaches will open the main R Help window, as shown in Figure 1.5.

Figure 1.5   The R Help Portal in RStudio

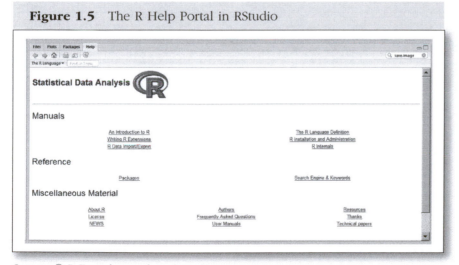

Source: © R Foundation, from http://www.r-project.org

The two most important help resources on that page are the Packages link and the Search Engine link. The Search Engine link will give you access to R Help searching, as shown in Figure 1.6. RStudio provides direct access to R Help searching in the top-right corner of the Help window, as shown in Figure 1.5.

All of R is built on packages, so the Packages menu is where the basic help pages reside, one for each R command or function. If you click on the Packages link from the main Help page, you will get a list of your installed R packages. Clicking on any package name will give you a clickable alphabetical list with a short description of every topic in the help file for that package. The most critical of these is the Base package, which contains the basic R commands. There are, at last count, 988 help topics in the Base package. It can be a little overwhelming, but browsing these can sometimes help you find what you're missing or even see other ways to do something. The other three foundational packages are the stats package, the graphics package, and the utils package.

A traditional approach to using Help for those who want to prove how tough they are is the **help(command)** facility in the R console. This approach makes the heroic assumption that you know the exact name of the command you need help with. Later on, this may be true. When you are starting out, it isn't so much. You can also use the shorthand help command just by placing a question mark before the name of the command.

Figure 1.6   The R Help Search Engine

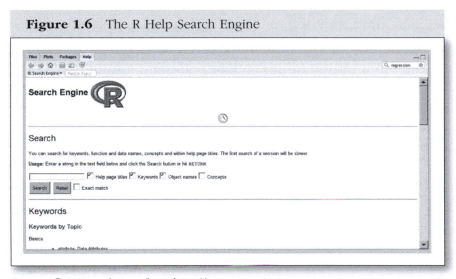

Source: © R Foundation, from http://www.r-project.org

To get help on the `getwd()` command, for example, just type `?getwd`. You can leave the parentheses off when you are calling for help on a function; that is, you can just use `?mean` instead of `?mean()`.

The object-oriented nature of R can cause some issues when looking for help on a relatively generic command like `plot()`. The `methods()` command will show all of the specialized versions of the command for different objects. You can then use these names to look up more specific help. For example, if you give the `plot()` command the name of a linear model, it will invoke the `plot.lm()` method. You can find out about that method by first typing in `methods(plot)`, which will give you a list of all the various plot methods. Looking down the list, you'll see a `plot.lm` method. Looking for help for that explicit method (`help(plot.lm)`) will give you the information you seek.

When you don't know the exact name of the command you need, you'll have to use the search facility. This is done from the R Console with the `help.search("searchterm")` function.

```
> help(getwd)
> ?getwd
> help(read)
No documentation for 'read' in specified packages and libraries:
you could try 'help.search("read")'
> help.search("read")
```

Note the difference between searching for an R object name, which does not require quotation marks, and searching for a text string, which does. Note also that when getting help with functions you do not need to include the parentheses (e.g., **getwd** *instead of* **getwd()***).*

The `apropos()` function finds all of the instances of the search term. You can use `apropos()` to help find the proper function or option names for which to get more specific help. This can be helpful when you know a piece of the command or want to know all of the different forms of a particular command. `apropos()` will give you a list of all of the commands containing the fragment you know. This is another way of getting all of the variants of a command, such as the **table** or **format** function families.

You can use regular expressions to make `apropos()` more powerful, but that is a separate and significant issue in itself. Whole books have been written about using regular expressions.[7] I will provide an introduction to regular expressions in Chapter 8.

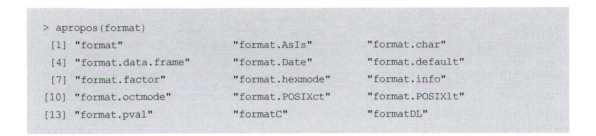

```
> apropos(format)
 [1] "format"              "format.AsIs"         "format.char"
 [4] "format.data.frame"   "format.Date"         "format.default"
 [7] "format.factor"       "format.hexmode"      "format.info"
[10] "format.octmode"      "format.POSIXct"      "format.POSIXlt"
[13] "format.pval"         "formatC"             "formatDL"
```

Sooner or later, you will find your way to an R Help page. As mentioned earlier, R Help is often a bit cryptic for novices. Once you have learned the basics and have a bit more experience under your R belt, you will start to find that it makes more sense. In the meantime, it is useful to understand a little about the structure of the Help page. The Help pages are almost always formatted the same way. Figures 1.7 and 1.8 are examples of R Help pages. Figure 1.7 is the help for the relatively simple standard

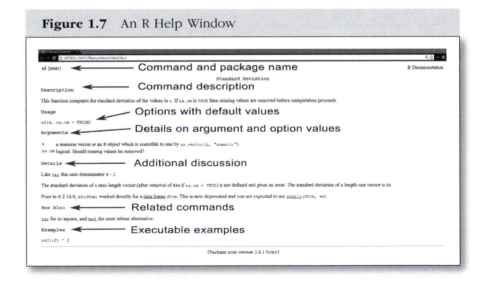

Figure 1.7 An R Help Window

---

7. See, for example, *Mastering Regular Expressions* (Friedl, 2006), or the more promisingly named *Beginning Regular Expressions* (Watt, 2005). If you are really pressed for time, you can get *Sam's Teach Yourself Regular Expressions in 10 Minutes* (Forta, 2004), although I'm a bit skeptical.

Figure 1.8 Another R Help Window

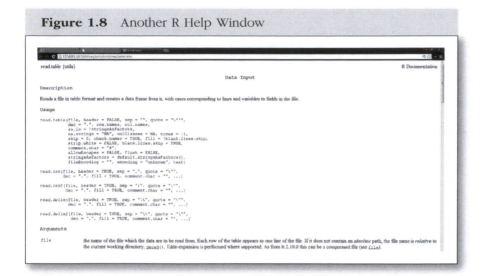

deviation command (**sd()**). It includes some annotations showing the basic Help page formatting. Figure 1.8 shows the first bit of the Help window for the more complex **read.table()** command.

You can use Cut and Paste to run specific examples from the Help page in the R Console window. Or if you want to see all the examples at work, use the **example()** command.

```
> example(mean)                        # Example from mean() help page

mean > x<-c(0:10, 50)

mean > xm<-mean(x)

mean > c(xm, mean(x, trim = 0.10))
 [1] 8.75 5.50
```

Though at first you may find the R Help challenging, it is important to struggle with it a bit. It is impossible for any one book to capture all of the intricacies and options of the many R commands across the various packages. At some point, you will need to turn to the R Help pages. When that time comes, you will want to have played around with them to be sure you have the hang of it.

Help With R Packages

The help material for packages can be directly accessed from the help portal (**help.start()**). You can also access the help content page for a specific package by using the command **help(package = PackageName)**. Some R packages, which are usually for more specialized statistical procedures, also provide various kinds of help materials and more detailed examples in what in R-speak are called "vignettes." To see a list of the available vignettes for the packages you have installed, use **vignette()**—with the parentheses empty. Then, to read a particular vignette, put its name in quotations in the **vignette("PackageName")** command. You can also use the **browseVignettes()** command to open a browser window with links to the available vignettes.

Error Messages

R Help is sometimes cryptic. R error messages take this to another level entirely. You will need to have a significant degree of R expertise before these things start to make sense to you. For most of your early days with R, the simple truth is that error messages will be a binary indicator: There is an error or there isn't. Here are some examples of R error messages that you may find less than helpful:

```
Error in "[<-"('*tmp*`, i, value = character(0)) :
      nothing to replace with

Error in stripchart(x1, ...) : invalid plotting method
```

One of the things that make R error messages difficult to interpret is that R functions are themselves built from sets of R commands. The error message returns the language within the function where the error occurs. Sometimes it is helpful to track the problem down by looking at the component language of the function. For many functions, you can do this by simply typing the function name without the parentheses—for example, **ifelse** to get the code for the **ifelse()** function

Another useful element in the error messages is that when you are working from a batch file or from a block of commands the error message will indicate the line on which the error occurs. After that, I'm afraid you are largely on your own. If the error message language is distinct enough, you can paste it in quotation marks into a web search and see if anyone else has had the same problem. Often they have, which brings us to a broader and exceedingly important source of help for all things R: the large and growing R community.

Help From the R Community

The R Help search facility is limited to searching the R Help pages and to looking for predefined key terms. You will, therefore, often need to move to a more general Internet search. There is a large R community online, and you can often find answers just by searching a few keywords to describe your issue. This sometimes increases your frustration because the R masters often see things as obvious that you may still be struggling with. The other unfortunate catch in looking things up online is that *R* is such a generic search term that it can sometimes be difficult to isolate R topics. I suppose we have to be grateful that they didn't name the program "a" or "XXX."

When you search for help, you will quickly discover the R-help mailing list, which is now a huge archive of questions and answers. Do a web search including the term *R-help*, and you'll often be able to find relevant threads from the R Help forums. Even more useful is the stackoverflow.com website. This is a site for programmers to ask and answer questions. It can tend toward the esoteric and advanced but allows easy searching and has a voting mechanism that helps the more useful answers float to the top. Just include "[r]" in the stackoverflow.com search box to isolate the R questions. There is also a Google group site that isolates R topics at rseek.org.

ORGANIZATION OF THIS BOOK

This book is structured around the central problems of learning R, the challenges of getting your data organized and ready for analysis, and the creation of R graphics. It spends relatively little time on statistical processes. You will find that material in other books and will learn it in statistics classes (I have provided a brief review of the most common and basic statistical procedures in Chapter 2 and in Appendix B). As I have argued, statistics is often the easy part. Once you get your data clearly organized around variables and observations, running a simple regression is a relatively quick affair. Moreover, learning the basics of R in the process of data management and visualization will give you the foundation from which it is much easier to learn R's statistical functions and make sense of the official R Help files and the numerous expert discussions of R procedures online.

Chapter 2 offers a quick example of an R session, working quickly through the kinds of problems that might be encountered in a beginning statistics course. This taste is organized around a simple set of functions operating mostly in their default mode on preset data. The primary purpose of the remainder of the book is to move beyond those limiting defaults and prepare for working with the complexities of real-world data.

R is an object-oriented language. In my experience, confusion about object types is one of the most common sources of frustration for new users. Chapter 3 builds the foundation we'll need to understand and work with R object types.

In our information-overloaded world, data can be found in many different places and in widely different forms. Chapter 4 covers the basics of getting data from a variety of sources into the R environment.

In Chapter 5, we look at approaches to summarizing and reviewing your data, to be sure that they are what they are supposed to be. I will also introduce here a few of R's very powerful graphic capabilities, because some quick plotting is a particularly good way of reviewing your data.

There is an appendix to Chapter 5, in which I offer some troubleshooting tips for the inevitable frustrations that will be arising by this time in your R journey.

Chapter 6 covers the techniques for sorting your data and selecting subsets of the data.

Chapter 7 looks at procedures for transforming your data, for systematically changing or rescaling variable values for any number of important analytic purposes. It also introduces R programming techniques for building your own functions and for doing repetitive analytic tasks.

Chapter 8 reviews some of the processes and idiosyncrasies involved in working with textual data and provides an introduction to the use of regular expressions.

Chapter 9 focuses on some of the unique problems of date and time data.

In Chapter 10, I suggest and demonstrate some approaches for merging data sets of either similar or quite disparate forms. Chapter 10 also reviews some of the procedures for aggregating data.

Chapter 11 looks at the problem of missing data. Different R procedures are more and less sensitive to missing data, so it is important to have a few different skills for managing data sets that may have various gaps.

The last four chapters, Chapters 12 to 15, provide an extensive discussion of R graphics. Chapter 12 demonstrates the use of some of the built-in plotting routines. Chapter 13 covers the foundations of customizing graphics output: setting the plot area, using different output devices, and the like.

Chapter 14 moves on to modifying textual elements, such as labels, legends, and axes. Chapter 15 covers both the ad hoc and the systematic placement or customization of shape elements on R graphics, such as points, lines, polygons, and images.

There are four appendices with additional material you may find of help. Appendix A discusses the installation of R and related programs. Appendix B summarizes the R procedures for doing basic statistics. Appendix C looks at some of the most prominent packages for enhancing R. Appendix D is a discussion of style practices for programming in R.

CHAPTER 2

A SAMPLE SESSION

So here's the thing: Before we can really get into the interesting stuff with R, we've got to spend a little time looking at object types. That is, I'm afraid, somewhat tedious stuff. It is, however, exceedingly important. Failure to pay attention to object types is the surest route to R despair. To make that medicine a little more palatable, we're going to start here with a brief walkthrough of basic R statistics. We'll go through a sample session of R that will include many of the procedures that would be required in an introductory statistics class.[1] We'll do this in as spare a manner as possible, using mostly R's defaults. The remainder of this book will get us started on the vast power of R to systematically manage, analyze, and visualize data. In that process, I hope we'll start to get a handle on the things we need to dramatically improve on the work we do in this initial session.

The data and code for this exercise are available at http://www .sagepub.com/gaubatz, so you can follow along. Do try this at home! If you haven't worked up the courage to install R yet, you should go get the instructions for that in Appendix A.

This exercise uses some country-level data about economic strength (measured as gross domestic product [GDP] and GDP per capita [GDPc]), military spending as a percentage of GDP (milSpend), female life expectancy (FemLife), education spending as a percentage of GDP (EdSpend), and press freedom, which is measured with two variables: PressStat, a variable measured on a 100 to 0 scale, where 0 is the most press freedom, and PressFree, a categorical variable indicated by F, PF, and NF, for Free,

---

1. These procedures are discussed in more depth in Appendix B.

Partly Free, and Not Free, respectively. The data come from The World Bank (2013),[2] except for the press freedom variables, which come from Freedom House (2013).

REVIEWING YOUR DATA

We'll look here at the relationships between female life expectancy, as a general indicator of social well-being and the status of women; national economic wealth; and the freedom of the press. We start by downloading the data, which are in a tab-delimited format, and reading them into an R data frame named **myDF**.

```
myDF = read.delim("http://www.sagepub.com/gaubatz/data/Chapter2Data.txt",

   header = TRUE,                    # Data has headers for var names
   colClasses = c("character",      # Set storage modes of variables
      "numeric", "numeric", "numeric", # This is just a convenience and
      "numeric", "factor", "numeric")) #   could be adjusted afterwards
```

We can quickly review the data along with some basic descriptive statistics using the **summary()** command.

```
> summary(myDF)                      # Summarize data set
  Country.name           GDPc            MilSpend          EdSpend
  Length:213        Min.   :   245   Min.   :0.100   Min.   : 5.5
  Class :character  1st Qu.:  1536   1st Qu.:1.100   1st Qu.:14.7
  Mode  :character  Median :  5330   Median :1.500   Median :20.9
                    Mean   : 14765   Mean   :1.944   Mean   :21.9
                    3rd Qu.: 14474   3rd Qu.:2.500   3rd Qu.:27.6
                    Max.   :163026   Max.   :8.400   Max.   :51.4
                    NA's   :26       NA's   :89      NA's   :108
```

---

2. The military spending data are originally from the Stockholm International Peace Research Institute (SIPRI; 2013) but were provided through The World Bank. More details on the variables and sources are available at http://www.sagepub.com/gaubatz.

```
      FemLife              PressFree          PressStat
Min.     :47.00              :18        Min.     :10.00
1st Qu.:65.75        F  :64            1st Qu.:25.50
Median :76.00        NF:59            Median :49.00
Mean     :72.22        PF:72            Mean     :47.52
3rd Qu.:80.00                           3rd Qu.:64.00
Max.     :87.00                           Max.     :97.00
NA's     :21                              NA's     :18
```

Right off the bat, we can learn a lot of important things. The **summary()** function gives us a list of the variables and shows their types. We can see the number of missing values for each variable, which range from 18 for PressFree to 108 for EdSpend. What we can't see here, irritatingly enough, are the standard deviations. That requires an additional step. We'll brute force it here, doing one variable at a time. In Chapter 7, we'll learn about the **apply()** family of functions, which will allow us to do it a little more elegantly in one fell swoop. Notice that R is willing to give us a standard deviation for the press freedom variable PressFree, even though it is a categorical variable. We'll talk at some length about this little anomaly in the next chapter.

```
> sd(myDF$GDPc, na.rm = T)              # Get standard deviations
[1] 23115.1

> sd(myDF$MilSpend, na.rm = T)          #    removing missing values
[1] 1.369662

> sd(myDF$EdSpend, na.rm = T)
[1] 9.51568

> sd(myDF$FemLife, na.rm = T)
[1] 10.56439

> sd(myDF$PressFree, na.rm = T)
[1] 0.9817179
```

The **sd()** *command requires removal of the missing values, which we do with the* **na.rm = TRUE** *option.*

DATA VISUALIZATION

We will probably want to visualize some of these relationships, which is easily done with the **plot()** function. By way of example, let's look at the relationship between the free press rating and the life expectancy of females (Figure 2.1).

```
plot(myDF$PressFree, myDF$FemLife)     # Plot: femlife by free press
```

Apart from the possible cluster of high press freedom, high female life expectancy states in the upper-left corner, it doesn't look like much.

Figure 2.1   Female Life Exepectancy and Press Freedom

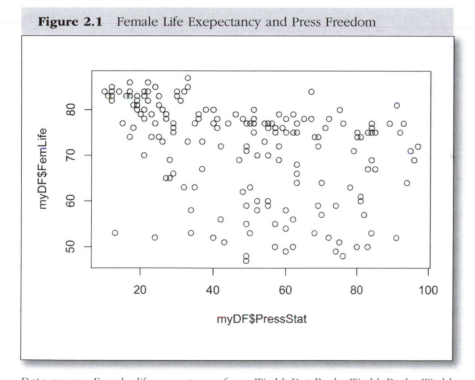

Data source: Female life expectancy from World DataBank. World Bank, World Development Indicators, http://databank.worldbank.org/data/home.aspx; and Press freedom from Freedom House, http://www.freedomhouse.org/report-types/freedom-press.

HYPOTHESIS TESTING

With the basic descriptive statistics in hand, you will likely move on to hypothesis testing (albeit blithely ignorant of the heated debates going on about the shortcomings of traditional hypothesis testing). Let's check on the difference in mean female life expectancy between countries with and without a free press (dropping, for the moment, the "partly free" category). We need to start by checking whether the variances are plausibly equal. We do that with the **var.test()** command. We'll set this up to compare female life expectancy for the two different kinds of states. We select those states by putting a condition, the relevant value of the PressFree variable, in brackets after the name of the variable.

```
> var.test(                              # Run a test comparing variances
+   myDF$FemLife[myDF$PressFree == "F"],    # FemLife in states w/ free press
+   myDF$FemLife[myDF$PressFree == "NF"])   #  compare w/states w/o free press

        F test to compare two variances

data:  myDF$FemLife[myDF$PressFree == "F"] and myDF$FemLife[myDF$PressFree == "NF"]
F = 0.515, num df = 55, denom df = 57, p-value = 0.01457
alternative hypothesis: true ratio of variances is not equal to 1
95 percent confidence interval:
 0.3037603 0.8755024
sample estimates:
ratio of variances
        0.5150451
```

We see here that the p value for the F test is less than .05, so we have to reject the null hypothesis that the two variances are equal. We'll run our t test assuming unequal variances, which is the default anyway.

```
> t.test(                                # A t-test for the hypothesis that

+   myDF$FemLife[myDF$PressFree == "F"], # states w/ press freedom and
```

```
+  myDF$FemLife[myDF$PressFree == "NF"])#  states w/o press freedom have
>                                        #  the same female life expectancy

        Welch Two Sample t-test

data:  myDF$FemLife[myDF$PressFree == "F"] and myDF$FemLife[myDF$PressFree == "NF"]
t = 6.5946, df = 103.507, p-value = 1.84e-09
alternative hypothesis: true difference in means is not equal to 0
95 percent confidence interval:
  7.649842 14.229468
sample estimates:
mean of x mean of y
 78.75000  67.81034
```

Here, we can see that the difference between the mean female life
expectancy in the two kinds of states is quite significant. Average female
life expectancy in states with high press freedoms is close to 79 years, com-
pared with 68 years in states with low press freedom. We can confidently
reject the null hypothesis of no difference (p value < .0001). We can display
this graphically with a simple box plot (Figure 2.2).

```
> boxplot(myDF$FemLife ~ myDF$PressFree)# Plot f life by free press status
```

The box plot confirms the significant difference between the free press
and non–free press states. In this quick form, however, it leaves much to
be desired. It awkwardly includes both the partially free category and the
observations missing from the press freedom data. This highlights the problems that can emerge from R being allowed to set up factor coding on its
own, which is something we'll come back to in much more depth in
Chapter 3.

The partially free states look very similar to the not free states.
Interestingly, far from being missing at random, those states without a press
freedom rating appear to be a virtual paradise for women. We'll need to
look at that. We'll pull out the names of the states that have data for female
life expectancy but are missing the free press metric.

Figure 2.2 Female Life Expectancy by Free Press Status

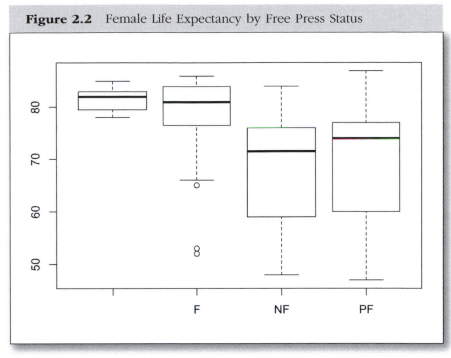

Data source: Female life expectancy from World DataBank. World Bank. World Development Indicators, http://databank.worldbank.org/data/home.aspx; and Press freedom from Freedom House, http://www.freedomhouse.org/report-types/freedom-press.

```
> myDF$Country.name[myDF$PressFree == "" # List states missing press status
+    & !is.na(myDF$FemLife)]              # but not missing f life exp.
[1] "Bermuda"            "Faeroe Islands"        "French Polynesia"
[4] "Guam"               "Macao SAR, China"      "New Caledonia"
[7] "Puerto Rico"        "Virgin Islands (U.S.)"
```

It looks like mostly very small states and pseudostates with reasonably high incomes and excellent beaches. That explains that.

We can force a little more discipline in the way R treats the Free Press factor by specifying the levels and their sort order explicitly. Also by specifying just the three real levels, the missing values (NA) are treated as missing instead of as a distinct level.

```
> str(myDF$PressFree)                  # Show current structure of factor
  Factor w/4 levels "","F","NF","PF": 3 4 3 1 1 2 3 4 4 3 ...
> myDF$PressFree =                      # Reorder factor levels in
+    factor(myDF$PressFree,             #  substantive rather than
+    levels = c("F", "PF", "NF"))       #  alphabetical order
> str(myDF$PressFree)                   # Show current structure of factor
  Factor w/3 levels "F","PF","NF": 3 2 3 NA NA 1 3 2 2 3 ...
```

A REGRESSION MODEL

Of course, we need to move toward multivariate analysis to really get at this. It is pretty likely that press freedom correlates with a lot of other factors that could be more important explanations. National wealth, GDP per capita, is an obvious candidate. Let's also pull in the proportion of GDP that goes toward defense to give us a rough sense of national priorities. Here, then, is a simple multiple regression model trying to capture those relationships:

```
> model1 = lm(FemLife ~ GDPc+MilSpend + PressFree, data = myDF)

> summary(model1)

Call:
lm(formula = FemLife ~ GDPc + MilSpend + PressFree, data = myDF)

Residuals:
    Min      1Q  Median      3Q     Max
-22.848  -4.022   3.438   6.119  11.150
```

```
Coefficients:
              Estimate Std. Error t value Pr(>|t|)
(Intercept)  7.039e+01  2.346e+00  30.000  < 2e-16 ***
GDPc         2.773e-04  5.322e-05   5.210 8.28e-07 ***
MilSpend     2.318e-01  6.233e-01   0.372   0.7107
PressFreePF -1.443e+00  2.333e+00  -0.618   0.5376
PressFreeNF -4.928e+00  2.637e+00  -1.869   0.0642  .
---
Signif. codes:  0 '***' 0.001 '**' 0.01 '*' 0.05 '.' 0.1 ' ' 1

Residual standard error: 8.799 on 116 degrees of freedom
  (92 observations deleted due to missingness)
Multiple R-squared:  0.3489,    Adjusted R-squared:  0.3265
F-statistic: 15.54 on 4 and 116 DF,  p-value: 3.293e-10
```

Not surprisingly, this model shows a strong relationship between GDP per capita and female life expectancy. The model can account for about a third of the variation in female life expectancy (adjusted R^2 = .33), which isn't terrible for a simple three-variable model in the social sciences. Note that since press freedom is a categorical variable (a "factor," in R's terminology) it is split up into its various levels. This shows the impact of the difference between each of these two levels and the default level of "F" (high press freedom). Lack of press freedom still has a large substantive impact (female life expectancy is expected to be almost 5 years less in states without a free press), but this effect just barely fails the conventional threshold for statistical significance (p = .06).

Before fully embracing this model, we have to be concerned that values like life expectancy and GDP are rarely linear. We can see this very clearly in the bivariate relationship between GDP per capita and female life expectancy (Figure 2.3).

```
plot(myDF$GDPc, myDF$FemLife)        # Plot: femlife by free press
```

Figure 2.3   Female Life Expectancy and GDP per Capita

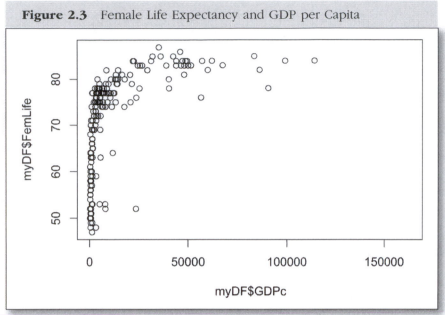

Data source: Female life expectancy from World DataBank. World Bank, World Development Indicators, http://databank.worldbank.org/data/home.aspx.

A NONLINEAR MODEL

The relationship between GDP and female life expectancy is clearly not linear. A log transformation is the obvious first step.[3] This can be done simply within the **plot()** command itself.

```
plot(log(myDF$GDPc), myDF$FemLife)     # Plot: femlife by ln of GDPc
```

This is a lot more plausible as a nonlinear relationship (Figure 2.4). We can now run our model again with the same log transformation. While we are at it, we'll log military spending as well.

---

3. A log relationship is also conceptually appropriate. We would expect a much larger effect from a $1,000 increase for a country with a GDP per capita of $4,000 than for a country with a GDP per capita of $40,000.

Figure 2.4   Female Life Expectancy and Log of GDP per Capita

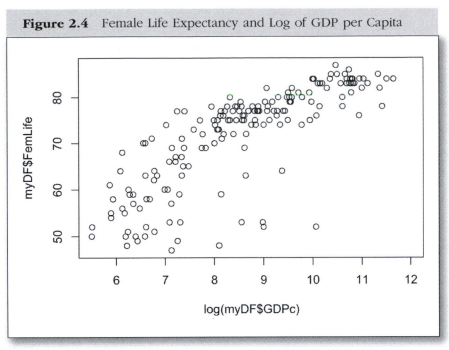

Data source: Female life expectancy from World DataBank. World Bank, World Development Indicators, http://databank.worldbank.org/data/home.aspx.

```
> model2 = lm(FemLife ~ log(GDPc) + log(MilSpend) + PressFree, data = myDF)

> summary(model2)

Call:
lm(formula = FemLife ~ log(GDPc) + log(MilSpend) + PressFree,
    data = myDF)

Residuals:
    Min      1Q  Median      3Q     Max
-22.953  -2.049   1.030   3.896  13.740

Coefficients:
              Estimate Std.  Error t value Pr(>|t|)
(Intercept)    18.2589       5.2448   3.481 0.000704 ***
log(GDPc)       6.2300       0.5216  11.944  < 2e-16 ***
```

```
log(MilSpend)    -2.3477      0.9602   -2.445 0.015989 *
PressFreePF       2.3644      1.6908    1.398 0.164666
PressFreeNF       1.6852      2.0150    0.836 0.404681
---
Signif. codes:  0 '***' 0.001 '**' 0.01 '*' 0.05 '.' 0.1 ' ' 1

Residual standard error: 6.567 on 116 degrees of freedom
  (92 observations deleted due to missingness)
Multiple R-squared:  0.6374,    Adjusted R-squared:  0.6249
F-statistic: 50.97 on 4 and 116 DF,  p-value: < 2.2e-16
```

That about doubles our adjusted R^2, and interestingly it makes military spending plausibly statistically significant ($p < .05$). Controlling for overall wealth (GDPc), when military spending goes up, female life expectancy goes down. Meanwhile, in this model, the effects of the two levels of lower press freedom largely evaporate.

There is, then, a lot that can be done with a fairly limited set of R tools. But this initial foray also must be somewhat dissatisfying. It is in the mode of the typical statistics class, in which the data are passed out in a format that is all cleaned up and ready to analyze. We need to know how to manage and prepare more complex data. Even with this bit of data, it would be nice to get a better handle on the missing values. We might want to merge data from some other data sources. There are several avenues for combining or interacting our variables that could be of interest.

So, too, while these graphs have been adequate for getting a broad sense of the data, they are not as analytically helpful as they might be. The axes are something of a mess. Some color or other variation in the point symbols could help identify regional or other variation. Regression lines would be informative, as would identification of some of the outliers. At the end of the day, these graphs are far from publication quality.

Still, we have done a lot of analysis in just a few pages. And, importantly, we've done it all with explicit code that allows the analysis to be reproduced and easily modified.

To go further, though, we need to buckle down and get schooled on R object types. R is an object-oriented language. If you don't come to terms with R object types, you will be in for a world of hurt.

CHAPTER 3

OBJECT TYPES IN R

Having seen the kinds of things R can do, I'm sure everyone is anxious to get right on to revolutionary statistical discoveries and the production of eye-popping, full-color graphics. Before going there, we've got to stop for a moment and talk objects. This, I'm afraid, may be unpleasant. But objects are at the center of the R worldview, and misunderstanding them is the central cause of frustration for new, and even not so new, R users.

For better or worse, R is an object-oriented language. Being object oriented means that R procedures recognize the kind of object they are being called to process and behave differently depending on the object type. This is a great thing in that one command can adapt to many different situations. The **summary()** command, for example, recognizes whether you are trying to summarize a data set or the results of a regression analysis and adjusts to the differences between these two kinds of output. This can also be the source of some frustration in that the same command will do different things depending on the nature of your object. While R always has very strong views about what your object is, you will sometimes be confused on this point. This can lead to some unpleasantness in as much as R isn't really interested in your opinions on the subject.

When something isn't working the way you expect, object type is one of the first things you should check. In this chapter, we'll go over a taxonomy of object types and their basic care and feeding. I have to warn you up front that I am going to propose an approach to thinking about R objects that is mostly straightforward and coherent and, therefore, is not precisely consistent with R's own internal logic and terminology.[1]

There is a lot of technical detail surrounding objects, much of which I hope we will be able to avoid here. Part of the confusion about R objects comes from the fact that the term *objects* is really used for several different things that have different dimensions, characteristics, and purposes. Some of these concepts are technical legacies from the historical development of R. Others stem from the internal needs of the R program but are relatively remote from the experiences of everyday users. I'll point out a few instances where you may observe some inconsistency between my approach and R's more official notions; but I believe that the object schema I am going to propose will help you work through most of the object issues you are likely to encounter up through a relatively advanced level.

We'll start with a little housekeeping on naming and managing objects generally, and then I'll set out my approach to understanding R objects.

R OBJECTS AND THEIR NAMES

Objects in R can be thought of as simply the things that the program is keeping track of for you. These can be individual values, data sets, statistical outputs, or specialized functions. If it is something to which you can assign a name, it is an object.

Naming objects in R is subject to just a few rules. R names can be any combination of letters and numbers. No special characters (&, ^, %, $, #, @, etc.) are allowed except for periods and underscores. R names cannot start with a number; that will just confuse R. (This may give you some brief satisfaction in the sense that turnabout is fair play, but ultimately, confusing R always hurts you more than it.)

No spaces are allowed in R names. If you want to string words together for your variable name, the two most common practices are to demarcate the words with either periods or "camel capitalization." If different variables are for different years, for example, you could use a series of names like `result.2005`, `result.2006`, `result.2007`. Another common convention is to use an extension after a period to help keep track of the kind of object: `result.df` for a data frame, `result.f` for a function, and so

---

1. If you want the official view, use `help(mode)`, `help(type)`, `help(class)`, and `help(method)`. Good luck!

on. You can use as many periods as you want for clarity, but more than two is probably going to start looking silly. If the variable names in an imported data set have spaces, R will helpfully replace them with periods (see Chapter 4 on importing data).

Camel capitalization is the practice of capitalizing the first letter of different strung-together words: NormalizedValue, FirstCut, AnnualRate. Just remember R's sensitivities around the issues of case. MyVariable has to be always MyVariable. R will feign ignorance if you ask it to do something with myVariable, Myvariable, or myvariable.

That's the deal on naming. Now we need to think about the things that you can give names to. Let's start with the simple dichotomy of data objects and nondata objects. The nondata objects shouldn't cause you too much grief. There are just two kinds that you are likely to encounter on a regular basis: functions and the output from statistical procedures. I'll go over customized functions in Chapter 7. The output from a statistical procedure is really just a list, one of the data types we'll look at in a moment. Everything we are going to learn about working with lists can be applied to working with statistical output. The most interesting things to do with statistical output involve treating it as a data source in itself, so there isn't too much else that needs to be said about that at this point. I do demonstrate a number of statistical procedures and discuss working with their output in Appendix B, if you are anxious for that.

The real place where object-type problems are going to arise is in working with data objects. R's approach to classifying data objects is, in my view, hopelessly confusing for new users. I am going to propose an alternative schema that largely parallels the official R approach but slightly shifts some of the concepts and terminology. There are, of course, some dangers in doing this. I'll try to point out some of the places where you may observe differences between official R and my approach. In practice, though, I don't believe that you will encounter operational problems with the approach I lay out here until you reach a very high level of R programming. By then, you will be more than ready to deal with the technical details on their own terms.

 ## How to Think About Data Objects in R

I propose that we think about R data objects as containers that hold data. There are, in this schema, just four types of containers we need to focus on. Each of these types of containers has three critical characteristics. The first characteristic is which of the four types of container it is. We'll label this the "object type," recognizing that officially R uses the term *object type* a little more broadly. The four object types we'll use are vectors, matrices, data frames, and lists.

The second characteristic of each object type is a description of the kinds of things that the container is holding. We'll call this characteristic the object "storage mode." This is a term that R uses as well, but we'll apply it slightly differently. For us, the storage mode is a description of the kinds of things that can be held in one of our data containers. There are three main storage modes in this approach: logical, numeric, and character. The numeric category can be further divided into the integer and the double mode. I am also going to identify two of what I call "pseudo storage modes": dates and factors.

Here is where the R overlords are beginning to squirm. They know that in official R, a list is really a storage mode. But I find it more sensible to think of lists as data containers. As we'll see, lists hold all kinds of data (and other things) and, thus, are more like containers than like data elements. Until you get into pretty high-level programming, this alternative conceptualization won't cause any problems. Meanwhile, while you will find much about dates and factors in the R literature, you won't find anything about pseudo storage modes. I just made that up. If you will indulge me for the time being, I will make the case for that characterization after we have covered the more conventional parts of my typology.

The third descriptor for our R objects is the object class. The object class is a label that provides more specialized information on how R should work with an object. While the number of object types and storage modes is quite limited, there are a wide variety of classes. The good news is that they rarely cause problems, so we can deal with them more generically.

Every R data object type, our data containers, can be described by what kind of container it is, what kind of data elements it contains, and the class descriptor that provides more specific information about how it should be treated. This approach to understanding R objects is illustrated in Figure 3.1 and summarized in Table 3.1.

All this would be pretty straightforward, except for the two pseudo storage modes that you can see lurking under the gray shading on Figure 3.1 and Table 3.1. We would prefer not to talk about these in polite company, but they are so critical and so widely used that we cannot exclude them from our discussion. Still, let's hold off on that for a bit. As is customary, let's start by talking about the well-behaved kids.

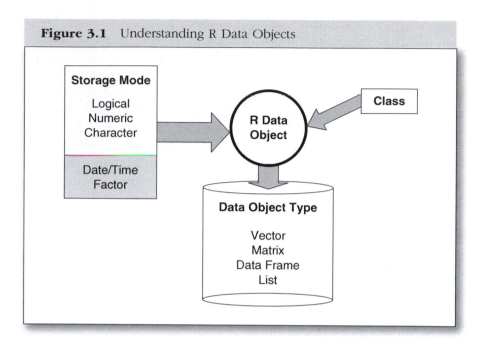

Figure 3.1   Understanding R Data Objects

R Object Storage Modes

I propose thinking of object modes as the way R has the computer store the individual pieces of data that make up an object. For our purposes there will be three of these: logical, numeric, and character. The numeric storage mode can be further divided into integer and double values. I give a short description of each of the storage modes in Table 3.2.

The commands **typeof()** and **mode()** will usually tell you the storage mode, again with the caveat that R officially considers "list" a storage mode as well. The **mode()** command lumps together integer and double under the "numeric" label, while **typeof()** makes those distinct.

```
> # Data objects
> myInteger = as.integer(4)              # An integer (whole number)
> myWholeNumber = 5                      # A whole number stored as double
> myDouble = 3.7                         # A numeric-double number
> myOtherInteger = as.integer(3.7)       # Non-whole num convert to integer
```

```
> myLogical1 = TRUE                    # A logical value set to TRUE
> myLogical2 = FALSE                   # A logical value set to FALSE
> myCharacter = "Hello World!"         # A character string
```

Table 3.1 A Typology of R Objects

			Description
Nondata objects		Functions	Sets of commands bundled together in a custom function
		Output	The results of a statistical procedure
Data objects	Storage mode	Logical	TRUE/FALSE values
		Numeric (integer or double)	The integer mode holds whole numbers. The double mode can hold any number.
		Character	Textual data
		Date/POSIX	Numbers that can be interpreted as dates or times
		Factor	Categorical variables
	Data object type	Vector	A set of data elements all of the same storage mode
		Matrix	A two-dimensional array of data elements all of the same storage mode
		Data frame	A set of vectors in which the vectors (columns) do not all have to be of the same storage mode
		List	A collection of other objects
	Data object class		An indicator that tells R what specialized methods to use on an object

Table 3.2   R Storage Modes

Storage Mode	Subcategory	Description
Logical		TRUE/FALSE values
Numeric	Integer	Numbers without fractional parts
	Double	Numbers that may have fractional parts
Character		Text values e.g., "Horse", "Alligator", "Four score and seven"
Date	Date	Calendar dates
	POSIX	Dates and times
Factor	Unordered	Categorical values without a clear ordering e.g., "Dog", "Cat", "Wombat"
	Ordered	Categorical values with an order e.g., "short", "tall", "grand", "venti"

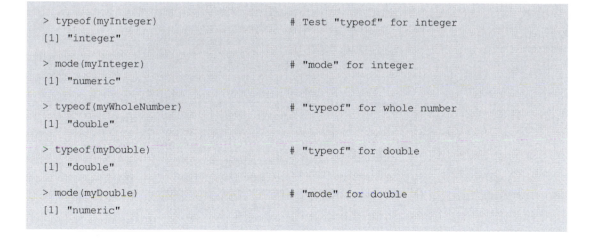

```
> typeof(myInteger)              # Test "typeof" for integer
[1] "integer"

> mode(myInteger)                # "mode" for integer
[1] "numeric"

> typeof(myWholeNumber)          # "typeof" for whole number
[1] "double"

> typeof(myDouble)              # "typeof" for double
[1] "double"

> mode(myDouble)                # "mode" for double
[1] "numeric"
```

```
> myOtherInteger               # Show 3.7 converted to integer
[1] 3

> typeof(myOtherInteger)       # "typeof" for convert to integer
[1] "integer"

> mode(myOtherInteger)         # "mode" for convert to integer
[1] "numeric"

> typeof(myLogical1)           # "typeof" for logical
[1] "logical"

> typeof(myCharacter)          # "typeof" for character
[1] "character"
```

Again, I've left the two pseudo storage modes in the gray shading for later. Officially, there are also a few other R object storage modes that you don't want to encounter down some dark programming alley the night before a statistics assignment is due: Complex, NULL, Raw, Closure, Special, Builtin, and Environment, for example, are either for special cases or for R's own internal purposes. For now, let's look more closely at the character, numeric, and logical storage modes.

The Character Storage Mode

The character storage mode is used for strings of text. You will see these referred to by all of those terms: "character," "text," or "string." You can usually tell that a value is in character mode when it is surrounded by quotation marks. You can check for character mode with **mode()** or **typeof()**, or with **is.character()**. There are two things of note to be careful about here. First, the backslash is R's escape character, so you can't include it in a text string without some extra steps.[2] You'll have problems, then, if you are trying to import data that include backslashes. This, happily,

---

2. I will go over this and much more about working with text data in Chapter 8.

is a relatively rare situation. The second, and more common, issue is that R can store numbers in character mode. This is highly vexing in that it often happens without your knowing it and you cannot perform numeric operations on character data. You can tell when a number has been stored as a character because it will be displayed within quotation marks. As we'll see in a moment, this happens because all the objects in a vector or a matrix have to be of the same storage mode. If you try to create a vector or a matrix with a set of values that has character data in it, it will convert the whole set to the character storage mode. We'll come back to the problem of number/character confusion and what to do about it after we've confronted factors, which complicate the story even further.

The Numeric Storage Modes

The numeric storage modes are pretty straightforward. On occasion, you'll have to be a little careful about the distinction between integer and double mode. An integer, of course, is a whole number, a number that doesn't have a fractional part (1, −3, 7, 2,568,482, as opposed to 1.65, 2.9, −4.002). In R, integers can be stored either in integer or in double mode.[3] This can be a little confusing since, for example, the command **as.integer()** truncates the fractional component of a number to turn it into and store it in the integer mode. But **is.integer()** is a test of mode that returns **FALSE** unless the number is, in fact, stored in R's integer mode. If you need to test for whether something is an integer, in the sense of not having a fractional part, use **is.wholenumber()**. The good news is that since both double and integer are numeric modes, this difference shouldn't cause problems.

The Logical Storage Mode

The logical storage mode registers whether something is true or false. Logical values look a little like character values but act a little like numeric values. They look like character values in that R displays logical values as either TRUE or FALSE. In accord with their existential importance, TRUE and FALSE are always capitalized in R. Likewise, note that they do not use

---

3. The "double" label comes about because most programming languages use a distinction between "single" and "double" precision for how much space is dedicated to storing a number.

quotation marks (which is how you can tell that they are not really in character mode). You can shorten logical values to T or F (again with no quotation marks). Just be careful that you don't ever name any variables T or F, in which case, things will get seriously confused.

The logical storage mode acts like numeric values in that for some operations R will treat them as zeros and ones. You can, for example, add or multiply logical values. You can use them in **sum()** or **mean()**, or in a regression model. In all these cases, they act just like numbers, with TRUE = 1 and FALSE = 0.

Once you have a group of character, numeric, or logical values, you will want to keep them in one of our data containers: the R data object types.

R DATA OBJECT TYPES

In my approach, the basic object types are containers that can hold some collection of data. For this purpose, I propose focusing on four basic object types: vectors, matrices, data frames, and lists. These object types hold particular data structures, as shown in Table 3.3.

Table 3.3   Basic Data Object Types in R

Object Type	Description
Vector	A one-dimensional set of values All values have to be of the same storage mode
Matrix	A two-dimensional array A matrix will be indexed by rows and columns. All elements have to be of the same storage mode
Data frame	A data set organized with variables in the columns and observations in the rows May hold objects with different storage modes, although each variable (column) has to be of the same storage mode
List	A collection of other objects Can mix all other types and storage modes

Again, my approach is a little different from that of official R. For official R, a list is a storage mode. If you enter **mode(myList)**, the answer you will get is "list." A data frame is stored as a list. If you enter **mode(myDataFrame)**, the answer will also be "list." For our purposes, a list is more like a data container than a storage mode. It is something in which you keep data. Meanwhile, the data frame is such a special form of list that it is worth treating it independently as one of our object types.

There is no regular R function that quickly tells you the object type in the sense that I use here. There are, however, individual tests you can use to figure each of these things out: **is.vector()**, **is.matrix()**, **is.data.frame()**, and **is.list()**. Jumping ahead a bit, we'll look at a custom function in Chapter 7 that is a simple procedure to join these individual tests together to indicate the object type. I think it is sufficiently straightforward to reproduce here, even though we are still some distance from doing custom functions.

```
DOType = function(x){                   # DOType function ------------------+
# This is a function to identify data object types. I think             |
# of object type as a characterization of objects that hold collections |
# of things. These object types are vectors, matrices, data frames,     |
# and lists.                                                            |
# If none of those types fit, then the function returns a statement      |
# that it is not a recognized data type.                                 |
#                                                                        |
   DOT = ""                               # Set default value for DOT     |
  if(is.vector(x)){DOT = "vector"}        # Check if is a vector          |
  if(is.matrix(x)){DOT = "matrix"}        # Check if is a matrix          |
  if(is.data.frame(x)){                   # Check if is a data frame       |
     DOT = "data frame"}                  #                               |
  if(is.list(x) & !is.data.frame(x)){    # Check if is a list (and not a |
     DOT = "list"}                        #     dataframe)                |
                                          #                               |
   if(DOT == ""){DOT = paste("Not a",    # Print a message if it is none |
     "recognized data object type")}      #     of the above              |
   return(DOT)                            # Return the appropriate value  |
 }                                        # End of function ------------------+
```

Once set up, the **DOType()** function can be used to indicate data object types. Now, let's look a little bit more into the care and feeding of each of these data object types.

THE BASIC DATA OBJECTS: VECTORS

When we are thinking about data structures in R, it is particularly important to understand the basic concepts of vectors and matrices. R is a vector-based language. This is the source of much of its power, but it also contributes to making R confusing for new users.

A vector is simply a grouped set of values. It is like a list, except that I won't call it a "list" because, as we've seen, that is another specific object type in R. When you import data from an external source, R usually brings it in as a set of vectors: one for each variable. The power of vector-based operations in R comes from the fact that when you specify an action to take with a vector, R applies that action to every element in the vector. A single command operates on the whole group of elements.

For our purposes, vectors can be made up of elements from any of the four object storage modes: logical values, numbers (integers or double precision), or characters. As I have emphasized, all of the elements in any one vector have to be of the same storage mode. In R's view, the vector itself has a mode that it inherits from the data it contains.

The concatenation function, **c()**, is used to package a set of things up into a vector. **myVector = c(1, 2, 7, 9)** tells R to create a vector with the numbers 1, 2, 7, and 9 and to assign it to an object named **myVector**.

```
> myLogicalVector = c(T, F, T, T)       # Set up a logical vector
> myNumericVector = c(1, 2, 4, 7)       # Set up an integer vector
> myTextVector = c("a", "b", "7", "x")  # Set up a text vector
> typeof(myLogicalVector)               # Show type for logical vector
[1] "logical"

> typeof(myNumericVector)               # Show type for numeric vector
[1] "double"

> mode(myTextVector)                    # Show type for text vector
[1] "character"
```

The special case of a vector with only one element is called a scalar. You can think of scalars as constants. Since scalars have only a single element, they don't need to be concatenated and can be created without using the **c()** function.

```
> myScalar = 1              # Create a scalar with value 1
> yourScalar = 2            # Create a scalar with value 2
> myScalar + yourScalar     # Add the two scalars
[1] 3
```

Because vectors must contain data with the same storage mode, if you create a vector **my.vector = c(1, 2, 7, "Smith")**, R will have to do something to make those elements consistent. R's approach to this is to assume that 1, 2, and 7 are characters rather than numbers, because "Smith" is clearly a character element. If you create such a vector and then try to add the first two elements, you will get an error that this is nonnumeric data.

There is a little more fluidity between logical and numerical data. If you try to use logical data in a numerical context, they will be treated as 1s and 0s. Likewise, if you try to use numerical data in a logical setting, they will be interpreted as TRUE wherever the numerical value is not zero and as FALSE wherever it is zero. While you'll get an error trying to mix operations with character and numeric vectors, logical vectors can be used in operations with numeric vectors. The former may be more frustrating, but the latter can be more dangerous, since you can think that something is working properly when it is not.

```
> myVector1 = c(0, 5, 18)          # Set up a numeric vector
> typeof(myVector1)                # Check vector type
[1] "double"

> myVector2 = c(TRUE, TRUE, FALSE) # Set up a logical vector
> typeof(myVector2)                # Check vector type
[1] "logical"

> myVector3 = c("Fred", "Joe", "Simon") # Set up a character vector
> typeof(myVector3)                # Check vector type
[1] "character"
```

```
> myVector1 + myVector3              # Add num & char vectors (error)
Error in myVector1 + myVector3: non-numeric argument to binary operator

> myVector1 + myVector2              # Add numeric & logical vectors
[1]  1   6  18

> as.logical(myVector1)             # Treat numeric as logical
[1] FALSE   TRUE   TRUE
```

In this example, we see the different data types and how logical values are treated as 0 or 1.

Vector Indices

The particular elements within a vector are identified with an index number enclosed in brackets at the end of the vector name. If **myVector = c(3, 9, 5)**, then **myVector[2]** is the second element, 9, and **myVector[3]** is the third element, 5.

```
> myVector = c(3, 9, 5)              # Set up vector of numeric values
> myVector[2]                        # Get the vector's 2nd element
[1] 9

> myVector[3]                        # Get the vector's 3rd element
[1] 5
```

You can also use another object to identify the element in the vector, as in the following example:

```
> myVector = c(3, 9, 5)              # Set up vector of numeric values
> myIndex = 1                        # Set up a selection index
> myVector[myIndex]                  # Use index for selection
[1] 3
```

Here is another example with a vector of text elements and a selection vector:

```
> myVector = c("Bob", "Mary", "Fred")    # Set vector of character values
> myVector[2]                            # Show 2nd element
[1] "Mary"

> myIndex = c(1, 3)                       # Set up an index variable
> myVector[myIndex]                       # Select vector elements w/index
[1] "Bob"   "Fred"
```

This method of element selection is very powerful because it allows us to choose vector elements conditionally. We'll get to that in much more depth in Chapter 6.

Vector Operations

When vectors are used in operations, there are four main ways in which the operation can work. Most of the time, these modalities are reasonably intuitive. Every once in a while, they'll jump up and bite you when you aren't being careful.

Vectorized functions work on each element of the vector and produce a new vector with the same number of elements. For example, **log()** creates a new vector with the log of each element from the input vector.

```
> myVector1 = c(1, 2, 3)                 # Create vector with 3 elements
> myVector2 = log(myVector1)             # Create new vector with log
> myVector2                              # Print new vector
[1] 0.0000000 0.6931472 1.0986123
```

Nonvectorized functions can only work on the individual elements of the vector. In this case, you have to be explicit about which element in the vector you want R to use. For example, **if()** requires a single element, while **ifelse()** is vectorized.

```
> myVector = c(1, 2, 3)                   # Numeric vector with 3 elements
> if(myVector == 1) print("Answer is 1") # This produces a likely error
[1] "Answer is 1"
Warning message:
In if (myVector == 1) print("Answer is 1") :
  the condition has length > 1 and only the first element will be used

> if(myVector[1] == 1)                    # This time specify 1st element
+    print("Answer is 1")
[1] "Answer is 1"

> myAnswer = ifelse(myVector == 1,        # Here is the vectorized ifelse()
+    "Answer is 1",                       #    it operates on each vector
+    "Answer is not 1")                   #    element individually
> myAnswer                                # Show results
[1] "Answer is 1"      "Answer is not 1" "Answer is not 1"
```

The difference between vectorized and nonvectorized functions is critical. Failure to understand which way a function works will lead to much grief. In Chapter 7, we'll look at the **apply()** family of functions, which can help nonvectorized functions operate on vectors.

A third kind of operation works on the whole vector: **min()** and **max()**, for example, return a single value that is the minimum or maximum element from the vector; **sum()** gives the sum of all the elements of the vector.

```
> myVector = c(1, 2, 3)              # Create a vector

> min(myVector)                      # Get the vector minimum
[1] 1

> max(myVector)                      # Get the vector maximum
[1] 3
```

```
> sum(myVector)                        # Sum the vector elements
[1] 6
```

Finally, there are operations that work on multiple vectors. Addition, for example, adds the elements of one vector to the elements of another with pairwise matching: The first element of the first vector is added to the first element of the second vector, and so on. Reasonably enough, there need to be the same number of elements in each vector.[4] Multiplication and division work the same way: element by element.

```
> myVector1 = c(1, 2, 3)               # A vector with 3 elements

> myVector2 = c(10, 20, 30)            # Another 3-element vector

> myVector1 + myVector2                # Vector addition
[1] 11 22 33

> myVector1 * myVector2                # Vector multiplication
[1] 10 40 90

> myVector2/myVector1                  # Vector division
[1] 10 10 10

> myVector5 = c(10, 20, 30, 40, 50)    # A vector with 5 elements

> myVector1 + myVector5                # Add different-length vectors

Error in myVector1 + myVector3 : non-numeric argument to binary operator

> myVector6 = c(10, 20, 30, 40, 50, 60) # A vector with 6 elements
```

———————

4. To be perfectly honest, it requires that either the same number of elements or the number of elements in the longer vector is a multiple of the number of elements in the shorter vector, in which case, addition keeps reusing the shorter vector. (Did you get that?)

```
# Add different-length vectors where one length is a multiple of the other
> myVector1 + myVector6
[1] 11 22 33 41 52 63
```

In this example, we see element-by-element mathematical operations. Note the error when the two vectors are of different lengths. But different lengths are okay if one is a multiple of the other.

Vectors are unidimensional. They contain one set of data elements, all of the same type. Matrices add a second dimension. Unlike vectors, you actually won't use matrices all that much; as we'll see, a data frame is a much more useful container for two-dimensional data. Nonetheless, matrices are conceptually important, and there are some operations that only work with matrices.

THE BASIC DATA OBJECTS: MATRICES AND THEIR INDICES

A matrix has two dimensions, a row dimension and a column dimension. You can think of it as a single object that contains a set of row vectors or a set of column vectors. In fact, it contains both, overlapping. You will recall from our discussion in Chapter 1 that a data set is usually a two-dimensional structure with observations and variables. A data set, then, is essentially a matrix in which each variable is a column vector and each observation is a row vector (see Table 3.4).

Table 3.4   A Data Matrix

	Variable 1	**Variable 2**	**Variable 3**
Observation 1	15	3.5	2
Observation 2	10	2.1	5.8
Observation 3	8	5	7

Anyone who has played the game Battleship understands the indexing for the elements of a matrix. A matrix is indexed by two values: a row index and a column index: **myMatrix[row,column]**. By convention, the row index always comes first. This is important. You've got to commit this to memory right now: *row first, then column*. **myMatrix[3,19]** is the element in the 19th column of the 3rd row of the matrix **myMatrix**.

We can isolate a specific row or column vector by leaving one of the two indices blank:

myMatrix[,4] references the 4th column of **myMatrix**.

myMatrix[12,] references the 12th row of **myMatrix**.

Thinking in terms of a data set, we could say that **myMatrix[,4]** is a list of the values for the fourth *variable* for every observation in the data set. **myMatrix[12,]** is a list of all of the variable values for the 12th *observation* in the data set.

As with vectors, basic mathematical operations work on the corresponding individual matrix elements. **myMatrix + 7** adds 7 to *every* element in **myMatrix**. **myMatrix1/myMatrix2** divides each element in **myMatrix1** by the corresponding (i.e., same row and column) element in **myMatrix2**. R's normal matrix operations are all by corresponding element, which means, as with vectors, that the two objects have to be either of the same dimensions or a multiple thereof. Those of you looking for authentic matrix algebra, as is likely in a more advanced statistics class, need to enclose the operator in percent signs (see Chapter 7 for more discussion on mathematical operators).

```
> myMatrix = rbind(c(3, 8), c(23, 33))    # Create matrix by binding 2 rows
> myMatrix                                # Display myMatrix
        [,1] [,2]
[1,]     3    8
[2,]    23   33

> myMatrix1 = myMatrix + 7                 # Add 7 to each myMatrix element
> myMatrix1                                # Display myMatrix1
```

```
        [,1] [,2]
[1,]    10   15
[2,]    30   40

> myMatrix2 = rbind(c(2, 5), c(3, 2))    # Create another matrix
> myMatrix2                              # Display myMatrix2
        [,1] [,2]
[1,]     2    5
[2,]     3    2

> myMatrix3 = myMatrix1/myMatrix2        # Divide myMatrix1 by myMatrix2
> myMatrix3                              # Display myMatrix3
        [,1] [,2]
[1,]     5    3
[2,]    10   20

> myMatrix4 = myMatrix2 %*% myMatrix3    # Matrix algebra multiplication
> myMatrix2                              # Display myMatrix2
        [,1] [,2]
[1,]     2    5
[2,]     3    2

> myMatrix3                              # Display myMatrix3
        [,1] [,2]
[1,]     5    3
[2,]    10   20

> myMatrix4                              # Display myMatrix4
        [,1] [,2]
[1,]    60  106
[2,]    35   49
```

Mathematical operations with matrices work on a corresponding ele-ment-by-element basis. This is different from real matrix algebra. Be careful!

R matrices, like R vectors, can only be made up of the same kind of data, for example, character, logical, or numeric data. So R matrices don't work for data sets that include mixed data. For that, we need to turn to data frames, which are a more flexible matrix-like structure that can hold variables with different storage modes.

 # The Basic Data Objects: Data Frames

Data frames are the central structures for holding and organizing data in R. Data frames look like matrices. They use the same **[row,column]** indexing but are more useful both because they can hold variables with different storage modes and because they allow referencing of variables by name. Note that while the data frame can hold variables of different storage modes, all of the elements of a given variable (column) still have to be of the same mode.

The ability to hold data with different storage modes is important, but it is the referencing by name that is the real key to the power and utility of data frames. In the following example, we create a data frame with the **data.frame()** command. We can then access the variables with several kinds of notation.

```
myData = read.table("mydata", header = TRUE)
myDataframe = data.frame(myData)

myDataframe$variablename
myDataframe["variablename"]
myDataframe[,"variablename"]
myDataframe[,column number]
myDataframe[column number]
```

All five of these approaches do the same thing. The first is the clearest and the most commonly used.

The second and last approaches show how the columns (variables) are privileged in a data frame: If there is only one index, it is assumed to refer to the columns rather than the rows. If you try all these ways, you'll see that the printing behavior changes. When you use the variable names, R prints the data in a table with the row names as well as the column names. When you use the numeric identifiers, it just prints the vector of values.

R assigns both variable names and observation names to the data frame. The variable names can be drawn from headers if you are reading in a table of data from an external source.

Unless you change them, the row names will just be observation numbers. You can give the observations names to help identify them, for example, the names of states, experiment numbers, or names of students. To set the row names, you can use the **rownames(myDataframe)** command. The same approach also works for column names: **colnames (myDataframe)**. In this example, I show how to set column names independently and to set them to be the same as the values in the first row of the data frame.

```
rownames(mydata) =                        # Add row names by hand
   c("Mary", "Michael", "Mia", "Michelle", "Mark")

rownames(mydata) = mydata[,3]      # Row names = third col. in data frame
colnames(mydata) = c("sex", "age")  # Add column names by hand
colnames(mydata) = mydata[1,]        # Set col names to values in 1st row
                                    # Note that this keeps 1st row as
                                    #    1st obs in the data frame
```

Referencing Data Frame Elements

The use of the **myDataframe$myVariable** convention can get cumbersome. It puts a real premium on short data frame and variable names. The most common alternative is to "attach" the data frame using the **attach()** command. This tells R to look for objects in the attached data frame, so the data frame name is no longer required.

```
> myData.df = read.csv("mydatafile.csv", header = TRUE)

> attach(myData.df)
```

*Note that no quotation marks are required for **mydata.df** because it is an R object, while **mydatafile.csv** is an external object and so is referenced as a text name within quotation marks.*

If you have used the **attach()** method and are having regrets, or are simply ready to move on to another data frame, you can detach the data frame with the **detach()** method.

```
> detach(myData.df)
```

attach() is a popular and convenient approach, and is therefore frowned upon by some of the R cognoscenti. To be fair, there are two problems with the **attach()** method. In the first place, **attach()** copies the variables from the data frame into the R workspace. Any changes you then make to the variables only affect the copies in the workspace, not the originals in the data frame. Second, if you are using multiple data sets with any overlapping object names, it is easy to get confused about where the objects are coming from and make mistakes. You should appreciate these concerns since, if I may be snide, it is not always the case that the R cognoscenti are observably concerned about the confusion of new users.

My recommendation would be to go ahead and use **attach()** if you are certain that you will only be using one data frame that hasn't simply been built from other objects that are already in memory. Otherwise, there are two other ways beyond the **dataframe$vName** approach to let R know which data frame a variable is associated with, which are a little less cumbersome than the **dataframe$vName** construction but are only applicable in certain circumstances.

You can sometimes specify the appropriate source for a variable within the command itself using the **data=** option. The command to construct a linear model, **lm()**, for example, allows the **data=** option to indicate the data frame. The **plot()** command, on the other hand, does not.

For a larger section of work, for example, the complex instructions for a plot, you can use the **with(dataframe, {commands})** function. This allows you to group a set of commands that utilize the same data frame. As with the attach method, however, you have to be careful in that any transformations to the data are only applicable within the **with({})** statement.

The **with({})** approach is useful for reasonably contained operations where you can keep track of the fact that a larger set of commands is contained within the **with({})** command. I wouldn't recommend it for more extensive processes where you might lose track of the data source and the need for a closing brace and parenthesis. The **with({})** approach is also constrained by allowing only one object to be the output.

Note also the somewhat unusual use of the parentheses and braces in the **with({})** process. The commands have to be one per line and are grouped both within the braces and the larger set of parentheses.

Here are a few demonstrations of all four methods of referencing variables within a data frame:

```
> myDF = data.frame(                   # Create a data frame
+    myVar1 = c(seq(0, 100, by = 5)),  # Set up variable 1
+    myVar2 = c(0:20))                 # Set up variable 2

> # 1. the $ construction ----------------------------------------------
> mean(myDF$myVar1)                    # $ Always works, minimizes errors
[1] 50

> # 2. The attach() method ----------------------------------------------
> attach(myDF)                         # Attach the data frame
>    mean(myVar2)                      # Do something with the data frame
[1] 10

>    myVar2 = myVar2 * 2               # Here is a transformation
>    mean(myVar2)                      # Mean of transformed variable
[1] 20

> detach(myDF)                         # Detach the data frame
> mean(myDF$myVar2)                    # Transform lost outside of attach
[1] 10

> # 3. The data = method ----------------------------------------------
> lm(myVar1 ~ myVar2, data = myDF)     # Run a linear model w/data frame

Call: lm(formula = myVar1 ~ myVar2, data = myDF)

Coefficients:
(Intercept)          myVar2
   1.551e-15       5.000e+00
```

```
> # 4. The with() method -------------------------------------------------
> with(myDF, {                        # with() to indicate data frame
+    myVar1 = myVar1/2                 # Transform myVar1
+    sd(myVar1)                        # Std dev. of transformed myVar1
+ })                                   # Note close brace & paren finish
[1] 15.51209

> sd(myDF$myVar1)                      # Transform lost outside with()

[1] 31.02418
```

This example shows the four different methods for referencing data frame elements. The $ construction is the safest and most reliable, but it can get unwieldy. The data= method only works in some commands and functions. Variable tranformations made within the attach() and with() methods are only local, they don't persist outside that immediate environment.

All of these methods work. My own view is that your default method should be the **dataframe$variable** construction. It is a little more cumbersome, but it always makes it clear what variable you are using and where it has come from. The other approaches should only be used where the gains in efficiency don't come at too high a price in terms of this clarity.

Displaying the Contents of a Data Frame

You can display the names of the variables in your data frame with the **names()** command. The whole data frame is displayed simply by typing its name. This isn't so helpful for big data sets. If you are using RStudio, just click on the name of the data frame in the workspace window (top-right quadrant) to see the data frame in a spreadsheet format. You can accomplish the same thing with the **View(myDataframe)** command (note the capitalization of **View()**). Summary statistics are available through the **summary()** command. In Chapter 5, we'll go over some other ways of viewing and reviewing larger data sets.

```
> myVar1 = c("a", "b", "c")          # Create char variable
> myVar2 = c(10, 11, 12)             # Create numeric variable
> myDF = data.frame(myVar1, myVar2)  # Combine into data frame
> myDF                               # Print data frame
  myVar1 myVar2
1      a     10
2      b     11
3      c     12

> names(myDF)                        # Show names of variables in myDF
[1] "myVar1" "myVar2"

> summary(myDF)                      # Summarize vars in data frame
    myVar1              myVar2
 Length:3          Min.   :10.0
 Class :character  1st Qu.:10.5
 Mode  :character  Median :11.0
                   Mean   :11.0
                   3rd Qu.:11.5
                   Max.   :12.0
```

The **summary()** *command gives the basic descriptive statistics for the numeric variable, but it cannot do much with the character variable.*

THE BASIC DATA OBJECTS: LISTS

Lists are perhaps both the most and the least important object types in R. They are the most important because lots and lots of things are packaged as lists. They are the least important because you don't often need to work with them directly. Still, for the former reasons, we have to spend a little time on them. Moreover, understanding a bit about lists will help you avoid some other potentially painful object lessons.

Lists are groups of objects. The important thing about lists is that they are pretty free form. A list can package together objects of different types (vectors, data frames, other lists, etc.) and of different storage modes (character, numeric, etc.). And all of those things can be of different lengths. For example, when R runs a linear model using the **lm()** command, it creates a list with the output. That list will include short elements with character data, such as the model used in the function call, and long elements with numeric data, such as a vector of residuals.

You can't find out what is in a list just by entering its name. R, in its infinite wisdom, decides what kind of list you've got (based on the class attribute, if it is included in the list) and then prints it out accordingly. If it is a data frame, it just prints the data. If it is a model, it prints the most relevant model output. To see what really lurks within a list, you need to use the **attributes()** command, which we'll look at in more detail shortly. **attributes(myList)** will display all the elements within the list, which you can then access by either using the **myList$element** construction or indicating the slot number of the item in the list: **myList[3]**. A linear model, for example, generates a set of residuals that are included in the second slot of a list that holds the output from the model. That element can be accessed with either **myModel$residuals** or **myModel[2]**.

```
> myVar1 = c(1:8)                        # Set up a y variable
> myVar2 = c(3, 5, 4, 6, 7, 9, 2, 9)     # Set up an x variable
> myModel = lm(myVar2 ~ myVar1)          # Create a linear model
> myModel                                # Print the model output

Call:
lm(formula = myVar2 ~ myVar1)

Coefficients:
(Intercept)          myVar1
     3.3214          0.5119

> attributes(myModel)                    # Show elements in model output
$names
[1] "coefficients" "residuals"  "effects"  "rank"   "fitted.values"
[6] "assign"  "qr"  "df.residual"  "xlevels"  "call"  "terms"  "model"
```

```
$class
[1] "lm"

> myModel$residuals                              # Show model residuals
     1        2        3        4        5        6        7        8
-0.8333   0.6547  -0.8571   0.6309   1.1190   2.6071  -4.9047   1.5833
```

There is also a double-bracket approach to accessing the elements of the list, for example, **myModel[[2]]**. This is an important distinction because the double-bracket notation (along with the **$** demarcation) gives you access to the individual components within the list element, while the single-bracket approach only gives you access to everything in the list slot all at once. You can think of the single brackets showing you the box, while the double brackets give you access to the things inside the box.

The fact that data frames are lists usually shouldn't cause any problems, but if you are trying to automate something using the bracket method to get inside a data frame, you may need to recall the distinction between single- and double-bracket indexing.

```
> myModel[2]                           # Single-bracket index result
$residuals
     1        2        3        4        5        6        7        8
-0.8333   0.6547  -0.8571   0.6309   1.1190   2.6071  -4.9047   1.5833

> myModel[[2]]                         # Double-bracket index result
     1        2        3        4        5        6        7        8
-0.8333   0.6547  -0.8571   0.6309   1.1190   2.6071  -4.9047   1.5833

> myModel[2][1]                        # Single bracket won't open list item
$residuals
     1        2        3        4        5        6        7        8
-0.8333   0.6547  -0.8571   0.6309   1.1190   2.6071  -4.9047   1.5833
```

```
> myModel[[2]][1]                    # Dble [[]] allow list item access
    1
-0.8333

> myModel$residuals[1]               # $ referencing works the same way
    1
-0.8333
```

You can package things up in a list yourself using the **list()** command. Even lists can be included in other lists. The names of the slots in the list can be attached with the **names()** command. Then you can even build stacked descriptions to retrieve elements from specific slots. The following example puts the model output, itself a list, into another list with some additional information about the model:

```
> myList = list(1,                   # List starting with model num (1)
+    myModel,                         # Then the myModel list
+    "This is a discussion of myModel") # Then some discussion of myModel

> names(myList) = c("ModelNumber",   # Create the list names
+    "ModelOutput", "ModelDiscussion")
> myList                             # Show myList
$ModelNumber
[1] 1

$ModelOutput

Call: lm(formula = myVar2 ~ myVar1)

Coefficients:
(Intercept)        myVar1
     3.3214        0.5119
```

```
$ModelDiscussion
[1] "This is a discussion of myModel"

> myList$ModelOutput$residuals          # Residuals from myModel in myList
     1       2       3       4       5       6       7       8
-0.8333  0.6547 -0.8571  0.6309  1.1190  2.6071 -4.9047  1.5833
```

This example shows how to bind together a new list that includes a preexisting list as one of its elements. We address an element in the list within a list in the final line with the two(!)-$ construction.

You can remove objects from a list with the **unlist()** function. But be forewarned that this will create a character vector with one entry for each of the things that were in the list. Except for the simplest of lists, you'll likely have to do some careful transformations to make anything useful out of it.

```
> myList = list(c(1, 2, 3), c("a", "b", "c"), "It's numbers and letters!")
> typeof(myList)                        # Show object type for myList
[1] "list"
> myList                                # Print myList
[[1]]
[1] 1 2 3
[[2]]
[1] "a" "b" "c"
[[3]]
[1] "It's numbers and letters!"

> myNotList = unlist(myList)            # New object = unlisted myList
> typeof(myNotList)                     # Show type of new unlisted object
[1] "character"
```

```
> myNotList                          # Show my new object
[1] "1"                    "2"                    "3"
[4] "a"                    "b"                    "c"
[7] "It's numbers and letters!"
```

In this example, we create and then disassemble a list.

Ò   A Few Things About Working With Objects

You can get a list of all of the objects in your current R session with either the **objects()** or the **ls()** command. Neither of these commands requires an argument, so you just leave the parentheses empty.[5]

```
> objects()                          # Show all active objects
[1] "myNumber"     "myRandNum"     "myVar"
```

One of the benefits of RStudio is that it shows a list of your current objects in the upper-right quadrant (see Figure 1.2). You can see what is in an object by clicking on it.

You can remove an object with the **rm(myObject)** function. You can remove all of your objects with **rm(list = ls())**. We'll learn about lists a little later. In the meantime, be a little careful with that one!

```
> myVector = 1:10                    # Create some objects
> myNewVector = myVector + 3
> myAnimal = "aardvark"
> objects()                          # List the objects
[1] "myAnimal"     "myNewVector"   "myVector"
```

---

5. Keeping track of your objects is another useful feature of the RStudio interface. Its object window lets you see the objects and display them in a spreadsheet-like format.

```
> rm(myVector)                        # Remove an object
> objects()                           # List the objects

[1] "myAnimal"      "myNewVector"
> rm(list = ls())                     # Remove ALL objects
> objects()                           # List the objects
character(0)
```

In this example, we tell R to remove myVector and then list the objects again. Note that "character(0)" is R's clumsy way of telling us that there are no objects left in the workspace.

If you are using RStudio, you can also remove all objects with the Clear Workspace option under the Session menu or with the little broom button above the workspace window on the top right. In the plain R Console, there is a "remove all objects" option under the Misc menu.

It is important to remember that objects can be overwritten by new objects with the same name. This is a nice feature when you use it to keep redundant objects from piling up in your project. It isn't so nice if you lose track of your object values because you weren't aware that R was overwriting them. Here is a demonstration.

```
> myNumber = 5                        # Assign value 5 to myNumber
> myNumber = 7                        # Assign value 7 to myNumber
> myNumber                            # Show that 7 replaced 5
[1] 7

> myNumber = 5                        # Assign value 5 to myNumber
> myNumber = myNumber + 4             # Add 4 to myNumber
> myNumber                            # Show new value for myNumber
[1] 9
```

OBJECT ATTRIBUTES

R data objects are defined by a set of attributes. One of the most critical strategies when you get in trouble is to be sure you understand your objects. There are, inexplicably, two distinct commands for looking at the attributes of your objects: **attributes()** and **attr()**. They are very similar but work in slightly different ways. The **attributes()** function takes just one argument: the name of the object you want to look at. The **attr()** function takes two arguments: (1) the name of the object and (2) the name of the specific attribute. With the **attributes()** function, the specific attributes are appended with the **$name** approach, for example, **attributes(myObject)$class**.

The **attributes(myObject)** function is the most straightforward way to get a complete list of object attributes, while the **attr(object, "attribute")** approach might be a little quicker for setting individual attributes.

```
> myData = data.frame(cbind(        # Create data frame w/2 vectors
+   c(1, 0, 1, 1, 0),               #    Vector 1
+   c(24, 38, 22, 51, 17)))         #    Vector 2

> # The attr approach
> attr(myData, "names") =           # Set col names to identify vars
+   c("sex", "age")
> attr(myData, "row.names") =       # Set row names to identify obs
+   c("Mary", "Mike", "Mia", "Mish", "Mark")
> myData                            # Display the data frame
      sex  age
Mary   1   24
Mike   0   38
Mia    1   22
Mish   1   51
Mark   0   17

> # The rownames/colnames approach
> rownames(myData) =                # Add row names
+   c("Mary", "Mike", "Mia", "Mish", "Mark")
> colnames(myData) = c("sex", "age")    # Add column names
```

This example shows two ways to set column and row names. Note the use of quotation marks for the attribute names in the **attr()** *approach. These approaches can also be used to set the row or column names to be equal to one of the existing rows or columns. For example,* **colnames(myData) = myData[1,]** *will set the column names to the values in row 1.*

You can erase an object's attributes individually by using **attr(object, "attribute") = NULL**. Alternatively, you can strip out all of the attributes with **attributes(object) = NULL**.

Another quick way to see the basic elements of an object is with the structure function: **str()**. It will give you a fast overview of what is in an object and the storage mode of the objects that make it up.

```
> str(myData)                    # Show data frame structure
'data.frame':                    5 obs. of  2 variables:
$ sex: num   1  0  1  1  0
$ age: num   24 38 22 51 17
```

OBJECTS AND ENVIRONMENTS

Before ending the discussion of R data object types, a word needs to be said about environments. An environment can be thought of as the space in which objects are defined. This usually won't be an issue for you, but it is important to be aware that R objects are stored within a specific environment. Most of your work will be in the "global environment," which is the overarching environment that is opened when you start R. Functions usually have their own environment, and thus, objects that are defined or manipulated within a function aren't necessarily available in the global environment.

This finishes our discussion of the basic R data object types: vectors, matrices, data frames, and lists. Our model, so far, is object types as containers that hold a group of objects that are characterized by their storage mode. The third element of this approach is object classes, which pass on more specific information about how an object should be treated.

R OBJECT CLASSES

In addition to the storage mode and data type, most R objects have a class, which gives R more detailed information about how the object should be treated. Unlike our short lists of storage modes and basic object types, there are a very large number of possible classes. Indeed, you can even create your own classes. (But please don't!) A variety of R procedures use the class information to set up different behaviors. If you run a linear model with the **lm()** function, the output of that model will be a list. One of the elements of that list is the class, "lm," which tells R to deal with that object as the output of a linear model. The class of any object will be listed in the **attributes()** function and can also be accessed directly with the **class()** command.

```
> x = 5                          # Create an object
> class(x)                       # Show object class
[1] "numeric"
> class(mean)                    # Show class of existing R command
[1] "function"
> class(x) = "my made up class"  # Set new custom class for x
> attributes(x)                  # Show attributes of x
$class
[1] "my made up class"

> str(x)                         # Show structure of x
Class 'my made up class'  num 5
```

For the more generic commands like **summary()** or **print()**, which are almost always dependent on class information, you can use the **methods()** function to tell you which classes it will recognize. Here is a truncated list of the classes for which **summary()** has a distinct routine (there are 60 in all).

```
> methods(summary)
  [1] summary.aareg*          summary.agnes*
  [3] summary.aov             summary.aovlist
  [5] summary.areg.boot       summary.aspell*
  [7] summary.cch*            summary.clara*
  [9] summary.connection      summary.coxph*
 [11] summary.coxph.penal*    summary.data.frame
```

You can also give methods the class information to see which generic functions are set up to work with them. For example, here is the list of functions that have a specialized approach to the results of a linear model (**class = lm**).

```
> methods(class = lm)
  [1] add1.lm*            alias.lm*           anova.lm
  [4] attrassign.lm*      case.names.lm*      confint.lm*
  [7] cooks.distance.lm*  deviance.lm*        dfbeta.lm*
 [10] dfbetas.lm*         drop1.lm*           dummy.coef.lm*
 [13] effects.lm*         extractAIC.lm*      family.lm*
 [16] formula.lm*         hatvalues.lm        HTML.lm*
 [19] influence.lm*       kappa.lm            labels.lm*
 [22] logLik.lm*          model.frame.lm      model.matrix.lm
 [25] nobs.lm*            plot.lm             predict.lm
 [28] print.lm            proj.lm*            qr.lm*
 [31] residuals.lm        rstandard.lm        rstudent.lm
 [34] simulate.lm*        summary.lm          variable.names.lm*
 [37] vcov.lm*

Nonvisible functions are indicated with an asterisk
```

We don't need to say much more about classes. They mostly work quietly in the background and don't cause too many problems. Most of what you have to know about objects and most of the more serious object problems will have to do with the basic object types and with confusion about the storage modes. This brings us back to our much delayed discussion of what I have called the two "pseudo storage modes."

THE PSEUDO STORAGE MODES

As indicated above, we need to deal with the complexities of fitting two other important kinds of objects into our schema: (1) date/time data and (2) factor data. Date and time values are obviously critical to many kinds of data projects. So too, "factor" is just the name R uses for categorical data, which is as common as it is critical.

The conceptually sensible home for both factors and date/time values is as storage modes. It makes sense to think of both as a characteristic of a data element, like the logical, numeric, and character storage modes. We would frequently expect to use dates or factors to fill one of our data containers. Indeed, we can use the `c()` function to create what look and behave like vectors of date/time or factor data, although R's `is.vector()` function won't officially recognize them as such. They can be packaged up and worked with as variables in a data frame. You can put them in a list.

The one container they don't fit into so well is matrices. If you put date/time or factor values into a matrix, they will be converted to a numeric storage mode, losing the critical information that makes date/time and categorical data distinctive. Mostly, we can work with date/time and factor values as if they were storage modes. But as we shall see, and as intimated by the way matrices refuse to acknowledge their character, dates and factors can cause significant problems if you aren't careful.

DATE AND TIME AS STORAGE MODES

I will spend just a little time on date/time data at this point. I've dedicated all of Chapter 9 to the issues you may confront when working with dates and times. Date and time values are obviously critically important for many data projects. Conceptually, the logical place for date and time values in our objects typology is as a storage mode. Date and time data can be thought of as individual elements that you would want to keep in a data container;

some of your variables are numeric, some are character, and some are dates or times. It makes the most sense to think of date and time as a distinct storage mode, like logical, numeric, or character data.

Officially, R does not see dates or times this way. It stores dates as simple numeric values and then uses the class information to associate those values with instructions for how they should be interpreted to act and look like dates or times.

I'll go into much more detail on this process in Chapter 9. The one other thing to note now is that there are two kinds of date/time modes: (1) the Date mode and (2) the POSIX mode. The main difference is that POSIX values allow measurement down to even fractions of a second, while the Date mode only measures down to days. And POSIX values are more amenable to being broken up into component parts (e.g., days, minutes, or seconds).

Again, the important thing to keep in the back of your mind is that both POSIX and Date objects are technically stored as numeric data, with class and formatting information that translates them from raw numbers into recognizable date and time information.

Because date and time values are reasonably distinctive, these complexities are less likely to get you into trouble. You usually know when you are working with dates or times. Once you learn how R deals with them, as I'll cover in much more detail in Chapter 9, you should be able to manage them pretty well. Factors, I regret to say, can be a little trickier.

FACTORS

Factors are conceptually straightforward. They are just categorical variables. That means they are variables that can take on a discrete number of values or levels. They are very important in R because of their role in labeling, grouping, and sorting data and because of their ability to screw things up if you don't realize you are working with them.

As with dates, I think it makes the most conceptual sense to think of factors as a storage mode. A categorical variable is similar to the characterization of data as either numeric or character: A "factor" describes a unit of data that is stored as a categorical variable. This is not precisely how R sees it, which is why I have labeled this a pseudo storage mode.

Here is the critical thing: R really sees factors as two (or three) connected vectors (Figure 3.2). The first vector is a set of levels, which is all of the possible values the factor can take. The second is a set of pointers that tells R which of the levels to connect to each data point. Suppose we were categorizing things as made of metal, plastic, or wood. As a factor variable, this would have a vector of three levels ("metal", "plastic", and "wood") and a vector of pointers indicating which level to apply to each observation. The levels vector will be the length of the number of unique levels (three in this case). The pointer vector will be the length of the number of observations. Since in our current example there are three different levels, the pointer vector will have a 1, 2, or 3 for each observation. Problems arise when you get confused about when R is working with the levels and when it is working with the pointers. If you use **typeof()** on a factor, it will look at the vector of pointers and return "integer." **attributes()**, **str()**, and **is.factor()** are, therefore, more reliable tests for figuring out that you have a factor.

There is a third, optional, vector that is a set of labels to match up to the levels. The levels attribute is a vector of all the possible values that a factor variable can take. The labels attribute is a vector of labels corresponding to those levels. When you don't provide the labels vector, R just

Figure 3.2   The Structure of Factor Variables

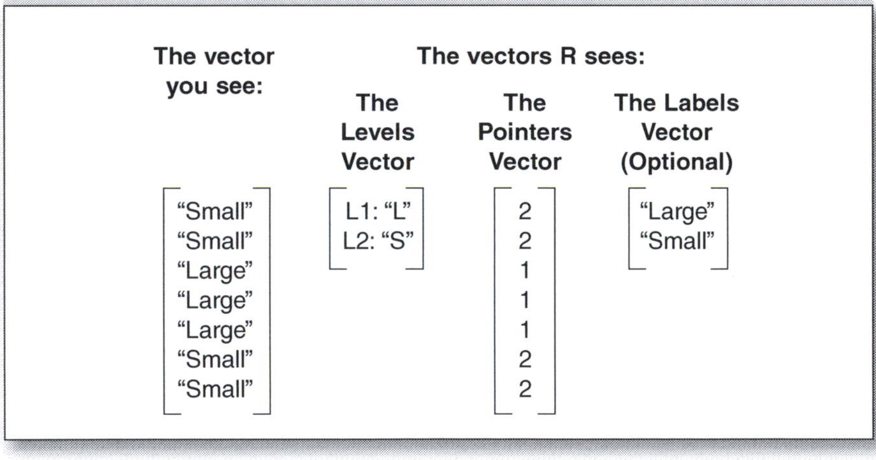

The vector you see:	The vectors R sees:		
	The Levels Vector	The Pointers Vector	The Labels Vector (Optional)
"Small"	L1: "L"	2	"Large"
"Small"	L2: "S"	2	"Small"
"Large"		1	
"Large"		1	
"Large"		1	
"Small"		2	
"Small"		2	

Note: This factor is created with the code: **myFactor = factor(c("S", "S", "L", "L", "L", "S", "S"))**. The labels are optional. Because the **"ordered = TRUE"** option isn't specified, the levels are simply sorted alphabetically.

uses the levels as labels. If the names of your levels are self-explanatory, you don't need to add the labels vector. If, as in the following example, you would like to provide more explicit labels, you can include them as an option in the **factor()** command, and R will switch to using them instead of the original levels.

```
> c2ltr = c("FR", "UK", "SW",         # Create a variable with 2 letter
+    "NK", "SO")                        #    country abbreviations
> cname = c("France", "U.K.", "Sweden", # Create a variable with
+    "North Korea", "Somalia")          #    country names
> country = c("UK", "SW", "FR",        # Create a variable w/country codes
+    "SO", "NK")
> regime = c(rep("dem", 3),            #    and democratic status
+    rep("nondem", 2))
> nations.df =                         # Join into a data frame
+    data.frame(regime, country)
> nations.df                           # Print the new data frame
   regime country
1    dem      UK
2    dem      SW
3    dem      FR
4 nondem      SO
5 nondem      NK

> #now add labels
> nations.df$country =                 # Create a country factor
+    factor(nations.df$country,
+        levels = c2ltr,               # Connecting 2-letter codes
+        labels = cname)               #    with country names

> nations.df                           # Print data frame
   regime    country
1    dem        U.K.
2    dem      Sweden
3    dem      France
4 nondem     Somalia
5 nondem North Korea
```

This example shows the application of factor labels to a data frame.

As shown in Figure 3.2, R's default behavior is to sort factors alphabetically. In that case, we would probably rather list "Small" before "Large." We can exercise more control over how a factor gets set up by using the **levels=** and **labels=** options with the **factor()** command. The following example shows these procedures. Note in the second of these examples how the **labels=** option is dependent on the preexisting order of the levels and how it changes the levels themselves.

```
> # Set up the factor from figure 3.2
> myFactor = factor(c("S", "S", "L", "L", "L", "S", "S"))
> str(myFactor)                       # Show factor structure
Factor w/2 levels "L","S": 2 2 1 1 1 2 2

> # Change the ordering of the levels
> myFactor = factor(myFactor,         # Use values from current factor
+    levels = c("S", "L"))            # Specify the levels
> str(myFactor)                       # Show factor structure
Factor w/2 levels "S","L": 1 1 2 2 2 1 1

> myFactor = factor(myFactor,         # Use values from current factor
+    labels = c("Small", "Large"))    # Specify labels
> str(myFactor)                       # Show factor structure
Factor w/2 levels "Small","Large": 1 1 2 2 2 1 1
```

We can use the same **factor()** approach to add new levels to the factor. Or we can use the **levels()** function to do it more directly. Note in the second case how the **levels()** function can be used both to display and to modify the levels of the factor.

```
> # Add additional level
> myFactor = factor(myFactor,        # Use values from current factor
+   levels =                         # Specify the levels w/addition
+     c("Small", "Medium", "Large"))
> str(myFactor)                      # Show factor structure
Factor w/3 levels "Small","Medium",..: 1 1 3 3 3 1 1

> levels(myFactor) =                 # Use levels() to add new level

+     c(levels(myFactor), "X-Large") # Combine old levels with new

> summary(myFactor)                  # Summarize myFactor w/new levels

   Small   Medium    Large   X-Large

       4        0        3         0
```

Unfortunately, adding new observations to a factor is not as straightforward. With concatenation, R just tries to add to the pointers vector, and in so doing, it changes the storage mode from factor to the storage mode of whatever you are trying to add.

```
> myFactor2 = c(myFactor, "Medium")  # Can't concatenate w/new values
> myFactor2                          # Show result
[1] "1"  "1"  "3"  "3"  "3"  "1"  "1"  "Medium"

> myFactor2 = c(myFactor, 2)         # Can add to pointer vector
> myFactor2                          # But, dumps us out of factor mode
[1] 1 1 3 3 3 1 1 2
> is.factor(myFactor2)
[1] FALSE
```

The odd trick here is that the data frame object type is smart enough to know how to add things to a factor when you use the row bind (**rbind()**) tool (we'll talk more about that in Chapters 4 and 10). This is an example of the class attribute working quietly and efficiently in the background. This data frame ability is a very good thing, since it means that factor data can be correctly handled when you are joining together more complex data sets. Here, it is in action.

```
> myDF = data.frame(myFactor)           # Put the factor into a data frame
> myDF = rbind(myDF, "Medium", "Small") # Add 2 new observations
> myDF                                   # Show result
   myFactor
1     Small
2     Small
3     Large
4     Large
5     Large
6     Small
7     Small
8    Medium
9     Small

> myFactor2 = myDF$myFactor              # Return to vector status
> myFactor2                              # Confirm result
[1] Small  Small  Large  Large  Large  Small  Small  Medium Small
Levels: Small Medium Large
```

The **levels()** command can also be used to combine levels. Just duplicate the level names where you want to merge previously distinct levels, as in the following example:

```
> myFactor2                              # Display the factor
[1] Small  Small  Large  Large  Large  Small  Small  Medium Small
Levels: Small Medium Large
> levels(myFactor2)                      # Show the current levels
```

```
[1] "Small"   "Medium" "Large"
> levels(myFactor2) =                  # Modify the levels to combine
+   c("Small", "Large", "Large")       #   Medium with Large.
> myFactor2                            # Show the new version
[1] Small Small Large Large Large Small Small Large Small
Levels: Small Large
```

Finally, we should note that as intimated in Table 3.2, there are two kinds of factors: ordered and unordered. An ordered factor provides R with an explicit ordering for the different factor levels. To tell R to interpret your factor as ordered, you just include the **ordered = TRUE** option when setting up the factor, as shown in the following example:

```
> mySize = c("Small", "Medium",       # Create variable of all sizes
+   "Large", "X-Large")
> sort(mySize)                         # Sort (alphabetical default)
[1] "Large"   "Medium" "Small"   "X-Large"
```

This regular sort is simply alphabetical.

```
> mySize = factor(mySize,             # Set as factor
+   levels = mySize,                  # Set factor levels from variable
+   ordered = T)                      # Make it an ordered factor

> sort(mySize)                        # Sort (now ordered)
[1] Small   Medium Large   X-Large
Levels: Small < Medium < Large < X-Large
```

*When we set it up as a factor and use the **levels=** option, then R can sort in the desired order.*

```
> myData = c("Small", "Large",        # Here is some data w/sizes
+   "Small", "X-Large", "Medium")
```

```
> sort(myData)                          # Sort (alphabetical default)
[1] "Large"    "Medium"  "Small"   "Small"   "X-Large"

> myData = factor(myData,               # Make it a factor
+    levels = mySize)                    # Use levels from mySize
> sort(myData)                          # Sort-now based on factor levels
[1] Small    Small   Medium  Large  X-Large
Levels: Small Medium Large X-Large
```

In this last example, we use our first factor as an ordered set of levels for sorting other variables.

You can already specify the order in which things are displayed by setting up the **levels=** option. There is a more important substantive distinction between ordered and unordered factors in that some basic statistical procedures, for example, **lm()** and **anova()**, make use of the ordering information and treat the factor quite differently (this gets into the statistics of contrasts).[6] We'll get into ordering and sorting of objects in much more detail in Chapter 6.

I'm sure, you are now thinking that these factors seem pretty useful and are wondering what the big deal is. And indeed, they are very useful. But here is why factors so often cause troubles: The *default* behavior in R is to turn character variables into factors whenever you import them into R or incorporate them into a data frame.[7] This makes it much more likely that you'll be caught unawares that what you think are characters R thinks are factors. There is a significant danger of getting confused between the factor, numeric, and character storage modes.

———————

6. You may also encounter situations where you need to specify the first element in a factor to serve as the reference level. You can control this with the **relevel()** command setting the **ref=** option to the number of the level you want to serve as the reference level.

7. R does this because it is often much more efficient to store string variables as factors. In Appendix A, I show how to change this default behavior by using the **stringsAsFactors** option. This approach, however, comes at some cost both in efficiency and in reproducibility.

COERCING STORAGE MODES

Before going further into the nature of the confusion that can arise between the factor, character, and numeric storage modes, it may be reassuring to say a little bit about our ability to coerce storage modes. Sometimes, you will want to force an object to retain its storage mode when incorporating it into a data frame. For example, you may want a set of character variables to retain their character mode rather than be forced into factors. To preserve a variable's mode, use the **I()** function. You can also use the **as.** modifier to force a type of object. In the following example, I create a vector that is turned into a vector of character elements because of the one clear bit of character data. You can see that prevents us from doing mathematical operations. I then force the vector to be numeric, which requires the character data to be left out as a missing value (**NA**).

```
> myVector = c(1, 15, 7, "Smith")        # Set up a vector
> typeof(myVector)                        # Show type for vector
[1] "character"

> myVector[2] + 1                         # Try math w/2nd element in vector
Error in myVector[2] + 1 : non-numeric argument to binary operator>

> typeof(myVector[2])                     # Type for 2nd element in vector
[1] "character"

> myVector = as.numeric(myVector)         # Vector forced to numeric

> myVector                                # Print vector
[1]  1 15  7 NA

> typeof(myVector)                        # Type for forced numeric vector
[1] "double"
```

In this example, we see that if any element in the vector is nonnumeric, R converts the whole vector to nonnumeric. If we force the vector to be numeric, the one nonnumeric element is turned to a missing value (NA). R will give us a warning that it was forced to create an NA value.

I should also mention here the **asis()** modifier. This modifies an object type so that it isn't transformed by certain operations. Most important, as we'll discuss in the next chapter, it can be used to prevent data frames from converting character or numeric data to factor data. This is part of a larger source of confusion that we need to address presently.

 ## THE CURSE OF NUMBER/CHARACTER/FACTOR CONFUSION

One of the most confusing (and often frustrating) experiences is when you have character data that look like numbers. The character "7" is different from the number 7. If for some reason R has interpreted a variable as a set of characters, rather than as numbers, you need to be careful to transform it back to its numeric values before performing operations. Suppose you import the following data from a CSV (comma separated) file: 7, 8, missing, 8. R will put this into a vector. But recall that vectors can only hold things that are all of the same storage mode. Because of the word *missing*, R will force all of the data to be character data rather than letting the 7s and 8s be numbers.

```
> myData = c(7, 8, "missing", 8)        # Here we simulate the csv input
> sum(myData)                            # If we sum myData we get an error
Error in sum(myData) : invalid 'type' (character) of argument

> myData[1]                              # We see the value is a character
[1] "7"

> myData[1] + 2                          # Errors w/numeric operations
Error in myData[1] + 2 : non-numeric argument to binary operator

> as.numeric(myData[1])                  # Fix with transform to numeric
[1] 7

> as.numeric(myData[1]) + 2              # Now we can do numeric operation
[1] 9
```

Watch for the quotation marks, which are a dead giveaway that R thinks something is a character rather than a number.

As shown in this example, you have to convert the character variable to numeric to use it as a number.

This problem becomes even more acute when working with factors. When R imports character data or incorporates them into a data frame, its default behavior is to convert it to a factor. R keeps track of factors as a set of values (the levels) and a set of pointers to those values. If you have a data set of kangaroos and koalas, the kangaroo/koala factor will have just two levels, "kangaroo" (1) and "koala" (2). The values in the factor itself will just be 1s or 2s to point to either "kangaroo" or "koala." Here is an example:

```
> animal = (c(rep("kangas", 4),        # Create a character variable
+   rep("koalas", 5)))
> myData = data.frame(animal)          # Putting the data in a data frame
> levels(myData$animal)                #   converts character to factor
[1] "kangas" "koalas"

> aninum = as.numeric(myData$animal)   # Create a numeric version

> myData = cbind(myData, aninum)       # Add that to the data frame
> myData                               # Show results
  animal  aninum
1 kangas       1
2 kangas       1
3 kangas       1
4 kangas       1
5 koalas       2
6 koalas       2
7 koalas       2
8 koalas       2
9 koalas       2
```

The **levels()** *function shows us that the animal variable has been converted to a factor with two levels.*

This makes reasonable sense. The two levels of the factor are given the numbers 1 and 2. These are the pointers to the two levels of the factor. The problem comes if you have what you think are numbers but what R thinks are factor levels, as in the following example:

```
> myVar = (c(rep(7, 4),          # Create variable w/"missing"
+    "missing", rep(8, 5)))      #   value which forces to character
> myData = data.frame(myVar)     #   & becomes factor in data frame
> levels(myData$myVar)           # Show levels of unwanted factor
[1] "7"          "8"          "missing"

> myVar2 = as.numeric(myData$myVar)   # Convert to numeric
> myData = cbind(myData, myVar2)      # Add to data frame
> myData                              # Show data
       myVar  myVar2
1          7       1
2          7       1
3          7       1
4          7       1
5    missing       3
6          8       2
7          8       2
8          8       2
9          8       2
10         8       2
```

You might think these are numbers, but R treats them as factors because of the character value in observation 5.

As you can see, because of the one value with character data, R coerced all the data to character data. The data became a factor when placed into a data frame.[8] The factor has three levels: 7, 8, and "missing". When converted to numeric data, it is the pointers to those values (1, 2, and 3), rather than the interpreted values, that are used. If you try to do numeric operations on the **as.numeric(myVar)** values, you will be sorely disappointed.

---

8. If you are aware of the potential problem, you can prevent this transformation with the **I()** function for individual variables or the **stringsAsFactors = F** option for data files. See Appendix A for instructions on the use of this option.

To convert factors to numeric, you cannot use **as.numeric(myFactor)**. That will just give you the values of the pointers. R Help (look up **?as.factor** to find this) recommends the following, somewhat cumbersome, approach:

```
as.numeric(levels(myFactor))[myFactor]
```

It is a little less efficient, but I think it a bit more intuitive to convert the factor to a character object and then to numeric. You can do this in two steps to keep everything very clear:

```
myTemp = as.character(myFactor)
myNum = as.numeric(myTemp)
```

Or you can put it all in one step:

```
myNum = as.numeric(as.character(myFactor))
```

Now that we have squared away the number/factor confusion, it's time to face up to the factor/character confusion. Here is where we really enter the twilight zone: You have to be careful about the distinction between factor and character variables.

Let's go back to our koalas and kangas data.

```
animal = (c(rep("kangas", 4), rep("koalas", 5)))
myData = data.frame(animal)
```

Let's find out what kinds of animals are in observation 4 and then change them to the other type.

```
> myData$animal[4]                    # Let's take a look at obs 4
[1] kangas
Levels: kangas koalas
```

```
> myData$animal[4] = "koalas"           # Now we'll change it to "koalas"
> myData$animal[4]                       # Another look at num 4
[1] koalas
Levels: kangas koalas
```

Okay, no problem. Now let's try a different change.

```
> myData$animal[4] = "hippopotami"
Warning message:
In `[<-.factor`(`*tmp*`, 4, value = "hippopotami") :
   invalid factor level, NAs generated
```

Yikes! No hippopotami allowed! It isn't that R has some kind of marsupial filter. It's just that it kindly converted our character variable into a factor when we created the data frame. Once a factor is created, it can only deal with its existing levels. We can get around this in at least three ways (actually, since this is R, there are probably 47 ways around, but we'll stick to these 3).

First, we could have forced R to keep the animal variable as a character variable when setting up the data frame by using the **I()** function.

```
> myData = data.frame(I(animal))
> typeof(my.data$animal)                 # confirm that animal is a character
variable
[1] "character"
> myData$animal[4]
[1] "kangas"
> myData$animal[4] = "hippopotami"
> myData$animal[4]
[1] "hippopotami"
```

Second, we could allow R to make the conversion to a factor, and then we could add another level to the factor.

```
> animal = (c(rep("kangas", 4), rep("koalas", 5)))
> myData = data.frame(animal)           # Put the data in a data frame
> typeof(myData$animal)                 # which converts it to a factor
[1] "integer"
```

Note: *This is a bit misleading. This is a factor! So here R is just telling us about the vector of pointers.*

```
> myData$animal = factor(myData$animal, # We'll add a new level to the mix
+    levels =                           #   with the levels option
+       c(levels(myData$animal),        # Combining old levels
+         "hippopotami"))               #   with our new entry
> myData$animal[4]                      # Let's look at animal[4]
[1] kangas
Levels: kangas koalas hippopotami
> myData$animal[4] = "hippopotami"      # We can add "hippopotami" because
> myData$animal[4]                      #   that is included in the factor
[1] hippopotami
Levels: kangas koalas hippopotami
```

Finally, we could just make the conversions ourselves.

```
> animal = (c(rep("kangas", 4), rep("koalas", 5)))
> myData = data.frame(animal)           # Putting the data in a data frame
> typeof(myData$animal)                 # Check on the data type
[1] "integer"
> myData$animal =                       # Force variable back to character
+    as.character(myData$animal)
> typeof(myData$animal)                 # Recheck the type -- that works!
[1] "character"
```

```
> myData$animal[4]                        # Show observation 4 value
[1] "kangas"

> myData$animal[4] = "hippopotami"        # Now make the change to obs 4
> myData$animal[4]
[1] "hippopotami"
```

Which of these approaches you choose will depend on your patience and on whether you want the variable to end up as a factor or a character vector.

CONCLUSION

I am sorry that we have had to spend so long disentangling R objects. Objects are at the core of how R works; building this foundation has been critical for everything that will follow. At the end of the day, the schema I have offered here, built on a mostly straightforward distinction between data object types, storage modes, and object classes, will carry you a very long way in the R world. This approach isn't quite regulation, but until you are ready to integrate your work in R with other high-level computer languages or need to worry about microsecond differences in efficiency, it will get you by.[8]

Every R data object, then, can be characterized by its type, its storage mode, and any class information that might be attached to it. You need only worry about the four data object types: vectors, matrices, data frames, and lists. The data stored within these containers will be characterized by one of five storage modes: logical, numeric, character, date/time, or factor. The last two of these are what I have called "pseudo storage modes." You have to be a little more careful when you encounter date/time or factor values. In Chapter 9, we'll get into the idiosyncrasies of date and time data. In the meantime, be particularly aware of where R has taken its own initiative to convert between characters, numbers, and factors without your explicit permission. Object classes shouldn't cause you much grief. When things aren't being displayed or processed as you would expect, you might use **class()** to check to be sure there isn't something amiss in the class information.

Data object types, storage modes, and classes. You've got this. And now we are ready to move on to the process of getting real data into R. Someday shortly beyond that, we'll get to the fun stuff.

---

8. It is interesting to note that official R ends up in this same place for reading in data. The read family of commands includes a **colClasses=** option, which lumps together date and factor variables with the more traditional logical, numeric, and character storage modes.

CHAPTER 4

GETTING YOUR DATA INTO R

Data management and analysis starts with data. The world is increasingly full of data; but it doesn't do you any good if you can't get them from where they are to where you need them, which is in some R objects. Needless to say, if the data don't come into R correctly, it is even worse than not having them at all. In this chapter, we'll go over the most important and common methods for getting data into the R environment. These methods fall into three basic classes: (1) entering data by hand, (2) creating data within the R environment, and (3) importing data from other data sets.

ENTERING DATA

The first way to build a data set in R is simply to type it in. Except for very small data sets, this is generally a dreadful idea. Having provided that warning, here is how it is done.

Entering Data With the Concatenate Functions

The concatenate function is critical for a number of data management actions, as we'll see throughout this book. It is also the most rudimentary approach to entering data. In this case, concatenation means that a string of numbers or other data should be put together into a vector.

```
> myVar = c(1, 7, 3, 5, 9, 21, 8)        # Entering data with concatenate
> myVar                                   # Print data
[1]  1  7  3  5  9 21  8
```

We'll talk about concatenation as a process for putting text together in Chapter 8. When used for creating a data vector, the **c()** function can also create a vector of text values.

```
> myWords = c("ant", "ball", "clown")    # Concatenate words into variable
> myWords                                 # Print variable
[1] "ant"    "ball"   "clown"
```

Joining Vectors Into Matrices and Data Frames

Vectors can then be joined together into matrices with the **cbind()** and **rbind()** functions. **cbind(vector1, vector2)** joins two or more columns into a matrix. If you have several variables and want to combine them into a data set, use **cbind()**. Remember, though, that they have to be sorted in the same order if you want the observations to line up in the correct rows. Likewise, the number of elements in each vector needs to be the same. If it isn't, R will give you a warning, but then it will just repeat values to fill in the missing values.

```
> # cbind
> temp = c(78.4, 65.3, 72.9, 81.2)       # Setup some data
> rain = c(.025, .001, 0, 1.2)
> day = c(1, 2, 3, 4)
> weather1 = cbind(day, temp, rain)      # cbind demonstration
> weather1                                # Show results
     day temp  rain
[1,]   1 78.4 0.025
[2,]   2 65.3 0.001
```

```
[3,]   3 72.9 0.000
[4,]   4 81.2 1.200

> # rbind
> day1 = c(.025, 78.4)                # Setup some data
> day2 = c(.001, 65.3)
> day3 = c(0, 72.9)
> day4 = c(1.2, 81.2)
> weather2 =                          # rbind demonstration
+   rbind(day1, day2, day3, day4)
> weather2                            # Show matrix
        [,1] [,2]
day1 0.025 78.4
day2 0.001 65.3
day3 0.000 72.9
day4 1.200 81.2

> colnames(weather2) = c("rain", "temp")   # Add variable names for columns
> weather2                            # Show weather2 matrix w/names
        rain temp
day1 0.025 78.4
day2 0.001 65.3
day3 0.000 72.9
day4 1.200 81.2
```

Note that cbind incorporates the variable names as column labels and rbind incorporates the variable names as row labels. The other appropriate labels can be added with **rownames(myData) =** or **colnames(myData) =** as in the rbind example.

Here is an example where one of the vectors has a different length. Temperature and rain have four values, but day only has two. You can see how this could be handy for something like entering the 7 days of the week over and over, but it is dangerous if it happens inadvertently. Note that we also have to combine these vectors into a data frame, since regular R matrices cannot include objects with different storage modes (i.e., numeric and character variables). If we tried to put them just into a matrix, it would force all the numbers to be character variables, with the resulting grief we looked at in Chapter 3.

```
> temp = c(78.4, 65.3, 72.9, 81.2)        # Setup some data
> rain = c(.025, .001, 0, 1.2)
> day = c("Saturday", "Sunday")
> weekend.weather = data.frame(            # Combine unequal length vectors
+     cbind(day, temp, rain))              #     with cbind

> weekend.weather                          # Show results
        day temp   rain
1 Saturday 78.4  0.025
2   Sunday 65.3  0.001
3 Saturday 72.9      0
4   Sunday 81.2    1.2
```

In this example, the day vector is shorter than the others, so it gets repeated to fill in. This is very helpful as long as that is what you really wanted.

If you have *observations* in their own vectors, you can concatenate them into a matrix with the **rbind()** function. Again, if you want the columns of the resulting matrix to represent variables, you need to be sure that the row vectors are all the same length and are sorted the same way.

R usually doesn't care whether vectors are rows or columns. If push really comes to shove, it will treat a vector as a column. But you'll need to be careful to keep track of whether a vector of values is conceptually a variable (a column) or an observation (a row) for the more frequent case where it doesn't matter to R. You can force a default column vector to be a row vector (more precisely to be a matrix with just one row) with the transpose function, **t()**.

Entering Data With the R Spreadsheet

If you are used to working with Excel, you'll be glad to know that R does have a primitive spreadsheet sort of thing for entering data. If you are used to working with Excel, you'll be more than a little disappointed with the limited nature of this method. But it can be acceptable for some quick data entry or editing. You access it in a couple of ways. The most straightforward is just with the **data.entry()** command. The argument for that command (what goes in the parentheses) is a matrix or a list of vectors.

```
myX = c(1, 2, 3)                        # Create variable 1
myY = c("a", "b", "c")                  # Create variable 2
myData = cbind(myX, myY)                # Combine in data frame
data.entry(myData)                      # Open in data entry spreadsheet
```

This will open a spreadsheet where the data can be edited.

You cannot create a new data set with the **data.entry()** command, so if you aren't working on existing data, be sure to create even just one variable to get started.

```
x = 1
data.entry(x)
```

Once you get the spreadsheet open, working with the data and creating new variables is pretty straightforward, even if it is decidedly lacking in the features we have come to expect from modern spreadsheet software. The **data.entry()** spreadsheet does not preserve the data frame form, which is another significant limitation of this approach. If you feed it a data frame, it returns a list with each variable as a component object. The R manual also warns that the spreadsheet is implemented differently on different platforms, which may further limit your enthusiasm for this approach.

The `data.entry()` method does change the underlying data. The `edit()` method also opens a spreadsheet and has the advantage of working on data frames. It does not, however, change the underlying data. For this method, you need to assign the edited data to a new name (or overwrite the old name).

```
myX = c(1, 2, 3)                        # Create variable 1
myY = c("a", "b", "c")                  # Create variable 2
myData.df = data.frame(myX, myY)        # Combine in data frame
myData.df = edit(myData.df)             # Use edit() to open spreadsheet
```

The `edit()` command is another way to open the spreadsheet for data entry and editing.

The bottom-line message for all of these methods is that R really isn't the place to be entering data. The better ways to get your data into R are either inputting a data file, which we'll get to in just a minute, or, in some special cases, automating data creation, which we'll turn to now.

CREATING DATA

Our second method for getting data into R is to convince R to automatically create variable sequences. This is a hugely useful thing for statistics professors or people writing books about R, who often need to create a quick data set to illustrate a point. It is somewhat less useful for everyone else, who will generally be limited to working with data from their favorite version of the real world. Still, there are important occasions where one needs to generate new data as part of an analysis, so you'll need to pay attention.

Simple Sequences and Repetitions

We can start by creating a simple sequence of whole numbers using the colon construction.

```
> myVar1 = 0:10                         # A variable w/0-10 sequence
> myVar1                                # Show result
[1]  0  1  2  3  4  5  6  7  8  9 10
```

```
> myVar2 = 10:22                        # A variable w/10-22 sequence
> myVar2                                # Show result
[1] 10 11 12 13 14 15 16 17 18 19 20 21 22

> myVar3 = -5:5                         # A variable w/-5 to 5 sequence
> myVar3                                # Show result
[1] -5 -4 -3 -2 -1  0  1  2  3  4  5
```

The sequence function, **seq()**, allows you to set the size of the step between numbers. The function arguments are the starting value, the ending value, and the step size: **seq(from=, to=, by=)**.

```
> myVar4 = seq(0, 5, by = .5)          # A sequence from 0 to 5 by .5
> myVar4                                # Show result
 [1] 0.0 0.5 1.0 1.5 2.0 2.5 3.0 3.5 4.0 4.5 5.0

> myVar5 = seq(7, 5, -.25)             # A sequence from 7 to 5 by -.25
> myVar5                                # Show result
[1] 7.00 6.75 6.50 6.25 6.00 5.75 5.50 5.25 5.00
```

In the first example, we specify the **by=** *value explicity. The second example just uses the order of the arguments.*

The repeat function, **rep()**, can also be helpful for quick data entry. The two primary arguments are the values and the number of times to repeat them.

```
> myVar1 = rep(7, 3)                    # Create variable w/3 7's
> myVar1                                # Show result
[1] 7 7 7

> myVar2 = c(rep(1, 5), rep(2, 3))      # Create variable w/ 5 1's & 3 2's
> myVar2                                # Show result
[1] 1 1 1 1 1 2 2 2
```

```
> myVar3 = c(                          # Create variable with
+    rep("Fred", 2),                   #    2 "Fred" and
+    rep("Wilma", 4))                  #    4 "Wilma"

> myVar3                               # Show result
[1] "Fred"   "Fred"   "Wilma" "Wilma" "Wilma" "Wilma"
```

Generating Factors

When you need to create a factor on your own, you can do so with the **factor()** command. At a minimum, you need to give it a vector, which it will then turn into a factor variable. You can also provide an explicit set of levels and labels with the **levels=** and **labels=** options.

The generate levels, **gl()**, command is another approach to this same process. **gl()** normally takes four arguments. The first (**n=**) is the number of levels in the factor. The second (**k=**) is the number of times those levels should each be repeated. The third, which is optional, is the total length of the result (**length=**). The fourth, which is also optional, is a set of labels for the levels (**labels=**). You would think that the total length should be a multiple of the number of levels times the repeats, but as usual, if it is less, R will just keep repeating the whole sequence until it fills in the length, as in the second example below. The second example also shows the command setup without the explicit argument labels.

```
> myFactor = gl(n = 3,                 # Set up 3 levels
+    k = 2,                            # Each repeats twice
+    length = 6,                       # Total length is 6
+    labels = c("small", "med", "large")) # Matching labels for 3 levels

> myFactor                             # Display factor
[1] small small med   med   large large
Levels: small med large

> myFactor2 = gl(2, 4, 10, c("y", "n")) # Set 2 levels w/4 repeats
> myFactor2                            # Display factor
[1] y y y y n n n n y y
Levels: y n
```

Random Numbers and Statistical Distributions

Finally, it is often useful in statistical analysis to generate a series of values stochastically (i.e., randomly drawn) from a known probability distribution. Most commonly, you'll need either random numbers or values from a normal distribution.

Generating truly random numbers is a surprisingly tricky thing. The intricacies are beyond this book (more to the point, they are probably beyond this writer). Suffice it to say, the problem is that you need some kind of seed value to start your random number generator. This value itself needs to be random, so you can see that there is a bit of a recursive problem. R allows several different seeding algorithms. You can get a little clue as to the nature of this literature and the controversies it engenders knowing that one of R's seed generators is called the "Super-Duper" and that even with a name like that, the writers of the R manual warn that it still "does not pass the MTUPLE test of the Diehard battery." **help(RNG)** will clue you in on all this stuff, if that is where you want to go.

Those of you aspiring to design encryption protocols for nuclear weapon launch codes will want to spend a little more time on this subject. For most of the rest of us, pseudo-random will do.

runif(n) generates n random numbers from a uniform distribution. This means that any number is as likely to be drawn as any other. The default range is from 0 to 1. You can change this with the **min=** and **max=** options. These can be either spelled out or just included in order, as shown in the following example (I use the **round()** function to limit the display to two decimal places).

```
> myRand = runif(10)                    # 10 random numbers between 0,1
> round(myRand, 2)                      # Print rounded to 2 places
[1] 0.74 1.00 0.44 0.72 0.31 0.00 0.65 0.69 0.29 0.46

> myRand2 = runif(5, min = 0, max = 100)# 5 random values between 1, 100
> round(myRand2, 2)                     # Print them
[1] 52.85 23.11 24.79 82.33 91.69

> myRand3 = runif(3, 0, 10)            # 3 random values between 0, 10
> round(myRand3, 2)                     # Print them
[1] 3.13 2.29 8.50
```

To produce values from a normal distribution, we use the **rnorm(n)** function. At a minimum, you have to specify the number of values to generate *n*. You can also specify the mean and the standard deviation with the **mean=** and **sd=** options. Otherwise, they are taken to be 0 and 1, respectively. Figure 4.1 displays a simple histogram of a normal distribution using R's built-in **hist()** function.

```
> myNorm = rnorm(10)                        # 10 values from std normal dist
> round(myNorm, 2)                          # Print them
[1] -0.03  1.52  0.19  1.31  0.22 -0.43 -1.03 -0.19  0.18 -1.42

> myNorm2 =                                 # From normal distribution
+    rnorm(10, mean = 50, sd = 10)          #    with mean = 50 & std dev = 10

> round(myNorm2, 2)                         # Print them
[1] 50.43 26.50 46.92 45.13 60.58 47.01 37.03 45.03 42.03 47.06

> myNorm2 = rnorm(10000)                    # 10,000 values from std norm dist
> hist(myNorm2)                             # Display in histogram>
```

In the same basic manner, R will generate values from a number of other probability distributions (Poisson, binomial, Weibull, etc.). You can get the full list and instructions from **help(distributions)**.

There are lots of other fancy ways to generate even quite complex data by adding options to the **seq()** function or using the **rep()** function and the various distributions. If you become a statistics professor or write an R book, you'll definitely want to learn about them. But now let's get real. You aren't going to be inputting or creating much of your data directly in R. You already have a spreadsheet or some other kind of a file that is just teeming with data. You just need to get them into a form that R will recognize. Even if your data are still floating around on small scraps of paper, for all but the most hardened R user or the smallest data set, it is almost always easier to do the basic data entry in a spreadsheet. Let's finally turn, then, to the real work of importing data from other sources.

Figure 4.1   Histogram of Random Normal Values

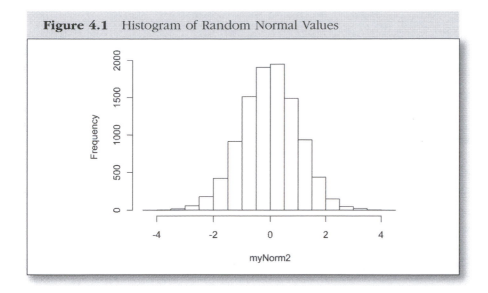

IMPORTING DATA

One of the great advantages and disadvantages of R is that it does not have a proprietary file format. R can work with data files in a number of different formats. Those of us who have worked with other statistics programs are used to the frustrations of the annual version upgrade, which often entails both significant expense and new, incompatible data formats. R works particularly well with simple text files, which means that you can easily go back and forth between different programs for working on your data set. The disadvantage of this generic approach is that you cannot just double-click a file and have it open up in R. A bit more work is involved in getting your data into R, which is the subject of the remainder of this chapter.

Working With the Working Directory

The first problem you are likely to encounter in importing data is telling R where your data are hiding. R keeps track of the location of a working directory where it assumes it will find things and where it puts anything you want it to save. If you need to know what R thinks the current working directory is, you can use the **getwd()** command. If all of your data are someplace simple like a c:\data folder, this is pretty straightforward: You can set up a working directory with the **setwd()** command.[1] Note, how-ever, that while your computer usually works with backslashes (\) for directory names, R uses forward slashes (/).[2]

```
> setwd("C:/data")
> getwd()
[1] "C:/data"
```

*Note that the parentheses for the **getwd()** function are empty. They are always empty. But you still can't leave them off.*

In the real world, your computer is likely to have a more complex set of folders that is a pain in the neck to keep track of, let alone to type with no errors. This is not too difficult a problem if you are using RStudio or one of the other interfaces that allow you to interact with R. These programs have a menu button for setting the working directory to be the same as the directory for the current R script file you are using. In RStudio, you'll find this in the Sessions menu.

If you need to set the working directory by hand, either because you are not using one of these editors or because your data are somewhere different from your command file, the easiest approach is probably to use the **file.choose()** function. This will let you browse to the folder you would like to use for your working directory.

```
setwd(dirname(file.choose()))
```

I wish I could tell you there was a way to do this without typing all those parentheses. Though aesthetically preposterous, they all make sense if you think in terms of the **file.choose()** function embedded in the **dirname()** function, embedded in the **setwd()** function. If you get all the parentheses right, this command will open a window that will allow you to browse to the directory of your choice. When you get there, choose any file just to set the working directory.

Alternatively, you can browse to the file in the Windows file manager, copy the directory name using Ctrl-C, and then paste it into your R command

---

1. I discuss resetting the default working directory in Appendix A.

2. We'll see later that backslashes play a special role as R's escape character.

file using Ctrl-V. If you do this, you have to then put it in quotation marks and switch the backslashes to forward slashes.

Typing the **getwd()** command will confirm that you have set the working directory where you want it. If you are setting up a file of R commands for a project that will use a given directory, you can then cut and paste the results of the **getwd()** command into a **setwd()** command, so that in the future, the command file will automatically go to the correct directory.

```
> setwd(dirname(file.choose()))
> getwd()
[1] "C:/Documents and Settings/Kurt/My Documents/Data"
```

Use Copy and Paste to move the directory name from the **getwd()** *function to the* **setwd()** *command.*

```
> setwd("C:/Documents and Settings/Kurt/My Documents/Data")
```

You can confirm the contents of the working directory with the **list.files()** command.

There are two basic philosophies for working directories. One approach is to set up a directory that you always use as your R working directory. A **setwd()** command pointing to that directory can then always be a part of the boilerplate you use at the beginning of any R session. Alternatively, if you will be reading or writing several data files in a single directory, you can set that directory as the working directory. Using the first approach, you have to set the working directory and then provide directory information or use the **file.choose()** method every time you read or write a file from somewhere else. Using the second approach, you may use the **file.choose()** method up front in setting up the working directory, and from then on, you can just use the filenames alone, as long as they are all in that particular working directory.

Once the working directory is set up, we can turn to the real issue of importing data.

THE READ COMMAND: OVERVIEW

The **read.table()** command tells R to read in some data. R can work with a number of different data formats. The read command has to be modified to tell R the form of the data. The most common and transparent forms of data are blank-, comma-, or tab-delimited files and data organized in fixed-width columns.

```
Space delimited:
129 8 55 32 6.3509 284.333 78 56 689 42 846 0.1 0.798

Comma Separated Values (CSV):
129,8,55,32,6.3509,284.333,78,56,689,42,846,0.1,0.798

Tab separated:
129     8       55      32      6.3509          284.333         78

Fixed Width:
1298755032 6.3509284.333Nebraska    7856 689428460.10.798
```

The data in the table can be numeric, factor, or textual (character) data. R expects the data in any given column to all be of the same storage mode (logical, character, or numeric). If any of the elements in a given column (with the exception of the first row when there is a header row with the variable names) is a character element, then the whole column will be interpreted as character elements or, worse yet, as a factor. This can be particularly important when dealing with different notations for missing data. If your data set uses text to indicate missing values, you may need to tell R this explicit formulation in order to prevent it from interpreting the whole column as text.

If your data set just uses blanks for missing data, you won't have any problem. But if it uses some other character code—"NA," "#N/A," "Null," "missing," etc.—then you need to let R in on the plan with the **na.strings = "myNAstring"** option. This is particularly important since if R encounters a character representation of missingness, it will treat the whole variable as a character variable.

As we saw in Chapter 3, for R, as in many computing environments, there is a difference between a numeric representation of a number and the character representation of the same number. The number 5 is different from the character "5." It is important to keep this distinction in mind. If you need it, return to Chapter 3 for a discussion on making the conversions between numeric, character, and factor variables.

When character data are read in using the **read.table()** family of functions or when a data frame is created using the **data.frame()**

function, character variables are by default turned into factors.[3] You can turn them back into regular character values using the **as.character()** function, or you can force R to leave them as vectors of character elements by using the **as.is = TRUE** parameter.

It can be a little more tedious for you, but it is more efficient for R, if you include the **colClasses=** option in your read statement. While this uses the term *classes*, it is actually about what I have called R data storage modes. The argument for **colClasses=** is a character vector listing the object storage modes for each column in your imported data: for example, **colClasses = c("character", "numeric", "numeric", "factor", "date")**. You can save a lot of typing here if you remember that you can just use NA for any column for which you want to allow R to decide the appropriate storage mode.

THE READ COMMAND: READING FROM THE CLIPBOARD

I am going to show you how to get data from the clipboard into R, even though I don't want you to do this. It is easy and quick to copy your data onto the clipboard and then use the shorthand **"clipboard"** in the place of a filename in a read command.[4] Here is what it looks like.

```
myData = read.delim("clipboard", header = TRUE)
```

This should be a pretty straightforward process, but there are several problems and significant dangers to this approach. From the start, you have to be sure that you have what you want on the clipboard. The clipboard can contain a lot of different kinds of information with significantly different formatting. A more general problem with the clipboard approach is that you can't include it in a command file and be confident the next time around that the clipboard is still holding the desired data. Hence, reproducibility takes a big hit in this process. I think it is better and safer to stick to the

---

3. I discuss changing this default behavior in Appendix A.

4. There is also a **readClipboard()** method, but in this approach, the contents of the clipboard are always interpreted as character strings, so an additional step is required to translate to numeric data. If what you want to bring in is just text, this can be an efficient, though still irreplicable, method. (See the discussion in Chapter 3 on converting character values to numeric values.)

approaches described below, particularly the use of the **read.table()** method with tab- or comma-separated files.

 ## The Read Command: Blank-Delimited Tables

The default table format is for the data in each row to be separated by one or more blank spaces. R doesn't actually care how many blank spaces. Nor does the number of blank spaces have to be consistent between the different columns. The thing to be careful about is text variables that have meaningful spaces in them. If you have a textual variable with the names of countries, then "France" is no problem, but "North Korea" will be read as two distinct variables, "North" and "Korea." If there is any danger of spaces in your data that will cause these problems, you need to manipulate the data set so that you can use comma-delimited, tab-delimited, or fixed-width read methods, as discussed later.

A table with blanks separating the variables can be read with the **read.table()** function. There are a number of options you can use for things such as skipping blank lines or comments, and how to handle missing values, but the most important options are simply the file name (in quotation marks) and the indicator for whether or not the file contains the variable names in the first row. If there is no header row, you will need to set the header option to false (**header = FALSE**), and R will assign default variable names (*V*1, *V*2, *V*3, . . .).

```
myData = read.table("myDataFile.txt", header = FALSE)
```

Sometimes, the beginning of a data file has more than one row before the start of the actual data. You can tell R to skip as many rows as necessary with the **skip=** option. Just set it to the number of rows to skip before starting to input.

Two other attributes that can be useful to know about are **col.names=** and **row.names=**. These two attributes are used to tell R the names that should be used to identify the variables (columns) or observations (rows). You only need to use **col.names=** if you don't have a header. **row.names=** can tell R that one of the columns contains names that can be used to identify the rows. **col.names=** needs to be a vector with one unique name for each column (variable). **row.names=** can be either a vector of names or a single number that tells R which column should be interpreted as the row names. If the third column of the data set contains the names of the subjects, for example, then you could use **row. names = 3** to pass that information to R.

If you are working with a large data file and just want to test whether you have set up the read statement correctly, you can use the **nrows = X** attribute to tell R to only read the first *X* rows.

THE READ COMMAND: COMMA-SEPARATED VALUES

If the data are in a comma-separated file, then the appropriate command is **read.csv()**.

```
myData = read.csv("myDataFile.csv", header = TRUE)
```

You can easily create a comma-separated values (CSV) file with most spreadsheet and database programs by using the Save As command under the file menu to save as a CSV file.

Your CSV file should be set up with one observation per row and one variable per column. If your data are in a more complex form that involves several lines per observation or has the observations in the columns, you will need to see the discussion on importing contingency tables in the section "Dealing With Multidimensional Data" or the discussion on transposing data sets at the end of Chapter 10.

Europeans, Latin Americans, and other sophisticates may need to use the **read.csv2()** command, which changes the decimal point separator from a period to a comma and the value separator from a comma to a semicolon. Each of these things can be controlled individually. Conceptually, it is useful to note here that **read.csv2()** and indeed all of the read command variants, are just different versions of the **read.table()** command with different options selected as the defaults. You can see a list of these options and their defaults below. If you have particularly unusual data, you will need to wade into the help files for the **read.table()** command to get the details on the options and switches that can be included.

```
read.table() options:

header = TRUE
sep = ","
```

```
quote = "\" ' "
dec = "."
row.names=
col.names=
as.is = TRUE
na.strings = "NA"
colClasses = NA
nrows = -1
skip = 0
check.names = TRUE
fill = !blank.lines.skip
strip.white = FALSE
blank.lines.skip = TRUE
comment.char = "#"
allowEscapes = FALSE
flush = FALSE
```

This list of the available options for the read.table command gives you a sense of the flexibility of that command. Note the use of the backslash in the quote option. As we'll see in Chapter 8, this tells R to treat the next character literally.

As with blank-delimited files, with comma-separated data you'll have to be careful if there are meaningful commas within any of the variables. The comma-separated approach will choke, for example, on country names like "Korea, North." If that is your situation, you'll probably want to go with tab-separated data.

THE READ COMMAND: TAB-SEPARATED DATA

Another common data format is to use tabs to separate data values. Again, there are many available options for particular situations, but for most data sets, the defaults will work fine. Usually all you will need are the file name and the reminder that your file has the variable names in the first row (**header = T**).

```
myData = read.delim("myDataFile.txt", header = TRUE)
```

As always, you have to be careful about missing values. If your data set uses a special character or other code for missing, you have to pass that information on to R with the **na.strings = "myNAstring"** option. Failure to do this will cause R to treat any variable with missing data as a character variable.

For the Europeans and their friends, there is a **read.delim2()** for data sets using commas as the decimal separator.

Again, all of these elements are just variations on the underlying **read. table()** command. The difference between comma-separated and tab-separated files is indicated by the **sep = " "** option, with the desired separator character between the quotation marks. Comma-separated values would be indicated as in the following.

```
myData = read.table("myDataFile.txt", header = TRUE, sep = ",")
```

Tab-separated values can be indicated with the "\t" value.

```
myData = read.table("myDataFile.txt", header = TRUE, sep = "\t")
```

It seems unlikely, but if you have data—perhaps passed on by aliens—that are separated by percent signs, the appropriate code would be as follows:

```
myData = read.table("myDataFile.txt", header = TRUE, sep = "%")
```

The Read Command: Fixed-Width Data

In the early days of computing, programs and data came on punch cards that were limited to 80 characters each. The standard approach to dealing with input in languages like Fortran was to assign fixed widths to data fields. That is, each variable was assigned a set number of the 80 characters. You will still come across such formatting if you are working with older, or "classic" if you prefer, data sets. Fixed-width files are difficult to disentangle visually because there will often be no spaces or other separators between the different variable values (Figure 4.2). A codebook with a list of the field

Figure 4.2   A Fixed-Width Data Set

```
       V1    V2  V3     V4  V5 V6    V7 V8 V9
       17932.78944    CTI05.768.3210 53
       18225.63112    ABDV13.641.5231221
       19073.84274MXABCC14.629.3116510
```

widths is necessary to figure out where each variable starts and stops. Fixed-width data can be directly imported into R with the **read.fwf()** command. This requires a vector setting out the width of each variable.

If you have such a vector or are working with similar data repeatedly, this is a worthwhile approach. Frankly, for a one-off, you may find it easier to transfer the file into a spreadsheet like Excel, which makes it very easy to correctly import fixed-width files. You can then save it from there as a tab- or comma-separated file.

The width vector is specified with the **width=** option. If the data for a single observation come on multiple lines (e.g., there was too much to fit in just 80 spaces), you need to use the **width = list(line1vector, line2vector)** specifications for each line.

```
Data:
123.459875502Pac        34589
38.0 56 3892Eminem      17840
256.4948733150cent      20945

myData = read.fwf("myDataFile.txt", width = c(5, 2, 3, 2, 15, 3, 2))
```

This will return the values shown in Table 4.1.

Table 4.1   Parsed Fixed-Width Data

V1	V2	V3	V4	V5	V6	V7
123.4	59	875	50	2Pac	345	89
38.0	56	38	92	Eminem	178	40
256.4	94	873	31	50Cent	209	45

Here is an example for the case of data on multiple lines:

```
Data:
0011123.459875502Pac
001234589
002138.0 56 3892Eminem
002217840
0031256.4948733150cent
003220945

line1 = c(3, -2, 5, 2, 3, 2, 15)          # Use -2 to skip line numbers
line2 = c(-3, -2, 3, 2)                    # Now skip obs and line numbers
myData = read.fwf("myDataFile.txt", width = list(line1, line2))
```

This will return the data shown in Table 4.2.

Table 4.2 Parsed Multiline Data

V1	V2	V3	V4	V5	V6	V7	V8
001	123.4	59	875	50	2Pac	345	89
002	38.0	56	38	92	Eminem	178	40
003	256.4	94	873	31	50Cent	209	45

Another potential pitfall to watch for in fixed-width data is the presence of spaces at the end of a line. When this happens, you will need to put in a dummy variable with the number of spaces as its width to prevent R from treating them as other missing variables.

IMPORTING FOREIGN FILE TYPES

It is possible to import data directly from other statistics programs. This can be dangerous and difficult, so sometimes it is easier to first export the data to a text-based file type, such as a comma- or tab-delimited file, or even to bounce it through a common format like Excel and then to save it as a comma- or tab-delimited file. But if a critical data set is only available in a file type suited for a statistics program that you don't own and for which you are unenthusiastic about shelling out $900, you may find the importation process worth pursuing.

Here, we have no choice but to turn to a package, which I have mostly tried to avoid, for the reasons outlined in Chapter 1. To import from other statistics formats, you will need to download and load the foreign package. We do this with the **library(foreign)** function.[5]

The most common of the currently supported file flavors include the following:

read.dta("myDataFile.dta") for Stata files

read.mtp("myDataFile.mtp") for Minitab portable worksheets

read.systat("myDataFile.syd") for Systat files

read.ssd("myDataFile.sd7") for SAS files

read.spss("myDataFile.sav") for SPSS[6] files

To read a Stata file, for example, we just need to issue the instruction to load the foreign package and then use a read statement.

```
> library(foreign)
> myData = read.dta("c:/data/mydata.dta")
```

We can drop the full file path if we have set the working directory with the **setwd()** *command.*

Several of these formats include a number of complexities. For example, most programs have their own rules about translating variable names and promulgate a variety of missing data indicators. Moreover, companies that make money from selling upgrades to their software packages often change their file formats, so one has to be careful about that as well. Bottom line, the comma- or tab-delimited approach is often safer. If you have to work with foreign formats, you will probably want to consult the online manual for the details on the foreign package. You will find that at http://cran.r-project.org/web/packages/foreign/foreign.pdf

---

5. Instructions for installing and working with packages are included in Appendixes A and C.

6. SPSS was acquired by IBM in October 2009.

Exporting Data in Foreign Formats

The foreign package also allows you to write files to the format for several other statistics programs. For example, **write.dta(dataframe)** creates a Stata data set. But don't do this. All of these other programs can also import tab- and comma-delimited files. If you need to save a data set, just save it as a comma- or tab-delimited file, which will be more transparent and universally accessible. Then, it is easy enough to import that file into whatever program you care to.

INTEGRATING STRUCTURED QUERY LANGUAGE WITH R

The use of a Structured Query Language (SQL) interface to work directly with a relational database or spreadsheet can really open up an integrated approach to working with data across different programs. It is, however, beyond the scope of this book, since SQL adds another layer of data management language. It requires installing an additional package for R, usually either the RODBC or the RMySQL package. These, in turn, will need specific drivers for the kind of file you are trying to read from (and the version, e.g., Excel 2007 and 2003 are different). It will also be necessary to set up DSN (Data Source Name) administration on your computer, a process that can differ depending on your operating system.[7]

EXTRACTING DATA FROM COMPLEX DATA SOURCES

R can be used to extract data from more complex data sets. The most common mode for this is to import the data as textual data and then use text-parsing commands to break the data down into the appropriate observations and variables. Many data sets available on web pages, for example, are broken up with HTML tags. These can be systematically analyzed and used to organize data. We'll go over the process for parsing complex textual data, including data scraped from the web, in Chapter 8.

There are several projects and packages out there for various degrees of integration of R with Excel. This is an attractive notion for those who have already invested in developing their Excel skills, and as I have said, the spreadsheet environment is very effective for a lot of basic kinds of data

---

7. The R-Data manual at http://cran.r-project.org/doc/manuals/R-data.html and the vignettes for the specific packages, such as RODBC and RmySQL, provide more detail on these connections.

manipulation. The problem with Excel and with the approaches that seek to pull data directly from Excel is that Excel can hide a lot of trouble in its individual cells. Excel's formatting and equation options often mean that the numbers that you are looking at in Excel aren't the values that other programs will see. Again, the safe way to deal with this is to save your Excel data as a clean .csv (comma delimited) or .txt (tab delimited) file and then import it to R.

 ## Web Scraping

Increasingly, data come from the web. Often, that just means downloading a file and then reading it in using one of the methods outlined earlier. Other times, a data set is displayed directly on a webpage and is acquired by what is called "web scraping." Basically, this involves extracting the relevant data from the underlying HTML code that controls the webpage.[8] This code can be read with the **readLines("http://www .myWebsiteURL")** command. Filtering the relevant data from all the other background HTML requires some skill at working with text data, which we'll get to in Chapter 8. I provide a worked-out example and a tutorial on using R for web scraping at the end of Chapter 8.

 ## Dealing With Multidimensional Data

Sometimes a data set comes in a form that collapses several dimensions into a two-dimensional spreadsheet. Consider the following data about voting patterns by state (Table 4.3). This combines three dimensions— the state, the party, and the year—into a two-dimensional representation. Both the state and the party are represented on the rows. This violates the principle articulated in Chapter 1 that the unit of observation has to be consistent with just one unique observation on each line. In this case, when the state is the unit of observation, each observation requires three lines.

As I have said, R is very flexible and powerful. There are several ways to import these kinds of data directly. In particular, you can look at the **scan()** commands and the **read.ftable()** commands. My suspicion is that you will find these difficult to use, and there will be considerable danger

---

8. Be aware that there can be important privacy and copyright issues in extracting and analyzing some website data.

Table 4.3   Example of a Multidimensional Contingency Table

		1960	1964	1968	1972
Alaska	Dem. vote				
	Rep. vote				
	Ind. vote				
Vermont	Dem. vote				
	Rep. vote				
	Ind. vote				

Note: Dem. = Democratic, Rep. = Republican, Ind. = Independent.

of mangling the data in the process of trying to set up the import (did I mention yet the importance of maintaining a safe backup of your original data files?). Unless you are repeatedly using the same kinds of data structures, it probably isn't worth it to work out all the details of the necessary **scan()** statements. It may be safer to import the data as a .csv file and then use conditional statements and other data manipulation functions (Chapter 7) to sort the data out into the appropriate units of observation.

When the input file is relatively straightforward, **read.ftable()** can be very efficient. The definition of *straightforward* here is that there is a single column that defines the variation of the data by row.

IMPORTING PROBLEMATIC CHARACTERS

We'll get more into the intricacies of working with character values in Chapter 8, but for the time being, I'll point out that for the rare occasion when you need to include quotation marks in your data, you can prevent R from treating them as text delimiters by using double quotation marks. Suppose the data string you want to import is

The friendly computer said "hello"

You would need to adjust this string by doubling the quotation marks before the data import:

The friendly computer said ""hello""

You can make this change with the find-and-replace facility in a spreadsheet or text-processing program.

As we saw earlier, if your data have commas that you need to maintain, you will need to just use the **sep=** option to specify an alternative separator.

By default, R interprets the crosshatch character (#) as a comment line, whether it occurs in a batch file or a data file. If your data set has cross-hatches, you will need to tell R to turn off the comment character. You do this with the option **comment.char = ""**. You could also set up an alternative comment character this way, but the unfortunate reality is that there aren't very many characters left that don't have other important functions. If you are having trouble here, it might be better to change the cross-hatches with Find and Replace before trying to import the data.

A final issue is dealing with text strings that include some amount of leading or trailing spaces. Using the option **strip.white = T** in the read command can take care of this problem. This requires that the separator character be explicitly specified with the **sep=** option. **strip.white=** only deals with leading and trailing spaces and will not remove the spaces between words (for more on these kinds of manipulations, see Chapter 8).

```
myData = read.delim("myDataFile.txt",    # Read some data
   sep = "\t",                           # Separator = tab
   strip.white = T,                      # Remove spaces
   header = T)                           # Data have headers
```

 ## MORE RESOURCES

The most important resource for understanding importing data into R is the R-Data section of the online R manual. It can be found at http://cran.r-project.org/doc/manuals/R-data.html.

The specific instructions for importing foreign file types are available at http://cran.r-project.org/web/packages/foreign/foreign.pdf.

Now that we've got a data set in, it is time to start doing something with it. The first thing to do is to make sure that it is all there and looks like it is supposed to. With a small data set, that is pretty easy. With larger data sets, we'll need to call on the powers of R for summarizing, authenticating, and visualizing data.

CHAPTER 5

REVIEWING AND SUMMARIZING DATA

Once you have your data imported or (heaven forbid) inputted into the R environment, you will need to know how to view it and how to check it to be sure that it is what you want it to be. That is the subject of this chapter. Fortunately, many of the same tools that we might use for analyzing and visualizing data are also available for checking and validating data. As the size of your data set increases, the ability to do automated and sample-based checking becomes ever more important. In the realm of really Big Data, these methods become a science all their own. For now, I trust you are learning R on data sets that are a little more manageable, even if they have already surpassed what can be easily proofed visually on a spreadsheet. We'll start with some of the most basic techniques for summarizing data. Then, we'll look at some tools for data sampling. We'll end with some of the simplest visualization tools, although those skills will really depend on the much more in-depth treatment we'll get to in Chapters 12 to 15.

At the end of this chapter, you will likely be ready for a little break. I've added an appendix for Chapter 5 that goes over some of the most common R traps that you have most likely begun to fall into already.

While the subject of this chapter is data sets that have gotten too large to review visually, for the purpose of learning these techniques, we'll begin by creating some synthetic data to work with in this chapter and in Chapter 6. This data set will be small enough so that we can see just how things are working. Here, I create four variables for some zoological data demonstrating various methods within a single data frame.

```
ch5data = data.frame(                      # Create a data frame
  year = c(1935:1959,                      # First variable is years
    1940:1949,                             # Sequence with colon
    1935, 1942, 1958, 1964, 1970),         # Some more years with commas
  animal = c(rep("Mouse", 25),             # Next variable is animal type
    rep("Kangaroo", 10),                   # 25 mice, 10 Kangaroos
    rep("Elephant", 5)),                   #    5 Elephants
  weight = round(c(                        # Next is plausible weights
    rnorm(25, mean = .06, sd = .006),  #    normally distributed
    rnorm(10, mean = 100, sd = 14),    #    around a mean
    rnorm(5, mean = 12000,             #    and std dev
      sd = 700)), 3),                  #    and rounded to 3 digits
  captive = rep(                           # Finally a captivity status from
    c(TRUE, FALSE, FALSE, FALSE), 10)) #    a repeated TRUE/FALSE pattern
```

To view your data on the screen, simply type in the name of the data frame (or any object). This is a quick way to see what you have for very small data sets. It isn't very helpful if it is a large data set, which will just whiz by on the monitor. The **print()** and **format()** commands give you a little more control over how things are displayed. For now, we just want to be able to get a sense of the data that we are working with.

We can get an overview of our data either by looking at the characteristics that define how R stores the data or by looking at statistical summaries of the data. We saw in Chapter 3, how to use the **attributes()** and **str()** functions to display the basic storage characteristics of a data frame or other object. That's a good starting point for making sure that you and R are in basic agreement about the object type and its defining elements, such as column and row names.

```
> attributes(ch5data)                    # Show data frame attributes
$names
[1] "year"    "animal"  "weight"  "captive"
```

```
$row.names
 [1]  1  2  3  4  5  6  7  8  9 10 11 12 13 14 15 16 17 18 19 20 21 22 23 [24] 2
26 27 28 29 30 31 32 33 34 35 36 37 38 39 40

$class
[1] "data.frame"

> str(ch5data)
'data.frame':    40 obs. of  4 variables:
 $ year     : num  1935 1936 1937 1938 1939 ...
 $ animal   : Factor w/ 3 levels "Elephant","Kangaroo",..: 3 3 3 3 3 3 3 ...
 $ weight   : num 0.059 0.06 0.065 0.06 0.056 0.056 0.055 0.067 0.058 ...
 $ captive  : logi  TRUE FALSE FALSE FALSE TRUE FALSE ...
```

Note that animal was entered as a character variable but was automatically converted to a factor, which is R's default behavior.

If you want to look at some of the more critical components on their own, **names()**, as we have seen, will give you a list of your variables (columns). **length()** will tell you how long a vector is (i.e., the number of observations). **length()** can also be used for matrices, in which case it gives you the longest dimension. Better, for that, to use the **dim()** function to see how many rows and columns there are in a vector, matrix, or data frame. You can get the number of rows or columns alone with the **nrow()** and **ncol()** functions. You can also use the **dim()** function to return one or the other dimensions. It is a little ungainly, but you add a 1 or a 2 in brackets to the end of the function to return either the numbers of rows, [1], or the number of columns, [2]. **dim(myData)[1]** is the same as **nrow(myData)**. **dim(myData)[2]** is the same as **ncol(myData)**. The **dim()** command can also be used to force the dimensions of a data set.

```
> dim(ch5data)                   # Show dimensions (rows x cols)
[1] 40   4

> nrow(ch5data)                  # Show num of rows (observations)
[1] 40
```

```
ᴏl(ch5data)                          # Show num of columns (variables)
1] 4
```

SUMMARY FUNCTIONS

Once you and R are in agreement about object types and characteristics, you can turn to the more interesting questions about what your data actually look like. The most basic way to check on your data integrity is to look at some statistical summary functions. There are several useful functions for this purpose:

length(x) returns the number of elements (observations) in the variable x

mean(x) returns the mean (average) of the variable x.

median(x) returns the median of the variable x.

sum(x) returns the sum of all the values of the variable x.

max(x) returns the largest value of the variable x.

min(x) returns the smallest value of the variable x.

range(x) returns the smallest and largest values of the variable x.

sd(x) returns the standard deviation of the variable x.

unique(x) returns a vector with the unique values in x.

For most of these (most important **mean()** and **sd()**), you have to specify the **na.rm = T** option if you have any observations with missing values. This confirms for R that you really want to generate these statistics without the missing values.

```
> myVar = c(1, 2, 3, 4, NA, 5)          # A variable w/ missing values
> mean(myVar)                           # Mean function returns NA
[1] NA
> mean(myVar, na.rm = T)                # Mean without missing values
[1] 3
```

Alternatively, you can generate the minimum, median, mean, and first and third quintiles for a whole data frame with the **summary()** command. It generates a table displaying these values for every numeric variable in the data frame.

```
> summary(ch5data)                          # Summary statistics for ch5data
       year              animal        weight             captive
 Min.   :1935     Elephant: 5    Min.   :     0.050    n:26
 1st Qu.:1942     Kangaroo:10    1st Qu.:     0.060    y:14
 Median :1946     Mouse   :25    Median :     0.065
 Mean   :1947                    Mean   :  1538.618
 3rd Qu.:1952                    3rd Qu.:    92.000
 Max.   :1970                    Max.   : 12638.400
```

Factors (categorical variables) are summarized with the number of observations for each value. This is very helpful for summarizing something like sex (male/female) but is irksome if one of your variables is something like the person's name, or even the state or country, where there may be dozens or hundreds of possibilities. It can also get you into trouble, but acts as an alarm bell, if one of the variables you thought was numeric is read in as a factor. (See the discussion at the end of Chapter 3 on dealing with factor/number/character confusion.)

CHECKING A SAMPLE OF YOUR DATA

If you have a large data set, it will be difficult to look it all over at once. The **head(dataframe, number of observations)** command allows you to work with just the first several observations.

```
> head(ch5data, 7)                          # Display first 7 observations
   year   animal  weight captive
1  1935   Mouse   0.065       y
2  1936   Mouse   0.054       n
```

```
$row.names
 [1]  1  2  3  4  5  6  7  8  9 10 11 12 13 14 15 16 17 18 19 20 21 22 23 [24] 24 25
26 27 28 29 30 31 32 33 34 35 36 37 38 39 40

$class
[1] "data.frame"

> str(ch5data)
'data.frame':    40 obs. of  4 variables:
 $ year     : num   1935 1936 1937 1938 1939 ...
 $ animal   : Factor w/ 3 levels "Elephant","Kangaroo",..: 3 3 3 3 3 3 3 ...
 $ weight   : num 0.059 0.06 0.065 0.06 0.056 0.056 0.055 0.067 0.058 ...
 $ captive  : logi   TRUE FALSE FALSE FALSE TRUE FALSE ...
```

Note that animal was entered as a character variable but was automatically converted to a factor, which is R's default behavior.

If you want to look at some of the more critical components on their own, **names()**, as we have seen, will give you a list of your variables (columns). **length()** will tell you how long a vector is (i.e., the number of observations). **length()** can also be used for matrices, in which case it gives you the longest dimension. Better, for that, to use the **dim()** function to see how many rows and columns there are in a vector, matrix, or data frame. You can get the number of rows or columns alone with the **nrow()** and **ncol()** functions. You can also use the **dim()** function to return one or the other dimensions. It is a little ungainly, but you add a 1 or a 2 in brackets to the end of the function to return either the numbers of rows, [1], or the number of columns, [2]. **dim(myData)[1]** is the same as **nrow(myData)**. **dim(myData)[2]** is the same as **ncol(myData)**. The **dim()** command can also be used to force the dimensions of a data set.

```
> dim(ch5data)                      # Show dimensions (rows x cols)
[1] 40   4

> nrow(ch5data)                     # Show num of rows (observations)
[1] 40
```

```
> ncol(ch5data)                        # Show num of columns (variables)
[1] 4
```

SUMMARY FUNCTIONS

Once you and R are in agreement about object types and characteristics, you can turn to the more interesting questions about what your data actually look like. The most basic way to check on your data integrity is to look at some statistical summary functions. There are several useful functions for this purpose:

length(x) returns the number of elements (observations) in the variable x

mean(x) returns the mean (average) of the variable x.

median(x) returns the median of the variable x.

sum(x) returns the sum of all the values of the variable x.

max(x) returns the largest value of the variable x.

min(x) returns the smallest value of the variable x.

range(x) returns the smallest and largest values of the variable x.

sd(x) returns the standard deviation of the variable x.

unique(x) returns a vector with the unique values in x.

For most of these (most important **mean()** and **sd()**), you have to specify the **na.rm = T** option if you have any observations with missing values. This confirms for R that you really want to generate these statistics without the missing values.

```
> myVar = c(1, 2, 3, 4, NA, 5)         # A variable w/ missing values
> mean(myVar)                          # Mean function returns NA
[1] NA
> mean(myVar, na.rm = T)               # Mean without missing values
[1] 3
```

Alternatively, you can generate the minimum, median, mean, and first and third quintiles for a whole data frame with the **summary()** command. It generates a table displaying these values for every numeric variable in the data frame.

```
> summary(ch5data)                      # Summary statistics for ch5data
      year              animal        weight            captive
 Min.    :1935    Elephant: 5    Min.    :    0.050    n:26
 1st Qu.:1942    Kangaroo:10    1st Qu.:    0.060    y:14
 Median :1946    Mouse    :25    Median :    0.065
 Mean    :1947                   Mean    : 1538.618
 3rd Qu.:1952                    3rd Qu.:   92.000
 Max.    :1970                   Max.    :12638.400
```

Factors (categorical variables) are summarized with the number of observations for each value. This is very helpful for summarizing something like sex (male/female) but is irksome if one of your variables is something like the person's name, or even the state or country, where there may be dozens or hundreds of possibilities. It can also get you into trouble, but acts as an alarm bell, if one of the variables you thought was numeric is read in as a factor. (See the discussion at the end of Chapter 3 on dealing with factor/number/character confusion.)

CHECKING A SAMPLE OF YOUR DATA

If you have a large data set, it will be difficult to look it all over at once. The **head(dataframe, number of observations)** command allows you to work with just the first several observations.

```
> head(ch5data, 7)                       # Display first 7 observations
   year   animal  weight  captive
1  1935   Mouse   0.065      y
2  1936   Mouse   0.054      n
```

```
3 1937   Mouse   0.052        n
4 1938   Mouse   0.050        y
5 1939   Mouse   0.064        n
6 1940   Mouse   0.056        n
7 1941   Mouse   0.058        y
```

Random sampling may be an even more helpful solution for this problem. The **sample(vectorname, samplesize)** function works very nicely on one-dimensional vectors (i.e., a single variable).

```
> myVector = c(1:1000)          # Create a vector
> sample(myVector, 5)           # Random sample of 5 observations
[1] 835 937  10 314 403
```

Unfortunately, **sample()** doesn't work directly on data frames. If you want to sample from a matrix or a data frame, it takes two steps. First, you have to set up a vector that contains the observation numbers for a random sample. Second, you can display those observations. In the following example, I create a vector of five random observation numbers. I do this using **nrow(my.dataframe)** to set the maximum observation number. This vector is then used to select observations to view from the data frame. This whole thing could be done in one step, as in the final line of the example, but that is likely to be more confusing and more prone to error.

```
> sample5 = sample(1:nrow(ch5data), 5)  # Create vector of 5 sample values
> ch5data[sample5,]                     # Print sample of data
     year     animal    weight captive
24 1958      Mouse     0.060       n
28 1942   Kangaroo    91.700       y
```

```
29 1943 Kangaroo     92.900       n
19 1953   Mouse       0.062       y
38 1958 Elephant  12638.400       n

> ch5data[sample(1:nrow(ch5data), 5),]     # All in one line
```

sample() can also be used to do probabilistic or weighted sampling. The default assumption is that the sampling process is based on a uniform random distribution. In that case, there should be an equal probability of drawing any observation. It is not uncommon, however, to need to weight different observations differently. The **prob=** option for the **sample()** function gives R a vector of probabilities to associate with each element in the sample vector. This is also a good place to mention the **replace=** option for **sample()**, which tells R whether or not to sample with replacement, that is, to draw each element of the sample from the whole vector rather than from only the remaining elements as each additional sample element is drawn out. The default is sampling without replacement (**replace = FALSE**).[1]

Another nice use for the **head()** or **sample()** approach is to use them within other operations to speed up trial runs on just a subset of the data while you are getting your programming working efficiently.

REVIEWING DATA BY CATEGORIES

It can be very helpful to review your data broken out into different strata or groups. There are several ways to do this. At a basic level, one of the easiest is the **table()** function, which can set out the number of observations that occur on two dimensions. It takes two variables for its main arguments, the first for the row dimension and the second for the column. This will work best with factors, or at least variables that aggregate with some frequent values. It's not so good for things that have a lot of unique values. Here is an example that works with our dummy data set and then runs a couple of tables on it.

---

1. The survey package provides several helpful functions if you are doing weighted survey analysis.

```
> table(ch5data$animal, ch5data$captive) # Create animal x captive table

            n   y
  Elephant  3   2
  Kangaroo  7   3
  Mouse     16  9

> table(ch5data$captive, ch5data$animal) # Create captive x animal table

      Elephant Kangaroo Mouse
  n        3        7      16
  y        2        3       9
```

These same things can be done with the crosstab function, **xtabs()**, which has the advantage of also allowing you to compute chi-square statistics. It is formulated a little bit differently, however, and I deal with that in the statistics discussion in Appendix B.

We'll spend a lot more time later coming to grips with the apply family of functions (Chapter 7), but it's worth a quick preview here of using the **lappy()** function to summarize data split into different categories by a factor or other variable. The apply functions apply another function to a data set. For these purposes, we use the **lapply()** function in combination with the **split()** function, which divides the data up by a factor variable. Here is the basic syntax to apply the **summary()** function to **myData** split up by the **myFactor** variable:

```
lapply(split(myData, myFactor), summary)
```

If you just want one of the component functions, you could just replace summary with the mean or standard deviation, or the like. In those cases, you can pass the **na.rm = T** option along after another comma, as in this construction:

```
lapply(split(myData, myFactor), mean, na.rm = T)
```

Another method for dividing up data is the **cut()** function, which can be used to split up a data set by the critical values of a continuous variable. The **cut()** function converts a numeric variable into a factor at a set of cut points. These dividing lines either can be provided to the function explicitly or you can simply indicate how many bins you want, and R will divide the data up evenly. Once a continuous variable has been converted to a factor, it can then be included in the **lapply(split())** approach, as shown here:

```
> lapply(                            # Apply a function to a data frame
+  split(ch5data,                    # Split up data before applying
+    cut(ch5data$weight,             # Variable to use as factor
+      breaks = c(0, 50, 500, 100000),    # Break points (including ends)
+      labels =                      # Labels for the different levels
+        c("small", "large", "huge"))),
+  summary)                          # Function to apply
$small
      year         animal         weight          captive
 Min.   :1935   Elephant: 0   Min.   :0.05000   n:16
 1st Qu.:1941   Kangaroo: 0   1st Qu.:0.05700   y: 9
 Median :1947   Mouse   :25   Median :0.06100
 Mean   :1947                 Mean   :0.06044
 3rd Qu.:1953                 3rd Qu.:0.06500
 Max.   :1959                 Max.   :0.06900

$large
      year         animal         weight          captive
 Min.   :1940   Elephant: 0   Min.   : 72.50    n:7
 1st Qu.:1942   Kangaroo:10   1st Qu.: 89.53    y:3
 Median :1944   Mouse   : 0   Median : 92.30
 Mean   :1944                 Mean   : 96.61
 3rd Qu.:1947                 3rd Qu.:104.12
 Max.   :1949                 Max.   :127.90

$huge
      year         animal        weight         captive
 Min.   :1935   Elephant:5   Min.   :11702    n:3
 1st Qu.:1942   Kangaroo:0   1st Qu.:11708    y:2
```

```
Median :1958    Mouse   :0    Median :12151
Mean    :1954                 Mean    :12115
3rd Qu.:1964                  3rd Qu.:12377
Max.    :1970                 Max.    :12638
```

We can do this graphically and somewhat more automatically with the histogram function.

Ò DISPLAYING DATA WITH A HISTOGRAM

R is an extremely powerful graphics program. As we'll see in Chapters 12 to 15, this can get quite complex. It is, however, relatively simple to produce the basic built-in charts and graphs. We'll review the use of the basic built-in plots in Chapter 12. But for now, a histogram is a great way to do a quick review of many kinds of data. A histogram is just a graph showing the frequency of different values of a variable. If you do not specify them explicitly, R makes a guess about the appropriate bins to put the data in.

There is more detail on histograms and their customization in the discussion of R graphics in the final four chapters, so I won't go into the details of manipulating histograms or other charts at this point. In the meantime, Figure 5.1 is a simple histogram set up mostly with the default values.

```
myVar = seq(-3, 3, .0001)        # Set variable with .0001 intervals
myNormVar = rnorm(myVar)         # Create random normal variable

hist(myNormVar, main = NA)       # Histogram plot of normal variable
                                 #  with title (main=) turned off
```

Another useful summary plot can be generated quickly with the **density()** function. A density plot shows the continuous probability of the variable taking a specific value. This is done with kernel density

Figure 5.1 Histogram of a Normally Distributed Variable

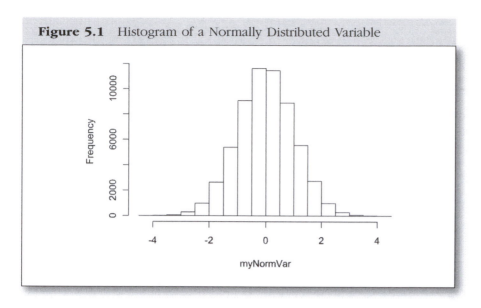

estimation, which is more complicated than we need to get into here. The syntax is simply **plot(density(myVariable))**. The following example shows the density plot for a random normal variable (see Figure 5.2).

Figure 5.2 Kernel Density Plot of Normally Distributed Variable

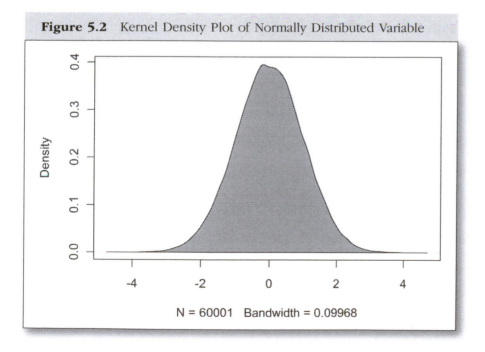

```
> x = seq(-3, 3, .0001)              # Set up var with .0001 intervals
> normX = rnorm(x)                    # Create random normal var on x
>
> plot(density(normX))               # Density plot of normal variable
> polygon(density(normX), col = "gray")  # Fill it in with gray if you want
```

○ DISPLAYING DATA WITH A SCATTERPLOT

A simple scatterplot, as seen in Figure 5.3, is another quick way to visualize your data. For this, all you need to know is the **plot()** command. The minimum plot formulation requires just the *x* and *y* variables. The *x* variable goes on the horizontal axis, and the *y* variable goes on the vertical axis.

```
> myX = c(1, 5, 19, 7, 6, 18, 11, 10)   # Create an x variable
> myY = c(4, 3, 12, 7, 8, 9, 15, 9)      # Create a y variable
> plot(myX, myY)                         # Simple scatterplot of x & y
```

Figure 5.3   A Basic Scatterplot

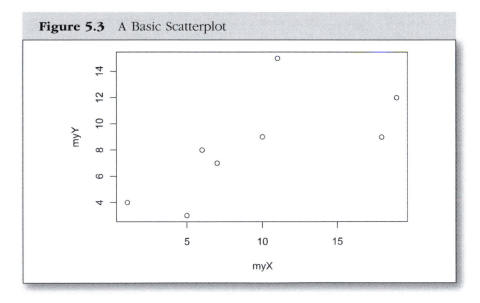

It can also be useful to put point labels on a graph to confirm that the data set is as it should be. We will get at this more seriously in Chapter 14, but it is straightforward enough to play with a bit now (see Figure 5.4).

Labeling the points is done with the **text()** command. To add point labels, we need to use the original *x*, *y* data to tell R where to print each label. In its default formation, R prints the labels centered on the *x*, *y* coordinates. If we want them offset, so that they don't cover up the points, we can use the **pos=** option. **pos = 1** puts the label below the point, **pos = 2** puts the label to the left of the point, **pos = 3** puts the label above the point, and **pos = 4** puts the label to the right of the point. We also use here the **xpd = TRUE** option to allow our labels to spill outside the main plot region. There are also options for varying the font (**font=**) and font size (**cex=**), but we'll look at those with the graphics discussion in Chapter 14.

```
myLabels = c(                          # Add vector of labels for each obs

   "Bach", "Beethoven",

   "Brahms", "Mozart", "Chopin",

   "Tchaikovsky", "Satie", "Bartok")

plot(myX, myY)                         # Simple scatterplot of x & y

text(myX, myY,                         # Add labels using x & y coords

   labels = myLabels,                  # The labels to add

   pos = 3,                            # Put labels above points

   xpd = TRUE)                         # Allow printing outside plot
```

Figure 5.4   Scatterplot With Labels

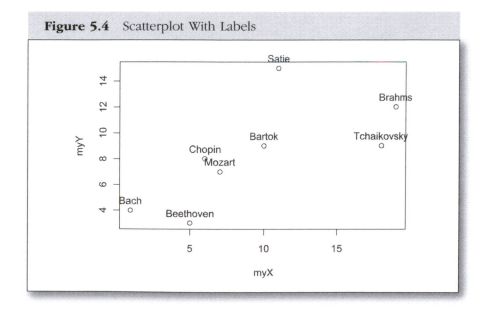

SCATTERPLOT MATRICES

You can easily create a matrix of scatterplots with the **pairs()** function. This creates a scatterplot for every combination of variables. If you just specify the data frame as the argument to the **pairs()** function, you will get a matrix with every combination of variables in your data set (see Figure 5.5). Obviously, this is not a great approach if you have a lot of variables. Likewise, this is one of those functions that won't work if any of the data are nonnumeric. In either case, you should just select the variables you want to include.

Figure 5.5   A Basic Pairs Plot

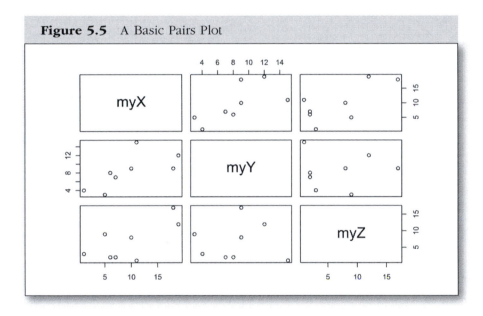

```
> myZ = c(3, 9, 12, 2, 2, 17, 1, 8)        # Add z to x & y
> myData = data.frame(myX, myY, myZ)       # Combine x, y, z into data frame
> pairs(myData)                            # Pairs plot for data frame
```

By now, we should have some data set up in R and be able to review it to be sure that all is as it should be. We'll now turn to the critical issues of sorting and selecting data. But first, we'll make a brief detour to consider the sources and solutions for a few of the common frustrations that might be arising by this point.

APPENDIX: IN CASE OF EXASPERATION, READ THIS! ⊙

Okay. So R is giving you some grief. Welcome to the club. Learning R can often prove a frustrating experience. Take some deep breaths. Get up and walk around the room. Go do something else for a few minutes. If you have already been up for 2 days trying to figure out why R won't select the x values less than −7 when you use $x[x < -7]$, then go get some sleep, and when you come back, read little tip 7.

Here are a few suggestions for trying to track down problems, sorted out between the big concepts and the little things that can drive you crazy.

The Big Things

1. Make sure you have the function right.

The quickest way to check that you have the right function and have spelled it correctly is to try to find help on it. Use **?FunctionName**. If you have got it right, R will open up the Help page, which will help with further debugging. If it is wrong, alas, it will just issue the suggestion that you do a **help.search("phrase")**. But, at least, now you know something about where your problem lies. While you are on the Help page, make sure you have the appropriate package loaded that contains the function. The top-left corner of the Help page shows the package in brackets right after the name of the function.

2. Check your object storage modes and types.

As I've said, I suspect object types are the number one source of problems and frustrations. Make sure you know what your object types are and what object types your functions are expecting or will accept. It is particularly important to know whether the function you are using is vectorized: Does it operate on the whole vector or on individual values? Also, be careful about the difference between factor and character data. As we have seen, this distinction can cause all kinds of mischief. Use **str(myObject)** or **attributes(myObject)** to be sure you understand your objects' structure and type.

3. Work it out on some sample data.

Here's a place where R really shines. The ability to create a very small analogous data set on the fly is enormously helpful. It is always tempting to jump right into the real data. For people unfamiliar with or still learning R (which is almost all of us), complex operations on complex data can get out of control pretty quickly. It is almost always more time efficient to get your code working on sample data first. You can slowly add in the complexities of your real-world data, such as missing values or unbalanced hierarchical data. Once the code is working, it is easy to switch it over to apply it to the real data.

4. Break up nested operations, and check the intermediate steps.

The ability to nest functions in R can make for very efficient code. Consider the following monstrosity:

```
gnp.mn2 = mean(sample(as.numeric(gsub(",", "", gnp[year > 1945])), 25), na.rm = T)
```

I think this takes the mean of a sample of 25 observations of GNP (gross national product) data that are currently formatted as character data with commas separating the 1,000s. If you can make it work without errors, that's terrific. Mere mortals are less likely to make mistakes if they break this up into individual steps. R will then tell you more clearly in which step the syntax error occurs. Breaking it up also allows you to print out the intermediate values so you can see where it might have gone awry. Here is the same project broken into discrete steps:

```
gnp.postwar = gnp[year > 1945]
gnp.postwar.temp1 = gsub(",", "", gnp.postwar)
gnp.postwar.temp2 = as.numeric(gnp.postwar.temp1)
gnp.postwar.temp3 = sample(gnp.postwar.temp2, 25)
gnp.test.mean2 = mean(gnp.postwar.temp3, na.rm = T)
```

5. Annotate it.

Excessive annotation is not considered good programming style. Elegant programming code should speak for itself, this line of reasoning goes. Those are fine ideals. But, on the steep part of the learning curve, you may find that R code doesn't really speak to you. In my view, it is unlikely that there is any level of annotation that is too much at this stage.

Force yourself to explain what you think each step in your code is doing. This can help you see where the more complex steps are and ensure that you understand what it is you are trying to do. It also makes it easier for other people to help you catch errors when they can see the difference between what you think you are doing and what R thinks you are doing.

Annotation can be particularly helpful when you have copied some snippet of code from someone else's example. It forces you to think through his or her logic.

Finally, annotation is very helpful when you return to a project 6 months later and need to remember what it is you were doing and why.

6. Check on your missing values and how they are being handled.

Some functions will just skip observations with missing values, while others insist that you make an explicit decision to do so. Most notoriously, by default `mean()` returns NULL if it encounters even one small and insignificant missing value. This is a feature. There is an important substantive difference between the mean with and without the missing values. So you have to give R explicit permission to ignore the missing value cases: `mean(x, na.rm = T)`. Other functions make other assumptions. See the earlier tip on sample data for a good way to get a handle on this. We'll come back to missing data in much more depth in Chapter 11. In the meantime, be careful!

7. Run the function with the minimum required options.

The default values for the function options are usually reasonably sensible. If you're having problems, it is a good idea to check and make sure your option choices aren't the issue. If you have a larger nested command, you can also try running just pieces of it to make sure they are doing what you expect. In RStudio when the cursor is on a line in the editor, the Run button sends the whole line to the R Console. But if you highlight just a piece of your code, the Run button will send just that piece to the console.

8. Search for help online.

There is a huge community of R users online, and over the years, they have helped new users out with a variety of issues. Put some piece of your error message or a description of your problem into a Google search, and you will likely find that someone else has already encountered this particular headache. You may find many of the online answers are pitched toward higher-level users, but with a bit of persistence, you are likely to find some helpful material.

The Little Things

1. Check your object types and storage modes.

This was listed under the big things as well, but it is worth repeating. Make sure you know what kind of objects you are working with at each step of your analysis (numeric, factor, or character; matrix, data frame, or list).

2. Check your parentheses.

As commands get more complex, parentheses proliferate. Make sure the open and close parentheses are matching up properly. An effective programming text editor like RStudio highlights the matching parentheses and makes this pretty easy. One way to avoid parentheses errors is to always create the opening and closing parentheses at the same time and then fill them in with the appropriate content. Also watch for the difference between parentheses, ( ); brackets, [ ]; and braces, { }.

3. Check your commas.

Make sure your commas between options or values aren't missing. For me, this is particularly a problem when I break commands up on multiple lines. Also, be careful that commas go between things in quotes and don't get caught up in the quotation marks. If R says that the error is that there is an argument missing, that is probably really about an extra comma making R think there should be an argument.

4. Check your quotation marks.

As with parentheses, you first just have to check that they are there and are nested properly. But you also have to be careful about where R wants values in quotation marks and where it doesn't. When in doubt, this is something that is relatively easy to discern from the function help files.

5. Check your capitalization.

R is very sensitive to case. Forget this at your peril.

6. Make sure you use == instead of = for checking equalities.

There are few things that will cause more insidious problems than reassigning the values of a variable when you think you are just testing for equality. Don't do it. If you make this mistake too often, you may need to return to the **<–** assignment operator as penance. Also, be aware that having mistakenly used the = operator for comparison changes your data, so you have to retrace your steps to fix this problem.

7. Beware of testing for less than a negative number.

For all the principled arguments that the R lords make about the virtues of the **<–** assignment operator rather than the = assignment operator, one of its unalloyed drawbacks is that R can screw up if you attempt to test for numbers that are less than a negative number with a **<-myNumber** construction. You have to add either a space or parentheses to separate the less-than sign and the minus sign, so that R knows you are doing a comparison rather than an assignment. In general, whether you use the assignment operator or conduct less-than operations, you should be in the habit of surrounding both symbols with spaces.

CHAPTER 6

SORTING AND SELECTING DATA

Sorting and conditionally selecting parts of a data set is central to most R projects. R is a very effective tool for both of these processes. Unlike a click-and-drag spreadsheet program, it has the advantage of allowing you to leave the original data unaltered. A record of data transformations is maintained in an R command file that will allow for quickly re-creating specific forms of the data set for analysis. Replicability is ensured.

In this chapter, we'll start by looking at several techniques for selecting specific sets of variables and observations. The important thing about this process is that it can, itself, be data driven. We'll learn how to set up selection vectors to automate the process of filtering data, either for modifying data sets or more locally within the execution of specific functions. We'll also look at splitting up variables and data sets into groups. And we'll finish with a discussion on sorting and ordering data.

Data selection is something we may need to do in either or both of the two dimensions of our data frames: rows and columns. With rows, we are selecting particular observations. With columns, we are selecting particular variables. Sorting is usually about the order of the observations (rows) based on some values of the variables (columns), although on occasion, we may want to put the variables in a certain order for displaying results.

USING INDEX VALUES TO SELECT DATA

I hope you recall the discussion in Chapters 1 and 3 of indices for vectors and matrices. If so, that's great, because we are going to use them now. If not, you might want to go back and review those concepts. Up to this point, we have mostly used a single numeric value as the index. As we have seen, the most straightforward way to select particular values is to use the appropriate index for the object. If you want the fifth element of the vector **myVector**, just use **myVector[5]**. Matrix or data frame indexing is done by **[row,column]**. But note that if only one number is used to index a data frame or a matrix, R will treat it as the column. The third column can be indicated either by **myMatrix[,3]** or by **myMatrix[3]**. Because of the column assumption, the row index always has to have its comma. The seventh observation (row) in a data frame, for example, is isolated with **myDataframe[7,]**. Especially while you are still learning, I would recommend always using the commas whether you are indexing rows or columns to help avoid confusion.

We can use a range to select a set of elements. If you want to use just the first 20 observations in **myDataframe**, you can select them with **myDataframe[1:20,]**. Likewise, **myDataframe[,1:20]** would give you the first 20 variables (columns). More varied selections can be indicated with a vector or values, either set up previously or created on the fly.

```
> selection = c(1, 5, 7, 11:14)          # Set a vector of rows to select
> myDF = ch5data[selection,]             # Create data frame w/select rows
> myDF = ch5data[c(1, 5, 7, 11:14),]     # Create data frame w/select rows
> myDF                                    # Print myDF
   year  animal weight captive
1  1935  Mouse  0.065       y
5  1939  Mouse  0.064       n
7  1941  Mouse  0.058       y
11 1945  Mouse  0.065       n
12 1946  Mouse  0.067       n
13 1947  Mouse  0.060       y
14 1948  Mouse  0.067       n
```

Using a minus sign before an index reverses the process and tells R to exclude values.

```
> myDF[-2,]                              # Print myDF w/o observation 2
    year  animal weight captive
1   1935  Mouse  0.065        y
7   1941  Mouse  0.058        y
11  1945  Mouse  0.065        n
12  1946  Mouse  0.067        n
13  1947  Mouse  0.060        y
14  1948  Mouse  0.067        n
```

We can eliminate specific variables from the data frame by using the inverse of the concatenate function, -c(). This example tells R to eliminate columns (variables) 1 and 3.

```
myDF2 = myDF[,-c(1, 3)]                  # Drop columns 1 & 3
```

We can do the same thing to eliminate observations 1, 3, and 7.

```
myDF4 = myDF[-c(1, 3, 7),]               # Drop rows 1, 3 & 7
```

The placement of the comma is very important in both of these operations to tell R whether you are eliminating rows or columns. The comma is optional in the first case, since R presumes columns, but it is helpful to keep your intent clear.

USING CONDITIONAL VALUES FOR SELECTING

We can use logical phrases to set up a selection index. In the following example, we select all of the cases where x is greater than 4.

```
> x1                                    # Print x1
 [1]   5   6   7   8   9 10 11 12 13 14 15 16 17 18 19 20

> x1[x1 > 8]                            # Print x1 where x1 > 8
 [1]   9 10 11 12 13 14 15 16 17 18 19 20
```

This is where the real power of index selection comes in. Suppose we return to our quick animal data from Chapter 5—the mouse, kangaroo, and elephant data—and we want to select only the kangaroo data. You could jump around looking for those observations. But if one of the variables, Animal, contains the animal names, you could just use that to select all of the kangaroo observations in one step (note, again, the comma placement to indicate rows).

```
kDF = myDF[myDF$animal == "Kangaroo", ] # Select all kangaroos
```

We can do more complex selections by building statements with logical (Boolean) operators. The primary logical operations used in R are listed in Table 6.1.

Table 6.1 Logical Operators in R

! x	Not x
x & y	x and y by element
x && y	x and y by object
x | y	x or y by element
x || y	x or y by object
x or (x, y)	x or y but not x and y

Here is an example with the Chapter 5 data, selecting only those kangaroos that weigh more than 165 pounds.

```
bigkDF =                                # New data frame for big kangaroos
   myDF[myDF$animal == "Kangaroo" &     # Select all kangaroos
   myDF$weight > 100, ]                 #   weighing more than 100 lbs
```

This example also serves to reemphasize the use of the double equals sign to test equality. A single equals sign makes the thing on the left of the equals sign equal to whatever is on the right; it is an assignment operator. The double equals sign is for testing whether the stuff on the left side is really the same as the stuff on the right.

Another way to approach this kind of selection is with the **which()** function, which returns the set of observation numbers for which an expression is true. The **which()** function creates a vector with the observation numbers for the cases that satisfy a criterion.

```
> myDF = ch5data                        # A short DF name for convenience
> kDF = myDF[myDF$animal == "Kangaroo",]# Select all kangaroos
> head(kDF, 3)                          # First 3 kangaroo observations
    year   animal weight  captive
26 1940 Kangaroo   89.9        n
27 1941 Kangaroo   83.0        n
28 1942 Kangaroo   91.7        y

> bigkDF =                              # New data frame for big kangaroos
+   myDF[myDF$animal == "Kangaroo" &    # Select all kangaroos
+   myDF$weight > 100,]                 #    weighing more than 100 lbs
# The which() approach -------------------------------------------------
> kselect = which(myDF$weight > 100 &   # Create a vector of obs numbers
+   myDF$animal == "Kangaroo")          #    with Kangaroos > 165 lb
> kselect                               # Print selection vector
[1] 32 33 34

> bigkDF2 = myDF[kselect,]              # Create data frame w/selected
> bigkDF2                               # Print data frame
    year   animal weight  captive
32 1946 Kangaroo  106.5        n
33 1947 Kangaroo  115.3        n
34 1948 Kangaroo  127.9        y
```

As in the preceding example, **which()** can be exceedingly useful since you can embed the **which()** command, or the vector it creates, inside the brackets following an object name to specify a data subset.

Using subset ( ) to Select Data

The **subset()** command can also be used to select rows (observations). The main argument, after the data frame or matrix name, is a logical expression, so ultimately, this isn't a lot different from just subsetting with the bracket construction. It is a little more explicit, so it may make it easier to keep track of what you're doing. Here are some simple examples.

```
> myData = data.frame(
+    myV1 = c(10, 20, 30, 40),          # Set up 3 vars in a data frame
+    myV2 = c("a", "b", "c", "d"),
+    myV3 = c(1, 2, 3, 4))

> myData                                # Display the data frame
  myV1 myV2 myV3
1   10    a    1
2   20    b    2
3   30    c    3
4   40    d    4

> # Subset by rows
> myData1 = subset(myData, myV1 > 20)   # Select rows with myV1 > 20
> myData1                               # Display results
  myV1 myV2 myV3
3   30    c    3
4   40    d    4
> myData2 = myData[myV1 > 20,]          # Same selection w/bracket method

> myData2                               # Display results
  myV1 myV2 myV3
3   30    c    3
4   40    d    4
```

The **subset()** function can be used to select columns by their variable names. For this, we use the **select=** option and a list of the variable names. Here are some examples using a single value for the selection.

```
> myData3 = subset(myData,          # Create a subset of the dataframe
+    select = myV1)                  #   with only the variable myV1
> myData3                           # Display the result
  myV1
1   10
2   20
3   30
4   40


> myData 4 = subset(myData,          # Create a subset of the dataframe
+    select = -myV3)                 #   without the variable myV3
> myData4                           # Display the result
  myV1  myV2
1   10    a
2   20    b
3   30    c
4   40    d
```

As we've seen, selecting columns can also be done with the bracket construction. This is very straightforward with the column numbers. If you want to use column names, you have to put them within quotation marks and cannot use the minus sign approach. Here are the bracket versions of the preceding example.

```
myData3b = myData[,1]               # Select column 1 w/bracket approach
myData4b = myData[,-3]              # Remove column 3 w/bracket approach

myData3c = myData[,"myV1"]          # Use variable name to select column
myData4c = myData[,c("myV1", "myV2")] # Use var names for column selection
```

You can use a vector as the argument for the **select=** option to subset by a larger group of variable names. This could either have been defined earlier or in the select operation itself. Note that within the select operation you don't need to use the **myData$** prefix because R knows that that is where the data are coming from. But when setting up a vector of variable names outside of the **select()** function, we need to put the variable names in quotations so that R interprets them as names rather than as the variables themselves.

```
> myData5 = subset(                  # Create a subset with just
+    myData, select = c(myV1, myV3)) #    myV1 and myV3
> myData5                            # Display the result
   myV1  myV3

1    10     1
2    20     2
3    30     3
4    40     4

> myData6 = subset(                  # Create a subset without
+    myData, select = -c(myV2, myV3)) #   myV2 and myV3
> myData6                            # Display the result
   myV1

1    10
2    20
3    30
4    40

> mySelector = c("myV1", "myV3")     # Create vector to select vars
> myData7 = subset(                  # Subset the data using
+    myData, select = mySelector)    #    the mySelector vector
> myData7                            # Display the result
   myV1  myV3

1    10     1
2    20     2
3    30     3
4    40     4
```

SPLITTING A DATA SET INTO GROUPS

It is often the case that we want to analyze a data set broken up into relevant subgroups. Suppose, for example, we again have our Chapter 5 data set with information about mice, kangaroos, and elephants and we want to run parallel analyses of each. There are several ways to do this, but **by()** is the most straightforward.[1] The **by()** function lets you run another function on a data set divided up by some factor. It takes three primary arguments: (1) the data frame (**data=**), (2) the factor by which you want to categorize the results (**INDICES=**), and (3) the function (**FUN=**). If the function requires some specific options, you can include those at the end after a comma. Here is a summary broken up by animal type.

```
> by(myDF, myDF$animal, summary)          # Summary by animal type
myDF$animal: Elephant
      year            animal          weight          captive
 Min.   :1935    Elephant:5    Min.   :11702    n:3
 1st Qu.:1942    Kangaroo:0    1st Qu.:11708    y:2
 Median :1958    Mouse   :0    Median :12151
 Mean   :1954                  Mean   :12115
 3rd Qu.:1964                  3rd Qu.:12377
 Max.   :1970                  Max.   :12638

--------------------------------------------------------------------

myDF$animal: Kangaroo
      year            animal          weight          captive
 Min.   :1940    Elephant: 0    Min.   : 72.50    n:7
 1st Qu.:1942    Kangaroo:10    1st Qu.: 89.53    y:3
 Median :1944    Mouse   : 0    Median : 92.30
 Mean   :1944                   Mean   : 96.61
 3rd Qu.:1947                   3rd Qu.:104.12
 Max.   :1949                   Max.   :127.90

--------------------------------------------------------------------
```

---

1. **by()** is actually just a shortcut to the **tapply()** function, which we'll discuss in Chapter 7.

```
myDF$animal: Mouse
        year            animal          weight          captive
  Min.   :1935    Elephant: 0    Min.   :0.05000    n:16
  1st Qu.:1941    Kangaroo: 0    1st Qu.:0.05700    y: 9
  Median :1947    Mouse   :25    Median :0.06100
  Mean   :1947                   Mean   :0.06044
  3rd Qu.:1953                   3rd Qu.:0.06500
  Max.   :1959                   Max.   :0.06900
```

Multiple factors can be combined using the **interaction(var1, var2)** function, which generates every combination of factor levels. This works very well, though obviously things can get out of control pretty quickly if you are trying to combine too many levels of too many factors. In the following example, we break up the animal data by both animal type (three levels) and captivity status (two levels).

```
> by(myDF,                         #
+    interaction(myDF$animal,      # Interact 2 factors: animal type
+      myDF$captive),              #   and captivity
+    summary)                      # Apply the summary function

interaction(myDF$animal, myDF$captive): Elephant.n
        year            animal          weight        captive
  Min.   :1935    Elephant:3    Min.   :11708    n:3
  1st Qu.:1946    Kangaroo:0    1st Qu.:12042    y:0
  Median :1958    Mouse   :0    Median :12377
  Mean   :1952                  Mean   :12241
  3rd Qu.:1961                  3rd Qu.:12508
  Max.   :1964                  Max.   :12638
--------------------------------------------------------------------

interaction(myDF$animal, myDF$captive): Kangaroo.n
        year            animal          weight        captive
  Min.   :1940    Elephant:0    Min.   : 72.50    n:7
  1st Qu.:1942    Kangaroo:7    1st Qu.: 86.45    y:0
```

```
   Median :1944    Mouse    :0     Median : 92.90
   Mean   :1944                    Mean   : 93.87
   3rd Qu.:1946                    3rd Qu.:101.75
   Max.   :1949                    Max.   :115.30

   -----------------------------------------------------------------

interaction(myDF$animal, myDF$captive): Mouse.n
        year           animal         weight          captive
   Min.   :1936    Elephant: 0    Min.   :0.05200   n:16
   1st Qu.:1942    Kangaroo: 0    1st Qu.:0.05950   y: 0
   Median :1947    Mouse   :16    Median :0.06350
   Mean   :1947                   Mean   :0.06200
   3rd Qu.:1952                   3rd Qu.:0.06525
   Max.   :1958                   Max.   :0.06900

   -----------------------------------------------------------------

interaction(myDF$animal, myDF$captive): Elephant.y
        year           animal         weight          captive
   Min.   :1942    Elephant:2     Min.   :11702     n:0
   1st Qu.:1949    Kangaroo:0     1st Qu.:11815     y:2
   Median :1956    Mouse   :0     Median :11927
   Mean   :1956                   Mean   :11927
   3rd Qu.:1963                   3rd Qu.:12039
   Max.   :1970                   Max.   :12151

   -----------------------------------------------------------------

interaction(myDF$animal, myDF$captive): Kangaroo.y
        year           animal         weight          captive
   Min.   :1942    Elephant:0     Min.   : 89.40    n:0
   1st Qu.:1944    Kangaroo:3     1st Qu.: 90.55    y:3
   Median :1945    Mouse   :0     Median : 91.70
   Mean   :1945                   Mean   :103.00
   3rd Qu.:1946                   3rd Qu.:109.80
   Max.   :1948                   Max.   :127.90

   -----------------------------------------------------------------
```

```
interaction(myDF$animal, myDF$captive): Mouse.y
        year            animal          weight          captive
   Min.   :1935    Elephant:0    Min.    :0.05000    n:0
   1st Qu.:1941    Kangaroo:0    1st Qu. :0.05400    y:9
   Median :1947    Mouse   :9    Median  :0.05800
   Mean   :1947                  Mean    :0.05767
   3rd Qu.:1953                  3rd Qu. :0.06100
   Max.   :1959                  Max.    :0.06500
```

SPLITTING UP CONTINUOUS NUMERIC DATA

by() is great for analysis with a factor variable, but sometimes we want to divide the analysis up by value ranges for numeric data. One way to do this would be simply to create a new factor based on the numeric values by using a bunch of **ifelse()** statements.[2] This is pretty inelegant for all but the very simplest situation. R provides a faster way with the **cut()** command.

Use **cut()** to transform continuous variables into categorical factor variables. The central arguments for the **cut()** function are the input variable to be categorized and the break points. The break points argument is usually a number, which tells R how many categories the variable is to be divided into. It can also be a vector of interval dividers. The following example shows a variable cut into six 1-unit-wide categories from −3 to +3.

```
> myVar = rnorm(100)              # Create var from std. normal dist
> myVar2 = cut(myVar, -3:3)       # Cut into 6 1-unit segments
> table(myVar2)                   # Show num of obs in each segment
myVar2 (-3,-2] (-2,-1]  (-1,0]   (0,1]   (1,2]   (2,3]
             3      15      38      29      12       3
```

---

2. See Chapter 7 for a discussion of **ifelse()**.

Note that a closed bracket is inclusive while a parentheses is not inclusive. In this case, the top number of each range is included in the range, while the range starts just above the bottom number.

By default, the `cut()` command creates a character label for each interval, such as those seen in the preceding example "`(-3,-2]`", "`(-2,-1]`", and so on. If you would prefer to just create integer markers for each level, use the `labels = FALSE` argument.

```
> myVar2 = cut(myVar, -3:3,        # Cut myVar into bins of width 1
+    labels = FALSE)               #    without labels
> table(myVar2)                    # Show num of obs in each segment
myVar2
 1    2    3    4    5    6
 3   15   38   29   12    3
```

A powerful approach is to combine the `cut()` command with the `quantile(x, probs)` function. The `quantile()` function identifies cut points for distributing a variable into bins based on a vector of probabilities. The default number of bins is four (quartiles), but you can provide any reasonable number of bins (actually R doesn't care if you provide an unreasonable number of bins, but I do). The bins are identified with probabilities rather than simply the number of bins. This makes it a little more complex than just saying you want quartiles, quintiles, or deciles, but it gives you greater flexibility if you need some more exotic probability breakdown. You can do these manually (e.g., `probs = c(0, .2, .4, .6, .8, 1)`, but the easiest way to do these probabilities is with the `seq(from, to, by)` function. Quartiles, the default, are `probs = seq(0, 1, .25)`. Quintiles would be `probs = seq(0, 1, .2)`. There are several different methodologies for dealing with sorting out ties and other technical issues in this process. You can read about these in the help for `quantile()`, but they probably shouldn't be an issue for you.

```
> myVar = rnorm(n = 100)              # Set up data from normal dist
> quantile(myVar)                     # Default quantiles is quartiles

        0%          25%          50%          75%         100%
-2.97964291  -0.59052872  -0.07181196   0.81595661   2.58788054

> quantile(myVar,                     # Set up quintiles manually
+    probs = (c(0, .2, .4, .6, .8, 1)))

        0%          20%          40%          60%          80%         100%
-2.97964291  -0.74562746  -0.28529882   0.09542015   0.96082996   2.58788054

> quantile(myVar, probs = seq(0, 1, .2))    # Set up quintiles with seq()

        0%          20%          40%          60%          80%         100%
-2.97964291  -0.74562746  -0.28529882   0.09542015   0.96082996   2.58788054

> quantile(myVar,                     # Some cuts for normal curve
+    probs = c(.0001, .01, .025, .5, .975, .99, .9999))

    0.01%          1%         2.5%          50%        97.5%          99%        99.99%
-2.973633  -2.378688  -2.292355  -0.071811   2.044771    2.132795   2.583329
```

Here, then, is the **cut()** function combined with **quantile()** to divide the data first into quartiles (the default) and then quintiles. The result of this operation is a new factor sorting the original variable into the appropriate bins. The one little complexity here is that by design, **quantile()** starts its first bin at the lowest value in the data. **cut()** doesn't so much like this and leaves out the lowest value (marks it **NA**). The solution is to specify the **include.lowest = T** option with the **cut()** function.

```
> myVar = rnorm(n = 100)              # Set up data from normal dist
> myVarQ = cut(myVar,                 # Divide myVar into bins
```

```
+    quantile(myVar),              # Use 4 bins w/equal obs (default)
+    include.lowest = T)           # Include lowest value in 1st bin

> summary(myVarQ)                  # Show quartiles

 [-2.52,-0.969] (-0.969,-0.223]  (-0.223,0.576]    (0.576,2.76]
        25               25            25              25
> head(cbind(myVar, myVarQ))       # Show first 6 observations
          myVar     myVarQ
[1,]  -0.39064755      2
[2,]  -0.40289161      2
[3,]   1.47137825      4
[4,]   0.15488018      3
[5,]   0.08024616      3
[6,]  -0.03042930      3
>
> myVarQ2 = cut(myVar,             # Divide myVar into bins
+    quantile(myVar,               # Use 5 bins with an equal number
+      probs = seq(0, 1, .2)),     #    of observations in each bin
+    include.lowest = T)           # Include lowest value in 1st bin

> summary(myVarQ2)                 # Show quintiles

 [-2.52,-1.01]  (-1.01,-0.48] (-0.48,0.0447]  (0.0447,0.855]  (0.855,2.76]
       20            20            20              20             20

> head(cbind(myVar, myVarQ2))      # Show first 6 observations
          myVar   myVarQ2
[1,]  -0.39064755      3
[2,]  -0.40289161      3
[3,]   1.47137825      5
[4,]   0.15488018      4
[5,]   0.08024616      4
[6,]  -0.03042930      3
```

 ## SORTING AND ORDERING DATA

Sorting data is very straightforward with either the **sort()** or the **order()** function. The **sort()** function sorts a single variable (a single vector or factor), while the **order()** function works with the observation numbers and thus can be used to sort a data frame and do more complex sorting where secondary variables can come into play when there are ties in the values of the first sorting variable.

Sorting a Variable

The following example shows a simple sort for a single variable:

```
> numbers = c(1, 6, 5, 7, 8)          # Some numbers to sort
> sort(numbers)                        # Voila!  The numbers sorted
[1] 1 5 6 7 8
```

Important options for sorting and ordering are shown in Table 6.2.

R's case sensitivity for character data means that lowercase letters are ordered before uppercase letters.

```
> fruit = c("Apple", "banana",        # Some fruit data
+    "apple", "Banana")
> fruit = fruit[order(fruit)]          # Ordered by fruit
> fruit                                # Display in order
[1] "apple"  "Apple"  "banana"  "Banana"
```

Ordering a Data Frame

Returning to our sorting example, we can see the difference between the **sort()** and **order()** functions.

```
> numbers = c(1, 6, 5, 7, 8)          # Some numbers to sort
> sort(numbers)                        # Sort -> order of numbers
[1] 1 5 6 7 8

> order(numbers)                       # Order -> obs nums of sorted obs
[1] 1 3 2 4 5
```

Table 6.2   Sorting and Ordering Options

`decreasing = F`	(default) This means to sort in ascending order.
`decreasing = T`	This sets the sort in descending order.
`na.last = T`	(default) This puts the missing values at the end.
`na.last = F`	This puts the missing values at the beginning.
`na.last = NA`	This deletes the observations with a missing value for the sort variable(s)

The values returned by the **sort()** function are the ordered values of the variable, while the **order()** function returns a vector of the observation numbers that correspond to the ordered values. Using **order()** as an index for the data frame tells R to reorder the whole data frame based on the returned observation numbers.

We can build quite complex sort routines using the **order()** function. Returning to our animal data set (ch5data), we start by ordering it by year. (I'll work with just a subset of the data here to keep the printout manageable.)

```
> myDF2 = subset(ch5data,           # For tractibility in example
+    year > 1940 & year < 1945)     #   take subset of myDF
> myDF2 = myDF2[order(myDF2$year),] # Sort myDF2 by year
> myDF2                             # Display result
     year   animal    weight  captive
7    1941    Mouse      0.058       y
27   1941 Kangaroo     83.000       n
8    1942    Mouse      0.065       n
28   1942 Kangaroo     91.700       y
37   1942 Elephant  11702.300       y
9    1943    Mouse      0.066       n
29   1943 Kangaroo     92.900       n
10   1944    Mouse      0.061       y
30   1944 Kangaroo     97.000       n
```

Adding a second variable in the **order ()** list uses that variable to sort the ties in the first variable. If we wanted to sort the data by year and then by animal name, we could do it as in the following example. This first sorts by year and then sorts within each year by the animal name. You can keep on going if you need to sort by three, four, or more variables.

```
> myDF2 = myDF2[order(myDF2$year,        # Order first by year
+     myDF2$animal),]                     #     and then by animal name
> myDF2                                   # Show result
      year    animal    weight  captive
27    1941   Kangaroo    83.000        n
7     1941      Mouse     0.058        y
37    1942   Elephant 11702.300        y
28    1942   Kangaroo    91.700        y
8     1942      Mouse     0.065        n
29    1943   Kangaroo    92.900        n
9     1943      Mouse     0.066        n
30    1944   Kangaroo    97.000        n
10    1944      Mouse     0.061        y
```

Again, R is case sensitive for character data, so lowercase letters are ordered before uppercase letters.

With your data now appropriately sorted and selected, it is time to think about more extensive transformations.

CHAPTER 7

TRANSFORMING DATA

It is now time to come to grips with the unfortunate but unavoidable fact that the world does not actually revolve around you, an important life lesson that R will frequently reinforce. Unlike the warm and comforting world of a statistics class, real-world data rarely come to you prepackaged in the form in which you need them. You will have to transform and reshape your data in various ways to make them functional for your purposes. That is the subject of the next five chapters.

Consider, for example, a situation where you need to pull together data from different sources. One data set might be monthly, while the other is daily. One might use metric measurements, while the other is in imperial units. Some of the data might be qualitative instead of quantitative. In one data set, time might be the basis for the unit of observation, while in the other the unit of observation is a geographical unit or an event. One data set might reference plants by their scientific names, while the other uses the popular name. Even where you have collected the data yourself, you may have some data where the unit of observation is the time and other data where the unit of observation is the test tube. In each of these cases, the data will have to be transformed to be ready for analysis.

R is enormously powerful for transforming data. Almost any form of data can be transformed into the form you need. Alas, it isn't always easy. If it is any small consolation, many of these tasks are vexing in other statistics programs as well. The starting point is always sitting down and figuring out exactly what you want your data to look like. What are the variables you need? What is the unit of observation? What are the hierarchies and relationships in the data that are relevant to the analytic questions you want to answer? Needless to say, if you don't know where you need to go with your data, you are unlikely to get there.

In this chapter, we'll cover the basics of operating on data, the use of functions, and then the problems of rotating and reshaping data sets. In Chapter 8, we turn to the specific functions and procedures for working with character variables and textual data. Chapter 9 is about time and date issues. Chapter 10 confronts the critical problems of aggregating and merging data sets. Chapter 11 is about the problems of missing data. We'll start off here with the most basic elements of editing and adding and subtracting data.

CREATING NEW VARIABLES

As we have seen many times already, we can add new variables to a data frame with a simple assignment statement. If we currently have a data frame named myData with three variables—myV1, myV2, and myV3—we can create a new variable from an operation on the existing variables, as shown here:

```
myData$myV4 = (myData$myV1 + myData$myV2)/myData$myV3
```

The important thing is to include the data frame name with the **myDataframe$myVariable** construction if you want the new variable to be connected to the data frame. If you want the variable to be simply free-floating as an object in your R workspace, you can just give it its own name, free of the data frame connection.

You can use **length()** to shorten or extend a vector. If you extend a vector, R adds **NA** observations to the end. If you shorten it, it is just truncated. **length()** is handy if you want to make sure that you have the same number of observations, with the proviso that care is required to ensure that the observations line up correctly.

EDITING DATA

As with many operations in R, editing data can be done in a number of different ways. The first thing you will want to decide is whether the changes are more easily made in Excel or some other environment. A spreadsheet is a nice tool for small-scale data editing because it is easier to see the immediate results of your changes. But by and large, you will find that R is a more powerful tool for systematically editing and transforming data. And, as I have emphasized many times, R maintains a clear record of the transformations you have made, so that your steps can easily be retraced and replicability is ensured.

Since R overwrites data with an assignment statement, a single value can be changed by just assigning the new value to the particular observation.

```
myData[observation.number, myVariable] = newValue
myData$myVariable[observation.number] = newValue
```

The same thing can be done for a whole vector.

```
myData$myVariable = newVector
myData[,myVariable] = newVector
```

There are several ways to edit data in a spreadsheet-like form. The most important of these are **data.entry()** and **fix()**. These can be useful for looking at your data, but I don't really recommend them for regular use. This is both because they purportedly behave differently in different computing environments and because they lose the advantage of keeping track of your data transformations.

○ Basic Math With R

If the calculator on your cell phone is broken, the R command line can be used directly for arithmetic calculations.

Addition: +

Multiplication: *

Division: /

Exponentiation: ^

Just enter the equation, and then hit Enter.

```
>   3 + 2
[1]   5

>   3 * 2
[1]   6

>   3^2
[1] 9

>   3/2
[1] 1.5

> 7 + ((10^2)/(3 + 2))
[1] 27
```

Of course, the real purpose of these operators is to transform objects. Unlike your calculator, when these mathematical operations are performed on vectors, matrices, and data frames, they affect every element. **myMatrix + 4** adds 4 to every element in the matrix. I don't suppose you are likely to need to do these kinds of operations very often on matrices or data frames, but should you need to, there it is.[1] You are much more likely to need to conduct operations on column vectors—your variables.

```
> myData$myVariable5 = myData$myVariable2 + 8
```

Remember that you can replace variables with their transformed versions just by writing over the original.

```
> myData$myVariable3 = myData$myVariable3 * 10
```

Adding variables to each other adds by observation.

```
> myVariable1 = c(10, 20, 30, 40)        # Two data vectors
> myVariable2 = c(1, 2, 3, 4)
```

---

1. It is important, again, to note that for several operations this works differently than normal matrix algebra. R has a matrix algebra capability, but this requires distinctive operators. Matrix multiplication, for example, is %*%.

```
> myVariable1 + myVariable2          # Pairwise vector addition
[1] 11 22 33 44
```

If the two variables have different numbers of observations, R will start reusing the variable with the smaller number of observations (again, not a normal behavior in regular matrix mathematics). If the larger is not a multiple of the shorter, it will issue a warning that it has done so. If the larger is a multiple of the shorter, it will do so without complaint. This can be handy for adding repetitive elements, but it is dangerous if it takes you unawares.

```
> myLongVar = c(10, 20, 30, 40)
> myShortVar = c(1, 2, 3)            # Short var not a multiple of long
> myLongVar + myShortVar             #    generates a warning
[1] 11 22 33 41
Warning message:
In myLongVar + myShortVar :
  longer object length is not a multiple of shorter object length

> myLongVar = c(10, 20, 30, 40)
> myShortVar = c(1, 2)               # Short var is a multiple of long
> myLongVar + myShortVar             #    does not generate warning
[1] 11 22 31 42
```

These same pairwise rules apply to all the basic math operations. In vector multiplication, for example, the first element of vector x is multiplied by the first element in vector y, the second element in vector x is multiplied by the second element in vector y, and so on.

```
> myVar1 = c(10, 20, 30, 40)         # Two vectors of length 4
> myVar2 = c(1, 2, 3, 4)
> myVar1 * myVar2                     # Multiplied
[1]  10  40  90 160

> # Mismatched vectors: A vector of length 8 multiplied by a vector of length 4
> myVar3 = c(10, 20, 30, 40, 50, 60, 70, 80)
> myVar2 * myVar3
[1]  10  40  90 160  50 120 210 320
```

In the case of mismatched vectors, note how the four values of **myVar2** *get recycled to match up with the eight values of* **myVar3**.

R FUNCTIONS

Functions are simply procedures that operate on some object. There are many functions in R, which is one of the sources of its power, but this variety also contributes to its complexity. As we have seen already, it is not uncommon for there to be several different functions that can all accomplish the same thing.

All functions have a name by which they are called. Most functions accept some input, accept the function's arguments, and produce output. When entered by themselves, all functions are identified by having a set of parentheses for the list of arguments. Even those functions that don't take any arguments still include the parentheses, which is how R recognizes them as functions. An example of this is the **getwd()** function, which does not take any arguments. Typing the name of a function without the parentheses returns details about the function and its underlying code. Although often overwhelming, this can sometimes be helpful for seeing what a function does or how it does it.

This gets a little more complex when functions are used in other functions. When functions are just nested, they continue to use their parentheses form—that is, when you are running one function inside of another. When, however, a function calls for another function as an argument, then you use the name without the parentheses. We have already seen this in the **help()** function, although that seems to be indifferent to the presence or absence of the parentheses. The most common place for this problem is the family of **apply()** functions, which apply functions to subsets of data. This is a very important set of operations, which we'll discuss more fully later.

```
Examples:

getwd()
help(getwd) but help(getwd()) also works
apply(myArray, 1, sum) but not: apply(myArray, 1, sum())
```

Arguments to functions can be required—that is, the function won't work without them—or they can be optional, in which case R has a default value for the argument. You can see the default values in the Help page for any function. Look under the "Usage" heading, where R help will list each of the options and show its default value.

It is critical to know whether a function is vectorized—that is, whether it operates on single values or on all of the values of a vector or matrix. For nonvectorized functions, we need to use the **apply()** family of functions, which we'll review at some length after a quick tour of some math and logical functions and the basic rounding functions.

 ## Math and Logical Functions in R

The most commonly used functions may be the simple mathematical transformations. These are all relatively straightforward with R's built-in functions.

Natural logs use the **log()** function.

Base 10 logs use the **log10()** function.

The antilog for natural logs is **exp()**.

The square root function is **sqrt()**.

```
> log(10)                        # The natural log
[1] 2.302585

> log10(10)                      # Log base 10
[1] 1

> exp(2.302585)                  # Exponentiation
[1] 10

> sqrt(100)                      # The square root
[1] 10
```

Trigonometric functions are similarly straightforward: **sin()**, **cos()**, **tan()**, **acos()**, **asin()**, **atan()**, and **atan2()** work pretty much as you would expect. The one really important thing to know here is that angles are indicated by radians rather than degrees (recall that the angle in radians is the angle in degrees times $\pi/180$ while the angle in degrees is the angle in radians times $180/\pi$). **pi** is a built-in constant in R, so you can manage these transformations relatively easily.

```
> sin(.5235988)                      # Sine of 30 degrees (.52 radians)
[1] 0.5
> sin(30 * pi/180)                   # Sine of 30 w/conv to radians
[1] 0.5
> cos(.5235988)                      # Cosine of 30 deg (.52 radians)
[1] 0.8660254
> cos(60 * pi/180)                   # Cosine of 60 w/conv to radians
[1] 0.5
> tan(.5235988)                      # Tangent of 30 deg (.52 radians)
[1] 0.5773503
```

All of these math functions are vectorized. They will transform all the values of a given variable or other vector. For that matter, these functions are also matricized. They operate element by element on matrices as well. This also holds for data frames, as long as they have only numeric variables. If they include any nonnumeric values, R will quietly snicker and refuse the operation entirely.

```
> myMatrix =
+   array(c(1:6), dim = c(3, 2))     # Set up a 3x2 matrix
> myMatrix                           # Show matrix
      [,1] [,2]
[1,]    1    4
[2,]    2    5
[3,]    3    6

> log(myMatrix)                      # Show element-by-element log
           [,1]     [,2]
[1,] 0.0000000 1.386294
[2,] 0.6931472 1.609438
[3,] 1.0986123 1.791759

> myDF = data.frame(myMatrix)        # Switch matrix to data frame
> sqrt(myDF)                         # Take sq root of every element
```

```
        X1       X2
1 1.000000 2.000000
2 1.414214 2.236068
3 1.732051 2.449490

> myDF = data.frame(myDF,                # Expand data frame to include
+   myLogical = c(TRUE, TRUE, FALSE))    #   a logical variable.
> myDF                                   # Show new data frame
  X1 X2  myLogical
1  1  4       TRUE
2  2  5       TRUE
3  3  6      FALSE

> myDF^3                                 # All elements cubed
      X1  X2  myLogical
[1,]   1  64          1
[2,]   8 125          1
[3,]  27 216          0

> myDF = data.frame(myDF,                # Expand data frame to include
+   myString = c("One", "Two", "Three")) #   a character variable
> myDF                                   # Show data frame
  X1 X2  myLogical myString
1  1  4       TRUE      One
2  2  5       TRUE      Two
3  3  6      FALSE    Three

> myDF^3                                 # All elements cubed
Error in FUN(left, right) : non-numeric argument to binary operator
```

Note that R treats logical variables as numerics with values of 0 or 1.

There are two logical functions that can be very helpful in a variety of situations. **all()** returns a logical **TRUE** or **FALSE** depending on whether every value of the provided vector is **TRUE**. **any()** returns a logical **TRUE** if any of the values of the provided vector are **TRUE**. In both of these functions, you can include the **na.rm = TRUE** option to remove missing values.

```
> myVar = c(T, T, F)                # Set up some sample data
> all(myVar)                        # Are all of the values TRUE?
[1] FALSE
> any(myVar)                        # Are any of the values TRUE?
[1] TRUE
```

These functions work on logical vectors, but you can build the logical vectors as needed within the function. The following example does this. Note also the behavior regarding the **NA**. As long as the answer was **FALSE** anyway, R was willing to ignore the NA. But rather than return **TRUE** with the **NA**, R returns **NA** unless the **na.rm = T** option is selected. The opposite behavior obtains for **any()**. For **any()**, as long as any of the observations meet the condition, the **NA** is ignored and **TRUE** is returned. But if none of the observations meet the condition, **any()** returns **NA**, unless **na.rm = T** is included.

```
> myVar = c(7, 5, 9, NA)           # Set up some sample data
> all(myVar > 6)                   # Are all of the values > 6?
[1] FALSE

> all(myVar > 4)                   # Are all of the values > 4?
[1] NA

> all(myVar > 4, na.rm = T)        # Same removing NA's
[1] TRUE

> any(myVar > 6, na.rm = T)        # Are any of the values > 6?
[1] TRUE

> any(myVar > 10)                  # Note opposite behavior for NA obs
[1] NA

> any(myVar > 10, na.rm = T)       # Removing NA's
[1] FALSE

> any(myVar > 6)                   # NA removal doesn't matter here
[1] TRUE
```

TRUNCATION AND ROUNDING FUNCTIONS

trunc(x) returns x without any fractional value—that is, the whole-number component of x.[2] It is the largest number less than x for positive values of x and the smallest number greater than x for negative numbers. **round()** rounds a number off to the nearest integer. **floor()** and **ceiling()**, respectively, round off to the next lowest and the next highest integers. **signif(x, digits)** rounds a value, x, off to the number of digits specified. **abs()** takes the absolute value.

```
> x = c(-5.7284, -3.251, 3.251, 5.7284)     # Some values to work with
> rounding.demo = data.frame(x,
+    trunc(x),                               # Truncation to integer
+    round(x),                               # Round to nearest integer
+    round(x, 2),                            # Round to 2 digits
+    floor(x),                               # Round to next lowest integer
+    ceiling(x),                             # Round to next highest integer
+    signif(x, 1),                           # Round to 0 significant digit
+    signif(x, 2),                           # Round to 1 significant digits
+    signif(x, 3),                           # Round to 2 significant digits
+    abs(x))                                 # Absolute value

> row.names(rounding.demo) = c(              # Add function names as row names
+   "x", "trunc(x)", "round(x)", "round(x, 2)", "floor(x)", "ceiling(x)",
+    "signif(x, 1)", "signif(x, 2)", "signif(x, 3)", "abs(x)")

> rounding.demo                             # Table of rounding functions
              [,1]    [,2]   [,3]   [,4]
x           -5.7284 -3.251 3.251 5.7284
trunc(x)    -5.0000 -3.000 3.000 5.0000
round(x)    -6.0000 -3.000 3.000 6.0000
round(x, 2) -5.7300 -3.250 3.250 5.7300
floor(x)    -6.0000 -4.000 3.000 5.0000
ceiling(x)  -5.0000 -3.000 4.000 6.0000
signif(x, 1) -6.0000 -3.000 3.000 6.0000
```

2. **as.integer()** does the same thing as **trunc()**, but it also changes the type to an integer storage mode.

```
signif(x, 2)    -5.7000 -3.300 3.300 5.7000
signif(x, 3)    -5.7300 -3.250 3.250 5.7300
abs(x)           5.7284  3.251 3.251 5.7284
```

THE APPLY() FAMILY OF FUNCTIONS

As has been hinted on several occasions already, the **apply()** family of functions plays a significant role in R. These functions are used to apply other functions to the data in more complex (and useful) ways. For example, **apply()** functions allow you to apply a function to every row or every column of a matrix, a function to a subset based on factor values, or a nonvectorized function to a vector. The different **apply()** function flavors are summarized in Table 7.1.

The most basic is the **apply()** function itself, which applies a function to either the rows or the columns of a data array. The output of an **apply()** function is a vector of values resulting from the application of the function either to each row or to each column. **apply()** is usually the function of choice anytime you want to create margin values for a matrix (i.e., values you would place in either the right or the bottom margin of a table, aggregating by row or by column). There are three central arguments for the **apply()** function. The first, **X=**, is the name of the matrix on which you are working. The second, **MARGIN=**, indicates whether to apply the function to the rows (**1**), or to the columns (**2**). The

Table 7.1   Summary of **apply()** Functions

apply()	Apply a function either to every row or to every column of a matrix or data frame.
lapply()	Apply a function to every element in a vector or list (returns a list).
tapply()	Aggregate a numeric vector by a factor.
sapply()	Apply the function to every element in a vector or list (returns a vector when the result is numeric).
mapply()	Same as **sapply()** can work on a set of vectors or lists (returns a vector or matrix when the result is numeric).

third argument, **FUN=**, is the function to apply. This is another place where the functions go without their parentheses. If there are particular options that need to be included with the function (e.g., **na.rm = T**), those go in the fourth place, after another comma. If you put the function arguments in the specified order, you do not need to include the argument names.

```
> row1 = c(1:5)                      # Set up a first row of data
> row2 = c(seq(10, 50, by = 10))     # Set up a second row of data
> myData = data.frame(rbind(row1, row2))# Put rows together in data frame
> myData                             # Display the data frame
      X1 X2 X3 X4 X5
row1   1  2  3  4  5
row2  10 20 30 40 50

> apply(X = myData,                  # Apply a function to myData
+    MARGIN = 1,                     # Apply to each row
+    FUN = sum)                      # Use the summation function
row1 row2
  15  150

> apply(myData, 2, sum)             # Get the sums of the columns
X1 X2 X3 X4 X5
11 22 33 44 55
```

The options are explicit in the first **apply()**, *but they are implicit, based on order, in the second.*

As usual, you have to be very careful about object types with the **apply()** function. **apply()** works with matrices, so it converts whatever you give it into a matrix. This has the pernicious effect of changing everything to factor or character data if any of your observations are factor or character data. The functions you are applying will screw up if they are expecting numeric data. In this case, you'll need to filter out the nonnumeric data.[3]

```
> X6 = c("A", "B")                    # Create a character variable
> myData = data.frame(myData, X6)     # Add it to the data frame
> apply(myData, 2, sum)               # Apply sums to columns
Error in FUN(newX[, i], ...) : invalid 'type' (character) of argument
>                                     #    This generates error because
>                                     #    of non-numeric data in col 6
> apply(myData[,-6], 2, sum)          # Redo, filtering character data
X1 X2 X3 X4 X5
11 22 33 44 55
```

While **apply()** usually returns a vector of values, one for each row or column, if you are working with a function that is designed to return multiple values for a single row or column, R will then output an array rather than a vector.

```
> myRange = apply(myData[,-6], 1, range)# Apply funct w/multiple outputs
> myRange                              # Show resulting array
      row1 row2
[1,]    1   10
[2,]    5   50
```

There are four shortcut functions that work like **apply()** but bypass some of its complexities and are thus worth knowing about. **rowSums(myData)** and **colSums(myData)** create, respectively, vectors with the values of either the summed rows or the summed

---

3. For functions that are defined for different object types, **sapply()**, discussed momentarily, can fix the problem. The plyr package makes some of these apply issues more manageable. It works on data frames in a more consistent manner, applying functions to columns or rows as you instruct, without tripping on the object type problems.

columns. **rowMeans(myData)** and **colMeans(myData)** operate the same way but obviously produce means instead of sums. In both cases, the **na.rm = T** option can be used to control the treatment of missing observations. Be careful, as well, that these functions still require numeric variables. If your data frame includes nonnumeric variables, you'll again have to exclude those. The following demonstrates both these functions and a technique (jumping ahead to **sapply()**) for systematically filtering nonnumeric data.

```
> colSums(myData[,-6])               # Sum by col(filter non-numeric)
X1 X2 X3 X4 X5
11 22 33 44 55

> colMeans(myData[,-6])              # Means by column
  X1    X2    X3    X4    X5
 5.5  11.0  16.5  22.0  27.5

> rowSums(myData[,-6])               # Sums by row
row1 row2
  15   150

> rowMeans(myData[,-6])              # Means by row
row1 row2
   3    30

> # Select just numeric columns
> myN = sapply(myData, is.numeric)   # T/F for cols w/numeric data
> myN                                # Show vector
   X1    X2    X3    X4    X5    X6
 TRUE  TRUE  TRUE  TRUE  TRUE FALSE

> apply(myData[myN], 2, sum)         # Apply sum to numeric columns
X1 X2 X3 X4 X5
11 22 33 44 55
```

We could do this final operation all in one step by nesting the **sapply()** *function in the* **apply()** *function instead of the intermediate step of creating the myN selector variable.*

lapply(myObject, function) applies a function to a list, a matrix, or a vector. It requires only two arguments: (1) the name of the list, matrix, or vector and (2) the name of the function. It applies the function to every element in the supplied object. **lapply()** always returns a list, which may or may not be what you want. If it isn't, you'll need to use **unlist()** to fix that.

Here, you have to be careful that the definition of "every element" varies both by the nature of the object and by the function. For a data frame, every element is every column. For a matrix, every element is every object within the matrix. To add to the confusion, if the function is vectorized, then **lapply()** treats each column of the data frame as a vector and applies the function to every element of the vector. If the function is not vectorized but can operate on a whole vector, then it applies the function to each column of the data frame as a whole. In the following example, you can see that though the matrix and data frame look exactly alike, **lapply()** treats them differently. It sees three elements in the data frame (the columns) but six in the matrix (every cell of the table).

```
> row1 = c(1:3)                          # Set up a first row of data
> row2 = c(seq(10, 30, by = 10))         # Set up a second row of data
> myData = data.frame(rbind(row1, row2)) # Put rows together in data frame
> myData                                 # Display the data frame
        X1 X2 X3
row1   1  2  3
row2  10 20 30

> lapply(myData, is.numeric)             # lapply to a data frame (list)
$X1
[1] TRUE
$X2
[1] TRUE
$X3
[1] TRUE

> myMatrix = rbind(row1, row2)           # Create a matrix
> myMatrix                               # Display matrix
       [,1] [,2] [,3]
row1     1    2    3
row2    10   20   30
```

```
> lapply(myMatrix, is.numeric)          # lapply to a matrix
[[1]]
[1] TRUE
[[2]]
[1] TRUE
[[3]]
[1] TRUE
[[4]]
[1] TRUE
[[5]]
[1] TRUE
[[6]]
[1] TRUE

> lapply(myData, log)                   # lapply vectorized funct to list
$X1
[1] 0.000000 2.302585
$X2
[1] 0.6931472 2.9957323
$X3
[1] 1.098612 3.401197

> lapply(myMatrix, log)                 # lapply same function to matrix
[[1]]
[1] 0
[[2]]
[1] 2.302585
[[3]]
[1] 0.6931472
[[4]]
[1] 2.995732
[[5]]
[1] 1.098612
[[6]]
[1] 3.401197
```

sapply() also applies a function to a vector or a list, but it will try to return a vector or a matrix whenever the results are numeric. **mapply()** does the same thing, but where **sapply()** works on a single vector or list, **mapply()** can be done over a set of vectors or lists. Since data frames are really lists, either will work with a data frame. For some inscrutable reason, the arguments passed to **sapply()** and **mapply()** go in the opposite order.

```
sapply(myVector, function)

mapply(function, myVector)
```

Here, is an example of the use of **sapply()** to apply the **mean()** function to all of the variables in a data frame.[4] In this case, it works fine, but it provides a warning about the inapplicability of the **mean()** function to the nonnumeric variable in the data frame. Trying the same thing with the **sum()** function doesn't work at all because of the nonnumeric variable. The solution is to use **sapply()** to identify and filter out the nonnumeric data. This approach can be exceedingly useful when working with the many functions that work on only certain object types.

```
> myData = data.frame(          # Create a data frame
+    myV1 = c(1, 0, 1, 1),       # A numeric variable
+    myV2 = c("A", "B", "C", "D"),  # A character variable
+    myV3 = c(7, 9, 2, 4))       # Another numeric variable

> sapply(myData, mean)          # Apply mean fun. to data frame
myV1 myV2 myV3
0.75   NA 5.50
```

---

4. Note that for this particular function, the same thing can be accomplished with the **colMeans()** command.

```
Warning message:
In mean.default(X[[2L]], ...) :
  argument is not numeric or logical: returning NA

> sapply(myData, sum)                    # Won't work because non-num var
Error in FUN(X[[2L]], ...): invalid 'type' (character) of argument

> sapply(                               # Rerun, filtering out
+   myData[sapply(myData, is.numeric)], #   non-numeric data
+   sum)                                # Apply sum function

myV1 myV3
   3   22
```

If you are working with logical functions within an **apply()** command, it is worth noting that the negation (**!**) goes in front of the **apply()** function rather than in front of the logical function. That's not very logical to me, but it seems to be the way it works.

```
> sapply(myData, is.numeric)            # Identify numeric data
 myV1  myV2  myV3
 TRUE FALSE  TRUE

> !sapply(myData, is.numeric)           # Identify non-numeric
 myV1  myV2  myV3
FALSE  TRUE FALSE
```

Saving, perhaps, the best for the last, **tapply(X = myVector, INDEX = myFactor, FUN = function)** applies a function to a vector based on the values taken by a factor. This can be very helpful. If you have a variable like weight that is connected to a grouping factor variable like animal type, you can then apply the function to those individual groups. **myFactor** can be either a single factor or a group of factors, in which case R breaks the analysis down by the unique combinations of the listed factors. To use a group of factors, enclose them in a **list()** function, as in the example below, which works with the synthetic animal data we set up at the beginning of Chapter 5.

```
> tapply(ch5data$weight,            # Look at animal weights
+    INDEX = ch5data$animal,        #  grouped by animal type
+    FUN = mean,                    # Get mean weight by animal
+    na.rm = T)

   Elephant      Kangaroo         Mouse
11254.66680      97.52050       0.05876

> tapply(ch5data$weight,            # Look at animal weights
+    INDEX = list(ch5data$animal,   # Group by animal and
+       ch5data$captive),          # captivity status
+    FUN = mean,                    # Get mean weights by group
+    na.rm = T)                     # Remove any missing data

                 FALSE         TRUE
Elephant  1.118685e+04  1.152595e+04
Kangaroo  9.881800e+01  9.233050e+01
Mouse     5.855556e-02  5.928571e-02
```

With one or two factors, this is pretty straightforward. It gets a bit more cumbersome with more than two, since the array size grows exponentially and it gets packaged up as a list.

CHANGING VARIABLE VALUES CONDITIONALLY

There are a number of ways to change values. Our presumption here is that we want to make some conditional changes. For example, we might want to convert a continuous variable to a categorical variable or change the values of one variable depending on the values of some other variable.

Ifelse(test, yes, no), where **test** is a logical expression to be evaluated and **yes** and **no** are the values the function, should return for a yes or no answer to that test. Here is a quick example operating with simple scalars.

```
> myV1 = 7                          # A value
> myV2 = ifelse(myV1 == 7, 10, 20)  # If myV1 = 7, then myV2 = 10, else 20
> myV2
[1] 10
```

The real power of **ifelse()** comes in applying it to vectors. **ifelse()** operates on each element of the vector. It creates a new vector with the values specified in the **ifelse()** statement. This is in distinct contrast to the **if()** operation and to the combination of **if()** and **else()** commands, which only works on single values. I'll return to those operations later when we get to the discussion of R programming.

```
> myVar = c(1, 57, 5, 22, 84, 79, 100)  # A variable with some values
> myVarSize = ifelse((myVar > 50),       # Check if myVar is > 50
+    "big", "small")                     # If so, size is big, else small
> data.frame(myVar, myVarSize)           # Display result
   myVar myVarSize
1      1     small
2     57       big
3      5     small
4     22     small
5     84       big
6     79       big
7    100       big
```

The **ifelse()** function can also be nested. That can get dangerously complex, but if you are careful, it gives you a quick way to change three or four values with one command.

```
> myVar = c(1, 57, 5, 22, 84, 79, 100)  # Set up some values
> myVarSize = ifelse(myVar >= 70, "big",# If >= 70, then size is "big"
```

```
+    ifelse(myVar > 50 & myVar <= 70,    # If > 50 & <= 70 then "medium"
+       "medium", "small"))              # If neither then "small"

> data.frame(myVar, myVarSize)
  myVar myVarSize
1     1     small
2    57    medium
3     5     small
4    22     small
5    84       big
6    79       big
7   100       big
```

An alternative to the **ifelse()** approach for this particular problem is to use the **cut()** function we discussed in Chapter 6.

```
> myVar = c(1, 57, 5, 22, 84, 79, 100)  # Set up some values
> myVarSize = cut(myVar,                 # Use cut() to divide into levels
+    breaks = c(0, 50, 70, 120),         # Set break points for levels
+    labels =
+      c("small", "medium", "large"))    # Labels for each level

> data.frame(myVar, myVarSize)           # Show results
  myVar myVarSize
1     1     small
2    57    medium
3     5     small
4    22     small
5    84     large
6    79     large
7   100     large
```

Note that the **breaks=** option in the **cut()** function requires a top and a bottom value. You could automate that with **min(myVar)** and **max(myVar)**.

Both of these operations set up new text values from numeric data. There are many other conversions and transformations that we may need to conduct on textual data. That is of sufficient importance and complexity to merit its own chapter, so I have left working with text values to Chapter 8.

 ## CREATING NEW FUNCTIONS

One of the great advantages of R is its ability to do repetitive analytic tasks. One of the central mechanisms for doing this is through the creation of custom functions from a set of commands.

To create a new function, use the **function()** command. As with regular R functions, the parentheses of the function command contain the things on which you want your new function to operate and any other data or information the function needs to know to do its thing. The function is given a name in a regular assignment statement, and then, the commands that make up the function follow the **function()** statement. If, as is likely, it requires more than one line, enclose them in braces **{}**.

At the simplest level, a function can just execute a set of commands. This is terrific for creating a standardized display of analytic results or producing repetitive graphics. But remember that a function has its own data environment, so changes made to a variable within a function are not available outside the function unless you make that process explicit.

If you want a function to give you a particular value or data object instead of just executing commands, use **return()** to tell R what you want to take out of the function. If you don't provide an explicit **return()** statement, R will use the last evaluated expression in the function as the function's output value. If you need to return multiple things, just package them up in a vector, a data frame, a factor, or a list as appropriate. To illustrate, here is about as simple a function as you could imagine.

```
> addition = function(number1, number2){
+    sumValue = number1 + number2
+    return(sumValue)
+ }
```

Calling this new addition function would provide the admittedly unnecessary service of adding two numbers, but you get the point.

```
> newValue = addition(2, 4)
> newValue
[1] 6

> num1 = 7
> num2 = 3
> addition(num1, num2)
[1] 10
```

You can ask for user input in your custom function (or in any R programming) with the **readline()** command. The argument in the parentheses is just a prompt for the user. Suppose you want to give yourself a chance to pick out a particular observation in some process.

```
my.obs = readline("Input an observation number and then press Enter")
```

R will pause to wait for your input. The value of **my.obs** will then be the keyboard input. R always interprets **readline()** input as a character value, so you will have to use **as.numeric()** if you need to convert it to a number (see Chapter 3 on coercing storage modes).

Here, again, is the custom function we introduced in Chapter 3 to look at a data object and indicate whether it is a vector, a matrix, a data frame, or a list. It takes just one argument, *x*, which is the object to evaluate. It checks for each of the basic data object types and creates a string indicating that type. This version goes a little further than the one in Chapter 3 in that if there is no match it reports that and also prints the **typeof()**, **mode()**, and **class()** values for the object.

```
DOType = function(x){                      # DOType function --------------+
# This is a function to identify data object types. As in ch. 3, I think  |
# of object type as a characterization of objects that hold collections   |
# of things. These object types are vectors, matrices, data frames,       |
# and lists.                                                              |
```

```
# If none of those types fit, then the function reports that and returns   |
# some information about mode, typeof, and class.
#                                                                          |
DOT = ""                                 # Set default value for DOT       |
if(is.vector(x)){DOT = "vector"}         # Check if is a vector            |
if(is.matrix(x)){DOT = "matrix"}         # Check if is a matrix            |
if(is.data.frame(x)){                    # Check if is a data frame        |
  DOT = "data frame"}                    # |
if(is.list(x) & !is.data.frame(x)){      # Check if is a list (and not a   |
  DOT = "list"}                          #    dataframe)                   |
                                         #                                 |
if(DOT == ""){                           # If it is none of the above      |
  cat("This is not a recognized",        # Print out the typeof(), mode(), |
    "data object. Perhaps the",          #    and class() information       |
    "following information",             #                                 |
    "would help:",                       #                                 |
    "\n\ttypeof:", typeof(x),            #                                 |
    "\n\tmode:  ", mode(x),              #                                 |
    "\n\tclass:", class(x), "\n")        #                                 |
  } else{return(DOT)}                    # Else return appropriate value   |
}                                        # End of function --------------------+
```

Here it is in action.

```
> myVector = c(1:10)                         # Create a vector
> myMatrix = as.matrix(c(1:20),              # Create a matrix
+   ncol = 2)
> myFactor = factor(LETTERS[1:10])           # Create a factor
> myDF = data.frame(myVector, myFactor)      # Put together a data frame
> myList = list("This is a list", myDF)      # Put together a list

> DOType(myVector)                           # Test for data object type
[1] "vector"
```

```
> DOType(myList)                          # Test for data object type
[1] "list"

> DOType(myDF)                            # Test for data object type
[1] "data frame"

> DOType(myMatrix)                        # Test for data object type
[1] "matrix"

> DOType(myFactor)                        # Test for data object type
This is not a recognized data object. Perhaps the following information would
help:
        typeof: integer
        mode:   numeric
        class:  factor


> DOType(DOType)                          # Test with non-data object
This is not a recognized data object. Perhaps the following information would
help:
        typeof: closure
        mode:   function
        class:  function
```

In the last line of this example, we used the function to test itself. Since a function isn't one of our data object types, it returns the default values showing that **DOType** is a function ("closure," for the **typeof()** value is one of those R types for internal use).

There are a few critical things to keep in mind when working with your own functions.

The function is its own environment. That means that creating a variable or giving a variable a value within a function doesn't have a direct effect outside the function: What happens in the function stays in the function. Variables created within the function are not available outside the function unless you include them in the **return()** statement. Likewise, changing an object within the function doesn't change it outside the function. The lesson in both of these cases is that you have to always be careful about the difference between what is going on inside the function and what you want to happen outside the function.

You can set up default values for some of the argument functions by using the equals sign to indicate the default value. If a default value is indicated, then the function will not require that argument.

A good way to see how to build a function is to take a look at the code for some of R's existing functions. You can do this by issuing either the name of the function without its parentheses or the name followed by .**default**, as in **mean.default**.

Another minor irritation is that *function* is a reserved word in R, so if you need to get the help for **function()**, you have to use **help("function")**.

As mentioned earlier, functions don't have to return any value and can be great for repetitive plotting. If you have a particular format you want to use repeatedly for graphical analysis, you can just set it up as a function and then use it on different bits of data. At the risk of getting well into our discussion of customized plots in Chapters 14 and 15, here is an example of a function to overlay a normal curve and critical probability regions on top of a histogram (see Figure 7.1). It uses the **match.call()** function to extract the name of the variable for use in labeling the *x*-axis. **match. call()** returns a language object rather than a data object, so I convert it to character values with the **as.character()** function. This makes it into a character vector where the first element is the name of the function and the rest of the elements are the variable names or the values passed to each function argument.

```
# A function to overlay a normal curve and shaded probability regions
# (2-tailed) on a histogram.  The function has two inputs: a variable
# and the desired critical probability level. Note that this function
# does not do any error checking and requires that there be no missing
# values.
#
hist.norm = function(v, pr){          # Set up function --------------------+
                                      #                                     |
    vname =                           # Get variable name from the 2nd      |
        as.character(match.call())[2] #    element in match.call function    |
                                      #                                     |
    f.hist = hist(v,                  # Set up a histogram                   |
        xlab = vname,                 # Add var name as x axis label         |
        main = NA,                    # Turn off title                       |
        col = "light gray")           # Shade bars light gray                |
```

```
                                     #                               |
p = pr/2                             # For 2-tailed divide prob      |
  ztop =                             # Identify the z score at the top |
    mean(v) + qnorm(1 - p) * sd(v)   # Top z score                   |
  zbot =                             # Identify the bottom z score   |
    mean(v) - qnorm(1 - p) * sd(v)   # Bottom z score                |
                                     #                               |
  k = seq(min(f.hist$breaks),        # Set up sequence from bottom   |
    max(f.hist$breaks),              #   to top of histogram range   |
    length = 1000)                   #   with 1000 observations      |
  y1 = dnorm(k, mean(v), sd(v))      # Y from norm dist w/v1 mean & sd |
  y2 =                               # Y2 - scale Y1 to proportions of |
    y1 * (max(f.hist$count)/max(y1)) #   the histogram.              |
                                     #                               |
  lines(k, y2, lty = 2)             # Add dashed normal curve line   |
                                     #                               |
  abline(v = mean(v),                # Add vertical line at mean     |
    col = "darkgray", lwd = 3)       # Make the line gray and thicker |
                                     #                               |
  polygon(                           # Shade in the bottom prob region |
    c(min(f.hist$breaks),            # x values for shaded region    |
      k[k < zbot], zbot, zbot),      #                               |
    c(0, y2[k < zbot],               # y values for shaded region    |
      max(y2[k < zbot]), 0),         #                               |
    col = "darkgray")                # Color of shaded region        |
                                     #                               |
  polygon(                           # Shade in the top prob region  |
    c(ztop, ztop, k[k > ztop],       # x values for shaded region    |
      max(f.hist$breaks)),           #                               |
    c(0, max(y2[k > ztop]),          # y values for shaded region    |
      y2[k > ztop], 0),              #                               |
    col = "darkgray")                # Color of shaded region        |
}                                    # End of add.normal function  ------+

# Show the function at work

myVar = c(1, 7, 5, 5, 6, 3, 8, 9, 2, # Create a variable with
  6, 3, 4, 5, 5, 6, 8, 4, 3,         # a bunch of values
```

```
    5, 5, 6, 9, 0, 11, 4, 5, 6,
     3, 7, 11, 5, 7, 4, 3, 4, 5)
pr = .05                              # Set pr interval of interest

hist.norm(myVar, .05)                 # Call overlay normal curve function
```

Figure 7.1 A Custom Function at Work

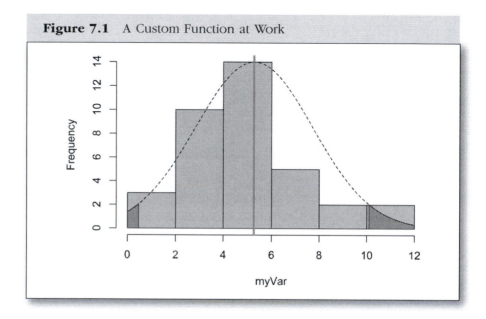

Once a function like this is set up, it can be used repeatedly for different variables. If one desires additional or different formatting, it can be accomplished by just changing the one function instead of having to track down parallel changes at disparate places in your R code.

6 ADDITIONAL R PROGRAMMING

Much of the power of R comes from its ability to serve as a programming environment for statistical analysis rather than just a tool for running basic statistical analysis. The material that we have covered is already well into a programming approach to managing and analyzing data with R. A full discussion of programming approaches to R is beyond the scope of this book. Nonetheless, there are some basic program control elements that are worth going over. These approaches can greatly increase your ability to use R effectively, especially for some of the repetitive tasks that are common to data management.

Loops

Loops are a basic programming structure that are used to generate repeated operations. Because the R language is designed around operations on vectors, loops are rarely required. Indeed, it is widely considered better to avoid loops; the consensus is that they will slow R down. Nonetheless, many people with some programming background are used to working with loops. For many basic data projects, speed is not a real issue, and loop structures can often be conceptually easier and clearer than various uses of the **apply()** function or other vectorized operations.

We use loops when we want to repeat a particular operation in a structured way. For example, we might have a complex data set that needs preprocessing, and we want to run through each observation making appropriate transformations or parsing out data with particular issues. We can do this without loops by building functions and then using something from the **apply()** family to apply the function to each observation. But it can also be done, and is sometimes more straightforward, with a loop architecture.

R uses **for()** to build loops. The instructions to be looped either are on the same line as the **for()** command or are contained in a set of braces. The loop is based on an index value, traditionally "**i**," but it can be most anything you want. Every time the loop gets to its end, R returns to the beginning of the loop and the index is incremented by 1. It keeps doing this until its value reaches the ending value. Then R moves on to the next line of code after the loop.

```
> for(i in 1:5) print("hello")          # This is a simple one-line loop
[1] "hello"
[1] "hello"
[1] "hello"
[1] "hello"
[1] "hello"
```

```
> for(i in 1:4){                      # This loop requires more lines
+    x = as.character(i)               #    so uses braces
+    y = paste("this is loop ", x)     # Print loopnumber
+    print(y)
+ }                                    # End of loop
[1] "this is loop  1"
[1] "this is loop  2"
[1] "this is loop  3"
[1] "this is loop  4"
```

You can use the **break** command to exit a loop early, although this makes the flow control more difficult to trace and is usually not considered good style.

```
> for(i in 1:4){                           # Set up loop to run 4 times
+    x = as.character(i)                    # Set x as character value of i
+    y = runif(min = 0, max = 100, n = 1)   # y = random variable btwn 0 & 100
+    print(                                 # Print
+        paste(                             #    a pasted together phrase
+           "This is loop ", x,             #    showing status of variables
+           " y = ", round(y)))
+    if(y > 75) break                       # Break out of loop if y > 75
+ }
[1] "This is loop  1  y = 43"
[1] "This is loop  2  y = 60"
[1] "This is loop  3  y = 92"

> print("All done with that loop")         # Print this after loop
[1] "All done with that loop"
```

You can use the **next** command to increment the loop on demand, but that also shouldn't usually be necessary. Note that neither **next** nor **break** requires parentheses to indicate that it is a command.

The **while()** command is another looping function that is constructed in the same basic way as the **for()** loop. **while()** loops can be helpful for situations where the number of desired iterations depends on some characteristic of the data.

`if(){} else{}`

We already saw the **ifelse()** function at work on vectors. More traditional program control is accomplished with the combination of an **if(){}** command and an **else{}** statement. The condition on which **if()** operates goes in the parentheses. The commands you want to run conditionally can just follow **if()** if they all fit on one line, or they can go in braces**{}** if more than one line is required.

One tricky thing about the **else{}** statement is that it has to be on the same line as the closing brace for the commands in the **if(){}** statement. Note also that **else** uses braces (**else{}**) rather than parentheses to group the things that happen when the **if()** condition is not fulfilled.

```
X = 1

if(x > 1){print("x is greater than one")

    } else{print("x is less than one")}
```

Note that the closing braces for the **if()** *statement and the* **else** *statement have to be on the same line.*

Character Strings as Program Elements

In just a couple of pages, we are going to turn much more intensely to the use and manipulation of text variables. In the meantime, it is worth noting the way in which character variables can be incorporated into the R programming process. R can dynamically interpret character strings as part of a program command. Going the other direction, it can also be helpful to interpret programming elements, for example, variable names, as text.

Dynamic Object Names

The most basic tool for creating dynamic object names is the **paste()** command. This command is the equivalent to text concatenation in most other programming languages, although as we'll see in the next chapter, it has some interesting characteristics for vectorized text concatenation. The basic paste function is to put together character data into a single unit. Its advantage for our purposes is that it can interpret certain kinds of R objects directly as text rather than returning their underlying value. The following example takes the natural log of every observation in a data frame (using **lapply()**). It then uses **sapply()** and **paste()** to change the names of each of the variables to include ".**log**" at the end.

```
> myData = data.frame(               # Set up a data frame
+    v1 = c(1, 2, 3),                #    with 3 variables
+    v2 = c(10, 12, 22),
+    v3 = c(4, 5, 9))

> # The apply approach
> myData.log = lapply(myData,log)    # apply log fun to every element
> names(myData.log)                  # Show variable names
[1] "v1" "v2" "v3"
> names(myData.log) =                # Change all of the names
+    sapply(                         # Paste function to create names
+        attributes(myData.log)$names,   # Use original var names
+        paste, ".log", sep = "")    # Paste on ".log" with no space
> myData.log = data.frame(myData.log) # Turn it into a data frame
> print(myData.log, digits = 2)      # Display
   v1.log v2.log v3.log
1     0.0    2.3    1.4
2     0.7    2.5    1.6
3     1.1    3.1    2.2
```

Note that **paste()** uses the name of the variable itself rather than the value that has been assigned to that name. The opposite can be accomplished with the **get()** command, which searches for an object with the indicated name and returns the value of that object. This can be useful for converting text constructions into program elements.

```
> v2 = c(10, 12, 22)                    # A variable
> myVar = paste("v", 2, sep = "")       # Construct text variable name
> print(myVar)                          # Print myVar
[1] "v2"
> print(get(myVar))                     # Value to which myVar points
[1] 10 12 22
```

Combining **paste()** and **get()**, you can build more elaborate programming routines that use object names dynamically in both directions.

The other helpful tool in this area is the **assign()** function. This does essentially the same thing as the equals or arrow sign. It is useful, however, when working with dynamic names that don't work properly with the shorter assignment operators. The first argument in the **assign()** function is a character string, so if you are assigning to a simple variable name, it has to be within quotations.

```
> v.4 = c(2, 4, 6)                      # Set up some data to work with
> assign("vNum", 3)                     # Use assign to set up a variable
> paste("v", vNum, sep = ".") = v.4     # Try to set v.3 = v.4
Error in paste("v", vNum, sep = ".") = v.4 :
   target of assignment expands to non-language object

> assign(                               # Same thing with assign function
+    paste("v", vNum, sep = "."), v.4)
> v.3                                    # Print v.3
[1] 2 4 6
```

assign() can be particularly useful for projects that involve the repetitive construction of a number of models. The following snippet suggests the logic of this approach:

```
mName = paste("model", n, sep = ".")  # Create name for model iteration n
assign(mName, lm(myV1 ~ myV2 + myV3))   # Assign the name to an lm model
```

Dynamic R Code

So far, we've only worked with dynamic object names. We can also make the R code itself dynamic. This actually requires stacking up two functions: **eval()** and **parse()**. **parse()** tells R to turn its **text=** argument into interpretable R code. **eval()** then evaluates that code. Here is an example.

```
> myV = c(1, 2, 3, 4)              # A vector to use
> myCode = "length"                # Some code language to work with
> eval(parse(text =                # Evaluate parsed character string
+    paste(myCode, "(myV)", sep = "")))   # A constructed character string
[1] 4
```

While these examples have been relatively trivial, the ability to go between text and program objects can be very powerful. Any string of characters you can build that is correct R code can be incorporated into your R program that way. Here is a more complex example. It gets a little ahead of our work so far on text objects, but it shows how this approach might be used to put together linear models with varying sets of independent variables.

```
> v1 = c(1, 2, 3, 5, 7, 8)                 # Set up a few variables
> v2 = c(10, 12, 15, 13, 22, 18)
> v3 = c(4, 7, 5, 9, 12, 18)
> eval(parse(text =                        # Evaluate/parse string
+    paste("model1 = lm(v1 ~ ",            # Paste a model statement together
+        paste(                            # Paste ind. var names together
+          paste("v", c(2, 3), sep = ""),  # Create independent var names
+            collapse = " + "),            # Connect ind. vars with + sign
+        ")", sep = "")))                  # Connect whole thing without gaps
> summary(model1)                          # Show lm model results

Call:
lm(formula = v1 ~ v2 + v3)
```

```
Residuals:
        1        2        3        4        5        6
 -0.2502  -0.8160   0.1511   1.2230  -0.0822  -0.2258
Coefficients:
             Estimate Std. Error t value  Pr(>|t|)
 (Intercept)  -2.6598     1.4282  -1.862    0.1595
 v2            0.2485     0.1243   1.999    0.1395
 v3            0.3563     0.1049   3.396    0.0426 *
 ---

 Signif. codes:  0 '***' 0.001 '**' 0.01 '*' 0.05 '.' 0.1 ' ' 1

 Residual standard error: 0.8765 on 3 degrees of freedom
 Multiple R-squared: 0.9414,      Adjusted R-squared: 0.9023
 F-statistic:  24.1 on 2 and 3 DF,  p-value: 0.01418
```

In this manner, any text you can construct, or bring in from outside R, can be interpreted as R instructions. To do this efficiently and effectively, we need to understand how textual variables are built and manipulated. This brings us at long last to the critical subject of working with character data.

CHAPTER **8**

TEXT OPERATIONS

As the world becomes increasingly digital, there are growing amounts of easily available textual data that can be used for all manner of analytic issues. It is also often the case that we have numeric data that are locked up in textual formats: for example, the output of other statistics programs, data lists in textual form or data tables from published sources.

As we have seen, R can deal with textual variables. It is not the most elegant or efficient program for this realm,[1] but as long as you are already learning R and using it for your statistical analysis, it is often the path of least resistance to incorporate text processing into your R work.

Once you have your text data in hand, you can do a wide range of processing with R's many text functions. In this chapter, we'll start by reviewing the most important of these functions. We'll then delve into the sometimes cryptic world of regular expressions, and we'll finish with a brief discussion on inputting and exporting text files. We need to start, however, by reiterating the message of Chapter 3 about the importance of knowing your object types. The character functions we are going to look at in this chapter can be inconsistent in the ways in which they treat different kinds of objects. Most of the dedicated character operations, **paste()** for example, translate noncharacter data into character data. Others can choke if you

---

1. My own personal preference for text manipulation is the open-source programming language REXX, but that is a bit old school. See http://www.rexxla.org/. The Python language is rapidly gaining popularity for working with text and has the decided advantage that it can be integrated with R using the RPy program (rpy.sourceforge.net).

feed them the wrong kind of data. In the following example, counting the number of characters in a string works fine for character objects, but for a factor, it counts the number of characters in the numeric value of the factor rather than in its label (see the factor discussion in Chapter 3). Once again, the lesson is to be very careful about your object types.

```
> myTxt = c("ab", "cdef")           # Here is some text data
> myTxt                             # Display it
[1] "ab"    "cdef"

> typeof(myTxt)                     # Show object type (character)
[1] "character"
> nchar(myTxt[2])                   # Num of characters in 2nd element
[1] 4

> myTxt3 = as.factor(myTxt)         # Change myTxt into a factor
> myTxt3                            # Display myTxt3
[1] ab    cdef
Levels: ab cdef

> typeof(myTxt3)                    # Show object type
[1] "integer"

> myTxt3[2]                         # Display myTxt3 element 2
[1] cdef
Levels: ab cdef

> nchar(myTxt3[2])                  # Num of characters in 2nd element
[1] 1
```

This example shows the danger (again) of confusing factor and character variables. **nchar()** *applied to a factor evaluates the length of the numeric factor vector (1) rather than the character labels.*

We should also highlight here the role of a few special characters that can cause some problems. There are two different reserved lists of characters we need to be careful about. One list contains the special characters for regular expressions. We'll come to those in a little while. The second list contains the problematic characters for R itself. This list has just two items: quotation marks and the backslash character.

Quotation marks are obviously problematic, since they themselves demarcate the presence of character values as distinct from program input. Nonetheless, they are relatively easily dealt with in R by alternating between single and double quotation marks. If you want to print a double quotation mark, you just have to enclose it in single quotations. If you want to print a single quotation mark, you have to enclose it in double quotations. To show how this works, we are going to jump ahead to the **cat()** function. **cat()** derives from concatenate and works like **paste()** to put string objects together. The difference is that it outputs to different devices (including the screen) and processes the new line and quotation symbols, so what you see is more likely to be the formatted output.

```
> doubleQuote = ""this is in quotes""     # This won't work--" encasing "
Error: unexpected symbol in "doubleQuote = ""
> doubleQuote = '"this is in quotes"'      # This will work-- ' encasing "
> cat(doubleQuote)                         # Print
"this is in quotes"


> SingleQuote = 'It's a conjugation!'      # This won't work-- ' encasing '
Error: unexpected symbol in "SingleQuote = '"
> SingleQuote = "It's a conjugation!"      # This will work -- " encasing '
> cat(SingleQuote)                         # Print
It's a conjugation!
```

That's all well and good, but right about now you are probably asking, "What if you want to print both?" I'm glad you asked. This brings us to the most special character of them all: the backslash.

The backslash, used within a string demarcated by quotation marks, tells R to interpret the very next thing as something special that either shouldn't be interpreted as a program element or is itself a special character. To print a double and a single quotation mark within the same string, you just have to use a backslash in front of one of them.

```
> mixedQuote = "Ron's mom said \"boo!\""  # If mixing ' & " use backslash
> cat(mixedQuote)                          # Print
Ron's mom said "boo!"
```

So how do you print a backslash? By preceding it with another backslash, of course. We'll see this in action shortly when we get to regular expressions. But first, let's review the most important of R's built-in character and string commands.

SOME USEFUL TEXT FUNCTIONS

We have already been introduced to the very important **paste()** function at the end of Chapter 7. **paste()** is used for putting character strings together and is important enough to be worth a little more time. We'll start with a simple example that just joins together three character objects into one.

```
> myTxt =                            # A vector of text values
+    c("peas", "potatoes", "carrots")
> myStr =)                           # Paste together peas and potatoes
+    paste(myTxt[1], "and", myTxt[2]
> myStr                              # Display
[1] "peas and potatoes"
```

paste() takes two main options: **collapse=** and **sep=**. As we saw at the end of the previous chapter, **sep=** tells R what to use to connect the pasted parts together. The default value for **sep=** is a space (" "), so if you want things butted right against each other, you'll have to use **sep = ""**.

```
> myTxt =                            # A vector of text values
+    c("peas", "potatoes", "carrots")
> myStr = paste(myTxt[1], myTxt[3],  # Paste peas and carrots
+      sep = " & ")                   # Join with " & "
> myStr                              # Display
[1] "peas & carrots"
```

The **collapse=** option tells **paste()** to take a vector of character objects and run them all together. The default value for collapse is "NULL," which tells R to keep distinct the individual vector elements.

When you give **collapse=** another value, R uses that value to connect the vector elements, just like **sep=**. If you want a space in between, then set **collapse = " "**. If you really want them merged smoothly, then use **collapse = ""**. As with **sep=**, you can put almost anything else in there as well.[2]

```
> letters[22:26]                     # Show last 5 of letters vector
[1] "v" "w" "x" "y" "z"

> lets = paste(letters, collapse = "")  # Collapse to text string
> lets                                # Show lets text string
[1] "abcdefghijklmnopqrstuvwxyz"
```

An interesting, and nice, thing about **paste()** is that it translates almost everything you throw at it into a character object. This means that you can give it numbers and factors without worrying about the number/character/factor conversion process that we obsessed over at the end of Chapter 3.

paste() is vectorized. If you apply it to a vector, it will operate on each element. If you give it two vectors, it will put them together element by element. Be careful here, though, because if the vectors are of unequal lengths, it will start recycling the shorter vector. If this is what you intend, it can be useful. Otherwise, not so much.

```
> alphabet = LETTERS[1:10]            # Use built-in uppercase letters
> numbers = seq(1:10)                 # A vector of 10 numbers
> paste(numbers, alphabet, sep = "")  # Paste together (vectorized)
[1] "1A"  "2B"  "3C"  "4D"  "5E"  "6F"  "7G"  "8H"  "9I"  "10J"

> myTxt7 = paste(myTxt, 7, sep = "-") # Another vectorized paste
> myTxt7                              # Show-note char conversion of 7
[1] "peas-7"     "potatoes-7" "carrots-7"
```

---

2. If you want to use one of the reserved characters, such as a quotation mark, you'll have to use the backslash approach, as discussed earlier.

```
> myTxt7new = paste(myTxt, c(1:2),        # Paste with vectors of unequal
+      "new", sep = "-")                   #  sizes:3 elements, 2, and 1
> myTxt7new                               # Display
[1] "peas-1-new"      "potatoes-2-new" "carrots-1-new"
```

Here is another example that uses repeated paste operations to insert punctuation into a list of any size and to build a sentence.

```
> commas =                                # A vector with commas
+   c(rep(", ", length(myTxt) - 2),       #   to build comma-separated list
+      ", and ", ".")                      #   then an "and" & a period
> myStr = paste(myTxt, commas, sep = "")  # paste commas into list
> myStr = paste(myStr, collapse = "")     # Collapse into one string
> myStr = paste("Veggie list:", myStr)    # Add start of sentence
> myStr                                   # Display
[1] "Veggie list: peas, potatoes, and carrots."
```

There are a few other useful text functions to know about in addition to **paste()**. **nchar()** tells you how long a string is (the number of characters). The only argument required is the string itself or a variable name for the string. **nchar()** is vectorized, so if you apply it to a vector of string elements, it will return a vector with the length of each of those strings.

```
> myString = ("peas and carrots")        # A string to work with
> nchar(myString)                         # How long it is
[1] 16

> myStrVector =  c("v-1", "v-2b", "v-3")  # A vector of strings
> nchar(myStrVector)                      # Length of each element in vector
[1] 3 4 3
```

strsplit() breaks a string into parts based on the appearance of a specific character or substring. Its arguments are the string and the breaking point(s), which are also characters. As you may be disappointed to learn, if you use **strsplit()**, the characters used for the split point disappear from the result. The result returned from **strsplit()** is a list. This is often not what you want, in which case you can use **unlist()** to turn the results back into a character vector.

```
> myStr = "peas and carrots"              # A text string to work with
> strsplit(myStr, split = " and ")        # Split at " and "
[[1]]
[1] "peas"     "carrots"

> strsplit(myStr, split = " ")            # Split up at blanks
[[1]]
[1] "peas"     "and"      "carrots"

> myStr2 = strsplit(myStr, split = "")    # Split into individual letters
> myStr2                                   # Show individual letters
[[1]]
 [1] "p" "e" "a" "s" " " "a" "n" "d" " " "c" "a" "r" "r" "o" "t" "s"

> typeof(myStr2)                          # Note that it is a list
[1] "list"
> myStr2[1]                               # First element is the whole thing
[[1]]
 [1] "p" "e" "a" "s" " " "a" "n" "d" " " "c" "a" "r" "r" "o" "t" "s"

> myStr3 = unlist(myStr2)                 # Make it not a list
> myStr3[1:6]                             # Now it is a more useful string vector
[1] "p" "e" "a" "s" " " "a"
> myStr3[1:8]                             # Now it is a more useful string vector
[1] "p" "e" "a" "s" " " "a" "n" "d"
```

If you use the empty character (**""**) as the argument for **split**, it will split the string into one-character units, as shown in the example.

strsplit() is vectorized, so if you apply it to a vector, it will split each element of the vector. strsplit() will split a string at every point where the split= value appears, so you do have to be careful with the vectorized version, where different elements might have different patterns of the split value. Finally, if you want to split on a period or on other reserved characters, you'll have to get into regular expressions, as shown here and discussed below. Notice, again, that the result of the strsplit() operation is a list. It is likely that you will need to transform it into a more useul data object.

```
> myStrVector = c("v-1", "v-2-b", "v-3")# A vector of strings
> strsplit(myStrVector, split = "-")    # Split at dashes
[[1]]
[1] "v" "1"

 [[2]]
[1] "v" "2" "b"

 [[3]]
[1] "v" "3"

> myStr = ("peas.carrots")              # A string with a period
> strsplit(myStr, split = "\\.")        # Regular exp. to split at period
[[1]]
[1] "peas"     "carrots"
```

Systematic character translation can be done with the chartr(x, old, new) function. Just give it the original and new values, and it will fix everything. This only works for individual characters. You can, however, package the elements together to translate a set of characters all at once, as shown in the following example:

```
> myTxt = c("peas", "carrots")          # A text vector to work with
> myNewTxt = chartr(myTxt, old = "s",   # Change lowercase s
+    new = "5")                         #    to the number "5"
> myNewTxt                              # Print the new vector
[1] "pea5"     "carrot5"
```

```
> myNewTxt = chartr(myTxt,          # Translate lowercase vowels
+    old = "aeiou", new = "AEIOU")   #     to uppercase vowels
> myNewTxt                           # Print the new vector
[1] "pEAs"      "cArrOts"
```

You can translate a set of characters if they are bound up in equal-length character strings. You cannot work with the old and new values in a vector of character strings. You can see how this works in the following example, which uses the built-in **letters** and **LETTERS** vectors.[3] In the first attempt, R only uses the first item in the vectors ("a" and "A"). In the second attempt, we collapse these vectors each into a single text string, and then it works.

```
> myTxt = c("peas", "carrots")      # A text vector to work with
> myNewTxt = chartr(myTxt,          # Try to translate lowercase
+    old = letters, new = LETTERS)   #     to upper using letter vectors
Warning messages:
1: In chartr(myTxt, old = letters, new = LETTERS) :
   argument 'old' has length > 1 and only the first element will be used
2: In chartr(myTxt, old = letters, new = LETTERS) :
   argument 'new' has length > 1 and only the first element will be used

> myNewTxt                           # Print the new vector
[1] "peAs"      "cArrots"

> lets = paste(letters, collapse = "")  # Letters vector to text string
> lets                               # Show lets text string

[1] "abcdefghijklmnopqrstuvwxyz"
> LETS = paste(LETTERS, collapse = "")   # Same for uppercase LETTERS vector
> myNewTxt = chartr(myTxt, old = lets,   # Translate lower case
```

----

3. These built-in vectors of all of the letters can be remarkably handy. Note that as preset data objects they don't require the following parentheses.

```
+   new = LETS)                    #     to uppercase
> myNewTxt                         # Print the new vector
[1] "PEAS"     "CARROTS"
```

chartr() can translate any character to any other character. For just changing the case, you can more easily use the **tolower()** and **toupper()** functions. These functions can be very helpful given R's particularity about case in variable names and the like.[4]

```
> VAR1 = c(1, 2, 4)               # Some data to work with
> Var2 = c(5, 7, 4)
> myData = data.frame(VAR1, Var2) # Combined into a data frame
> names(myData)                   # The data frame
[1] "VAR1" "Var2"

> names(myData) = tolower(names(myData)) # Lowercase for var names
> names(myData)                   # Show variable names
[1] "var1" "var2"

> names(myData) = toupper(names(myData)) # Uppercase for var names
> names(myData)                   # Show variable names
[1] "VAR1" "VAR2"

> names(myData) = chartr(names(myData), # Use chartr() to switch to just
+   old = "AR", new = "ar")       #   first letter capitalized
> names(myData)                   # Show variable names
[1] "Var1" "Var2"
```

FINDING THINGS

One of the most important things to be able to do with text is searching and replacing. As usual, there are a number of different approaches to search and replace in R.

---

4. There is also the **casefold()** function, which can go either way (depending on the value of the **upper=** option). But this is only there to maintain compatibility with the S-PLUS program.

grep(pattern, x) tells you whether and where a target character pattern can be found within a set of character objects. This function returns the observation numbers for where the pattern is found in the *x* vector and a 0 if it is not found anywhere. As usual in R, searches are case sensitive, but there is an **ignore.case = T** option if you want to search for either lower- or uppercase matches. If you use the option **value = TRUE**, it will return the value of the observation itself. You can build quite complex search patterns using regular expressions, which we'll get to in a moment.

```
> myTxt = c("Peas", "Carrots")          # A text vector
> grep("rr", myTxt)                      # Look for "rr" in myTxt
[1] 2

> grep("pe", myTxt)                      # Look for "pe" in myTxt
integer(0)

> grep("pe", myTxt, ignore.case = T)     # Look again ignoring case.
[1] 1

> agrep("peau", myTxt, ignore.case = T)  # An approximate look finds "peau"
[1] 1
```

Note that **integer(0)** *is R's somewhat subtle way of telling you that it can't find what you are looking for.*

agrep() works the same way but looks for approximate matches. This is a fine, but dangerous, thing. Obviously, you have to be very careful that close enough is good enough.

Here is another **grep()** example, this time returning values rather than observation numbers and then doing something with them.

```
> myText = c("Fred Smith", "Julie Brown", "Fred Jones")
> i = grep(pattern = "Fred", x = myText)
> cat("Freds are in: ", i)

Freds are in:  1 3

> i = grep(pattern = "Fred", x = myText, value = TRUE)
> cat("A list of Freds: ", i, sep = "\n")
```

```
A list of Freds:
Fred Smith
Fred Jones
```

Note that the **value** = **TRUE** option tells R to return the values of the observations in which a match is found instead of the number of the observation.

x **%in%** **y** returns **TRUE** or **FALSE** if *x* is in the object *y*. This is an unusual function both because it eschews the normal parenthesis format for functions and because it is one of the few functions that are sensibly insensitive to object type. It works for any kind of object, as the first thing this function does is convert its arguments into character strings.[5] On the other hand, it only works for the whole object, so in the following example, when one of the objects is "me and you," **%in%** returns false for a search for just "me."

```
> myData = c(1, 2, 3, 4, 5)        # A bit of data
> 3 %in% myData                    # Check if 3 is in the data
[1] TRUE
> "3" %in% myData                  # Check if "3" is in the data
[1] TRUE
> 6 %in% myData                    # Check if 6 is in the data
[1] FALSE
> myData2 = c("one", "two")        # Some more data
> "one" %in% myData2               # Check if "one" is in the data
[1] TRUE
> myData3 = c("one and two",       # Some more data
+    "this and that")
> "one" %in% myData3               # Check if "one" is in this data
[1] FALSE
> if("one and two" %in% myData3){  # Use %in% in an if() function
+    print("one and two are included")
+ }
[1] "one and two are included"
```

---

5. R help warns that this can be a slow process with large lists.

%in% does not work for finding a substring within a string. For that, use **substr()** to extract a specified piece of text or **regexpr()** to find a specific bit of text in a string. **regexpr()** returns both the starting position and the length of the matched text. That length is stored in an attribute called **match.length**. Since **regexpr()** is vectorized, it works on a whole vector of string variables at once, but it can be used on single strings of text as well (which it treats as vectors of length 1). Be careful that when **regexpr()** doesn't find what it is looking for it returns −1 rather than an NA or other more obvious missing value indicators.

```
> myTxt = c("alligator", "rat", "flat cat", "horse")

> regexpr(pattern = "at", text = myTxt) # Find "at" in myTxt
[1]   6   2   3  -1
attr(,"match.length")
[1]   2   2   2  -1
attr(,"useBytes")
[1] TRUE
```

regexpr() generates an object with two attributes. The regexpr() object itself is a vector of integers showing the starting position of the pattern in each string. The first attribute is the length of the pattern in each string (this is always the same here but can vary in more complex searches). The second attribute is an indicator that the useBytes= option was set to TRUE.

gsub() is R's real version of "find and replace." The arguments are the search string, the replacement string, and the object in which to search. Here is an example of using **gsub()** to deal with the common scourge of imported numeric data with commas.

```
> GDP = c("135,246,005",        # Here is some simulated data
+    "254,679,103",             #    you might have
+    "43,456,28")               #    read in as character data
>                               #    with those pernicious commas.
> typeof(GDP)                   # Confirm R thinks this text data
[1] "character"
```

```
> gdp = gsub(",", "", GDP)          # Replace commas w/nothing ("")
> gdp = as.numeric(gdp)             # Convert character to numeric
> typeof(gdp)                       # Check object type again
[1] "double"

> mean(gdp)                         # Try a calculation
[1] 131423579

> data.frame(gdp, GDP)              # Print out values side by side
        gdp           GDP
1 135246005   135,246,005
2 254679103   254,679,103
3   4345628    43,456,28
```

gsub() is vectorized, so it works over the whole vector in one step. It will work with any vector, so you can also use **gsub()** to make systematic changes in vectors of variable or row names.

substr() extracts a substring from a character vector. It takes three arguments: The first tells it which string to use, the second tells it the starting point for extracting the substring, while the third is the ending point.[6]

```
> # Example 1 -- a simple extraction
> substr("abcdefghijkl", 2, 5)     # Get characters 2-5 from string
[1] "bcde"

> # Example 2 -- a variable extraction
> myStart = 7                      # Set a start variable
> myStop = 11                      # Set a stop variable
> myText = "hello Fred!"           # Text to substring
> substr(myText, myStart, myStop)  # Substring operation
[1] "Fred!"
```

---

6. Remember that **regexpr()** can find these for you if you need to automate the process.

```
> # Example 3 - Extracting from a vector
> myText = c("Hello Fred!",               # A string to work with
+    "and hello Julia!")                   # Another string to work with
> nameStart = regexpr(                     # Find start of all names
+    pattern = "hello ",                   #    by locating "hello"
+    text = myText,                        #    in each string
+    ignore.case = TRUE)                   #    ignoring case

> nameStop = regexpr(                      # Find end of all names
+    pattern = "!",                        #    by locating !
+    text = myText)                        #    in each string

> myNames = substr(myText,                 # Extract substrings myText vector
+    start = nameStart +                   # Starting position plus
+      attributes(nameStart)$match.length, #    length of matched text
+    stop = nameStop -                     # Ending position minus
+      attributes(nameStop)$match.length)  #    length of matched text
> myNames                                  # Display result
[1] "Fred"   "Julia"
```

You can also use **substr()** to replace bits of text. Just set the **substr()** equal to a new value.

```
> greeting = "Hello Fred!"
> substr(greeting, 7, 10) = "Mike"        # Replace text from position 7 to 10
> greeting
[1] "Hello Mike!"
```

substr() is limited, in that it can only replace a segment of text with another segment of the same length. For more flexible replacements, you'll need to either return to the **gsub()** function or use a combination of **substr()** and **paste()**.

There is an alternative function, **strtrim()**, that truncates strings on the right to match a given length. It can work with matching vectors of strings and lengths if for some reason you were needing such a thing. The following example works on a vector of strings using a vector of lengths.

```
> strtrim("Hello World!", 5)                # Trim string after 5 characters
[1] "Hello"

> strtrim(
+    c("Hello World!", "World Hello!"),     # A vector of strings
+    c(1, 5))                               # A vector of lengths for trimming
[1] "H"       "World"
```

match(vector1, vector2) probably sounds more useful than it is. It returns a vector with the *first* positions of the objects in vector 1 in vector 2. This works with strings as well as other data types. I suppose the more creative types will have all kinds of things where this type of matching would be useful. If you have a sorted list, it could tell you the observation number where each of the vector 1 items begins. **match()** works with the whole character string or variable value.

```
> testData = c(rep("United States", 10),# Data w/a bunch of country names
+    rep("France", 4), rep("U.K.", 12))
> countries = c("France",                  # A vector with each name
+    "United States", "U.K.",
+    "Germany")
> countryPlace =                           # Identify first occurence of
+    match(countries, testData)            #    each name in testData
> countryPlace
[1] 11   1 15 NA
> countryPlace2 =                          # Join these results with the
+    data.frame(countries, countryPlace)   #    country names
> countryPlace2
        countries countryPlace
1           France           11
2    United States            1
3             U.K.           15
4          Germany           NA
```

Regular Expressions

Regular expressions are a set of tools for describing patterns in text. You wouldn't think it would be so complex, but it turns out that managing the myriad punctuations and the various special characters that are required for digital typography is actually very involved. It is beyond the scope of this book to go too far into the arcana of regular expressions. There are other books that tackle that, as well as many online resources (see, e.g., Forta, 2004; Friedl, 2006; Watt, 2005).[7] But regular expressions can be as useful as they are scary, so going over some of the basics is warranted.

Regular expressions are used in R to significantly enhance search-and-replace text operations. You can get the R help on regular expressions by using **help(regex)**. As usual, other online resources may be more immediately helpful, especially when you are just starting out.

The first thing to be aware of is that regular expressions aren't really very regular at all. They are implemented in different ways in different computer languages; so, alas, you can't always be confident that a regular expression from one context will work in another. Fortunately, there are only two flavors of regular expressions we need to be concerned about in the R environment: extended (the default) and Perl (named after the Perl programming language). You can tell R which version to use by including an option statement in the same function that uses the regular expressions.[8]

```
Extended = TRUE        (the default)

Perl = TRUE            (to use Perl regular expressions)
```

With one exception, we are mostly going to stick to the default extended expressions here, but if you come across something you want to do using the Perl set, you just need to add **perl = T** as an option in your **gsub()** or other find-and-replace operation.

The starting point for regular expressions is the set of characters that can have special meanings. These metacharacters (see Table 8.1) are the

---

7. http://www.regular-expressions.info/quickstart.html and http://www.funduc.com/regexp.htm are two of many online resources.

8. If **extended = FALSE**, R uses a lesser set of the basic regular expressions. That flavor shouldn't really be an issue for our purposes.

levers for making regular expressions work, but they'll cause all manner of grief if you don't keep them under careful control.

Table 8.1   Metacharacters for Regular Expressions

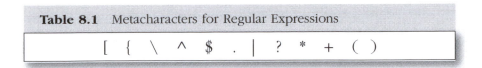

[{ \ ^ $. | ? * + ( )

As in R more generally, the backslash is key to identifying special characters in regular expressions. The backslash tells R that the following character requires special interpretation. Since R already uses the backslash for its own purposes, it often requires two consecutive backslashes to set up a regular expression. The first tells R that something special is coming; the second begins the regular expression sequence.

Essentially, backslashes are used in two opposite ways: For the special characters, the backslash tells R to interpret the following character as not special. For not special characters, the backslashes tell R to interpret the following character as special. So the backslash makes normal text special and special text normal. Let's look at some examples.

In this first example, we can see how searching for one of the special characters, in this case the dollar sign ($), goes awry because the dollar sign has a special meaning: It demarcates the end of a line.

```
> myText = " $ Hi There!"          # Character data with a $
> myText =
+     sub(myText,
+         pattern = "$",           # Try to find "$"
+         replacement = "X")       # Try to replace with X

> myText                           # Puts X at end indicated by $
[1] " $ Hi There!X"
```

We can successfully search for a $ in the string by protecting it with a backslash, demoting it to a regular character rather than a special character. But because the backslash is also a special character, we need another backslash to let R know that the following backslash requires special handling. For this purpose, we use a double backslash, one for the regular expression and one for R.

```
> myText = " $ Hi There!"                # Character data with a $
> myText =
+    sub(myText,
+       pattern = "\\$",                  # Find "$" protected with \\
+       replacement = "X")               # Replace with X
> myText                                  # Success!
[1] " X Hi There!"
```

Here is another example. The period in regular expressions is a wild-card character. Using a regular expression search for ".ee." will return every four-letter word with two *es* in the middle. You can see the problem here since there are so many other uses of periods in text. This is another case of a special symbol that we want to make unspecial. To indicate a normal period in a regular expression, you have to identify it as such with a preceding backslash (\.). But, as we have seen, R also takes special note of backslashes, so you have to use a backslash to indicate that the following backslash itself is a special character. So again you need to use "\\." If you want to change every period followed by a blank space with a question mark followed by a blank space, you would need to use the following commands (remember that **gsub()** replaces every occurrence, where **sub()** only replaces the first).

```
> myTxt = "This. Is. Over. Punctuated." # Some text to work with
> gsub(x = myTxt, pattern = "\\. ",      # The pattern to look for
+    replacement = "\\? ")               # The replacement
[1] "This? Is? Over? Punctuated."
```

In this search example, the period is made unspecial with a backslash. A backslash is made unspecial with another backslash. The final period isn't replaced because it doesn't have a space after it to match the **pattern=** *sequence.*

An example of making normal text special would be the use of "\n" to indicate a new line. If we wanted to put every sentence that ends in a period on its own line, we could use the following.

```
> myTxt = "This is sentence 1. This is sentence 2."
> myNewTxt = gsub(x = myTxt,              # Replace
+   pattern = "\\. ",                     #  period followed by a space
+   replacement = ".\n")                  #  with period & line break
> myNewTxt                               # Show with formatting codes
[1] "This is sentence 1.\nThis is sentence 2."
> cat(myNewTxt)                          # Show as it will print
This is sentence 1.
This is sentence 2.
```

In addition to **\n** for a new line, other examples of normal text that can be made special in searches include **\s** for space and **\t** for tab.

The backslash is the key, then, to building all manner of interesting and increasingly complex search-and-replace procedures. Here are two more examples that eliminate extraneous white space either at the beginning or at the end of a string. The beginning and end of strings are indicated with the special characters ^ and $, respectively. **\s** is also used to indicate a space. The first two special characters do not require a backslash to be treated as special. The use of "s" as a space indicator, however, is a special use of a normal character, so it does require the backslash. If we wanted to search for a regular ^ or $ within our text, we would need to backslash them to prevent R from interpreting them as the start or end of string indicators.

```
> # Removing leading white space
> myText = "    Hi There!"              # String w/leading white space
> myText =
+   sub(myText,
+     pattern = "^\\s+",                 # Find spaces (\\s+) from start(^)
+     replacement = "")                  # replace with nothing
> myText
[1] "Hi There!"

> # Removing trailing white space
> myText = "Hi There!    "              # String w/trailing white space
> myText =
```

```
+    sub(myText,
+       pattern = "\\s+$",              # Find spaces (\\s+) at end ($)
+       replacement = "")              # replace with nothing

> myText
[1] "Hi There!"
```

I hope these examples suggest the essential role of regular expression in find-and-replace operations. We can think more systematically about regular expressions in terms of two kinds of operations: location and repetition. Location operations tell R where to look in a string. Repetition operations tell R how many of something to look for.

Location Operators

As we have just seen, the dollar sign ($) indicates the end of a line. Searching for **X$** looks for lines that end with *X*.

```
> myTxt = "some text of interest"     # Some text to work with
> myNewTxt = gsub(myTxt,              # Set new text with find/replace
+    pattern = "t$",                  # Find t at end of line
+    replacement = "X")              # Replace with X
> myNewTxt                            # Display Result
[1] "some text of interesX"
```

The carat symbol (^) either indicates the beginning of a line *or* negates what follows it in a search. (Sorry. Not my fault.) **^X** alone finds lines that start with *X*. Using the carat symbol within brackets **[^X]** finds things that aren't *X*.

```
> myTxt = "some text of interest"     # Some text to work with
> myNewTxt = gsub(myTxt,              # Set new text with find/replace
+    pattern = "^s",                  # Look for s at start of line
+    replacement = "X")              # Replace with X
> myNewTxt                            # Display result
[1] "Xome text of interest"
```

```
> myNewTxt = gsub(myTxt,              # Set new text with find/replace
+    pattern = "[^s]",                # Find anything that isn't s
+    replacement = "X")              # Replace with X
> myNewTxt                           # Display result
[1] "sXXXXXXXXXXXXXXXXXXXsX"
```

The less-than and greater-than symbols (<, >) are used to locate the beginning and the end of words. Unlike the other locators, however, they are not special characters for regular expressions, so we have to make them special with the double backslash.

```
> # Beginning of words
> myTxt = "some text of interest"    # Some text to work with
> myNewTxt = gsub(myTxt,              # Set new text with find/replace
+    pattern = "\\<t",                # t's at beginning of words
+    replacement = "X")              # Replace with X
> myNewTxt                           # Display Result
[1] "some Xext of interest"

> # Ends of words
> myTxt = "some text of interest"    # Some text to work with
> myNewTxt = gsub(myTxt,              # Set new text with find/replace
+    pattern = "t\\>",                # t's at end of words
+    replacement = "X")              # Replace with X
> myNewTxt                           # Display Result
[1] "some texX of interesX"
```

The Repetition Operators

The repetition operators (?, *, +, and {}) allow you to do pattern recognition in find-and-replace operations based on the number of times a pattern appears.

The question mark makes R look for a pattern where the element that immediately precedes the question mark is present either zero or one time. "One time" is pretty easy to understand. "Zero times" just means that if the rest of the preceding pattern is matched, the element that immediately precedes the question mark doesn't have to be present.[9]

```
> myTxt = "ab aba abaa abaaa abaaaa"    # Some text with patterns
> myNewTxt = gsub(myTxt,
+    pattern = "ba?",                    # Every b followed by 0 or 1 a
+    replacement = "X")                  #   replaced by one X
> myNewTxt
[1] "aX aX aXa aXaa aXaaa"
```

Note that the first two patterns (ab and aba) are treated the same when looking for "ba"? The "a" doesn't have to be there.

The asterisk (*) works the same way as the question mark but matches any number of the element immediately preceding the asterisk. As with the question mark, this includes zero times. All of the repeated match elements are replaced with a single copy of the indicated replacement text.

```
> myTxt = "ab aba abaa abaaa abaaaa"    # Some text with patterns

> myNewTxt = gsub(myTxt,
+    pattern = "ba*",                    # Every b followed by any # of a's
+    replacement = "X")                  #   (including 0) replaced by one X

> myNewTxt
[1] "aX aX aX aX aX"
```

The plus sign (+) works the same way as the asterisk but doesn't include matches where the element preceding the plus sign is matched zero times.

---

9. The question mark can also be used within parentheses with the letter *i* to indicate case insensitivity. We'll get to that later.

```
> myTxt = "ab aba abaa abaaa abaaaa"     # Some text with patterns
> myNewTxt = gsub(myTxt,
+    pattern = "ba+",                     # Every b followed by any # of a's
+    replacement = "X")                   #   (not including 0) replaced w/X

> myNewTxt
[1] "ab aX aX aX aX"
```

Curly braces ({}) allow you to specify exactly how many times the element preceding the curly braces should be matched. This can be either a single number {3} or a range {1, 4}. If you include the comma but leave one or the other number off, it will do anything greater than or equal to the first number or anything less than or equal to the second number.

```
> myTxt = "ab aba abaa abaaa abaaaa"     # Some text with patterns

> myNewTxt = gsub(myTxt,
+    pattern = "ba{2}",                   # Every b followed w/exactly 2 a's
+    replacement = "X")                   #   replaced w/X

> myNewTxt
[1] "ab aba aX aXa aXaa"

> myNewTxt = gsub(myTxt,
+    pattern = "ba{1,2}",                 # Every b followed by 1 to 2 a's
+    replacement = "X")                   #   replace w/X

> myNewTxt
[1] "ab aX aX aXa aXaa"
```

One other thing to be careful about is that regular expression matching can be either "greedy" or "lazy." Greedy matching looks for the longest possible match, while lazy matching looks for the shortest match. The question mark modifies a search wildcard to be lazy. The following example shows the two alternatives. In the first instance (the greedy search), all of the contiguous *a*s are collapsed to be replaced by a single *X*. In the second instance (the lazy search), every *a* is replaced with its own *X*. The first one is greedy because it looks ahead and tries to pull as much into the match as it can. The second one is lazy because it makes the replacement as soon as it comes across a match, and then resumes searching until it comes to the next match.

```
> myTxt = "ab aba abaa abaaa abaaaa"    # Some text with patterns
> myNewTxt = gsub(myTxt,
+    pattern = "a+",                     # Every a (Greedy)
+    replacement = "X")                  #   replaced by X
> myNewTxt
[1] "Xb XbX XbX XbX XbX"

> myNewTxt = gsub(myTxt,
+    pattern = "a+?",                    # Every a (lazy)
+    replacement = "X")                  #   replaced by X
> myNewTxt
[1] "Xb XbX XbXX XbXXX XbXXXX"
```

Other Pattern Operators

There are a few other pattern operations that are useful to have in your regular expression toolbox.

The pattern **(?i)** is embedded in a search to indicate that the next element(s) can be case insensitive (i.e., either upper- or lowercase).

```
> myTxt = "abcde edcba"                 # Some text with patterns

> myNewTxt = gsub(myTxt,
+    pattern = "(?i)BC",                 # bc or BC or bC or Bc
+    replacement = "X")                  #   replaced by X

> myNewTxt
[1] "aXde edcba"
```

Parentheses, as one might expect, are used to group things together. A vertical separator line indicates a logical "or."

```
> myTxt = "abcde edcba"              # Some text with patterns

> myNewTxt = gsub(myTxt,
+    pattern = "b(cd|a)",            #  b followed by cd or a
+    replacement = "X")             #  replaced with X

> myNewTxt
[1] "aXe edcX"
```

Square brackets, [ ], are used to indicate alternative matches by character. R will match any of the things in the brackets. Note, however, that this is only for individual characters. Indeed, contrary to most other R syntax, since it is purely character based, you do not even need to provide commas (although R will not object if you do).

```
> myTxt = "abcde edcba"              # Some text with patterns
> myNewTxt = gsub(myTxt,
+    pattern = "[abc]",              # Every a, b, or c
+    replacement = "X")             #  replaced by X
> myNewTxt
[1] "XXXde edXXX"
```

The bracketed text can be combined with nonbracketed text.

```
> myTxt = "abcde edcba"              # Some text with patterns
> myNewTxt = gsub(myTxt,
+    pattern = "a[bc]",              # Every a with a following b or c
+    replacement = "X")             #  replaced by X

> myNewTxt
[1] "Xcde edcba"
```

You can indicate a range within the brackets by using a simple dash.[10] Even then, it is still a character-by-character replacement process.

```
> myTxt = "abcde edcba"            # Some text with patterns

> myNewTxt = gsub(myTxt,
+    pattern = "[a-d]",            # Every a, b, c, or d
+    replacement = "X")           #   replaced by X

> myNewTxt
[1] "XXXXe eXXXX"
```

Here, also, is where the carat symbol applies in its negation role. The carat before something in the brackets indicates that R should match everything *except* what comes after the carat.

```
> myTxt = "abcde edcba"            # Some text with patterns

> myNewTxt = gsub(myTxt,
+    pattern = "[^ce]",            # Anything except c or e
+    replacement = "X")           #   replaced with X

> myNewTxt
[1] "XXcXeXeXcXX"
```

Note that R replaces the space as well. **[^ce]** *would prevent that.*

R has a number of built-in character sets for use in the brackets. These are demarcated with a leading and trailing square bracket–colon combination. You can get these from the Help menu for Regular Expressions, but the most important are **[:alnum:]** for any alphanumeric character, **[:alpha:]** for any alphabetic character, **[:digit:]** for any numeric character, **[:punct:]** for any punctuation mark, **[:upper:]** for any uppercase letters, and **[:lower:]** for any lowercase letters.

---

10. If, perchance, you need to include a dash in your replacement list, just be sure that it is the first thing in the brackets.

```
> myTxt = "Punctuation: It's a fine thing!"
> myNewTxt = gsub(x = myTxt,
+    pattern = "[a[:punct:]]",           # Find any a or any punctuation
+    replacement = "X")                  #  Replace with X
> myNewTxt                              # Display result
[1] "PunctuXtionX ItXs X fine thingX"
> myNewTxt = gsub(x = myTxt,             # Find space
+    pattern = " [[:upper:]]",           #  followed by uppercase letter
+    replacement = "-X")                 # Replace with -X
> myNewTxt                              # Display result
[1] "Punctuation:-Xt's a fine thing!"
```

A Wisdom of Perl

I had hoped not to have to do this, but there is one feature of the Perl flavor of regular expressions that is worth noting. Perl regular expressions allow you to capture the matched text for reuse later. This can be very helpful for complex operations where you are doing things like processing and renaming variables.

The Perl options are invoked by adding **perl = T** to the statement where you wish to draw on Perl regular expression features. In Perl regular expressions, parentheses are used either for grouping or to capture matched text. The matched text is held in memory and labeled with a number. The first matched text is "\1". The second matched text is "\2", and so on. It is recalled with those patterns preceded by the usual extra backslash (\\1).

```
> myNames = c("varA", "varB", "varZ")   # Some variable names
> myNames2 = gsub(myNames,
+    pattern = "([A-Z])",               # search for any uppercase letter
+    replacement =  "-\\1",             # replace w/dash & matched item
+    perl = T)                          # Invoke Perl regular expressions
> myNames2                             # Show results
[1] "var-A" "var-B" "var-Z"
```

PROCESSING RAW TEXT DATA

Where do our text data come from? Most of the time, the text we need to work with is just character data sprinkled into a larger numeric data set. We've already seen how to work with that kind of input in Chapter 3. Remember, here again, the importance of distinguishing between character, factor, and numeric data. As we have seen, most of the text operations convert their input automatically to character data; a few, however, require that you make this adjustment yourself first.

R can also deal with purely textual files. To read in a text file, use the **readLines("filename")** command. **readLines()** reads the file into a character vector, with one observation for each line. A line will be all the text leading up to a hard return character. In some files, this might be a whole paragraph. The file needs to be simple text and not an encoded format, such as a Word document or PDF file. It is usually indicated by a .txt extension. Other kinds of files are often simple text as well, such as HTML or XML files. Be sure that the file you wish to read is in the current working directory, or you will have to provide the full path to find the file.

```
> myTxt = readLines("ozymandias.txt")    # Read in a txt file
> typeof(myTxt)                          # Show object type for myTxt
[1] "character"


> myTxt[5]                               # Display 5th element of myTxt


[1] "Who said: \"Two vast and trunkless legs of stone"
> lineNum =
+   c(0, 0, 0, 1:(length(myTxt)-3))      # Create line numbers
> ozy2 = data.frame(lineNum, I(myTxt))   # Data frame w/linenum & poem
> ozy2[5:8,]                             # Show data lines 5-8

  lineNum                                                myTxt
5       2 Who said: "Two vast and trunkless legs of stone
6       3        Stand in the desert. Near them on the sand,
7       4 Half sunk, a shatter'd visage lies, whose frown
8       5          And wrinkled lip and sneer of cold command
```

Note the use of **I()** *to prevent* **data.frame()** *from converting a character vector to a factor. Note also the backslashed quotation mark when displaying myTxt[5] but not when displaying the data frame version.*

A useful example of processing a raw text file comes from the increasingly common and important process of pulling data from webpages.

SCRAPING THE WEB FOR FUN AND PROFIT

Back in Chapter 4, I promised some guidance on web scraping. Now that we have learned a bit about text processing, we are ready to undertake that challenge.[11]

As I suggested in Chapter 4, the **readLines()** command can usually be used to fetch the raw HTML code that makes up a webpage. Beyond that, webpages can be structured quite differently, so there is no single way to extract the data. All of the tools we have worked through in this chapter can be used to facilitate this process.

To finish off this chapter, let's do an exercise in web scraping. In this case, I'll be using the intriguing ngrams data from the Google books project (Google, 2013). This is an effort to catalog every word and phrase that occurs in the millions of books that Google has scanned. You can explore the project at books.google.com/ngrams. Google has this nicely set up to produce comparative graphs of different phrases. It is limited, however, by not showing you the underlying data, by not allowing more complex searches, and by the fact that the web-optimized graphs are of pretty low resolution. If you run a search and then look at the underlying HTML code (most browsers have a "view source code" option), you can see that the raw data are there.[12] Here's what the source code looks like.

```
1    <html itemscope itemtype="http://schema.org/WebApplication"
2         xmlns="http://www.w3.org/1999/xhtml">
3
4    <head>
5
```

---

11. It is important to remember that there may be some research ethics and copyright issues in scraping websites for data.

12. Google also offers an ngram database download, but that is more than a little overwhelming if you are after just a few things.

```
 6        <meta http-equiv="content-type" content="text/html; charset=utf-8">
 7
 8
 9        <meta itemprop="url"
            content="https://books.google.com/ngrams/graph?content=
            R+package%2CSAS+output&amp;year_start=1970&amp;
            year_end=2008&amp;corpus=15&amp;smoothing=3&amp; "/>
10        <meta itemprop="name" content="Google Ngram Viewer">
11        <meta itemprop="description" content="Google Ngram Viewer,
            Ngrams: &#39;[R package]&#39;, &#39;[SAS output]&#39; between
            1970 and 2008 in English.">
12        <meta itemprop="image"
13              content="http://books.google.com/intl/en/images/
                logos/books_logo.gif">
14
15     <title>Google Ngram Viewer</title>
 .     ...
346 <script type="text/javascript">
347   var data = [{"ngram": "R package", "type": "NGRAM",
      "timeseries": [0.0, 0.0, 7.7456420906803672e-11,
      2.2690077594589297e-10, 2.2690077594589297e-10,
      ...
      1.3777201601783418e-08], "parent": ""},
      {"ngram": "SAS output", "type": "NGRAM",
      "timeseries": [1.7146718767069302e-10, 1.3717375013655442e-10,
      1.1431145844712869e-10, 9.7981250097538868e-11,

      ...

      1.2303092433718632e-08], "parent": ""}];
348   if (data.length > 0) {
349     ngrams.drawD3Chart(data, 1970, 2008, 1.0, "main");
350   }
351 </script>...
```

To run a Google ngram search, we need to start with the search URL constructed by Google. Here I have to interrupt our narrative to share a short and somewhat traumatic personal story that is instructive on two counts. Between the time I originally wrote this chapter and the time I received it back from the copy editor, Google significantly changed the ngram search page coding. The data were changed from being organized by the row (the year) to being organized by the column (the search phrase). And the webpage was changed from a regular http URL to a secure https URL. The first moral of this little story is that the Web is a fickle and unstable place in which to send your R scripts out to play. Be careful! The second moral comes from the fact that, by itself, R cannot access https websites. The hero for this part of the story is Duncan Temple Lang, a statistics professor at the University of California, Davis, and one of those beneficent R gods who in his great mercy has created for us mere mortals a specialized R package to quickly and easily do that job. So the second moral of our story is that the powers of R are greatly enhanced by a wealth of add-on packages. I have mostly avoided the use of R packages in this book to focus on the principles of working with basic R. But in this case, we are happy to have Temple Lang's RCurl package to help us out. Instructions for downloading and installing R packages are provided in Appendix A. Once RCurl has been downloaded, it can be loaded into R with the **library(RCurl)** command.

You can see the Google ngrams URL in your browsers' URL window at the top of the page. Here is the URL for a search comparing two phrases, "R package" and "SAS output," from 1970 to 2008 in English-language books.

```
https://books.google.com/ngrams/graph?content=R+package%2CSAS+output&year_
start=1970&year_end=2008&corpus=15&smoothing=3&direct_url=t1%3B%2CR%20
package%3B%2Cc0%3B.t1%3B%2CSAS%20output%3B%2Cc0
```

We could just cut and paste the URL into our R code, but since the purpose is to do some text processing, I've set it up more generically. We can re-create the Google ngram search URL by inputting the search terms and using **paste()** to build the URL.

```
> p1 = "R package"          # Phrase1: Enter words
> p2 = "SAS output"         # Phrase2: Enter words
> y1 = "1970"               # Set start and end years for search
> y2 = "2008"               # Must be between 1800 and 2008
```

```
> # The search terms occur twice in the URL. In the first instance we
> # need to replace spaces with + signs. I do this in pA and pB.
> # In the second instance we need to replace spaces with "%20",
> # which is the ascii code for a space. I make this replacement
> # in pC and pD.
> pA = gsub(pattern = " ", replacement = "+", x = p1)
> pB = gsub(pattern = " ", replacement = "+", x = p2)
> pC = gsub(pattern = " ", replacement = "%20", x = p1)
> pD = gsub(pattern = " ", replacement = "%20", x = p2)

> # The following search string pastes the dates and modified search terms
> # into the standard, if somewhat ungainly, ngram url.

> searchURL = paste("https://books.google.com/ngrams/graph?content=",
+     pA, "%2C", pB, "&year_start=", y1, "&year_end=", y2,
+     "&corpus=15&smoothing=3&direct_url=t1%3B%2C",
+     pC, "%3B%2Cc0%3B.t1%3B%2C", pD, "%3B%2Cc0", sep = "")
```

Were this a regular http URL, we would now be able to access the
webpage's source code with the **readLines("http://myURL.com")**
function. For the Google ngram https URL, we need the **getURL()** function from the RCurl package, with the **ssl.verifyPeer=** option set to
FALSE.

```
> library(RCurl)                      # Use the RCurl package to enable
>                                     #   reading https: webpages
> ngramdata = getURL(searchURL,       # Get webpage html from search URL
+     ssl.verifyPeer = FALSE)         #   turn off SSL verification
> ngramdata                           # Display webpage source code
[1] "<html itemscope itemtype=\"http://schema.org/WebApplication\"\n ...
```

As shown in the previous source code, there are 345 rows of HTML
stuff, and then line 346 starts the data. The data values are in scientific notation and at a level of precision more appropriate to the search for the Higgs
boson than the ngram frequency, but there it is. To pull these data out, we

are going to need to draw on several of our newly acquired text-processing skills.

You can see that the data are set off with a number of distinctive phrases. We can begin to isolate the actual data by searching for the phrase `'"timeseries": ['` to split up the source code. Since this involves searching for double quotation marks, we'll have to use single quotation marks to demarcate this character string. The bracket is a special character, so we have to protect it with a backslash. And the backslash is itself a special character, so we need a second backslash to set that up. Remember that **strsplit()** creates a list, so we need **unlist()** to turn the results back into a simple vector of character objects. Our unlisted **strsplit()** creates a vector of three elements. The first contains all of the preliminary HTML gobbledygook. The second contains our first data series, and the third contains our second data series.

```
> data1 = strsplit(ngramdata,            # Split the data series that are
+    split = '"timeseries": \\[')         #    demarcated w/timeseries label

> data1 = unlist(data1)                    # Undo strsplit list object
> data1                                     # Show sourcecode data
[1] "<html itemscope itemtype=\"http://schema.org/WebApplication\"\n ...
[2] "0.0, 0.0, 7.7456420906803672e-11, 2.2690077594589297e-10, 2.2690...
[3] "1.7146718767069302e-10, 1.3717375013655442e-10, 1.14311458447128...
```

Dropping the first element leaves us with character strings containing our two data series, but each of those has some extraneous coding at the end. Fortunately, that is demarcated with a closing bracket, so we can just do another **strsplit()** and eliminate that material.

```
> data2 = data1[-1]                         # Drop material before the data
> data3 = strsplit(data2, split = "\\]")   # Isolate material after the data
> data3 = unlist(data3)                      # Turn data back into text vector
> substr(data3, 1, 50)                       # Show 50 chars of each element
[1] "0.0, 0.0, 7.7456420906803672e-11, 2.26900775945892"
[2] ", \"parent\": \"\"}, {\"ngram\": \"SAS output\", \"type\": \""
[3] "1.7146718767069302e-10, 1.3717375013655442e-10, 1."
```

```
[4] ", \"parent\": \"\"}"
[5] ";\n   if (data.length > 0) {\n      ngrams.drawD3Chart("
[6] ";\n         _gaq.push(['_setAccount', 'UA-45098938-1'"
[7] ");\n         _gaq.push(['_trackPageview'"
[8] ");\n\n         (function() {\n      var ga = document.cr"
[9] "; s.parentNode.insertBefore(ga, s);\n         })();\n   "

data4 = data3[c(1, 3)]                    # Keep only elements 1 and 3
> data4                                   # Show data
[1] "0.0, 0.0, 7.7456420906803672e-11, ...
     1.1630148843977395e-08, 1.3777201601783418e-08"
[2] "1.7146718767069302e-10, 1.3717375013655442e-10, ...
     1.1732358817795329e-08, 1.2303092433718632e-08"
```

The data are now isolated, but they are trapped in two big and ugly text strings, which we'll need to parse out. Here, again, **strsplit()** does the job. In this case, we'll leave the result as a list, which will store each data series in its own list slot. We can then set up a new set of variables using those bins (note the double bracket notation to identify the list slots). It is at this point that we'll finally convert from character to numeric values. Thankfully, R is smart enough to handle the conversion, even with scientific notation. While we are at it, we'll multiply the values by 100 to convert from decimal to percentage notation and reduce the number of places after the decimal point a little bit.

```
> data5 = strsplit(data4, split = ",")   # Split up data at commas
> v1 = as.numeric(data5[[1]]) * 100      # Convert to numeric and make %
> v2 = as.numeric(data5[[2]]) * 100      # Convert to numeric and make %
> v1[1:3]                                # Display first 3 obs in v1
[1] 0.000000e + 00 0.000000e + 00 7.745642e-09

> v2[1:3]                                # Display first 3 obs in v2
[1] 1.714672e-08 1.371738e-08 1.143115e-08
```

Next, we need to create a series of years to add to the data. Then we can pull everything together in a data frame and add some more useful labels.

```
> year1 = as.numeric(y1)                # Create series of years

> year2 = as.numeric(y2)

> years = seq(from = year1, to = year2, by = 1)

> ngram = data.frame(years, v1, v2)     # Combine in data frame

> colnames(ngram) = c("Year", p1, p2)   # Add variable labels

> head(ngram)                           # Show the first few rows

   Year     R package     SAS output

1 1970  0.000000e+00  1.714672e-08

2 1971  0.000000e+00  1.371738e-08

3 1972  7.745642e-09  1.143115e-08

4 1973  2.269008e-08  9.798125e-09

5 1974  2.269008e-08  1.611064e-08

6 1975  2.269008e-08  2.546583e-08
```

The full data set is now assembled and ready for whatever we want to do with it. Some of the things we'll want to do with it likely will involve graphics. We haven't really gotten there yet (be patient . . . Chapter 12 is just around the corner), but here is the procedure for a quick plot to reproduce the Google output (see Figure 8.1):

```
plot(ngram$Year, ngram[,3],         # Plot the first ngram series
   type = "l",                      #    using a line plot
   lwd = 2,                         #    with line width = 2
   col = "gray",                    #    and a black line
   xlab = "Year",                   # Set X axis label
   ylab = NA,                       # Set Y axis label
   yaxt = "n",                      # Turn off automatic y axis values
   xaxt = "n")                      # Turn off automatic x axis values

points(ngram$Year, ngram[,2],       # Overlay second ngram series
   type = "l",                      #    using a line plot
   lwd = 2,                         #    with line width = 2
   col = "black")                   #    and a black line
```

```
axis(side = 1,                          # Set the labels for the X axis
   at = seq(min(ngram$Year),            #    from minimum year
     max(ngram$Year), by = 5))          #    to max year by 5

legend("topleft",                       # Add a legend at top left corner
   inset = .025,                        #    inset by .025
   legend = c(p2, p1),                  # Legend labels from phrase 1 & 2
   fill = c("gray", "black"))           # Fill colors to match plot
```

Figure 8.1   Google Ngram Plot

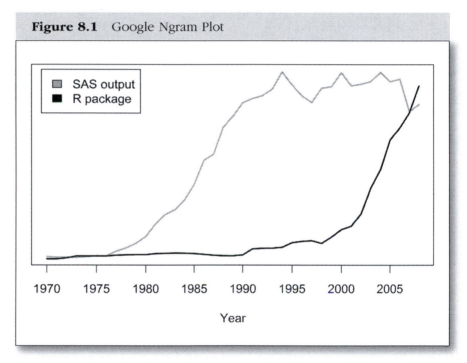

Data source: https://books.google.com/ngrams/graph?content=SAS+output%2C+R+package&year_start=1970&year_end=2008&corpus=15&smoothing=3&share=&direct_url=t1%3B%2CSAS%20output%3B%2Cc0%3B.t1%3B%2CR%20package%3B%2Cc0

Note: This plot shows the frequency of these two phrases as a percentage of all two-word phrases in the millions of English-language books scanned by Google. I've left off the labels for the actual percentages, which are vanishingly small. To be honest, in the grand scheme of things, not that many books talk about SAS or R.

All we've done here, of course, is to reproduce what Google's Ngram viewer already does. But we have done so in a way that now gives us control over the data and the graphing. You can easily see how this would allow us to do some more interesting things, like combining the data from different searches or other time series altogether.

Now that we've tackled the central issues in working with text, it is time to descend to the next circle: date and time values.

CHAPTER 9

WORKING WITH DATE AND TIME DATA

Dates have traditionally proven something of a problem for computer geeks. They are, after all, the clever folk who didn't realize when setting up their database programs in the 1970s that the year 2000 would likely come along and make two-digit date codes not only dysfunctional but also possibly catastrophic.

In this chapter, we are going to look at the general and surprisingly challenging problems of dealing with date and time data. We'll start by looking at the different ways R represents time measurements and facilitates operations on this kind of data. Then, we'll look at the associated issues of working with time series, which are data characterized by repeated measurements over regular time intervals.

The important thing about time is that it imposes both an order and a scale on the data. The order element is pretty easy to see. At least in the universe as we experience it, time moves in one direction, and time points tell you the order in which events occur. The scale element is also critical. Suppose you have the following data:

Dec. 5, 1953	4
May 21, 1968	5
Jun. 12, 1970	6
Apr. 2, 1980	6.2
Jan. 16, 1986	6.5
Feb. 28, 1987	6.7

Figure 9.1   Time Order and Scale

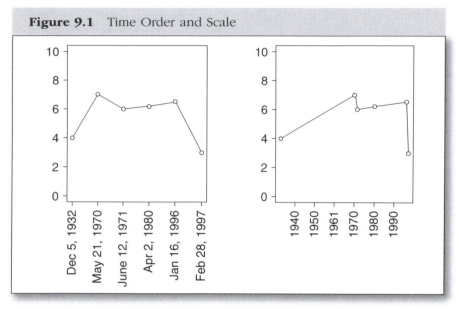

Note: Both of these plots use the same data. The plot on the left treats the data as ordered but ignores the time scale. The plot on the right is appropriately scaled for time.

These six measurements are scaled in time. The order is obvious. But as shown in Figure 9.1, the time scale also matters.

Thanks to our flexible human brains, we can usually just look at the data to understand the time dimension. It's a little harder in the arena of human–computer interaction, because we have many different ways of writing time data: 3/5/94, 9-2-2008, 15 JUN 06. All three of these dates are actually confusing even for us humans. It isn't clear if the first two dates are March 5 and September 2, or May 5 and February 9. The first and third dates don't indicate which century they are from. We can probably guess from the context, but this is something computers are less good at. If we want to add measures for hours, minutes, and seconds, or even fractions of a second, it becomes even more complex. To deal with these complexities, R has set up some special classes to hold time and date information.

DATES IN R

R's classes for holding date and time data facilitate operations on and between dates and times. For example, if you want to find out how many days there are between two dates or how many minutes between two times, you can simply subtract them from each other.

Dates in R, as in all computer programming approaches, are stored as numeric values that count the days from some origin. The problem with this is that while you might have religious convictions that tell you when the calendar should start, the people who have designed these systems seem to worship different gods. In Microsoft Excel for the PC, for example, the "zero day" is January 1, 1900. This strikes me as reasonable, but it makes doing historical analysis of the eighteenth or nineteenth centuries difficult. Try entering a date before 1900 into an Excel cell, and you will see what I mean. The geniuses who designed Excel for Apple computers decided that January 1, 1904, would be a better starting date. I'm not sure what they were smoking, but you can imagine the trouble that caused. Until the most recent version of Excel for Macintosh, which finally shifted to the 1900 date system, when you moved a file with dates from Excel for Windows to Excel for OSX, you would see it change before your eyes. The end of World War II would come in 1949 instead of 1945. The Soviet empire would survive an additional 4 years to 1993.

R, I regret to report, also has a few issues with dates. The default zero date for R is January 1, 1970. You can see this with the following example:

```
> testdate = as.Date("1970-01-01")      # Set up date value for 1/1/1970
> as.numeric(testdate)                   # Show numeric code for 1/1/1970
[1] 0
```

Unlike Excel, which returns an error on the use of negative date numbers, R is smart enough to count backward, so historical data sets are manageable. Alas, if you try to go back past R's numeric date −719529, which corresponds with January 1 in the year 0 of the Christian calendar, the date functions go to pieces. Classicists and archaeologists are still out of luck. (My apologies for having waited this far into the book to bring this up.)[1]

The purpose of this discussion is to warn you that there are a number of potential pitfalls in dealing with dates. I'll try to alert you about the most important of them here, but this is an area where it is particularly important to check over your data and make sure the dates haven't been mangled.

---

1. There is an inelegant work-around here using the **origin** = option, which lets you set your own starting point for the **as.Date()** function. You'll have to shift all of your pre-Jesus years to some post-Jesus period. When more classicists start using R, I'm sure someone will write a package to automate this.

If your dates are in Excel and you save them to a text file, they will be changed from their underlying numeric values to their character values. That is, "1/1/1900" will be recorded as the characters "1/1/1900" instead of as the numeric value 0. The good news about this is that it actually means that if you have a cell with "1/1/1800," it will have the same format in the text file as the more modern dates, where Excel will not have been able to deal with that as a date at all. The bad news is that it will take some extra steps to get R to treat those as dates instead of as simple character strings.

Dates as character strings will be fine if all you need to do is look at them or use them as labels to describe the data. If you need to do any operations on the dates, however, such as sorting the data by date (Chapter 6), aggregating by date (Chapter 10), or doing other date operations (this chapter), then you will need to convert these character strings to one of R's internal date classes. We do this by telling R that a variable is a date or time and by providing clear guidance as to the format of the date/time information.

FORMATTING DATES FOR R

R dates can be held in two different formats, POSIX dates and, well, Date dates. As noted in Chapter 3, these are technically classes rather than storage modes. The important differences between POSIX and Date are that (a) POSIX dates can carry information down to the fraction of a second, whereas Date dates are just days, and (b) POSIX dates can be more easily broken up into their component parts (more on this later).

In either case, R's default format for dates is YYYY-MM-DD. This is eminently logical, running from the largest to the smallest units, but as often with R, is at odds with how it is usually done in the real world.[2] Assuming that the dates in your data file were not formatted this way, you will need to tell R the explicit format of the dates. R has a number of specific codes for managing date and time formats. You can get the full list by using **help(strptime)**. The most commonly used ones are shown in Table 9.1.

If, for example, your dates are in the classic form "5/25/2010 3:25pm" and have been read in as character data, then you can convert them to regular dates with the **as.Date()** command and to POSIX dates with the **strptime()** command.

---

2. Actually, this just comes from a special place in the real world. It is the format dictated by the International Standards Organization (ISO) in their ISO8601 rules.

Table 9.1 `strptime` Formatting

%Y	Four-digit years, e.g., 1975, 2005, 1356
%y	Two-digit years, e.g., 75, 05, 56 (you can see the problem with this compared with the four-digit list)
%m	Numeric month, e.g., 01, 09, 12
%b	Abbreviated alphabetic month, e.g., Jan, Sep, Nov
%B	Full alphabetic month, e.g., January, September, November
%d	Day as a two-digit number, e.g., 07, 19, 28
%H	Hour as a two-digit decimal number on the 24-hour clock, e.g., 02, 08, 22
%I	Hour as a two-digit decimal number on the 12-hour clock, e.g., 02, 08, 10
%p	a.m./p.m. indicator (used with %I)
%M	Minute as a two-digit number, e.g., 05, 28, 53
%S	Second as a two-digit number, e.g., 22, 38, 57

```
> aDate = "5/25/2010 3:25pm"          # Set character string for date
> dFormat = "%m/%d/%Y %I:%M%p"        # Set up the format
> Date1 = as.Date(aDate, dFormat)     # Convert to R Date format date
> Date2 = strptime(aDate, dFormat)    # Convert to R POSIX format date
> Date1                               # Print the Date format date
[1] "2010-05-25"

> Date2                               # Print the POSIX format date
[1] "2010-05-25 15:25:00"
```

This example shows how the Date format (`as.Date()`) cut off the time information. Note the use of the uppercase, `%Y`, to indicate four-digit years. If your data were in the form "5/25/10," you would use lowercase,

%y. Note also the way that you add in any spacer or connector information (e.g., slashes or dashes) in the format statement.

Here are several examples of converting different date formats:

```
> d1 = c("January 1, 2000", "February 5, 2002", "May 12, 2003")
> date1a = as.Date(d1, "%B %d, %Y")
> date1b = strptime(d1, "%B %d, %Y")

> d2 = c("1/1/00", "2/5/02", "5/12/03")
> date2a = as.Date(d2, "%m/%d/%y")
> date2b = strptime(d2, "%m/%d/%y")

> d3 = c("01/01/2000", "05/02/2002", "12/05/2003")
> date3a = as.Date(d3, "%d/%m/%Y")
> date3b = strptime(d3, "%d/%m/%Y")

> d4 = c("1 Jan 2000", "5 Feb 2002", "12 May 2003")
> date4a = as.Date(d4, "%d %b %Y")
> date4b = strptime(d4, "%d %b %Y")

> d5 = c("1JANUARY00", "5FEBRUARY02", "12MAY03")
> date5a = as.Date(d5, "%d%B%y")
> date5b = strptime(d5, "%d%B%y")
> date5b
[1] "2000-01-01" "2002-02-05" "2003-05-12"
```

All of these approaches produce the same outcome as the one on the last line of the example. In every case, regardless of how the dates are formatted as characters, R is still storing them underneath as counts of days away from the origin date of January 1, 1970.

Another idiosyncrasy of date objects comes about if you have truncated date indicators—for example, just the year, or the year and the month. R will work with just the year but takes the missing components from the current date. R doesn't seem willing to recognize year and month formats alone.

```
> myDate = "1975"              # A date with just the year
> as.Date(myDate, "%Y")        # Convert to date class
[1] "1975-05-02"
```

```
> myDate = "Jan75"                    # A date with just year & month

> as.Date(myDate, "%b%y")            # Convert to date class
[1] NA
```

We see here that Date objects can deal with just the year but not with year and month alone. Be aware, though, that R adds in the current month and day to the provided year. I worked this example on May 2, so those values were added by R.

We can work around this problem by pasting the missing components onto our data.

```
> myDate = "1975"                         # A date with just the year
> as.Date(                                # Convert to date class
+    paste("01 01", myDate), "%d %m %Y") #  adding specific day/month data
[1] "1975-01-01"

> myDate = "Jan75"                        # A date with year and month
> as.Date(                                # Convert to date class
+    paste("01", myDate), "%d %b%y")      # adding specific day data
[1] "1975-01-01"
```

As discussed, Date class objects, created with the **as.Date()** function, are a straightforward count of the number of days before or after January 1, 1970. If you need times of day or need to work with individual date components (e.g., years or months), you'll probably find it easier to switch to POSIX dates.[3] That, however, involves a few additional costs.

WORKING WITH POSIX DATES

POSIX dates are created with the **strptime()** function. Before going any further, I should warn you that when I mentioned that I was trying to write

---

3. There are **weekdays()** and **months()** functions that will extract these elements from either Date or POSIX class objects, but you have much more control over POSIX dates.

about the POSIX date/time class to a friend who earns his living programming supercomputers for a very prominent high-energy physics laboratory, he mumbled something about Satan. That is a bit ironic since, if anyone, this is really God's fault. The problem is not so much with POSIX formats per se as with the irreducible complexities of time in the real world. The good news is that if you can stay away from the challenges of leap seconds and of time zone translation, you'll probably be okay here.

There are two kinds of date/time data that use the name POSIX: POSIXct and POSIXlt.[4] POSIXct is the calendar time, which, as I'm sure you have guessed, is simply the number of seconds since the beginning of 1970. POSIXlt gets its name from the idea of local time but is really just the same information as POSIX calendar time broken down into a more helpful format. POSIXlt dates are translated into a list of vectors that contain all the elements of the time, such as the year, month, day of the week, hour, minute, and so on. You can see all of these in the Help menu for DateTimeClasses (**help(DateTimeClasses)**). There is an additional virtual class, POSIXt, which allows you to mix the two types.

The trade-off for POSIXlt data is that because it is packaged as a list with all the different component vectors, it sometimes doesn't play well with other data. Trying to combine a POSIXlt date with a data frame of other date-organized data, for example, will bring up an error because R doesn't know which parts of the POSIXlt list to use. In this case, you can convert between POSIXlt and POSIXct using **as.POSIXlt()** or **as.POSIXct()**, respectively, to get the advantages of whichever format you need for a particular operation.

The advantage of the POSIX format is that you can work with the individual component parts of the date. If you run the **attributes(myDate)** function on a POSIX date, you'll get the list of component parts. Here, you have to be careful as well. As shown in Table 9.2, POSIX doesn't always count dates in the same way as you do. While the days of the month are counted in the normal 1 to 31 range, the month is counted from 0 to 11. January is 0, and December is 11. So, too, years are counted as an offset from 1900. The year 2010 is 110, 1994 is 94, and 1850 is −50. The days of the week run from 0 (Sunday) to 6 (Saturday).

---

4. The name POSIX comes from the IEEE (Institute of Electrical and Electronics Engineers) and is their set of standards for a portable operating system interface. These standards include the use of January 1, 1970, as the zero moment in time ("the Unix epoch") and then measure all other times as the number of seconds from that moment. Don't ask about how this deals with the inconvenience of leap seconds. Just be careful if your mission-critical data need to distinguish between the last second of 1998 and the first second of 1999.

Table 9.2   POSIXlt Vectors

Sec	Second (0–61)
Min	Minute (0–59)
Hour	Hour (0–23)
Mday	Day of month (1–31)
Mon	Month (0–11)
Year	Year (offset from 1970)
Wday	Day of week (0–6, Sunday = 0, Saturday = 6)
Yday	Day of year (0–365)
Isdst	Daylight Saving Time (0/1)

Working with these elements gives us a lot of control over the date/time data. In the following example, we first look at the date attributes, then show some of the individual components. Finally, we show how this approach allows us to make conversions, here changing just the day of the month to the first of the month.

```
> oldDate = "5/25/2010"              # Set up character string for date
> newDate2 =                         # Convert to POSIX format date
+   strptime(oldDate, "%m/%d/%Y")
> attributes(newDate2)               # Show available date components
$names
[1] "sec"  "min"  "hour"  "mday"  "mon"  "year"  "wday"  "yday"  "isdst"
$class
[1] "POSIXt"  "POSIXlt"

> newDate2$year                      # Show the year
[1] 110

> newDate2$mon                       # Show the month
[1] 4
```

```
> newDate2$wday                          # Show the day of the week
[1] 2

> newDate3 = newDate2                    # Make a copy of the date
> newDate3                               # Print to show date
[1] "2010-05-25"

> newDate3$mday = 1                      # Set day of the month to 1
> newDate3                               # Print to show date
[1] "2010-05-01"
```

You can include a time zone in POSIXlt specifications (`tz = "GMT"`). There is a standard set of time zone identifiers that include the appropriate offsets and information about daylight savings time rules. Be aware, however, that these can be a bit twitchy, since they are constantly being updated and depend on the implementation in your particular computer/operating system.[5]

```
> as.POSIXlt(Sys.time())                 # The time from my PC
[1] "2013-04-30 09:58:18 Eastern Daylight Time"

> as.POSIXlt(Sys.time(), tz = "GMT")     # Greenwich Mean Time
[1] "2013-04-30 13:58:18 GMT"
```

SPECIAL DATE OPERATIONS

You can subtract dates to get the amount of time between them, but reasonably enough, you can't add, multiply, or divide them. **difftime()** is another way of subtracting dates. The advantage of the **difftime()** function is that you can specify the units. Normal subtraction is just going to give you the number of days. With **difftime()**, you can specify the

---

5. Time zones are a notoriously difficult programming problem. The Olson Time Zone Library is the standard database for time zones (http://www.twinsun.com/tz/tz-link.htm). Good luck!

difference in terms of weeks, days, hours, minutes, or seconds (but not years or months, oddly enough).[6]

```
> date1 = as.Date("2010-05-25")        # Set up a date
> date2 = as.Date("1957-10-23")        # Set up another date
> date1 - date2                        # Get the days between dates
Time difference of 19207 days

> difftime(date1, date2,               # Get days using difftime()
+   units = "days")
Time difference of 19207 days

> difftime(date1, date2,               # Get weeks using difftime()
+   units = "weeks")
Time difference of 2743.857 weeks
```

There are a few additional operations you can perform on both POSIX and Date time variables. **seq.POSIXt()** or **seq.Date()** creates a regular sequence of date or time values. You give it a starting time, an ending time, and the incrementing unit, and it gives you a vector of the appropriate values. This can be very useful for generating plot scales for time series, as we'll see in Chapter 14. The unit for the increment can be either an integer for the number of days or a character string indicating the unit: "year", "month", "6 months", and so on. The values created by **seq.POSIXt()** do not contain the component vectors, but they can be created with the **as.POSIXlt()** function.

```
> myDates = seq.Date(                  # Set up a sequence of dates
+   as.Date("1/5/1924", "%m/%d/%Y"),   # Starting date
+   as.Date("3/7/1924", "%m/%d/%Y"),   # Ending date
+   by = "22 days")                    # Sequence by value
```

------

6. Years are relatively easy: Simply divide the days by 365 (except for leap years, alas). Months are a little trickier, of course, since their lengths differ. Note also that **difftime()** creates its own difftime class that associates the time unit (e.g., weeks) with the value. You'll need to get out of that if you want to switch to another time unit. Use **as.double()**, for example, to strip the special class.

```
> myDates                                # Show myDates
[1] "1924-01-05" "1924-01-27" "1924-02-18"
```

Date data can be consolidated with either the **trunc.POSIXt()**/ **trunc.Date()** or the **round.POSIXt()/round.Date()** functions. Both of these require two arguments: (1) the POSIX/Date variable and (2) the unit for rounding. The unit for rounding has to be "secs," "mins," "hours," "days," "months," or "years." Round will go up to the next unit, while truncate simply lops off the smaller units. Here are some examples to give you a feel for it.

```
> myT = "2009-12-23 10:38:15"            # Setup a date/time value
> myT2 = strptime(myT,                   # Convert to POSIX value
+    format = "%Y-%m-%d %H:%M:%S")        #    using this format
> c(myT2, round.POSIXt(myT2, "mins"))    # Round to nearest minute
> c(myT2, round.POSIXt(myT2, "hours"))   # Round to nearest hour
[1] "2009-12-23 10:38:15 EST" "2009-12-23 11:00:00 EST"

> c(myT2, round.POSIXt(myT2, "months"))  # Round to nearest month
[1] "2009-12-23 10:38:15 EST" "2010-01-01 00:00:00 EST"

> c(myT2, round.POSIXt(myT2, "years"))   # Round to nearest year
[1] "2009-12-23 10:38:15 EST" "2010-01-01 00:00:00 EST"

> c(myT2, trunc.POSIXt(myT2, "mins"))    # Truncate to minute
[1] "2009-12-23 10:38:15 EST" "2009-12-23 10:38:00 EST"

> c(myT2, trunc.POSIXt(myT2, "days"))    # Truncate to day
[1] "2009-12-23 10:38:15 EST" "2009-12-23 00:00:00 EST"

> c(myT2, trunc.POSIXt(myT2, "years"))   # Truncate to year
[1] "2009-12-23 10:38:15 EST" "2009-01-01 00:00:00 EST"
```

cut.POSIXt() or **cut.Date()** convert time/date data into factors. This is another way to put time variables into bins. If, for example, you have data in seconds that you want to group into minutes, you would use

breaks="min". For normal time divisions with POSIX formats, it will be quicker to do this with the truncation or rounding functions. The advantage of the cut method is both that it works with the R Date class and that you can set other nonstandard lengths of time for the bins. See **help(cut. POSIXt)** for the other kinds of intervals you can use. Note that this converts the data into a factor with one level for each bin. If you want to use it as time data, you'll have to convert it back to a POSIX variable.

FORMATTING DATES FOR OUTPUT

The same formatting schema used for **strptime()** and **as.Date()** can be used for printing and outputting time or date data. Here, the key is the **format()** function. Wrap your date data in a format function, and include the formatting option you want to use.

```
> format(newDate2, format = "%d %b %Y")  # Output a formatted date
[1] "25 May 2010"

> cat("The date is: ",                    # Include formatted date in output
+ format(newDate2, format = "%d %b %Y")   # Output a formatted date
The date is: 25 May 2010

> cat("The date is: ",                    # Insert date w/format in output
+    format(newDate2,                      # Format statement
+    format = "%d %b %Y"))                 # The format to use
The date is:  25 May 2010

> cat(format(newDate2,                     # Another example
+    format = "%b %d, %Y"),                # The format to use
+    "is a",                               # A snippet of text
+    weekdays(newDate2))                   # The day of the week in text
May 25, 2010 is a Tuesday
```

If you are interested in the name of the day of the week, as opposed to its numeric value in the POSIX schema, you can use the **weekdays()** function.

```
> newDate2$wday                        # Show day of week for newDate2
[1] 2

> weekdays(newDate2)                    # Show name of day of week
[1] "Tuesday"

> newDate2$mon                          # Show month for newDate2
[1] 4

> months(newDate2)                      # Show name of month
[1] "May"
```

Now that we have a handle on working with dates, we can turn to a few of the interesting, but sometimes vexing, issues that are associated with managing and analyzing time-series data. In so doing, however, I should warn you that we have to switch gears, because oddly enough, R's basic class for working with time series doesn't play well with either Date or POSIX class elements.

TIME-SERIES DATA

Time series are data that take repeated measurements on a set of variables at different points of time. They are important in a number of fields but present their own special problems for data management and analysis.[7]

R has a special data class for time-series data. All of that stuff we just learned about the complexities of times and dates doesn't really matter here because for the **ts** object class, R can only see a uniform set of ordered observations. The central logic is simply to connect a data series to an identified starting point, a finishing point, and the nature of the increments between those two points.

---

7. The R home page maintains a helpful task summary of packages and other tools for time-series analysis at http://cran.r-project.org/web/views/TimeSeries.html.

The first issue for working with time-series data in R is to let R know that your data set is a time series. This is accomplished with the **ts()** function.

```
> year = 1991:1996              # Create a series of year values
> x1 = c("CA", "VA", "NV",      # Create some char values for x1
+    "WA", "NM", "DC")
> x2 = c(10, 20, 30, 40, 50, 60)  # Create some num values for x2
> myTS = ts(cbind(year, x1, x2))  # Package as a time series
```

Many time-series functions automatically put data into this format, but it is probably better to do it explicitly yourself to avoid errors if you run across a function that does not (e.g., the **lag()** function). You can test to confirm that a data set has been set as a time series with the **is.ts()** function. The class values R is working with can be retrieved with **class()**.

```
> is.ts(myTS)                   # Confirm ts object class
[1] TRUE

> class(myTS)                   # Show class identifiers
[1] "mts"      "ts"       "matrix"
```

The time-series data frame is identified with the tsp vector, which has three values: (1) the starting point, (2) the ending point, and (3) the number of observations per year (i.e., 1 = annual data, 4 = quarterly data, 12 = monthly data, and 52 = weekly data). You can retrieve these values for your time series with the **tsp()** command. They are also displayed at the beginning if you print out the time-series data.

```
> tsp(myTS)                     # Show start obs, end obs, increment
[1] 1 6 1
```

```
> myTS                              # Show ts structure & values
Time Series:
Start = 1
End = 6
Frequency = 1
   year x1 x2
1 1991 CA 10
2 1992 VA 20
3 1993 NV 30
4 1994 WA 40
5 1995 NM 50
6 1996 DC 60

> attributes(myTS)                  # Show ts attributes
$dim
[1] 6 3

$dimnames
$dimnames[[1]]
NULL

$dimnames[[2]]
[1] "year" "x1"    "x2"

$tsp
[1] 1 6 1

$class
[1] "mts" "ts"
```

Because R expects the **ts** class data to hold a uniform sequence of observations, you need to take extra care about missing data. If you have missing data, you will need to create placeholders for the missing observations. The **seq()** function can be useful for just generating numeric years (i.e., **year = seq(1950:2000)**). To generate a series of formatted dates, you can use the **seq.Date()** or **seq.POSIXt()** function. But, again, those are not going to work directly in your time-series data frame.

○ Creating Moving Averages in Time-Series Data

Moving averages are created with the not very intuitive **filter()** command. It is capable of a few more complicated things, but for our purposes, it needs only three arguments: First comes the variable being averaged. That's pretty straightforward. The second argument is the filter, which is a vector of weights for the elements being averaged. If you want a four-period moving average with equal weights, it would be **c(.25, .25, .25, .25)**. You can shorten this with other R functions, for example, **rep(.25, 4)**, or by calling in another named vector. An easy way to apply equal weights is to set it up as **rep(1/n, n)**, where n is the number of periods over which you want to average. If you want to apply unequal weights, that can be done as well. The third element is the **sides=** value, which tells it either to just take past values (**sides = 1**) or to average both backward and forward (**sides = 2**). Remember that the moving-average process is going to create NA values at the beginning of the series. The filter process creates a list, so in the following example, I also demonstrate the use of **as.double()** to force it to be a simple double-precision numeric variable. The results are shown in Figure 9.2.

```
> year = 1990:1996              # Create a series of years
> x1 = c(10, 15, 14, 7, 14, 10, 18)   # Create some observation values
> x1ma = filter(x1,             # Create a 4 period moving average
+     filter = c(.25, .25, .25, .25),   # Equal weights for the 4 periods
+     sides = 1)                # Backwards looking moving avg.
> x1ma                          # Display list output
Time Series:
Start = 1
End = 7
Frequency = 1
[1]     NA     NA     NA 11.50 12.50 11.25 12.25

> as.double(x1ma)               # Display as forced to numeric
[1]     NA     NA     NA 11.50 12.50 11.25 12.25
```

Figure 9.2 Moving Averages[8]

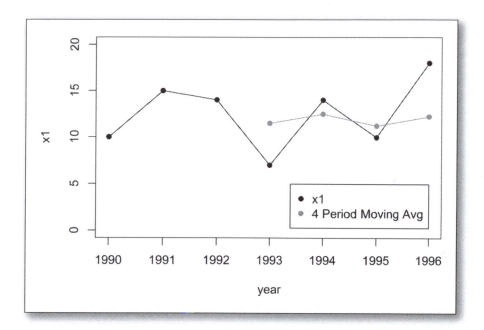

LAGGED VARIABLES IN TIME-SERIES DATA

In the analysis of time series, we are often interested in how things change over time and how things that happen at time $t - 1$ might affect things at time t. Using lagged variables creates missing values at the beginning of a time series. One of the most important things about the time-series data type is that it deals automatically with the missing-data problems at the beginning of data sets that have lag structures. Given that R doesn't always behave well with missing data, this can be a helpful feature (see Chapter 11).

If the data are set up as a time series using the **ts()** function, we can create lagged variables with the **lag()** function. The argument for the **lag()** function is set relative to the current period. If you want a previous period, you use a negative number. **lag(x.ts, -1)** is a traditional,

8. The code for this plot uses several elements that 08_GAUBATZ_A1A0088.pdf we won't get to until Chapters 14 and 15, but you can see it in the online code at http://www.sagepub.com/gaubatz.

one-period lag, while `lag(x.ts, 1)` is a future value, that is, the value for `x.ts` in the following period.

```
> year = 1990:1995                   # Create a variable with years
> x = c(100, 110, 120, 130, 140, 150) # Create an x value
> d = cbind(year, x)                 # Join in data frame
> d.ts = ts(d)                       # Set as time series
> x.lead1 = lag(x, 1)                # Set up 1 period leading value
> x.lead2 = lag(x, 2)                # Set up 2 period leading value
> x.lag1 = lag(x, -1)                # Set up 1 period lagging value
> x.lag2 = lag(x, -2)                # Set up 2 period lagging value
> x.ts = cbind(d.ts, x.lead1, x.lead2, # Join all together
+    x.lag1, x.lag2)
> x.ts                               # Display all
Time Series:
Start = -1
End = 8
Frequency = 1
     d.ts.year d.ts.x  x.lead1  x.lead2  x.lag1  x.lag2
-1         NA     NA       NA      100      NA      NA
0          NA     NA      100      110      NA      NA
1        1990    100      110      120      NA      NA
2        1991    110      120      130     100      NA
3        1992    120      130      140     110     100
4        1993    130      140      150     120     110
5        1994    140      150       NA     130     120
6        1995    150       NA       NA     140     130
7          NA     NA       NA       NA     150     140
8          NA     NA       NA       NA      NA     150
```

It is critical to be aware that by itself, the `lag()` function does not actually create new values. Instead, it creates a list that includes the original values and tells R how to change the tsp vector to shift the existing values forward or backward. If you try to operate on this thinking that it looks like a vector of lagged values, you will be disappointed.

DIFFERENCING VARIABLES IN TIME-SERIES DATA

Differencing is an important tool for removing the trend from time-series data. A differenced variable simply looks at the change in the variable value instead of its absolute value.

```
x.diff = diff(x)
```

By default, this is the first difference and uses one lag. If you need a different lag or differencing structure, you can specify those options. If, for example, you are trying to control trend in seasonal data—the sale of skis or the diet of wild animals—you might want to look at the change from one winter to the next (a lag of four seasons) rather than from autumn to winter (the default lag of one season).

```
x.diff = diff(x, lag = 4, difference = 1)
```

Phenomena with trends of trends—for example, a variable that is increasing at an increasing rate—may require second- or even third-order differencing. Both are easily accomplished.

```
x.diff2 = diff(x, lag = 1, difference = 2)
x.diff3 = diff(x, lag = 1, difference = 3)
```

If you prefer to create the differenced variables explicitly, you can take the same approach as was discussed for lagged variables. Just add one more step: A one-period differenced version of x, for example, is **xdiff = x - xlag**.

Beyond moving averages, lagging, and differencing, there are time-series functions that do forecasting, visualizations, all manner of ARIMA (autoregressive integrated moving average) modeling, and the like. These are mostly accomplished with an ever-expanding number of packages focused on time-series work, some of the more prominent of which we'll briefly review in Appendix C.

○ THE LIMITATIONS OF TIME-SERIES DATA

As mentioned earlier, the surprising reality is that the time-series data format stumbles over date/time data. The **ts** class is set up for regularly spaced time series, with no skips or uneven gaps. It thinks in terms of the **tsp()** values: starting point, ending point, and increment size. It is not really interested in days or months or leap seconds.

In the case of Date dates, you can see in the example below that **ts** just reports the raw number of days, rather than making the translation to years (the year 2 variable). The POSIX date (year 3) is even more problematic. It is seen as a list with all of the POSIX components and cannot be interpreted at all. This screws everything up, and R has to start recycling the original values in the data set to make everything match up. The following example shows both of these problems:

```
> x1 = c(100, 110, 120, 130, 140)        # Create some values for x1
> x2 = c("CA", "VA", "NV", "WA", "NM")   # Create some values for x2
> year = 1990:1996                       # Create a series of year values
> year = year[-3]                        # Drop 1992 as a skipped year
> year                                   # Show year variable
[1] 1990 1991 1993 1994 1995 1996

> year2 = as.Date(                       # Create year2 as Date class obj
+    as.character(year),                 #    Convert numeric to character
+    format = "%Y")                      #    Format = 4-digit year

> year2                                  # Show year2 Date variable
[1] "1990-03-25" "1991-03-25" "1993-03-25" "1994-03-25" "1995-03-25" "1996-03-25"

> year3 = strptime(                      # Create year3 as POSIXlt obj
+    paste("01 01", as.character(year)), #    Convert to char & fill mo/day
+    format = "%m %d %Y")                #    Format of date string

> year3                                  # Show year3 POSIX variable
[1] "1990-01-01" "1991-01-01" "1993-01-01" "1994-01-01" "1995-01-01" "1996-01-01"
```

```
> d = cbind(year, year2, year3, x1, x2)  # Join them together
Warning message:
In cbind(year, year2, year3, x1, x2) :
  number of rows of result is not a multiple of vector length (arg 1)
> d.ts = ts(d)                            # Set it up as a time series
> d.ts                                    # Print out
Time Series:
Start = 1
End = 9
Frequency = 1
  year year2     year3     x1   x2
1 1990  7388  Numeric,6  100  "CA"
2 1991  7753  Integer,6  110  "VA"
3 1993  8484  Integer,6  120  "NV"
4 1994  8849  Integer,6  130  "WA"
5 1995  9214  Integer,6  140  "NM"
6 1996  9580  Integer,6  100  "CA"
7 1990  7388  Integer,6  110  "VA"
8 1991  7753  Integer,6  120  "NV"
9 1993  8484  Integer,6  130  "WA"

> attributes(year3)                       # Show POSIXlt attributes
$names
[1] "sec"   "min"   "hour"  "mday"  "mon"  "year"  "wday"  "yday"  "isdst"

$class
[1] "POSIXlt" "POSIXt"
```

The problems in this example are, first, that year2 is reported as the number of days since January 1, 1970, rather than as years, and, second, that the POSIXlt date is a list with nine elements. This makes R try to expand the other variables to have nine elements as well. Not at all what we want.

The bottom line is that you can use the POSIX and Date classes to format and manage the dates in your time series, but you cannot actually include them in the time-series data frame.

Because a time-series data set is a list that is only connected to the set of explicit time-series operations, most operations on the data will have problems without a lot of careful work indexing (with brackets, the $ construction does not work) and converting to the appropriate numeric object type.

Alternatively, if you don't need the specialized time-series functions, you can just do the lagging and differencing by hand. This really isn't that hard. If x = c(x1, x2, x3, x4, x5), then a one-period lagged version of x is xlag = c(NA, x[-length(x)]).

If you need to keep track of the index values of your observations, you can use the index() function. To add explicit observation numbers to your data set, for example, you could use the following.

```
myDataframe$n = index(myDataframe)
```

With due care, R can be a powerful tool for time- and date-specified data. The important things are to keep track of what is going on with the initial assignment of dates from the zero value, to pay attention to formatting, and to watch out for the pernicious effects of missing values. It is to that last problem that we'll turn in Chapter 11, but first up, some consideration of the critically important procedures for data merging and aggregation.

CHAPTER 10

DATA MERGING AND AGGREGATION

For beginners, data merging and data aggregation are two of the most important and yet poorly understood processes of data management. Data merging is required when we want to put together data from different data sets. Data aggregation is the process we use when we want to build a data set from summarized values of other variables.

Consider, for example, the classic challenge of studying educational outcomes. We might have data on individual school performance that we want to combine with neighborhood demographics. If these data are in different places, they will have to be appropriately merged to be amenable to analysis. Alternatively, or in addition, we might have data from several different years that we want to aggregate or summarize to include in the analysis. Or we might want to make the unit of analysis the school when the available data are by classroom or even by student.

Let's start with the relatively simple situation of appending variables or observations from a second data set that is already set up in the same format and order as an existing data set (you should be so lucky!). Then we'll move through some progressively more difficult forms of data merging and aggregation.

DATA SET CONCATENATION

Concatenation is the fancy computer programmer's term for putting things together. The **paste()** function, for example, is a way of concatenating text objects. We have also seen concatenation with the **c()** function, which concatenates individual objects into a vector, and in the **cbind()** and **rbind()** functions, which add together columns or rows.

Adding New Variables: Column Concatenation

Concatenating in the column dimension—adding new columns to the data set—is how we add new variables. If we had one data set with the relevant performance metrics for each school in our hypothetical school district and we wanted to add a variable for some neighborhood demographic, and that neighborhood information was already collected by the school and was *in exactly the same order* as the complete school performance data set, we could concatenate the column of demographic data onto an existing data frame of school performance metrics (see Figure 10.1).

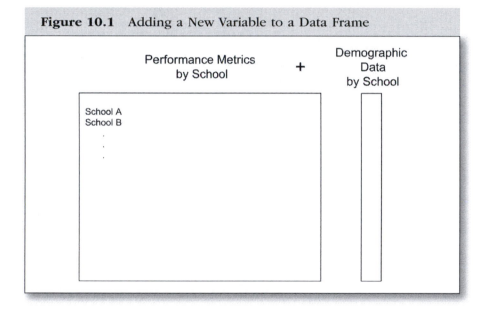

Figure 10.1   Adding a New Variable to a Data Frame

Performance Metrics by School   +   Demographic Data by School

School A
School B

There are two ways to add column data. The column concatenation function is **cbind()**.[1] It adds new columns to a matrix or data frame.

---

1. Those used to thinking in linear algebra terms, should note that R interprets the data as a row or column vector as appropriate to the **rbind()** or **cbind()** function. You can't expect linear algebra operations to work in their normal way unless you use the explicit matrix algebra operators: the normal operator surrounded by percent signs, for example, **%*%** for matrix multiplication.

Again, it is critical that the new column match up perfectly with the original data: It must have the same number of observations, and they must be sorted in the same order. Be careful, as well, that if you are using **cbind()** by itself to join columns or using **cbind()** to add columns to a matrix, it will force all objects to the same data type. If even one of your variables is a character object, everything in the matrix will become character data. If, however, you are using **cbind()** to add a column to an existing data frame, R will condescend to allow the objects to retain their original type.

```
> School = c("A", "B", "C", "D")        # Some data
> Test = c(68, 74, 82, 61)
> Change = c(7, -1, 5, -4)
> Size = c(340, 410, 275, 500)
> myData =                              # Create dataset in data frame
+   data.frame(School, Test, Change)
> myData2 = cbind(myData, Size)         # Add a column with cbind()
> typeof(myData2$Test)                  # Show myData2$Test object type
[1] "double"
> myData2                               # Show result
  School Test Change Size
1      A   68      7  340
2      B   74     -1  410
3      C   82      5  275
4      D   61     -4  500
```

You can also use the **data.frame()** command to do column concatenation directly. This also works without changing the object types. Again, with either approach, it is critical that the objects you are joining together have the same number of observations (rows) and that the observations exactly line up.

```
myData =                               # Create dataset in data frame
  data.frame(School, Test, Change)
myData2 = data.frame(myData, Size)     # Add a column with data.frame()
```

Adding New Observations: Row Concatenation

Concatenating in the row dimension—adding new rows to the data set—is how we add observations. If your object types are mixed across the different variables within one observation, then it is important that all the data that you are concatenating is in data frames rather than just vectors or matrices. As we have seen before, vector and matrix objects will force everything to the same object type. Data frames allow mixed object types and will have no problem joining together and keeping the object types straight.

Let's look at the basic concatenation logic first. If we had data for one set of schools and we wanted to add additional observations for another set of schools, we would concatenate the new rows onto the bottom of the original data. In this case, it is critical that the columns match up. That is, both data sets must have the same variables. Moreover, the variables have to have the same names. You can't just know that they are in the same columns. For example, if one data frame has the variable *year* and the other has the variable *Year*, you have to rename one of them. The payoff for matching variable names is that unlike **cbind()**, **rbind()** can then work with sets of observations that are not lined up the same way (see Figure 10.2). R will make sure that the matching name vectors are appropriately connected.

Here is the process in action. You can see that even though the appended data frame has its variables in a different order, R cleverly straightens that out in the merger:

```
> School = c("F", "G")                    # Create some more data
> Test = c(74, 83)
> Size = c(402, 386)
> Change = c(3, 11)
> NewObs = data.frame(School, Test, Size, Change)
> myData3 = rbind(myData2, NewObs)        # rbind new obs to data frame
> myData3                                 # Show data
  School Test Change Size
1      A   68      7  340
2      B   74     -1  410
3      C   82      5  275
4      D   61     -4  500
```

```
5       F    74     3   402
6       G    83    11   386
> str(myData3)                         # Show structure of new data frame
'data.fram': 6 obs. of  4 variables:
 $ School: chr  "A" "B" "C" "D" ...
 $ Test  : num  68 74 82 61 74 83
 $ Change: num  7 -1 5 -4 3 11
 $ Size  : num  340 410 275 500 402 386
```

Figure 10.2 Adding Observations With `rbind()`

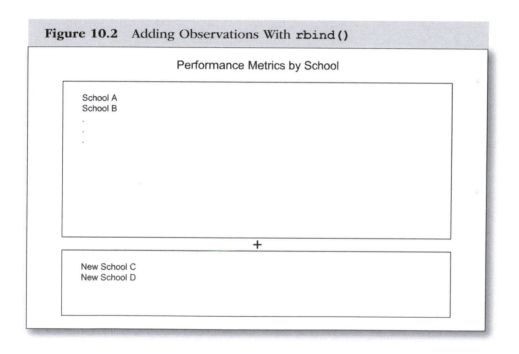

In the real world, data rarely come presorted and with all the right names. Let's look now at a more sophisticated and flexible process for adding columns (variables).

MATCH MERGING

The more interesting and more common merging problems come from having data sets that are similar but not exactly the same. There are two broad classes of merging operations for such data sets. The first case, match merging, is used when the two data sets have different variables that mostly match up on at least one shared variable. For example, returning to the schools example, we might have one data set with the schools data and another with demographic data, where both are organized by school but where the data do not line up in the perfect manner required for the **cbind()** approach (see Figure 10.3). The critical thing for this merging process is that there be a variable that is commonly specified and measured in both data sets (in this case, the school identifier).

Figure 10.3   Match Merging Data

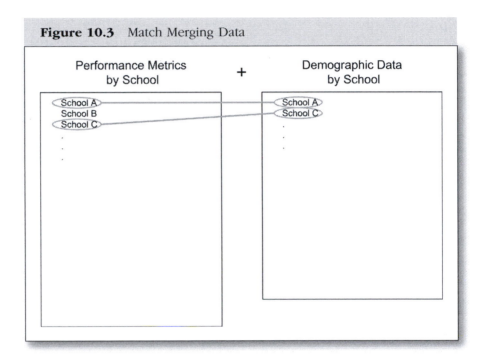

Not surprisingly, I suppose, the **merge()** command is the one used for this operation. Setting this command up with the appropriate options is critical to successful merging. You have to tell R which variables are common to both data sets. Here is the basic syntax:

```
merge(dataframe1, dataframe2, by.x = "variablename", by.y = "variablename")
```

The **by.x=** and **by.y=** options specify the names of the matching variables in the two data sets. "x" indicates the first data set and "y" the second. The matching variables don't have to have the same names; for example, it could be "School" in data frame 1 and "sch.num" in data frame 2. If there is just one matching variable and it has the same name in both of the data sets, this is pretty easy. In fact, the **merge()** command can be entered without the **by=** option, and R will look for the common variable name.

The **by.x=** and **by.y=** options can also specify more than one variable to match on from each data set. In that case, R will base the merge on the cases where both variables match. So, for example, you might match on both school name and class grade. In either case, the value or the combination of values used for matching has to occur just once in each data set. Otherwise, of course, R won't know which ones to use for the match.

The other critical options in match merging are the **all** settings. **all.x = TRUE** tells R to include every observation from the first data set, even if there are no matching values in the second data set. **all.y = TRUE** tells R to include every observation from the second data set,

Table 10.1   Match-Merging Data

School	Test	Change	Size
A	68	7	340
B	74	−1	410
C	82	5	275
D	61	−4	500

S	Inc	nBars
A	32	3
F	46	5
D	27	2
E	52	7
C	49	4

even if there are no matching values in the first data set. The default value for both of these is **FALSE**, so by default, the new data set will only include the observations that match between the two original data sets.

Let's do an example. Table 10.1 provides some made-up data about four schools. We'll merge these with some equally made-up demographic data about the school neighborhoods. In the first data set, the variable name for school is "School," while in the second it is just "S." Note that the second data set is not in the same order and doesn't have the same number of observations, so **cbind()** is not an option.

```
> School = c("A", "B", "C", "D")          # Some data to put together in the
> Test = c(68, 74, 82, 61)                #    Schools data frame
> Change = c(7, -1, 5, -4)
> Size = c(340, 410, 275, 500)

> SchoolsData = data.frame(School, Test, Change, Size)

> S = c("A", "F", "D", "E", "C")          # Some data to put together in the
> Inc = c(32, 46, 27, 52, 49)             #    S data frame
> nBars = c(3, 5, 2, 7, 4)

> DemData = data.frame(S, Inc, nBars)

> newData = merge(SchoolsData, DemData,   # Merge the two datasets
+      by.x = "School", by.y = "S")        # Matched variables: School & S
> newData                                 # Show the merged data
    School Test  Change Size Inc  nBars
1        A   68       7  340  32      3
2        C   82       5  275  49      4
3        D   61      -4  500  27      2
```

In this example, you can also see the effect of **all.x=** and **all.y=** being false. Only the three cases that have data in both data sets are included. Here are the other three possibilities: (1) including all of the observations from the first data set even if the second data set does not have the matching data, (2) including all of the observations from the second data set even if the first data set lacks the matching data, and (3) including all of the observations that occur in either data set.

```
> newData = merge(SchoolsData, DemData,   # Merge the two datasets
+       by.x = "School", by.y = "S",        # Matching variables: School & S
+       all.x = T)                          # Include all obs from School
> newData                                   # Show the merged data
  School Test  Change Size  Inc nBars
1      A   68       7  340   32     3
2      B   74      -1  410   NA    NA
3      C   82       5  275   49     4
4      D   61      -4  500   27     2

> newData = merge(SchoolsData, DemData,   # Merge the two datasets
+       by.x = "School", by.y = "S",        # Matching variables: School & S
+       all.y = T)                          # Include all obs from S
> newData                                   # Show the merged data
  School Test  Change Size  Inc nBars
1      A   68       7  340   32     3
2      C   82       5  275   49     4
3      D   61      -4  500   27     2
4      E   NA      NA   NA   52     7
5      F   NA      NA   NA   46     5

> newData = merge(SchoolsData, DemData,   # Merge the two datasets
+       by.x = "School", by.y = "S",        # Matching variables: School & S
+       all.x = T, all.y = T)               # Include all obs from School & S
> newData                                   # Show the merged data
  School Test  Change Size  Inc nBars
1      A   68       7  340   32     3
2      B   74      -1  410   NA    NA
3      C   82       5  275   49     4
4      D   61      -4  500   27     2
5      E   NA      NA   NA   52     7
6      F   NA      NA   NA   46     5
```

MERGING WITH A KEYED TABLE LOOKUP

A more complex situation arises when we have two data sets that have different organizational concepts. Suppose, for example, that we have our data set as earlier with the information about various schools and we have another data set with information about the locations. The key-value lookup matching approach is illustrated in Figure 10.4.

Merging with a keyed table lookup is a common data management approach because of the dominant relational database model. Efficient databases minimize the duplication of information. In the previous example, storing the city-based information about income and the number of bars in the schools database would be inefficient because the same values would be repeated over and over for all of the schools that are in the same city. Here, though, we are interested in setting up data for analysis rather than for efficient database structure. For that purpose, we usually need to have all of the data in one place. One of the strengths of R for data management is that the data can be stored in efficient database structures and

Figure 10.4   Merging With a Key-Value Lookup Table

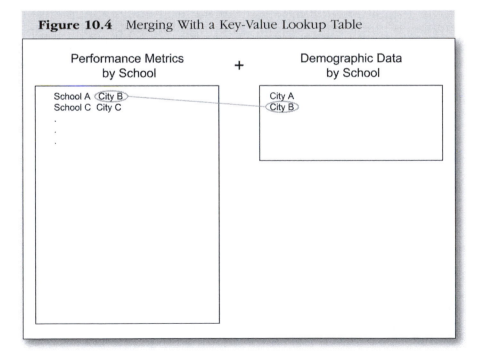

then brought together for analysis without creating persistent and ineffi-cient databases. R can build the necessary data set on the fly. Replicability is ensured by the maintenance of a record of the R code rather than by saving the constructed data sets.

The critical element of keyed-value matching is that one of the data sets has to have just one observation for each value of the key variable. This is the keyed table. The other data set will have the cases (observa-tions) you are analyzing. This is described in the language of relational databases as a many-to-one relationship. That is, there may be many observations with specific values of the key variable in the main data set, but there is only one observation per specific value in the data set that serves as a lookup table. If the keyed table had more than one observation for each value of the key variable, R wouldn't know how to do the merge.

The central R command for this operation is **match()**. The **match()** command works by giving you a vector that identifies where the values in your first table appear in your second table (the key-value lookup table). You can use that vector to pull out the lookup values from the key-value lookup table.

match() takes two main arguments. The first is the key variable in your main data set. The second is the key value in the key-value lookup table. We can see the process at work with a data example as in Table 10.2. The first table is the original data, and the second represents our key-value

Table 10.2   Keyed Table Lookup Data

School	City	Test	Change	Size
A	Littletown	68	7	340
B	Bigtown	74	−1	410
C	Bigtown	82	5	275
D	Littletown	61	−4	500

Town	Inc	nBars
Littletown	32	3
Bigtown	46	5

lookup table. The lookup is based on matching the "City" variable in the original data with the "Town" variable in the lookup table.

If we want to add information about income from the city lookup table to the schools data, we create a vector indicating where the matches are, and then we use that to pull out the relevant data. We then use that same matching vector to pull all of the city information into the school data set. This could be done all in one step, as shown in the example, by putting the **match()** command directly into the **cbind()** statements. That increases the possibility of scribal error, so we'll do it first in two steps, and then I'll show you the one-step code.

```
> # Create some original data
> School = c("A", "B", "C", "D")
> City = c("Littletown", "Bigtown", "Bigtown", "Littletown")
> Test = c(68, 74, 82, 61)
> Change = c(7, -1, 5, -4)
> Size = c(340, 410, 275, 500)
> SchoolsData = data.frame(School, City, Test, Change, Size)

> # Create the key-value lookup table
> Town = c("Littletown", "Bigtown")
> Inc = c(32, 46)
> nBars = c(3, 5)
> CityData = data.frame(Town, Inc, nBars)

> # Create the vector of lookup table connections
> myMatch = match(SchoolsData$City,      # Look-up value from main table
+    CityData$Town)                       # Match value from key-value table
> myMatch                                 # Show match vector
[1] 1 2 2 1

> # to bring in one new variable
> matchInc = CityData$Inc[myMatch]        # Vector of matched incomes
> nSchools =                              # Add Income vector to data
+    cbind(SchoolsData, matchInc)
> nSchools                                # Display new dataset
```

```
    School        City Test  Change  Size  matchInc
1       A Littletown   68       7   340        32
2       B   Bigtown    74      -1   410        46
3       C   Bigtown    82       5   275        46
4       D Littletown   61      -4   500        32

> # Same in one step
> nSchools2 = cbind(SchoolsData, matchInc = CityData$Inc[myMatch])

> # Merge all of the key-value lookup table information
> nSchools3 = cbind(SchoolsData, CityData[myMatch,])
> nSchools3
      School        City Test Change Size       Town Inc nBars
1          A Littletown   68       7  340 Littletown  32     3
2          B   Bigtown    74      -1  410    Bigtown  46     5
2.1        C   Bigtown    82       5  275    Bigtown  46     5
1.1        D Littletown   61      -4  500 Littletown  32     3

> # Everything in one step
> nSchools4 = cbind(SchoolsData,
+   CityData[match(SchoolsData$City, CityData$Town),])
```

AGGREGATING DATA

Another common data problem is to aggregate variable values by some other variable. For example, in the case of our schools data, we might need to pull together aggregate values by school from a data set that is originally organized by the classroom. The function for this is **aggregate()**. The central arguments for the **aggregate()** function are the variable to aggregate (**x=**), a list of the variables or factors by which to aggregate (**by=**), and the function used for aggregation (**FUN=**). You can also give instructions to work with a subset of the data (**subset=**), indicate a data frame from which the variables are taken (**data=**), and specify what to do about missing data (**na.action=**). The **by=** variable(s) has to be in the form of a list, so you'll need to use the **list()** function to achieve that: **by = list(myFactor1, myFactor2)**.

Table 10.3   Some Data in Need of Aggregation

School	Classroom	Test	Class Size
A	12	68	34
A	15	74	22
A	3	82	31
B	1	61	27
B	5	74	33
C	4	59	30

Table 10.3 offers some synthetic data to illustrate the problem and the process. Data have been collected for each classroom in each school, but we want to use the school as the unit of observation. The following example demonstrates the aggregation of the test scores with the mean and class sizes with the sum.

```
> School =                          # Create some data
+    c("A", "A", "A", "B", "B", "C")
> Classroom = c(12, 15, 3, 1, 5, 4)
> Test = c(68, 74, 82, 61, 74, 59)
> ClassSize = c(34, 22, 31, 27, 33, 30)
> sData = data.frame(School, Classroom, Test, ClassSize)

> meanTest = aggregate(x = sData$Test,    # Aggregate Test scores
+    by = list(sData$School),             #     by School
+    FUN = mean)                          #     using the mean function

> meanTest                          # Show aggregated variable
  Group.1        x
1       A 74.66667
2       B 67.50000
3       C 59.00000
> attributes(meanTest)$names =            # Change variable names
```

```
+    c("School", "mnTest")                # to make more sense
> meanTest                               # Show aggregated variable again
  School   mnTest
1      A 74.66667
2      B 67.50000
3      C 59.00000

> sumClass = aggregate(sData$ClassSize, # Aggregate Class Sizes
+   by = list(sData$School),            # by school
+    FUN = sum)                         # using sum function
> sumClass                              # Show aggregated variable
  Group.1  x
1      A 87
2      B 60
3      C 30
>
> attributes(sumClass)$names =          # Change variable names
+   c("School", "SchoolSize")           # to make more sense
> sumClass                              # Show aggregated variable again
  School SchoolSize
1      A         87
2      B         60
3      C         30
>
> sData2 = merge(meanTest, sumClass)    # Merge by common var School
> sData2                                # Show new dataset
  School    mnTest SchoolSize
1      A 74.66667         87
2      B 67.50000         60
3      C 59.00000         30
```

Another approach is to use the **tapply()** function, which was introduced in Chapter 7. **tapply()** applies a function to a table by a value. It takes three arguments: (1) the variable to aggregate, (2) the variable to aggregate by, and (3) the function to use for aggregation.

```
> mnTest = tapply(sData$Test,        # Get the mean test value
+    sData$School,                    #   by school
+    mean)                            #   with the mean function

> sSize = tapply(sData$ClassSize,    # Get the sum of class sizes
+    sData$School,                    #   by school
+    sum)                             #   with the sum function

> sData3 = data.frame(mnTest, sSize) # Join in new data frame
> sData3                             # Display new dataset
     mnTest sSize
A 74.66667    87
B 67.50000    60
C 59.00000    30
```

We might want to make this a little clearer by putting the row names back into the data set as school names. I'll do this in two steps, first using **cbind()** to add the row names to the beginning of the data frame. Then, I'll rename this new variable.

```
> # Add the row names as school identifiers
> sData3 = cbind(rownames(sData3),   # Add row names
+    sData3)                          #   to sData3 data
> # Rename this new school variable to "School"
> attributes(sData3)$names[1] = "School" # Rename School variable
> sData3                             # Display data
     School    mnTest sSize
A         A 74.66667    87
B         B 67.50000    60
C         C 59.00000    30
```

That worked fine in terms of the basic process of aggregation. We might be concerned, however, that we created the mean by simply adding the classroom test averages and then dividing by the number of classrooms. Since the number of students per classroom is different, this is the average by class for each school rather than the average by student for each school.

Which one we want is going to depend on what we are analyzing. If we are interested in teacher effectiveness, then the mean by classroom might still be appropriate. If we are looking at student performance, the mean by student will be more appropriate. To achieve this latter measure, we can redo the process, adjusting for class sizes.

```
> # Redo with mean test by student per school
> # Get sum of testscores time class sizes
> sumTest = tapply(sData$Test * sData$ClassSize,
+    sData$School,                          # by school
+    sum)                                   # with the sum function
> SchoolSize = tapply(sData$ClassSize,    # Get the sum of class sizes
+    sData$School,                          # by school
+    sum)                                   # with the sum function
> newSchool = data.frame(sumTest, SchoolSize)
> newSchool                                # Display new dataset
   sumTest SchoolSize
A     6482        87
B     4089        60
C     1770        30

> newSchool$meanTest2 = newSchool$sumTest/newSchool$SchoolSize

> # Add the row names as school identifiers
> newSchool = cbind(rownames(newSchool), # Add row names
+    newSchool)                            #  to newSchool data
> attributes(newSchool)$names[1] = "School"
> newSchool                                # Display data
   School sumTest  SchoolSize  meanTest2
A       A    6482          87   74.50575
B       B    4089          60   68.15000
C       C    1770          30   59.00000
```

We can compare the two results by merging the two files using the common variable School.

```
> newSchool2 = merge(sData3,          # Merge by class mean data
+    newSchool[,c(1, 4)])             #   with by student mean data
> newSchool2                          # Display the comparison
     School   mnTest sSize  meanTest2
1         A 74.66667    87   74.50575
2         B 67.50000    60   68.15000
3         C 59.00000    30   59.00000
```

Be very careful about missing values in these aggregation functions. We'll look more at those issues in the next chapter.

TRANSPOSING AND ROTATING DATA SETS

It is sometimes the case that we need to pull data from a table in which the observations are in the columns and the variables are in the rows. You can rotate (transpose) a matrix with the **t()** function.

```
> myX = (7:10)                        # Create 2 variables
> myY = (1:4)
> myMatrix = cbind(myX, myY)          # Join them into a matrix
> myMatrix                            # Display matrix
        myX myY
[1,]      7   1
[2,]      8   2
[3,]      9   3
[4,]     10   4

> myMatrix2 = t(myMatrix)             # Transpose myMatrix

> myMatrix2                           # Display transposed matrix
       [,1] [,2] [,3] [,4]
myX       7    8    9   10
myY       1    2    3    4
```

t() also works on data frames, but at the rather high cost of converting them to matrices. The object type of all variables in a matrix has to be the same. The transpose function will coerce all of the values to be character types if any of the original variables are nonnumeric.

As this scenario suggests, the problems of rotating data are often not so simple as just requiring transposition. Data may come in a form that requires rotating only a part of the data set. For example, the data might be formulated in a way that puts different variables for the same observational unit on different lines. For this, we often need to reshape the data more systematically.[2] We can't cover every contingency here, but in every case, the critical element is careful thinking about the unit of observation. When starting out, the best way to handle these situations is often to take the data set apart systematically and then put it back together the way you want it. It might, for example, be appropriate to split a data set into two pieces (return to Chapter 6 on sorting and selecting data), do some aggregating, and then put it back together using a key-value lookup table to get the data into the right form.

When you move beyond the warm and safe cocoon of the statistics class, you will quickly find that aggregating, merging, and transposing data are critical data skills for the real world. You will spend much time working these problems out. The only other issue likely to cause you as much grief is the reality of missing data: another rarity in statistics class but an ever-present issue in the real world. It is, finally, to that issue that we now turn.

---

2. The reshape2 package can help facilitate some of these operations, although it too has a bit of a learning curve. See Appendix C.

CHAPTER 11

DEALING WITH MISSING DATA

Dealing appropriately with missing values is a critical element of any data analysis project. Once again, this is an area that is often untaught in introductory statistics classes, where data sets descend from the heavens in nice neat packages. In the real world, missing data can often present significant problems. In some areas of work, missingness can be the norm rather than an exception (Allison, 2001).

In this chapter, we'll start with a review of the issues from Chapter 4 about reading in external data that may have missing values. Once the data set is in, we'll be ready to look at some techniques for summarizing your missing data and getting a sense of the big picture. This will be aided by some specific functions that can help manage "missingness." The next issue will be the tools for systematically recoding missing values. You'll recognize many of these tools from Chapters 6 and 7. Given its importance in the statistical lives of many users, and because it serves as a useful example for many other processes, we'll look briefly at some of the challenges in using R's basic linear regression tool in the presence of missing values. Finally, I'll suggest some approaches to visualizing missing data, although that is a process that won't really come to fruition until the next four chapters, when we, finally, take up R graphics in earnest.

The effects of missing data can be separated into two categories: (1) the analytical effects, which, though critical, are largely beyond the scope of this book, and (2) the effects on R, which is the focus of this chapter. At the end of the day, these two categories are related. It is precisely because missing data can affect analytic results that R is very careful about dealing with them. As was noted in Chapter 5, there are a number of basic R functions that are, by default, derailed by missing data. The problem is that R doesn't really tell you that it has encountered missing data and that that missingness is the reason for its recalcitrance. Instead, you often have to track this problem down by yourself. But, coming back to the substantive implications, it is important that you have a clear sense of the holes in your data set. R is a stern taskmaster on this front; you are usually required to give it explicit instructions to proceed with an operation despite the presence of missing data. Consider the following example.

```
> myVar = c(1:10)               # Some sequential data

> max(myVar)                    # The maximum value
[1] 10

> myVar[4] = NA                 # Insert a missing value
> myVar                         # Display new data
[1]  1   2   3 NA  5  6  7  8  9 10

> myVar + 2                     # Perform an operation
[1]  3   4   5 NA  7  8  9 10 11 12

> max(myVar)                    # Try to show new maximum
[1] NA
```

Note in this case that the addition operation is allowed on the data set with a missing value but the **max()** *function is not.*

As we have seen, missing data are indicated by **NA** (not available). In the example above, although R can conduct mathematical operations on the **myVar** vector, the function **max()** is unwilling to calculate the maximum value in the case that includes a missing value. The fix for this is to let **max()** know that you are aware of the missing values and are prepared to take responsibility for any untoward results that might come about as a consequence. This indemnification occurs by selecting the **na.rm = T** option for the **max()** function. Thus reassured, R will now do your bidding.

```
> max(myVar, na.rm = T)                    # Find max with NA removed
[1] 10
```

*With the NA values explicitly removed, the **max()** function can work.*

It is critical to remember that **NA** is a special value in R. (Object types, again!) It is a logical value rather than a character or numeric value. Note in particular that the string "NA" is not the same thing as the **NA** indicator. There are also three similar special values you may encounter in R: **NaN, NULL,** and **Inf**. **NaN** means "Not a number." If you try to take the square root of a negative number, for example, the result will be an imaginary number. These don't work so well in statistical operations, so R will generate a **NaN** indicator. **NULL** means that some element that R is looking for hasn't been defined. This is more likely to arise in the context of problems with your R code than in problems with your data. **Inf** just means infinity. If you divide a number by 0, you will generate an **Inf** result. Unless you have a good reason to expect one of these outcomes, **NaN** or **Inf** is usually a warning that something in your data is inappropriate for the operations you are trying to perform.

Before unpacking the processes for dealing with missing values in R functions, we should return to the procedures for reading data with missing values.

 ## READING DATA WITH MISSING VALUES

If you are reading in an external data set with missing data indicated by **NA** or simply by blanks, there will be little problem. R will know to interpret these as missing data. As we discussed in Chapter 3, the problem comes when missing data are indicated by some more imaginative coding, a not uncommon occurrence. The use of alternative text/character representations can be a particularly dangerous and confusing situation. When R encounters the text/character values, it becomes insecure about its coding for the whole variable, which it will now switch to be a factor, even if all the rest of the values are clearly numeric.[1]

---

1. This assumes that the **stringsAsFactors** option is set to its default **TRUE** value. If **stringsAsFactors** is set to **FALSE**, it will switch the whole variable to be a character rather than a factor or a numeric object. See Appendix A on setting R configuration options.

For the various incarnations of the **read()** command, you can include the **na.strings=** option to specify the identifier for missing data. If, for example, your data set uses –99 to indicate missing values, you would indicate this with **na.strings = "-99"**.

Here are some examples.

```
read.delim("mydata.txt", header = T, na.strings = "#N/A")
read.table("mydata.txt", header = T, na.strings = "-999")
read.csv("mydata.csv", header = T, na.strings = "X")
read.fwf("mydata.txt", header = T, na.strings = "Missing")
```

SUMMARIZING MISSING VALUES

summary(myData) will display the number of missing values for an individual variable or for each variable in a data frame. The **which()** function along with the **is.na()** function can be used to create a logical vector indicating which values are missing. You could then use that vector to explicitly exclude values from an analysis. The same thing can also be accomplished using the **na.rm = T** option, or the **[-is.na()]** or **na.omit()** approach, as shown in the following example:

```
> myVar = c(1, 2, 3, NA, 5, NA, 6)       # Set up a variable w/missing values
> summary(myVar)                          # Summarize variable
Min. 1st Qu. Median   Mean 3rd Qu.   Max.   NA's
 1.0    2.0    3.0    3.4    5.0    6.0    2.0

> mean(myVar)                             # Attempt mean w/missing data
[1] NA

> myMissing = which(is.na(myVar))         # Create a vector of missing obs nums
> myMissing                               # Show missing observation nums
[1] 4 6

> mean(myVar[-myMissing])                 # Mean w/missing values removed
[1] 3.4
```

```
> mean(myVar, na.rm = T)                    # Mean w/missing values removed
[1] 3.4

> mean(myVar[!is.na(myVar)])                # Mean w/missing values removed
[1] 3.4

> mean(na.omit(myVar))                      # Mean w/missing values removed
[1] 3.4
```

This example shows the failure of the **mean()** *function in the presence of missing data and several ways to exclude the observations with missing values.*

Data frames work in a similar fashion, but we have to account for the added complexity that different variables may be missing data for different observations. We'll come back to that in just a moment. First, we've got to look a little more closely at the missing values functions.

◌ THE MISSING VALUES FUNCTIONS

As we've seen, some R functions are flummoxed by missing values. Others take missing things in their stride. The regression modeling function **lm()**, for example, is rather indifferent to missing data. By default, it knows to skip any observation with missing data for any of the variables included in the model. The downside of this is that it is now up to you to be aware of the missing data issues and how they may be affecting your analysis.

For processes that choke on missing data, you can either pass specific instructions on missingness to the function or preprocess the data to remove or manage missingness.

The **complete.cases()** function will restrict a data frame to just the cases that have no missing values. This is a fine approach if you really want to eliminate all those cases. If you want to operate on an individual vector use either the **!is.na()** or **na.omit()** functions. In the example below, myVar2 is created by selecting the nonmissing values of myVar using the **!is.na()** function. myVar3 is created using the **na.omit()** function. For most purposes, the numerical results are the same for both methods. The difference is that myVar2 is a simple numeric vector, while myVar3 is now carrying some extra information that can be accessed and used by some functions.

```
> myVar = c(1, 2, 3, NA, 5, NA, 6)          # Set variable w/missing values
> myVar2 = myVar[!is.na(myVar)]             # New variable w/o missing values
> myVar2                                     # Show new variable
[1] 1 2 3 5 6

> mean(myVar2)                               # Calculate mean of new variable
[1] 3.4

> myVar3 = na.omit(myVar)                    # New variable w/o missing values
> myVar3                                     # Show new variable
[1] 1 2 3 5 6
attr(,"na.action")
[1] 4 6
attr(,"class")
[1] "omit"

> attributes(myVar3)$na.action              # Show list of NA obs
[1] 4 6
attr(,"class")
[1] "omit"

> mean(myVar3)                               # Calculate mean of new variable
[1] 3.4
```

The **is.na()** and **!is.na()** functions create a vector or array of true/false values identifying the missing and nonmissing values, respectively. We can see this for the data used above. The **is.na(x)** operation shows which values of x are missing (TRUE).

```
> is.na(myVar)
[1] FALSE FALSE FALSE TRUE FALSE TRUE FALSE
```

The **is.na()** family of functions works well with the **which()** function for identifying or selecting the observation numbers for the data that are missing or not missing. **which(is.na(myVector))** returns a vector with the observation numbers of all of the observations with missing values, while **which(!is.na(myVector))** returns all of the nonmissing values.

For a matrix or data frame, **is.na(myDataframe)** returns a matrix of TRUE/FALSE values indicating whether each element is missing or nonmissing. This is actually more useful than it might sound, since those TRUE/FALSE values are interpreted numerically as 1s and 0s. This means that summing the rows will give you a count of the number of variables missing for each observation. Summing the columns will give you a count of the number of observations missing for each variable. Here are a few approaches to that task, starting with a **summary()** to get an overview of the data.

```
> myData2 = data.frame(myVar1 = myVar,  # Add to our previous data to
+    myVar2 = c(4, NA, 5, 2, NA, NA, 5)) #   create a data frame

> summary(myData2)                        # Summarize data frame
     myVar1          myVar2
 Min.   :1.0    Min.    :2.0
 1st Qu.:2.0    1st Qu.:3.5
 Median :3.0    Median :4.5
 Mean   :3.4    Mean    :4.0
 3rd Qu.:5.0    3rd Qu.:5.0
 Max.   :6.0    Max.    :5.0
 NA's   :2.0    NA's    :3.0

> apply(is.na(myData2), 2, sum)           # Apply sum to is.na() columns
myVar1 myVar2
     2      3
> apply(is.na(myData2), 1, sum)           # Apply sum to is.na() matrix rows
[1] 0 1 0 1 1 2 0

> rowSums(is.na(myData2))                 # Sum is.na rows - missing by obs
[1] 0 1 0 1 1 2 0

> colSums(is.na(myData2))                 # Sum is.na cols - missing by var
myVar1 myVar2
     2      3
```

The **na.omit()** function is a little more versatile in that it operates on a vector, matrix, or data frame to remove every observation that has *any* missing value. A data frame or matrix, in this case, is reduced to the set of complete observations. This is quick and efficient, but you need to be careful that you aren't throwing away observations that might be complete for the variables of interest but are missing for other, less important variables. As always with missing data issues (and much else in life), the important thing is to be intentional and to think carefully about the effects of your actions.

```
> myData2                              # Show data with missing values
  myVar1 myVar2
1      1      4
2      2     NA
3      3      5
4     NA      2
5      5     NA
6     NA     NA
7      6      5

> na.omit(myData2)                     # Data with all NA obs removed
  myVar1 myVar2
1      1      4
3      3      5
7      6      5
```

na.fail() can be useful as an alarm in developing functions that might go wrong if there are missing values present. It returns an error if there are any missing values anywhere in your data. Otherwise, it just passes your data through.

```
> na.fail(myData2)                     # Produce error msg if any NA's
Error in na.fail.default(myData2): missing values in object
```

```
> na.fail(na.omit(myData2))               # Pass through data if no NA's
   myVar1  myVar2
1       1       4
3       3       5
7       6       5
```

RECODING MISSING VALUES

If you do not translate the missing values to **NA** when importing the data, you can always systematically change the values later. In this process, the important thing is that **NA** is a special logical value and not a character string, so it does not go within quotation marks.

For vectors or matrices, you can use **ifelse()** or **replace()** to do systematic replacements. The key to this operation is that both of these functions are vectorized: The functions operate on every element in the vector or matrix. Here, first, is the operation with **ifelse()**.

```
> myVector = c(1, 2, -9, 6)               # Set vector with -9 for missing
> myVector2 = ifelse(myVector == -9,      # Test every element for == -9
+    NA,                                   # If == -9 then replace with NA
+    myVector)                             # Else reuse myVector value

> myVector2                               # Display results
[1]  1  2 NA  6

> myMatrix = cbind(                       # Set up matrix w/-9 for missing
+    c(1, 2, -9, 6),                      # First column in matrix
+    c(4, 5, 3, -9))                      # Second column in matrix

> myMatrix2 = ifelse(myMatrix == -9,      # Test every element for == -9
+    NA,                                   # If == -9 then replace with NA
+    myMatrix)                             # Otherwise keep myMatrix value
```

```
> myMatrix2                            # Display results
       [,1] [,2]
[1,]     1    4
[2,]     2    5
[3,]    NA    3
[4,]     6   NA
```

The **replace()** function is pretty much the same concept, but it uses a list of the observation numbers that need replacement. **replace()** takes three arguments: first, the object on which to operate; then, the list of observations to operate on; and, finally, the replacement value. In this example, we use the **which()** function to select the observation numbers for the missing value cases. As the following example shows, this again works for both vectors and matrices.

```
> myVector2 = replace(myVector,       # Replace values in myVector
+    which(myVector == -9),           # Select obs that == -9
+    NA)                              # Replace with NA

> myVector2                           # Display myVector2
[1]  1  2 NA  6

> myMatrix2 = replace(myMatrix,       # Replace values in myMatrix
+    which(myMatrix == -9),           # Select obs that == -9
+    NA)                              # Replace with NA

> myMatrix2                           # Display myVector2
       [,1] [,2]
[1,]     1    4
[2,]     2    5
[3,]    NA    3
[4,]     6   NA
```

By themselves, **ifelse()** and **replace()** won't work for a data frame because a data frame is a list with a variety of different elements rather than just a set of vectors on which **ifelse()** or **replace()** could operate (use **attributes(myDataFrame)** if you want to see this structure).

The traditional way to overcome this problem is with nested **for** loops (see Chapter 7). The first loop indexes over each row and the second over each column. This, then, runs over every combination of row and column numbers and makes the replacements where appropriate.

```
> myDF = data.frame(cbind(          # Data frame with -9 for missing
+       c(1, 2, -9, 6),             # First column in data frame
+       c(4, 5, 3, -9)))            # Second column in data frame

> for (i in 1:nrow(myDF)) {         # Set index for every row in myDF
+       for (k in 1:ncol(myDF)) {   # Set up index for every column
+           if(myDF[i, k] == -9) {  # Test every element for == -9
+               myDF[i, k] = NA     # Replace -9 with NA
+           }                       # End of if
+       }                           # End of for k loop
+ }                                 # End of for i loop
> myDF                              # Display results
   X1 X2
1   1  4
2   2  5
3  NA  3
4   6 NA
```

This works, and has the advantage of being reasonably transparent, especially for those with some programming background. But the elegance of R comes from its ability to do vectorized operations. As you'll recall from the discussion in Chapter 7, we can use the **sapply()** functions to apply a function systematically to a data frame. This is a good place to exercise our **sapply()** chops. The **sapply()** function can apply **ifelse()** or **replace()** to the data array that is locked up in the data frame list. To do this, we need to set them up as customized functions.

```
> myDF2 = sapply(myDF,              # Use sapply to apply
+    function(x)                     #   new function (note no comma)
+    replace(x, which(x == -9), NA)) #   to replace all -9 with NA
                                     # Note: no comma with function(x)

> myDF2                             # Display result
     X1 X2
[1,]  1  4
[2,]  2  5
[3,] NA  3
[4,]  6 NA


> myDF2 = sapply(myDF,              # Use sapply to apply
+    function(x)                     #   new function (note no comma)
+    ifelse(x == -9, NA, x))         #   to replace all -9 with NA
> myDF2                             # Display result
     X1 X2
[1,]  1  4
[2,]  2  5
[3,] NA  3
[4,]  6 NA
```

Now that we've got the values appropriately marked with the **NA** notation, we can use the R missing value functions to help manage the missing values problems.

MISSING VALUES AND REGRESSION MODELING

Another minor, but common, headache comes from running regressions or other models on data sets with missing data and then trying to match up the original data and the regression output. Running a regression model generates a list with the regression output (see Appendix B). This includes valuable things such as a vector of the residuals and a vector of fitted values. Obviously, the regression model is going to leave out observations with missing values. If we want to connect these residuals back to one of the variables in the original data set (e.g., some observation identifiers), we have to let R know how to line things up.. The two vectors will be of different lengths because of the missing values. You can use the **na.omit()** function to bring the original data in line with the regression output. Just be sure to apply it to the whole set of model variables to account for the missingness across all of the relevant variables. Alternatively, one of the elements saved in the model output list is a vector of the original observation numbers that were used for the model. These are not saved in a particularly convenient format, but you can pull them out of the list as an attribute (**"row.names"**) of the model output. **attr(myModel$model, "row.names")** will produce the necessary vector.

Another approach is to use the **na.action = na.exclude** option in the **lm()** function (the default is **"na.omit"**). This tells R to keep track of the excluded observations and to pad the residuals and predicted values with NAs to correspond with the occurrence of NAs in the complete data set. See Appendix B for further discussion of the **lm()** function and its options.

As we have seen, other R functions treat missing values differently. The lesson, over and over again, is to be intentional and be careful. To this end, another helpful approach in dealing with missing values is to take advantage of R's visualization capabilities. We are going to turn to these issues in much more depth in the next four chapters. But we can jump a little ahead here to demonstrate a few different approaches to visualizing missing data.

VISUALIZING MISSING DATA

There are lots of interesting ways to visualize missing data. As is often the case with R, others have already done a lot of the work in this area. The VIM package, for example, provides a number of helpful missing observation plots, and it even has a built-in graphical user interface (which relies on the tcltk package).

R's default graphics are also easily recruited for visualizing missing data. We'll cover graphics a lot more in the next four chapters, but in the meantime, Figure 11.1 shows a reasonably simple approach for generating a missing value chart.

Figure 11.1   A Missing Values Dotchart

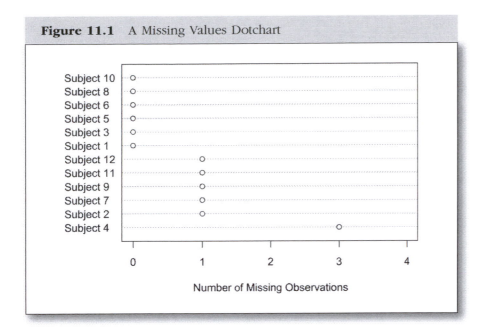

```
missobs = apply(myDF, 1,                  # Create new variable w/num missing
    function(x) sum(is.na(x)))             #   for each observation

missobs =
  sort(missobs, decreasing = T)           # Sort from most to least missing

dotchart(missobs,                         # Create a plot of missingness
  las = 1,                                # Rotate the y labels by 90 degrees
  xlim = c(0, length(myDF[1,])),          # Set range of x axis to num of vars
  xlab =                                  # Set X axis label
    "Number of Missing Observations")
```

If you prefer a barplot, just switch "dotchart" to "barplot." The data and graphics output instructions for this example can be found in the code file online.

Figure 11.1 is generated pretty easily with the default dotchart parameters. We can produce a more complex grid to show missing values if we

Figure 11.2   A Missing Values Grid

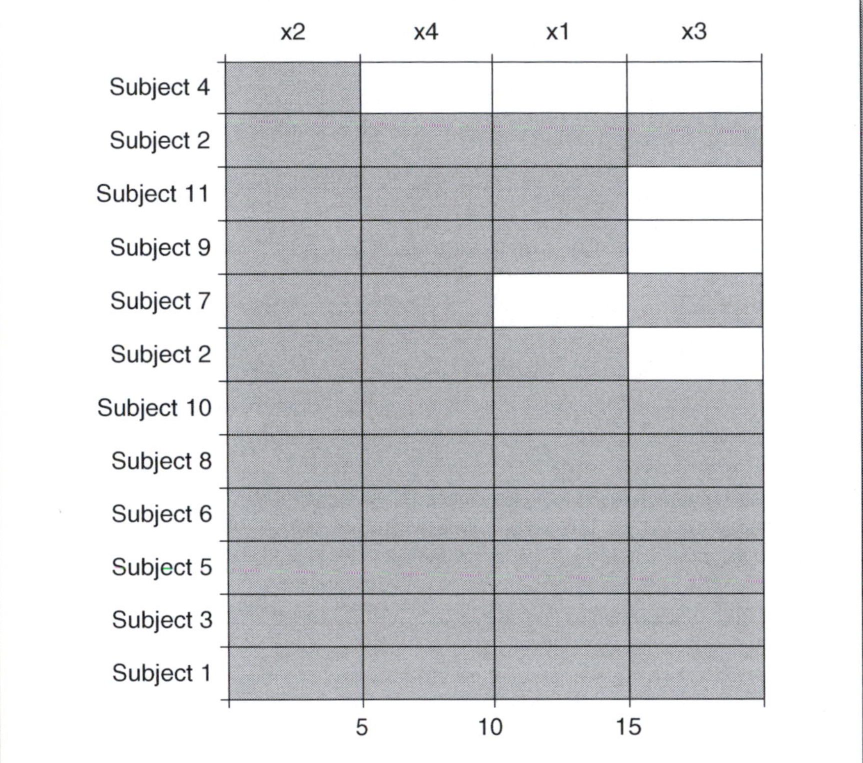

are willing to get into the customization techniques we'll get to in the following chapters (Figure 11.2). This figure plots the data set, with the observations running from those with the most missing values to those with the least and sorting the variables from left to right by those missing the fewest to those missing the most values. This doesn't get us that much for a 12 × 4 matrix, but as the size of your data set increases, this kind of approach can provide a quick visual sense of the overall missingness situation.

The code for Figure 11.2 is in the online code. I haven't included it here because it is mostly made up of graphics stuff we haven't covered yet. This is an appropriate place, then, to turn, at last, to the details of R graphics. We'll do that in four chapters, starting with the basic default plotting routines, then spending three chapters looking at the many ways in which R plots can be fully customized.

Chapter 12

R Graphics I

The Built-In Plots

Visualizations are an essential element for communicating quantitative data. R is a powerful and effective tool for generating high-quality and diverse graphics. It will generate quite simple plots with just a few commands but is sufficiently flexible to produce sophisticated and highly customized publication-quality plots. It is, for example, widely used by the graphics department of the *New York Times* for their consistently excellent data visualizations.

I would hope that sooner rather than later you will find yourself wanting to do things with graphs for which Excel just won't cut it. Once again, one of the big advantages of R is that precisely because it is a command language, you can develop and save routines that create a variety of replicable plots to meet your aesthetic and practical needs. This also makes it easy to model your graphics from the work of others who have made their code available.[1] Producing just the right plot can sometimes be a gruelling exercise, but the rewards can also be very high.

By this point in your learning process, it should not come as a surprise that the great power of R graphics comes at a certain cost in terms of complexity. The good news is that learning the basics that I present here will give you everything you need to produce effective and fully customized

---

1. I have provided a gallery of all the graphics from this book and a few others at http://www.sagepub.com/gaubatz. See also http://addictedtor.free.fr/graphiques/ for a variety of completed R graphs and their underlying code.

graphics. From here, you will also be prepared to interpret R's help facilities for those cases where you really need to go further. There are a growing number of add-on packages that attempt to enhance or simplify R's graphical capabilities.[2] This is something of a moving target, so as throughout this book, I won't get into the packages. But once you have a good handle on the underlying logic of R graphics, you should have relatively little difficulty adapting to the additional functionality provided by the packages.

My approach to the intricacies of R graphics will be to do it in four steps. In this chapter, we'll look at some of R's built-in plot styles. At this point, we'll try to hew as closely as possible to the default settings. But the real power of R graphics comes from the fact that *everything* can be customized. In the following three chapters, we'll go behind the scenes to get a handle on some of the most important ways in which R's plotting facility can be bent to your will.

For most of the examples in this chapter, we'll draw on a pretty standardized set of data from my own field of international relations. This is a data set that focuses on the relative degree of democracy/authoritarianism as measured by the Polity IV Project (Marshall, Gurr, & Jaggers, 2013). In this case, I've included a basic measure of economic activity (GDP per capita) from the World Bank (2013) and a measure of corruption (the Corruption Perceptions Index, CPI) from Transparency International (2013).[3]

SCATTERPLOTS

The generic plotting function in R is **plot()**. Give it an x variable and a y variable, and you are up and running with a scatterplot: **plot(myX, myY)**. In its basic mode, this deceptively simple-looking routine opens a plotting window and generates a plot. If you are using RStudio, it puts the plot in the plotting window in the lower-right quadrant.

When you produce these plots, there will be an option under the Edit menu in the plot window for copying the plot or under the "Save as" menu for saving it in any of several common formats. You can save it that way or simply copy and paste to get your output into a report. With RStudio, it is even easier. Just use the Export menu on the plot window, and you can save the image in one of several useful formats.

---

2. See Appendix C for a brief review of some of the more popular graphics add-ons.
3. The Polity Score (P4) is measured on a −10 to +10 scale, with +10 being the most democratic. The corruption score is measured on a 0 to 10 scale, with 10 being the least corrupt. A codebook and sourcing information for the data are available online at http://www.sagepub.com/gaubatz.

Figure 12.1   Regime Type and Corruption

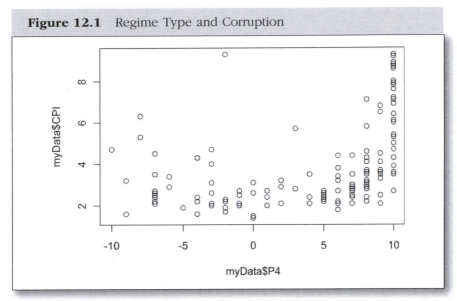

Data source: Regime type from the Polity Project, http://www.systemicpeace.org/polity/polity4.htm; Corruption data from Transparency International, http://www.transparency.org/research/cpi/overview.

Figure 12.1 is a simple bivariate scatterplot created with the straightforward **plot(myX, myY)** command.

```
> plot(myData$P4, myData$CPI)            # What could be simpler than that?
```

It's a little boring, I know. This isn't what we left Excel to do. Don't worry. Everything can be changed. We'll get there in the next three chapters.

PAIRS PLOTS

The **pairs(myDataFrame)** plot command creates a matrix of plots; it is rather like a visual correlation matrix. It is great fun, as long as you don't have too many variables in your data set, in which case it becomes rather indecipherable. The **pairs()** function requires that the input data all be numeric. If, as is common, you have some data that include some nonnumeric data, you'll have to filter them out.[4]

---

4. See the **sapply()** approach to this in Chapter 7.

```
> pairs(myData[-1])                        # Pairs w/all num vars in dframe
```

As can be seen in Figure 12.2, **pairs()** does not have any problem with categorical data, even where that doesn't really work very well in a bivariate scatterplot. Obviously, you can just exclude them. Figure 12.3 is another shot at the same thing, excluding the two binary variables.

```
pairs(myData[,c(2:4)])                     # Pairs plot w/o binary vars
```

Figure 12.2   A Pairs Plot

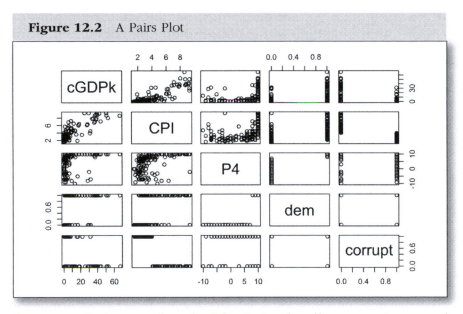

Data source: Regime type from the Polity Project, http://www.systemicpeace.org/polity/polity4.htm; Corruption data from Transparency International, http://www.transparency.org/research/cpi/overview; GDP data from World DataBank. World Bank. World Development Indicators, http://databank.worldbank.org/data/home.aspx.

 LINE PLOTS

A line plot is just like a scatterplot, but with the dots connected. Of course, the data have to be organized in a way that makes sense (i.e., the data may need to be sorted so that the *X* variable is steadily increasing along the *x*-axis).

Figure 12.3 Pairs Plot Without Binary Variables

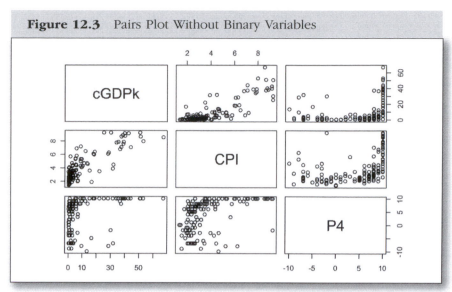

Data source: Regime type from the Polity Project, http://www.systemicpeace.org/
polity/polity4.htm; Corruption data from Transparency International, http://www.trans
parency.org/research/cpi/overview; GDP data from World DataBank. World Bank.
World Development Indicators, http://databank.worldbank.org/data/home.aspx.

Figure 12.4 Basic Line Plot

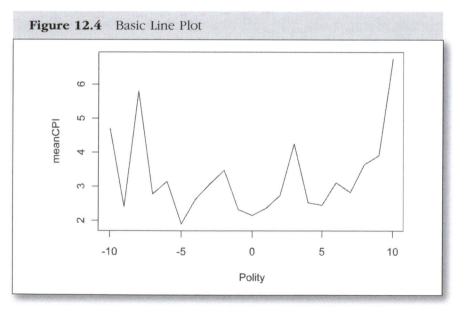

Data source: Regime type from the Polity Project, http://www.systemicpeace.org/
polity/polity4.htm.

Figure 12.5 Line Plot With Points Overlay

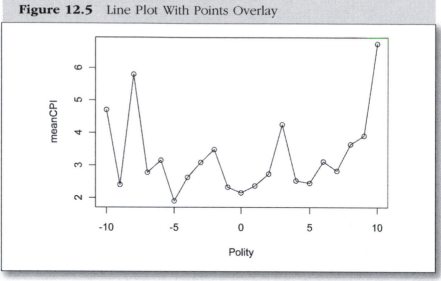

Data source: Regime type from the Polity Project, http://www.systemicpeace.org/polity/polity4.htm.

The line plot is created with the same **plot()** command as the scatterplot, but we add an option for the type of line (in fact, a regular scatterplot is really just a line plot without the line). The **type=** option can take five values:

type = "p"   A scatterplot

type = "l"   A line plot

type = "o"   Overlays the points on the line

type = "b"   Points with lines in between them

There is also a **type = "n"**, which suppresses the printing of any points on the plot. While this may sound a little silly, it's actually the way we start building much more sophisticated plots. We'll get to that in Chapter 15. Figures 12.4 through 12.6 are examples of simple line plots.

```
> meanCPI = tapply(myData$CPI,        # Create variable with mean CPI
+    myData$P4,                        #   at each level of P4
+    mean)

> Polity = as.numeric(                 # Create variable with P4 levels
+    row.names(meanCPI))               #   using row names from myMeans
>
```

```
> plot(Polity, meanCPI, type = "l")      # Basic line plot
> plot(Polity, meanCPI, type = "o")      # Line plot with points overlayed
> plot(Polity, meanCPI, type = "b")      # Plot with lines between points
```

Figure 12.6 Points With Line Connectors

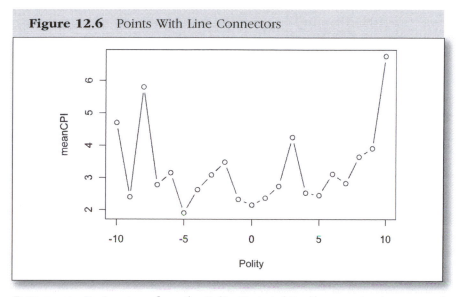

Data source: Regime type from the Polity Project, http://www.systemicpeace.org/polity/polity4.htm.

All that is nice enough in a quaint old-school kind of way. Again, we'll really learn how to make something of it in Chapters 14 and 15.

BOX PLOTS

A box plot is a very helpful tool for getting an initial sense of the data. It shows five different elements in the distribution of data. The box indicates the "interquartile range," which is the middle 50% of the data. The thick black line shows the median, that is, the value in the middle of the range. The "whiskers," the thin dashed lines on the top and bottom of each box, show the range of observations within 1.5 of the interquartile range above or below the box. Any observations above or below the whiskers are marked as potential outliers. Thus, the box plot also shows the smallest and largest values.

Figure 12.7 is a simple box plot for our CPI and Polity data. I've filtered out the two binary variables (dem and corrupt), since the box plot is pretty uninformative for dichotomous data. The scales for the two variables are close enough for this to work. If your variables have widely differing scales, you'll either have to rescale them or do each box plot separately (or use some of the more advanced options discussed in Chapters 13 and 14).

```
boxplot(myData[,3:4])          # Boxplot (leaving out binary data)
```

You can see from this that the CPI data are bunched toward the more corrupt end of the scale (closer to 0), such that the small number of non-corrupt states (closer to 10) look like outliers. The Polity Score (P4), on the other hand, has a more even distribution, but the median state still has a fairly high Polity Score.

While a single box can show the distribution of a single variable, the real leverage comes in comparing distributions across the values divided up by some factor or categorical variable. For this, there needs to be one continuous variable to display on the y-axis and a categorical/factor variable with a manageable number of levels to display on the x-axis. For our current data, this barely works with our measure of regime type on the x-axis and

Figure 12.7 A Simple Box Plot

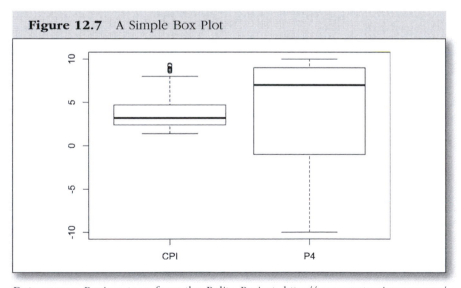

Data source: Regime type from the Polity Project, http://www.systemicpeace.org/polity/polity4.htm; Corruption data from Transparency International, http://www.transparency.org/research/cpi/overview.

Figure 12.8   Box Plot of Corruption by Regime Polity Score

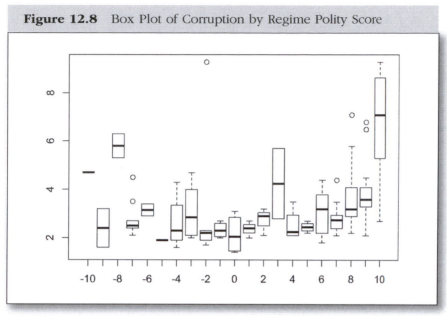

Data source: Regime type from the Polity Project, http://www.systemicpeace.org/polity/polity4.htm; Corruption data from Transparency International, http://www.transparency.org/research/cpi/overview.

the CPI corruption score on the *y*-axis (see Figure 12.8). This combination is created with the tilde (~), which one can interpret in R as a modeling statement: **y ~ x** means that *y* is a function of *x*. In our case, it is CPI score as a function of regime type.

```
> boxplot(myData$CPI~myData$P4)          # Boxplot of CPI by Polity score
```

This data set is clearly sparse in a number of the categories. A more effective approach would be to aggregate the Polity Scores (P4s) into quartiles (four bins with roughly equal numbers of observations) using the **cut(x, (quantile(x))** approach we saw in Chapter 5 (see Figure 12.9).

```
> boxplot(myData$CPI ~            # Boxplot of CPI by
+     cut(myData$P4,              # Polity score cut into 4
+         quantile(myData$P4),    #  quartiles w/ equal num of obs
+         include.lowest = T))    # Include lowest value in split
```

Figure 12.9   Box Plot of Corruption by Regime Type Quartiles

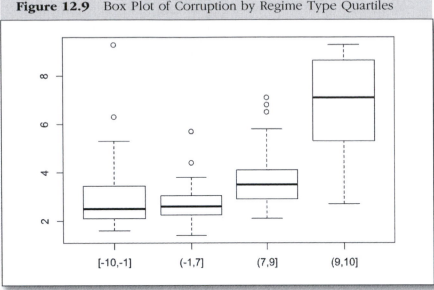

Data source: Regime type from the Polity Project, http://www.systemicpeace.org/polity/polity4.htm; Corruption data from Transparency International, http://www.transparency.org/research/cpi/overview.

These box plots suggest that most democratic regimes are much less corrupt and that there is not much difference in corruption levels between states at the lower levels of democracy. At the same time, there can be widely differing levels of corruption in even the strongest democracies.

Once again, with apologies to those who are anxious, we'll get to making these a lot prettier in Chapters 14 and 15.

Histograms, Density Plots, and Bar Charts

A histogram is a vertical bar chart that shows the frequency of variable values in a set of ranges. The command for this is simply **hist(myVariable, breaks)**. Left to its own devices, R will make some guesses about some good ranges. If you like those, great. Otherwise, you can easily change them with the **breaks=** option. R is surprisingly flexible about this option. It can either be the number of break points or the specific break points you wish to use. Figure 12.10 is the unadulterated R histogram for the polity data we've been working with (the default title can be turned off with the **main = NA** option).

```
hist(myData$P4, main = NA)          # Histogram of polity data
```

Figure 12.10   Simple Histogram of Polity Values

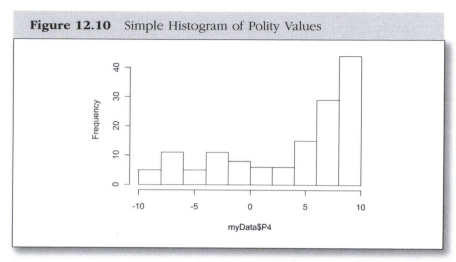

Data source: Regime type from the Polity Project, http://www.systemicpeace.org/polity/polity4.htm.

As we saw in Chapter 5, a smoothed version of the histogram can be generated as a density plot. R knows what to do when it sees the **density()** function embedded in a **plot()** command. The unadorned version is straightforward to produce, as shown in Figure 12.11.

```
plot(density(myData$P4), main = NA)    # Kernel density plot of polity data
```

The bar chart command, **barplot(height)**, is a more generic version of the histogram. It requires already aggregated input data showing the frequency for each bar: a vector with the height for each individual bar. Unless your data are already in this form, you'll want to go back to the Chapter 10 discussion of data aggregation and/or the discussion of **tapply()** in Chapter 7.

As an example, in Figure 12.12, we'll use **cut(x, breaks)** to generate a factor, putting our variable into subsets, and then we'll use **tapply()** to get the counts of the number of observations in each subset.

```
P4breaks = cut(myData$P4, breaks = 5)    # Create factor with P4 in 5 bins
newP4 = tapply(myData$P4,                # Create vector of bar heights
   P4breaks,                             #   based on the bins we created
   length)                               #   count number of obs in each bin
barplot(newP4)                           # Create a barplot
```

Figure 12.11 Density Plot of Polity Values

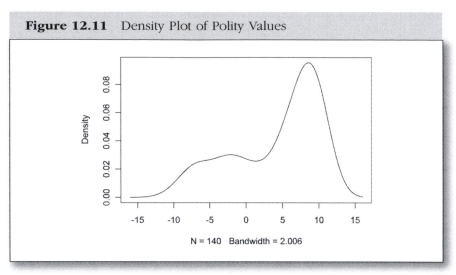

Data source: Regime type from the Polity Project, http://www.systemicpeace.org/polity/polity4.htm.

Figure 12.12 A Bar Chart of Polity Score (P4) Frequencies

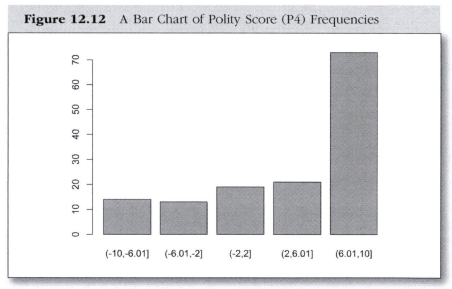

Data source: Regime type from the Polity Project, http://www.systemicpeace.org/polity/polity4.htm.

We can produce the same basic bar chart but rotated horizontally with the **horiz = T** option. In this case (Figure 12.13) we'll also add the option for an axis label, since the lack of labels in our previous plot is something of an abomination.

Figure 12.13 Horizontal Bar Chart of Corruption Measure

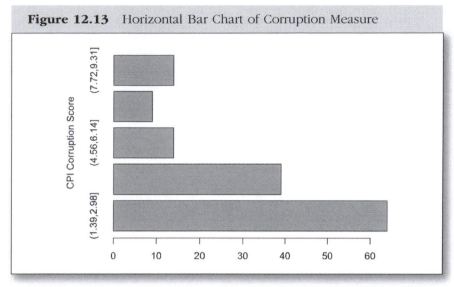

Data source: Corruption data from Transparency International, http://www .transparency.org/research/cpi/overview.

```
barplot(newCPI,                    # Create a barplot
   horiz = T,                      # Rotate to horizontal
   ylab = "CPI Corruption Score")  # Add y-axis label
```

R's **barplot()** function is hugely flexible. You can do stacked bar charts or side-by-side bar charts. You can change shading, bar widths, titles, axes, and really just about everything else. Still, at the end of the day, many would argue that you are better off doing a dot chart (Cleveland, 1993; Robbins, 2004).

DOT CHARTS

Dot charts are quite the rage these days. Their advocates argue that they can show more information in a cleaner and more efficient manner than the various incarnations of bar plots. I'm not sure I'm convinced, but you can decide for yourself. The command is simply **dotchart()**, where *x* is the variable to be plotted. As with **barplot()**, the vector of data to be plotted has to be aggregated. **dotchart()** directly plots the values you give it rather than combining things into bins, as we saw with **hist()**. In the following example (Figure 12.14), we do this aggregation by creating

Figure 12.14   Basic Dot Chart of Corruption Scores

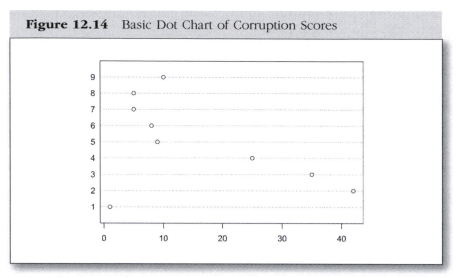

Data source: Corruption data from Transparency International, http://www.trans
parency.org/research/cpi/overview.

levels based on rounding the CPI scores to the nearest integer and then
using the **tapply()** function to count the number of observations at each
level. As you can see here, R is rather inconsistent about providing labels
and titles for the different plots. We'll take care of all of those important
elements in Chapter 14.

```
CPIcounts = tapply(myData$CPI,          # Aggregate CPI data
   as.factor(round(myData$CPI)),        #   in bins based on integer values
   length)                              #   count number of obs in each bin

dotchart(CPIcounts)                     # Produce basic dot chart
```

PIE CHARTS

I'm now going to show you how to do a pie chart. Please don't tell anyone
that I've done this. Pie charts are widely reviled by the graphics experts.
They are a relatively weak way to show relationships and are frequently
misused. Nonetheless, the public hungers for them, so here you go.

The command is simply **pie()**. The primary input for a pie chart has to be a vector indicating the relative size of each slice. The data vector can be either absolute or relative amounts (i.e., percentiles). If it is not already set up as percentiles (i.e., the shares add up to 100%), R will make the conversion. This is a nice service, but it also makes it easy to get into pie chart trouble. It is imperative that pie charts only be used for showing relative shares and that those relative shares add up to 100%.

If your data set is not already in the right form, the first thing you'll have to do is transform the data into a vector of relative shares. The code for Figure 12.15 shows one way to do that using **tapply(myVar, breaks, length)** to count the number of observations in each subset we want to appear on the pie chart. This example divides our corruption data into three categories—low, medium, and high—based on an equal division of the 0 to 10 range. Since the **pie()** function adds labels based on the names connected to the data vector, I've used the **names()** function to paste together some slightly more informative labels. I've also added a set of gray shades for the different slices, since the default setup uses colors (Figure 12.15).

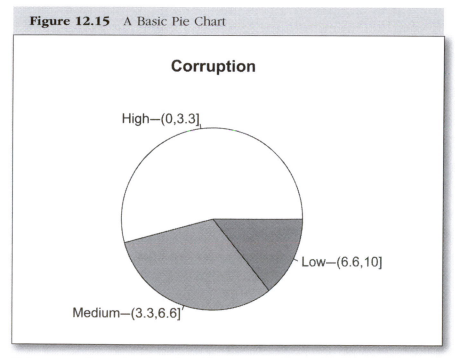

Figure 12.15 A Basic Pie Chart

Data source: Corruption data from Transparency International, http://www.trans parency.org/research/cpi/overview.

```
CPIbreaks = cut(myData$CPI,          # Create factor dividing CPI data
   c(0, 3.3, 6.6, 10))               #   into 3 bins

CPIcounts = tapply(myData$CPI,       # Create vector of bar heights
   CPIbreaks,                        #   based on the bins we created
   length)                           #   counting num of obs in each bin

names(CPIcounts) = paste(            # Create labels by pasting
   c("High Corruption",             #   low/medium/high text
      "Medium Corruption",
      "Low Corruption"),
   names(CPIcounts),                 #      to existing bin labels
   sep = "--")                       #      separated by "--"

pie(CPIcounts,                        # Create a pie chart w/CPI shares
   col = c("white", "gray", "darkgray"), # Set colors
   main = "Corruption")              # Add a title
```

Mosaic Plots

Mosaic plots provide a nice visualization for the interaction of two or more categorical variables. Basically, they show the whole data set as a square and then divide it up based on the percentage of the square represented by each combination of data values.

Producing a mosaic plot requires the data to be in the form of a contingency table: a table that has the possible values of the relevant variables in the margins and the number of observations at each intersection of possible values in the middle. This can be produced from raw data with the **table()** command.

Here are two examples using the democracy and corruption data. In the first (Figure 12.16), the data are first transformed into categorical objects (democratic/not democratic and corrupt/not corrupt), and then those data are used in a mosaic plot via the **table()** command to aggregate the counts in each combination of categories. The mosaic plot is set up with no modifications other than x- and y-axis labels and a title for the plot. We'll get into the kinds of modifications that might make this a lot more attractive in Chapters 14 and 15.

Figure 12.16   A Simple Mosaic Plot

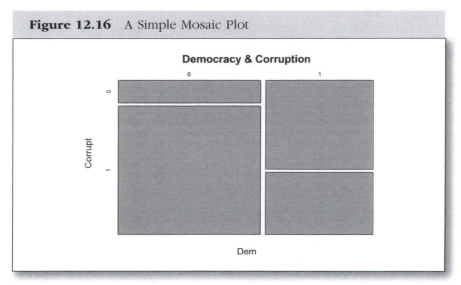

Data source: Regime type from the Polity Project, http://www.systemicpeace.org/
polity/polity4.htm; Corruption data from Transparency International, http://www
.transparency.org/research/cpi/overview.

```
> myTable = table(              # Create a contingency table
+   myData$dem,                 #    with x = dem/not dem
+   myData$corrupt)             #    and y = corrupt/not corrupt

> myTable                       # Display contingency table

     0  1
  0 12 69
  1 36 28

> mosaicplot(myTable,           # Create mosaic plot for myTable
+   main = "Democracy & Corruption",   # Set main title
+   xlab = "Dem",               # Set x axis label
+   ylab = "Corrupt")           # Set y axis label
```

We'll do another quick example to show the importance of the data
management skills we have been developing here (Figure 12.17). In this
case, we group the CPI measure into 10 levels with simple rounding. The

Figure 12.17   A More Complex Mosaic Plot

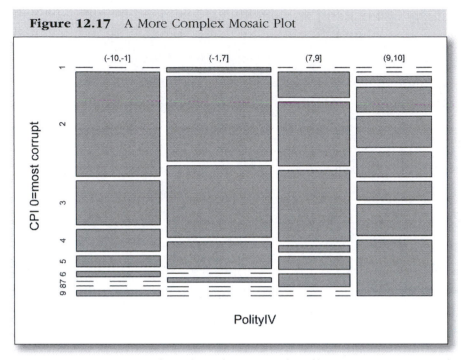

Data source: Regime type from the Polity Project, http://www.systemicpeace.org/ polity/polity4.htm; Corruption data from Transparency International, http://www .transparency.org/research/cpi/overview.

PolityIV democracy measure is grouped into four levels based on putting the same number of countries in each level. The graphics commands are no more complicated in this case. The big difference is the slightly more complicated data transformations setting up the table dimensions.

```
myTable2 = table(              # Create a contingency table
+   cut(myData$P4,             #   with x = polity score
+       quantile(myData$P4)),  #   cut in quantiles (i.e. same num
+                              #   of observations in each group)
+   round(myData$CPI, 0))      #   and y = rounded CPI score.
>
> myTable2                     # Display contingency table
```

```
>                2  3  4  5  6  7  8  9 10
   (-10,-1]  20  8  4  3  0  1  0  1  0
   (-1,7]    18 20  4  0  1  0  0  0  0
   (7,9]      3 16  9  1  2  1  1  0  0
   (9,10]     0  3  2  4  5  3  5  8  1
>
> mosaicplot(myTable2,              # Create mosaic plot for myTable2
+   main = NA                       # Turn off default plot title
+   xlab = "PolityIV",              # Set x axis label
+   ylab = "CPI 0 = most corrupt")  # Set y axis label
```

CONCLUSION

There are, then, many great plots that can be produced by R with only a minimal effort. The wide range of basic plots are easily produced at full publication quality and will serve a great many purposes. Nonetheless, the real strength of R graphics comes from the ability to automate and customize these charts. Every element in an R graphic can be adjusted. And even as they get quite complex, R's plots remain fully replicable. This is the direction we must turn next. The many approaches to chart customization are the subject of our next three chapters.[5]

---

5. There is a gallery with examples of some more complex graphs and the necessary code to produce them—available at http://www.sagepub.com/gaubatz.

CHAPTER 13

R GRAPHICS II

THE BORING STUFF

Now that we've got some basic graphs out, it is time to look a little more systematically at the process of customization. Pretty much everything in R graphics can be customized. While this can be a bit tedious in the first instance, one of the great virtues of command-line programming is that replication becomes trivial and the same customizations can be easily reused for other projects.

Graphics customization can look complex, but if taken step by step, it is really pretty straightforward. We are going to break it down into three big parts. First, in this chapter, we are mostly going to deal with a lot of boring, but essential, background and housekeeping issues: (a) the problem of graphics devices, (b) the general role of graphics parameters, (c) the layout of plot elements, and (d) the coordination of multiple plots in a single output (okay, those last two are a little more interesting). In the next two chapters, we'll finally turn to the more interesting customizations. In Chapter 14, we'll work through all of the things that can be done with text elements. In Chapter 15, we'll tackle colors and the manipulation of shape elements, such as points, lines, symbols, polygons, and images.

THE GRAPHICS DEVICE

The starting and ending point for R graphics is the graphics device. Where and how you want your graphics to be displayed affects how you set up the graphic at the beginning and how you get it out at the end. You can specify the graphics device either to open a new on-screen window or to directly write a graphics file. For casual graphics, you can just use the graphics window on RStudio.

The full list of available graphics devices is available from **help(Devices)**. Again, for most casual purposes, the plot window in RStudio will be sufficient. RStudio allows you to export plots (use the Export button on the plot window), which will be sufficient for many situations. When you need more fine-grained control and replicability, you will likely want to have more direct control over the graphics file output.

Screen-Based Devices

If you want to open a new independent window on your monitor, you can use the **windows()**, **quartz()**, **Cairo()**, or **x11()** functions, depending on whether you belong to the Microsoft, Apple, or Unix tribe. Here is an example of creating screen output in a new window (under Microsoft Windows):

```
myX = seq(1:10)                        # Some x values
myY = c(1, 3, 2, 2, 4, 8, 7, 1, 8, 10) # Some y values

windows()                              # Open graphics window
plot(myX, myY)                         # plot myX and myY
bringToTop()                           # Bring graphics window to front
dev.off()                              # Close graphics window
```

There are a few additional commands for controlling on-screen graphics devices that are worth pointing out.

The **bringToTop()** command is useful if your graphics window has gotten buried behind the R Console or RStudio window.

devAskNewPage() gets your input before continuing with any additional output. This is only for screen devices and is useful for forcing a pause between displaying different graphs.

plot.new() starts a new empty plot. The plot set up by **plot. new()** starts out based on a (0,1) coordinate system. This can be helpful for initializing some graphics devices for when you are developing more complex overlaid plots. You can see this approach, for example, in the code for Figure 13.1. You can also use it to skip plots in these kinds of overlays.

If you are a glutton for this kind of stuff, you can have multiple graphics devices open at once. You can choose which to use with the **dev.cur()** command. You can then close them all with the **graphics.off()** command. **dev.list()** will give you all the graphics devices that are currently in use.

Screen-based output is a fine thing for introverts, but eventually, you'll want to share your results. When you are ready to print your output or package it up in a file that others can use, you will need to switch to one of the devices that allows for that. RStudio and even the basic graphics windows devices have some basic abilities to export or save files. If you want more control over your output or want to have R create saved files automatically, you'll need to tell it the kind of output you want. For our purposes here, we can focus on two main output types: (1) bitmap/raster output and (2) vector-based output.

Raster/Bitmap Devices

Raster/bitmap images are based on providing instructions for setting individual pixels or squares to specific colors. These images can be perfectly adequate for publication-quality graphics, but they are set at a specific resolution and may only meet publication standards if they are kept at that size. The most common bitmap file types are accessed with the following commands: **jpg()**, **png()**, **tiff()**, and **bmp()**.

Within the graphics device command, you can specify, among other things, the file name, the size to be output, the default text size, the default font, and the background color. Be sure to set the file type correctly (.jpg, .png, .tif, .bmp) so that your output file will open appropriately. Most of these options are straightforward. Here are the most important at this point. (We'll go over all the parameter options in more detail in just a moment.)

filename= sets the file name. Just put the file name (and any path information) in quotes. It will be saved in whichever is set as your working directory. Annoyingly, some of the commands work with just **file=** for this option.

width= and **height=** set the size of the image. The default measure is pixels (**"px"**), but this can be changed with the **units=** option. The choices for units are inches (**"in"**), centimeters (**"cm"**), or millimeters (**"mm"**). If the units are other than pixels, you need to set the resolution with the **res=** option. This is measured in dots per inch (dpi). The default of 72 dpi is a fine number for screen output. For printed graphics, 144 to 300 dpi is better. Commercial printers prefer to work with 250 to 300 dpi. The limiting factor is that the file size goes up with higher resolutions. This is a triviality with simple black-and-white plots. With more complex projects, you will likely find the vectorized file types more efficient.

pointsize= sets the font size. The default is 12.

bg= sets the background color for the whole plot area. The default is **"white"**. **"transparent"** can also be useful on occasion. There are many others to choose from, although you probably shouldn't. We'll go over working with colors at the beginning of Chapter 15.

The **jpeg()** command also includes a **quality=** option, where the choices are a scale between 0 and 100. This tells R how much to compress the output. You won't want to go very low here. In any case, it probably isn't necessary unless you are creating something exceptionally large with some image- and color-intensive output.

I'll demonstrate the PNG device, but most of the other image formats work in a similar fashion. Here is a pretty straightforward example of setting up a PNG file.

```
png(filename = "myPlot300.png",      # Set filename for png output
    bg = "light gray",               # Set background to light gray
    units = "in",                    # Set units to inches
    res = 300,                        # Set resolution to 300dpi
    height = 4,                       # Set height to 4 inches
    width = 6,                        # Set width to 6 inches
    pointsize = 12)                   # Set default pointsize to 12

plot(myX, myY)                        # plot myX and myY
dev.off()                             # Close graphics device
```

This creates a PNG image file with the name "myPlot300.png." I set the background color to **"light gray"**, the height to 4 inches, and the width to 6 inches. The default font size will be 12 points. The **dev.off()** command at the end will close and output the new file.

Vector-Based Devices

Vector images are based on providing instructions for specific lines and shapes. These files are not set to a specific resolution, so they are excellent for publication-quality graphics and can, in theory, be scaled to any size. Note, however, that while these formats are capable of combining bitmap and vector output (see, e.g., Figure 15.16), the bitmap portions may not scale smoothly to very large sizes.

Here are the primary vector-based image formats:

1. **`win.metafile()`**. *Windows metafile output:* Windows metafile is a format that is effective and widely used for Windows programs. If you use Microsoft Word, PowerPoint, or Publisher for reporting your results, this is likely to be a useful format for you.

2. **`pdf()`**. *Adobe Portable Document Format (PDF) output:* The PDF is becoming increasingly widely used, so this may be a helpful mode of output if you work in that context. If you don't have a PDF editor to extract pictures or pages, you may find this a little less useful. But if you just want to share a single plot with someone else, the PDF format works very well.

3. **`postscript()`**. *Postscript output:* Postscript is another vectorized output, like Windows metafiles. That means that it scales up or down without becoming jagged. This is a particularly popular format for commercial printing (although PDF is increasingly moving into that realm). Encapsulated postscript (EPS) can also be produced with this command. If you are doing a lot of postscript graphics, you can set the postscript options just once with the **`ps.options()`** command.

4. *Scalable Vector Graphics (SVG) output:* I'm of the opinion that this is probably the future. SVG output is a vector-based graphic language based on XML textual descriptions of the graphical elements. SVG images are relatively efficient at all sizes and can be viewed in modern web browsers. The problem, at this point, is that they can't be directly imported into Microsoft Word documents. SVG output is directly accessible through the Cairo drivers on Linux and Mac computers. On Windows computers, you will need to install the Cairo package (Urbanek & Horner, 2012).

Most of these output formats are used in the same way as the bitmapped functions. Give it the output file name, set the size of the plot, and set up any special instructions about fonts, backgrounds, and the like.

The vector-based graphic devices have a few differences from the bitmapped functions as well as a few additional options. Instead of **`filename = "myFileName.pdf"`**, PDF files require just **`file = "myFileName.pdf"`**. The **`height=`** and **`width=`** options are measured in inches (trying to put these in pixels would not go well for you). The **`bg=`** option works the same way as in the other file types, except that here the default is **`"transparent"`**. In addition to the plot size indicated by **`height=`** and **`width=`**, you can specify the paper size with the **paper=** option. The default is **"special"**, which just sets the paper to the size of the plot. You may prefer to use **"letter"** to set the paper to 8½ inches × 11 inches if you are in one of those countries where that is the standard, or **"a4"** if that is the way your stationery works. For landscape printing, use **"a4r"** or the inelegant **"letterr"**. Other paper size options can be seen under the **pdf()** help topic.

For the moment, at least, many publishers are fond of EPS graphics. R's postscript output is compatible with EPS, but it requires a few specific options. **paper=** has to be **"special"**, and **horizontal=** has to be **FALSE**. These are both the defaults, so it shouldn't be a problem. More important, for EPS, you have to set the **onefile=** option to **FALSE**. This option tells the device whether it can accept multiple plots in a single file. The default is TRUE, which is okay for postscript but not for EPS. As this suggests, unlike the other output options, PDF and postscript files can contain multiple pages. When **onefile = TRUE** (the default), you can put several plots in a single file (one per page).

If you are using a process that generates multiple plots and you want to output a unique file for each of them with the **onefile = FALSE** parameter, then you need to include a dynamic file name under **file=**. A dynamic file name includes a percent sign followed by a regular expression to indicate how the file name should change for each iteration. You can get pretty fancy here, but trust me, you really just want to use simple numbers. Here's the step-by-step: first the percent sign (%), then a digit to indicate the filler for shorter numbers (0 is a good idea), then the number of counting digits to keep track of the separate pages (1 if you have less than 10 plots in the file, 2 if you have between 10 and 100, etc.), and finally the letter *d* to indicate the end of the phrase. If you want a 3-digit index with zero fillers (myfile001 .pdf, myfile002, . . .), then use **%03d**. For just 1 digit, use **%1d** (myFile1.pdf, myFile2.pdf, . . .). For 1 digit with a blank filler, use **% 1d** (myFile 1.pdf, myFile 2.pdf, . . .). For 17 digits with zero fillers, use **%017d** (not recommended: myFile00000000000000001, myFile00000000000000002, . . .).

Here is an example of an EPS device statement to output a simple plot:

```
postscript(file = "fig3.eps",        # create EPS file
   horizontal = FALSE,               # don't rotate to landscape
   bg = "white",                     # white background
   onefile = FALSE,                  # One picture per file,
   paper = "special",                # paper size = pic size
```

```
  width = 4.5, height = 3,          # set image size
  pointsize = 10)                   # set font size

plot(myX, myY)                      # plot myX and myY
dev.off()                           # Close graphics device
```

Note again the use of **dev.off()** at the end of this process. The device-closing command is critical to letting R know that you are done with the plotting commands and are ready to output the file.

The following example shows the printing of multiple files from a single **pdf()** command:

```
pdf(file = "MyGraphs%02d.pdf",      # Set up PDF files for output
    onefile = FALSE,                # Use one file per plot
    family = "Palatino",            # Set default font to Palatino
    paper = "letter")               # Set paper size

plot(x = c(1:10), y = log(c(1:10)))   # Create a plot
plot(x = c(1:100), y = log(c(1:100))) # Create another plot

dev.off()                           # Output and close device
```

We'll spend a lot more time on fonts in Chapter 14, but it is worth noting here that PDF files have a set of easy-to-use built-in fonts. The eight built-in PDF font families are shown in Figure 13.1. The font family is specified with the **family=** option. The font size can be controlled with **cex=**, as with the other R elements. Or you can specify the point size with the **pointsize=** option. Here are the PDF fonts and the R code that produced them.

```
pdf(file = "My-PDF-fonts.pdf",      # Set up PDF files for output
    family = "Palatino",            # Set default font to Palatino
    paper = "letter")               # Set paper size

plot.new()                          # Start new plot
text(x = .5, y = .8,                # Add text in the middle of the plot
```

Figure 13.1 Built-In PDF Fonts

AvantGarde

Bookman

Courier

Helvetica

Helvetica-Narrow

NewCenturySchoolbook

Palatino

Times

```
  "AvantGarde",                    # Text to print
  family = "AvantGarde",           # Use AvantGarde font
  cex = 2)                         # Set fontsize to 2

text(x = .5, y = .7,              # Add text in the middle of the plot
  "Bookman",                       # Text to print
  family = "Bookman",              # Use Bookman font
  cex = 2)                         # Set fontsize to 2

...

text(x = .5, y = .1,              # Add text in the middle of the plot
  "Times",                         # Text to print
  family = "Times",                # Use Times font
  cex = 2)                         # Set fontsize to 2

dev.off()                          # Output and close device
```

Unlike the other output options, **pdf()** won't overwrite existing files.
If there is an existing file with the same name, R will revert to the default
output, and you will get error messages for the specific **pdf()** options.

⬡ Graphics Parameters

Moving beyond the idiosyncrasies of output devices, the starting point for understanding the R graphics environment is the parameters function, **par()**, which allows you to change a number of appearance elements. There are currently 70 (!) graphics parameter settings. You can get the whole list, with the usual cursory and cryptic explanations, from **help(par)**.

As with several R commands, **par()** can be used both to set parameters and to find out the existing parameter settings. This can be very helpful when you aren't sure why something isn't working the way you expect it to. **par()** alone will give you the whole list. That can be a bit overwhelming, so if you know the parameter you are interested in, you can find its value by including it in quotation marks in the **par()** query. For example, use **par("usr")** to find out the current values for the plot area coordinates.

If you've got a set of parameters you want to reuse, you can make a copy simply by giving it a name: **myPar = par()**. You can then reuse these settings with **par(myPar)**.[1]

You can also set and query the par values with the **$** construction: **par()$usr**, for example. **par()** is a function, so you have to use the parentheses with **par()**, even though they remain empty in this case. On the other hand, your own set of saved parameters is a list, so it does not use parentheses; that is, it does not use **par()$font** but just **myPar$font**.

The **par()** settings are reset when you open a new graphics device. This has a couple of important implications. First, it means that you have to set **par()** after you open a device. Second, it means if you don't close a device, the **par()** settings will be sticky. This is particularly important for users of RStudio, since RStudio opens a plotting window that usually stays open for a whole session, with each new plot simply replacing the previous one. If you need to get back to the default settings, you can issue a **dev.off()** command to reset the RStudio plotting window.

We'll go into the details of most of the par value settings when we get to the discussion of working with text, points, lines, shapes, and colors in Chapters 14 and 15. For now, we can roughly sort the kinds of things you can do with the **par()** settings into four basic categories:

---

1. This will generate five warning messages for the five parameters that can only be queried and not set with **par()**. They are **cin**, **cra**, **csi**, **cxy**, and **din**. Duly admonished, you can safely ignore those warnings. If they really bother you, restrict **par()** to the non–read-only values with **myPar = par(no.readonly = TRUE)**.

1. Adjusting the placement, color, size, font, and rotation of text and symbols: **adj**, **ann**, **cex**, **cex.axis**, **cex.lab**, **cex.main**, **cex.sub**, **cin**, **col.axis**, **col.lab**, **col.sub**, **dra**, **crt**, **csi**, **cxy**, **family**, **font**, **font.axis**, **font.lab**, **font.main**, **font.sub**, **mgp**, **mkh**, **pch**, **ps**, **srt**.

2. Adjusting the placement, color, character, and size of lines and points: **cex**, **lend**, **lheight**, **ljoin**, **lmitre**, **lty**, **lwd**, **mkh**, **pch**.

3. Adjusting the plot axes: **fg**, **lab**, **las**, **mgp**, **tck**, **tcl**, **xaxp**, **xaxs**, **xaxt**, **xlog**, **yaxp**, **yaxs**, **yaxt**, **ylog**.

4. Setting the background characteristics and the plot size and placement: **bg**, **bty**, **din**, **fig**, **fin**, **mai**, **mar**, **mex**, **mfcol**, **mfrow**, **mfg**, **oma**, **omd**, **omi**, **pin**, **plt**, **pty**, **usr**, **xpd**.

The two important parameter settings I haven't put in any of these bins are (1) **col=**, which sets the default color for everything, and (2) **new=**, which, oddly enough, when set to **TRUE**, tells R to continue making additions to the current plot rather than start a new plot.

We can turn now to a more detailed discussion of setting the plot size and background characteristics.

THE PLOT LAYOUT

The plot layout can be thought of in terms of three concentric boxes. The inner box is the plot area: the space inside of the axes. The middle box is the figure area: the plot area plus space for titles, labels, and axes. The outer box is the device area. This is simply the total area available to put the plot for whatever kind of output device you are using. In the default setting, the figure area takes up the full device area. If you want to add an outer margin between the figure and the device areas, you can use the outer margin parameter settings: **oma=**, **omi=**, and **omd=**. These all work the same way. The difference between them is the unit of measure. **oma=** uses the number of text lines, **omi=** is the measure in inches, and **omd=** is the percentage of the device region. Each of these parameters is set with a vector of four values: **c(bottom, left, top, right)**. The default is to have no outer margin: **c(0, 0, 0, 0)**.

The figure and plot areas are manipulated the same way. For the figure area, the controlling parameters are **fig=** or **fin=**. **fig=** sets up the display region of the device in relative terms running from (0,0) on the lower left of the device to (1,1) on the upper right.[2] The coordinates are listed in a vector of the form `c(x1, x2, y1, y2)`, which defines the corners of the figure. You can think of these in terms of the proportion of the device region that should be between the edge of the device and the edge of the figure. The default `fig=` value is `(0, 1, 0, 1)`, which means that the figure will take up the entire device region.

`fin=` also sets the figure area within the device region, but in this case, it is measured in inches. While `fig=` uses a vector of corners, `fin=` takes just two parameters: the width and the height of the plot area measured in inches. `fig=` is probably easier to use if you think relative to the size of the device window, but `fin=` is probably better if you want to specify an exact size for publication. The default value for `fin=` is `(4,3)`.

If you are using RStudio, the size of the device region can be changed in the process of exporting the plot. The width and height in pixels can be set in the upper-right corner of the export box or by dragging the lower-right corner until you get the size you want. If you have used the `fig=` or `omg=` parameter settings, the boxes will change as you change the device area, since they are based on the device area. But if you have used the `fin=` or `omi=` settings, they will be constrained by the measurement in inches.

RStudio has a "Maintain aspect ratio" check box in the upper-right corner if you want to constrain how the device area shape changes (i.e., fixing the width to height ratio). You should set the pixel size based on the print resolution you are looking for. Again, the usual minimum standard for printed figures is about 144 pixels per inch, and up to about 300 pixels per inch for high-quality photo printing. The default of 72 pixels per inch is only sufficient for on-screen display.

`fig=` and `fin=` can only be used within a `par()` statement. When `fig=` or `fin=` gets set, it starts a new plot, unless you have used the `new = TRUE` option.

In Figure 13.2, a space is created between the device region margin (thick gray line) and the figure region margin (thick black line) with the `omi=` parameter setting. The figure region is set with the `fin=` parameter setting. There is a space between the inner device region margin (dashed line) and the figure region margin (thick black line) because the figure region is set to an absolute size that is less than the device size minus the outer margin (`omi=` setting). The distance between the plot region (thin black line) and the figure region (thick black line) is set with the `mai=` parameter

---

2. These are what are referred to as Normalized Device Coordinates (NDCs), if you were wondering.

Figure 13.2 Plot and Figure Areas

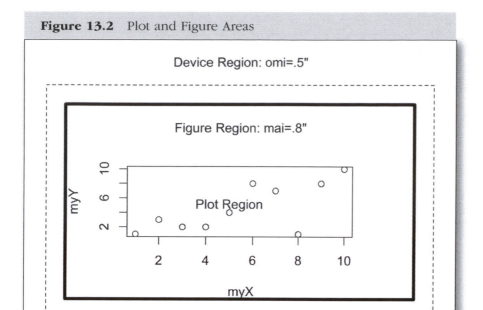

```
png(filename = "illustrations/fig-13-2-plot regions - BW.png",
    units = "in",                       # Set measurements in inches
    res = 1200,                         # Set resolution at 1200dpi
    width = 6,                          # Width at 6 inches
    height = 4)                         # Height at 4 inches

par(omi = c(.5, .5, .5, .5),           # Outer margin at .5 inches
    mai = c(.8, .8, .8, .8),           # Inner margin btwn figure & plot
    fin = c(4.5, 2.5))                 # Set the plot at 4.5 x 2.5 inches

plot(myX, myY)                         # Start new plot in device window
box("outer",                           # Create a box on outer margin
    col = "darkgray", lwd = 6)         #   with a thick dark gray line region
box("inner", col = "black", lty = 2)   # Dashed line for inner fig region
box("figure", col = "black", lwd = 4)  # Black line for figure region
box("plot", col = "black")             # Thin black line for plot region
mtext('Device Region: omi = .5"',      # Text in margin of device region
    line = 1, outer = TRUE)            #   indicating the outer margin
```

```
mtext('Figure Region: mai = .8"',    # Put text in the figure margin
   line = 2)                          #   on the 2nd line
text(x = 5, y = 5, "Plot Region")     # Place text in center of plot

dev.off()                             # Output png file
```

In this example, I have included the **png()** *command to set the plot size at 6 × 4 inches.*

Once you have the sizes set, there are two additional options to control the plotting area: (1) **bg=**, which sets the background color, and (2) **bty=**, which sets the style of the box around the plot. For **bg=**, you can use either a color name (e.g., white is the default for the bitmapped file types) or a hexadecimal color value. I'll go into more detail on all this in the more general discussion of colors in Chapter 15. For the box style (**bty=**), you have to use a set of letters that approximate the shape. **"o"** is the default and draws a border on all four sides of the plot. **"n"** tells R to draw no border.

Here is a summary of the primary commands for controlling the plotting region. The two things I have left out are (1) the **usr=** option, which sets up the coordinate system for placing objects on the plot, and (2) the **mfcol=** option, which sets up multiple plots. We'll come back to that a little later. In the meantime, for the rest of the options, I have included the default value in parentheses at the end:

bg= *Background color:* This can be set with one of the color names (see **colors()**) or with a hexadecimal color value. The coloring fills the whole plot area. If you want to set up different colors within the plot, you'll need to use the **rect()** or **polygon()** function and then use the **points()** and **axis()** functions to put your figure on top of the colored-in regions (as discussed in Chapter 15). (white)

bty= *Box type:* This sets the style of the box drawn around the plot. The argument is a letter or symbol that (very) roughly resembles which sides you want drawn ("o", "1", "7", "c", "u", "]"). For now, all you need is probably **"o"** for the full box and **"n"** for no box. (**"o"**)

mai= *Margin size in inches:* This sets the margins around the plot. This is a vector of the form (bottom, left, top, right). (0.561, 0.451, 0.451, 0.231)

mar= *Margin size in lines:* This works the same as **mai=** but sets the margins in terms of a number of lines of text. (5.1, 4.1, 4.1, 2.1)

oma=, omi=, omd= *Outer margin of a figure:* This is set with one of these parameters. **oma=** is measured in terms of a number of lines, while **omi=** is in inches and **omd=** is the share of the device region (e.g., .1 adds an outer margin using 10% of the device region). Each of these parameters is set with a vector of four values: **c(bottom, left, top, right)**. The default is to have no outer margin. (0, 0, 0, 0)

Once we have set up a plot area, we need to have a clear way to indicate what goes in it and where. We'll turn to the "what" in more detail in the next chapter. We need to address some things about the "where" right now.

GRAPHIC COORDINATES IN R

If you are going to add things to a plot, you need to have a way of telling R where to put them. There are several ways to do this. For many kinds of plots and for adding things that are going to be completely contained within the main plot area, the easiest coordinate system is simply to use the same *x* and *y* coordinates as the main plot. Figure 13.3 is a simple example adding some text, lines, arrows, and a rectangle to a plot using the *x* and *y* coordinates in the plotting area.

Figure 13.3 Objects Placed by Plot Coordinates

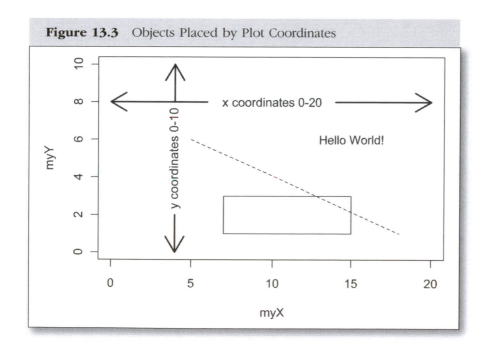

```
myX = c(0:20)                       # Create x var that runs 0 to 20
myY = myX * .5                      # Create y var that runs 0 to 10
plot(myX, myY, type = "n")          # Plot x & y, but suppress points
text(x = 15, y = 6, "Hello World!") # Add text at x = 15 and y = 6
polygon(x = c(7, 15, 15, 7),        # Add a rectangle at x coords
   y = c(1, 1, 3, 3))              #    and y coords
points(x = c(5, 18), y = c(6, 1),   # Add a dashed line between points
      type = "l", lty = 2)          #    at given x and y coordinates.

xtext = "x coordinates 0-20"        # Some text for adding to plot
ytext = "y coordinates 0-10"        # Some more text for plot

arrows(x0 = 7, y0 = 8, x1 = 0,      # Add a horizontal arrow
   lwd = 2)                        # Set line width to 2
text(x = 10, y = 8, xtext)          # Add coordinates text
arrows(x0 = 13, y0 = 8, x1 = 20,    # Add another horizontal arrow
   lwd = 2)                        # Set line width to 2

arrows(x0 = 4, y0 = 3, y1 = 0, lwd = 2) # Add a vertical arrow
text(x = 4, y = 5, ytext, srt = 90)     # Add rotated y coordinates text
arrows(x0 = 4, y0 = 7, y1 = 10,     # Add another vertical arrow
   lwd = 2)                        # Set line width to 2
```

A helpful tool for dealing with the standard x and y coordinates is the **locator()** function. This function identifies the coordinates for any point on the plot. Simply type **locator()** directly into the R Console (the lower-left box in RStudio). When you enter this command, a cross-shaped cursor will appear in the plotting window. Click on as many points as you want to identify, and then in RStudio, hit Escape (in other kinds of graphics windows, hit Stop, which you'll see at the top of the window, or right click, and then hit Stop). R will return the set of x and y coordinates for the points you clicked. You can then use these in your R program to place the elements you want to add to your plot.

A second approach to coordinate systems is to use proportional coordinates within the plot space. We can think of these as based on the percent distance along the x- or y-axis. Proportional coordinates have the advantage of being independent of the plot scale. So, for example, if you always want some annotation to be at the exact center of a plot no matter what the coordinate scale, this is the approach for you.

For proportional coordinates, we use the **usr=** parameter through the **par()** function. When a plot is set up, **usr=** is set in absolute terms based on the absolute x and y coordinates. Here is the coordinate system from the previous plot (Figure 13.3), which we can access with the **par()$usr** or **par("usr")** commands. As you can see, the absolute values for the plot area in Figure 13.3 run from −.8 to 20.8 on the x-axis and from −.4 to 10.4 for the y-axis.

```
> par()$usr                          # Show usr from previous plot
[1] -0.8 20.8 -0.4 10.4
```

The little overage R adds to the end of the x and y scale is there to make things look nice. If it irritates you, you can get rid of it with either the **xaxs = "i"** or the **yaxs = "i"** options.

When you need to overlay a second variable on a different scale or need to manipulate shapes or other additions to the figure, you can shift the **usr=** units. To use coordinates based on the proportion of the x- and y-axis, use **par(usr = c(0, 1, 0, 1))**. In Figure 13.4, we rerun the same plot but then change the **usr=** value and place the text and a polygon based on the percentage of the plotting area in each dimension. In this case, the text is in the exact center at the 0.5 mark for both the x and the y dimension, while the polygon is set up to be 0.25 (25%) from each plot border. You'll see again that the default dimensions add a little bit above and below the maximum range for each variable. In Figure 13.3 the arrows are drawn only for the x, y range, while for Figure 13.4 they are drawn for the entire range, including the little bit of overage on each end.[3]

```
plot(myX, myY, type = "n")        # Plot x & y, but suppress points
par(usr = c(0, 1, 0, 1))          # Set coords on % of plot area
text(.5, .5, "Hello World!")      # Place text in middle of plot
```

---

3. Figure 15.10 provides another example of shifting **usr=** units to facilitate particular drawing tasks.

Figure 13.4   Relative usr Coordinates

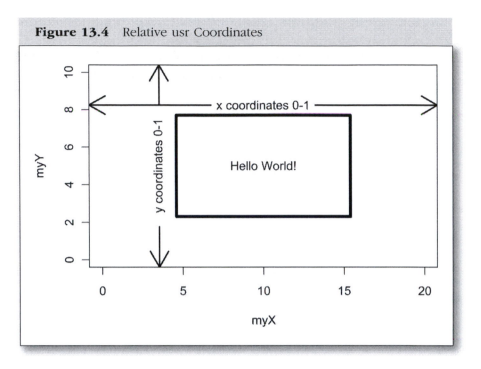

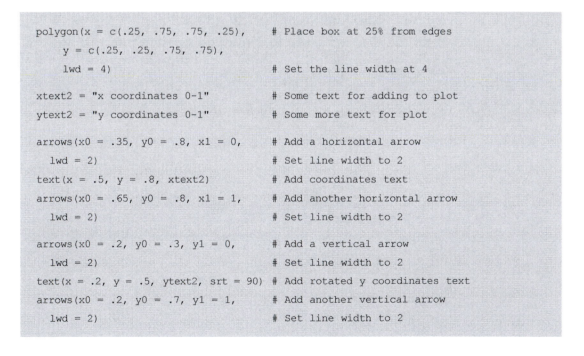

```
polygon(x = c(.25, .75, .75, .25),      # Place box at 25% from edges
    y = c(.25, .25, .75, .75),
    lwd = 4)                            # Set the line width at 4

xtext2 = "x coordinates 0-1"            # Some text for adding to plot
ytext2 = "y coordinates 0-1"            # Some more text for plot

arrows(x0 = .35, y0 = .8, x1 = 0,       # Add a horizontal arrow
  lwd = 2)                              # Set line width to 2
text(x = .5, y = .8, xtext2)            # Add coordinates text
arrows(x0 = .65, y0 = .8, x1 = 1,       # Add another horizontal arrow
  lwd = 2)                              # Set line width to 2

arrows(x0 = .2, y0 = .3, y1 = 0,        # Add a vertical arrow
  lwd = 2)                              # Set line width to 2
text(x = .2, y = .5, ytext2, srt = 90)  # Add rotated y coordinates text
arrows(x0 = .2, y0 = .7, y1 = 1,        # Add another vertical arrow
  lwd = 2)                              # Set line width to 2
```

The **usr=** coordinates are not limited to (0,1). You can set them up for whatever you want before pasting new text, lines, or points on to the plot. This doesn't make much sense for text or lines alone, but when you need to overlay points from a second data set, it can be a quick way to rescale it.

The lines can go out of the box if you set the **xpd=** option to **TRUE** (the default is **FALSE**). In the (0,1) coordinate systems, values less than 0 or greater than 1 will extend beyond the plot boundaries. You can see examples of **xpd=** at work in Figures 5.4, 15.8, and 15.10.

OVERLAYING PLOTS

A quick way to build more complex plots is to simply overlay multiple plots in a single frame (see Figure 13.5). The key to overlaying plots is using the **new = T** parameter setting. This has the counterintuitive meaning that when **new = TRUE**, it draws on the old plot instead of creating a new plot (the perverse logic behind this is that you are telling R to act like it is using a new plotting device when it isn't. Clever, huh?)

Figure 13.5   Overlaid Plots

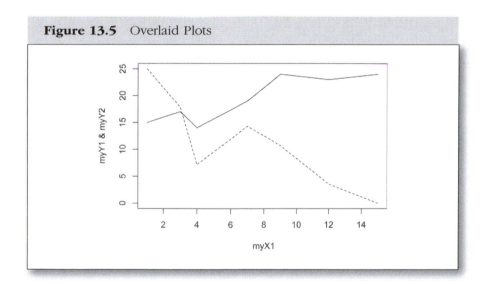

```
myX1 = c(1, 3, 4, 7, 9, 12, 15)
myY1 = c(15, 17, 14, 19, 24, 23, 24)
myY2 = c(8, 6, 3, 5, 4, 2, 1)
```

```
plot(myX1, myY1,                    # Plot myX1 and myY1
   ylim = c(0, 25),                 # Set Y axis range for both plots
   type = "l",                      # Line plot
   ylab = "myY1 & myY2")            # Set Y axis label

par(new = T)                        # Overlay the next plot
plot(myX1, myY2,                    # Plot myX1 and myY2
   type = "l",                      # Line plot
   lty = 2,                         # Set line type to dashes
   axes = FALSE,                    # Turn off the axes
   xlab = NA, ylab = NA)            # Turn off the labels
```

As shown in this example, the trick here is turning off or modifying the elements that would clash, such as axes and labels. We'll go into that process in more detail in Chapter 14. We'll also work there with much more powerful ways to add additional points, lines, shapes, and images to a plot.

Multiple Plots

One of the great plotting features of R is its ability to put multiple plots in a single output pane. This is done automatically, for example, in the **pairs()** command, which creates a matrix of scatterplots (see Figures 5.5, 12.2, 12.3, and B.4). More generally, there are two primary ways to place multiple plots. The easiest way is with the **mfrow=** or the **mfcol=** parameter. They both work the same way:

par(mfrow = c(1, 2)) puts two plots side by side.

par(mfrow = c(2, 1) puts two plots one over the other.

par(mfrow = c(2, 2)) creates a 2 × 2 grid of four plots.

The only difference between the **mfrow=** and **mfcol=** parameters is the order in which the plots are populated. **mfrow=** fills by the row, while **mfcol=** fills by the column. In both cases, the arrangement of plots is indicated by a two-element vector with the number of rows and the number of columns. There are several examples of this approach in other sections of

Figure 13.6 `mfrow(1,2)` for a Multiple-Plot Layout

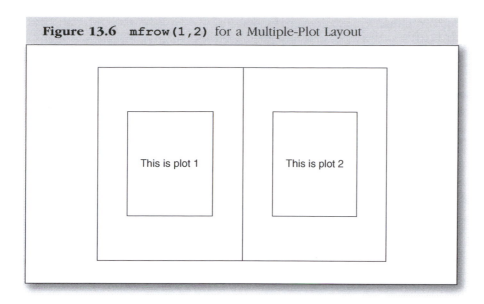

this book (see, e.g., Figures 9.1, 14.2, 14.3, and 15.5). Figure 13.6 demonstrates a simple 1 × 2 plot layout.

```
par(mfrow = c(1, 2))            # Set mfrow for 1 row 2 columns
plot.new()                      # New plot
box("plot")                     # Draw box around plot area
box("fig")                      # Figure area box
text(x = .5, y = .5,            # Put text in middle of plot
   labels = "This is plot 1",   #    identifying plot 1
   cex = 1.5)                   # Set font size

plot.new()                      # New plot
box("plot")                     # Draw box around plot area
box("fig")                      # Figure area box
text(x = .5, y = .5,            # Put text in middle of plot
   labels = "This is plot 2",   #    identifying plot 2
   cex = 1.5)                   # Set font size
```

When you need more complex arrangements, you'll need to use the
`layout()` function. **`layout()`** still thinks in terms of a grid of rows

and columns, but it allows independent control of the height and width of the columns and allows plots to span across multiple cells. With a little bit of thought, almost any arrangement can be developed through the **layout()** function.[4]

To create a grid with **layout()**, we use the **matrix()** function, which is nested within **layout()** and holds the following information: the number of cells, how many columns to place the cells into (**ncol=**), and whether they are organized by row or column (**byrow = TRUE** or **FALSE**). The trick with more complex layouts comes in setting the row heights and column widths. The **heights=** argument needs a vector with one height for each row. The **widths=** argument needs a vector with one width for each column. The challenge is that these heights and widths are expressed relative to the total vertical or horizontal space. If, for example, you have row heights of c**(0.5, 2, 5)**—that is, a total height of 7.5, the first row will take up 0.5/7.5 of the total vertical space available, the second row will take 2/7.5 of the total space available, and the third row will take 5/7.5 of the total space available (get it?). You have to think your grid through in terms of these relative numbers. The easiest way to do this is probably to make sure the sum of your row heights is 1, and then you can divvy them up as percentages. For the previous example, since 0.5/7.5 is about 0.07, 2/7.5 is about 0.27, and 5/7.5 is about 0.66, we could rewrite it as **heights = c(.07, .27, .66)** and get the same result (with a little rounding fudge). If you get the cells too small, you will get an error when you try to fill them. For Figure 13.7, I just put the cell numbers in order (the 1:15 in the **matrix()** command).

```
layout(                         # Setup a multiplot layout
   matrix(c(1:15),              # Create a matrix of 15 cells
      ncol = 3,                 #    in 3 columns (5 rows of 3 cells)
      byrow = T)),              # Order the cells by row
   heights = c(2, 2, .5, .5, 1))   # Set row heights

layout.show(15)                 # Show the layout grid
```

This sets the order in which the cells will be filled with the marvelous plots you are about to create. You can actually specify whatever order you

---

4. The Hmisc package has a nice function, **subplot()**, for placing plots within plots. The same thing can be done with the base graphics commands, as we'll see here, but the Hmisc approach might be more intuitive for some.

Figure 13.7 The Layout Method

1	2	3
4	5	6
7	8	9
10	11	12
13	14	15

Note: The layout for this set of plots is shown with the **layout.show(15)** command.

wish. For example, if you had six cells, you could use **c(1, 6, 5, 3, 2, 4)** in the **matrix()** command to fill the cells in that order. You can set up any cell, or even multiple cells, with a zero, which means that they won't be filled with anything. For example, **c(1, 4, 0, 3, 0, 2)** will fill the first cell, then the last cell, then the fourth cell, and then the second cell, and will leave the third and fifth cells empty. Even more interestingly, if you put the same number in a couple of adjacent cells, the plot will expand to fill all of the cells that have the same number (see Figure 13.8).

Use **layout.show()** to display the cells and their index numbers. The only argument for **layout.show()** is the number of cells to show. Most likely, you want to see everything, so just include the total number of cells (not including the zero cells).

The layout you develop will then be filled sequentially by the plots that you create. It's as easy as that. Figure 13.8 is an example of setting up four plots using a 2 × 3 grid. In this example, the first plot is extended across two columns, and the fourth plot is extended across both rows of the matrix, so the 2 × 3 matrix has only four boxes to fill in.[5]

---

5. Other examples of the **layout()** method can be seen in Figures 15.5 and 15.11.

Figure 13.8   Multiple Plot Layout

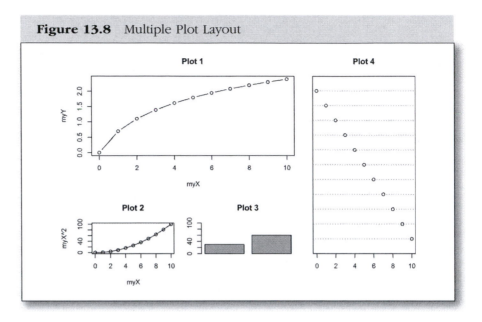

```
par(mai = c(.6, .6, .5, .1))            # Set margins around plots

layout(                                 # Set up a multiplot layout
  matrix(c(1, 1, 4, 2, 3, 4),           # Create a matrix of 6 cells
    ncol = 3,                           #   in 3 columns (3 cells per row)
    byrow = T),                         # Order the cells by row
  heights = c(.6, .4),                  # Set row heights
  widths = c(.34, .33, .33))            # Set column widths

layout.show(4)                          # Preview the layout grid

myX = c(0:10)                           # Some data for plots
myY = log(myX + 1)
myZ = c(30, 60)

# Some plots to fill in layout
plot(myX, myY, type = "b", main = "Plot 1")
par(mai = c(.6, .6, .5, .1))            # Change plot margins
plot(myX, myX^2, ylim = c(0, 100), type = "o", main = "Plot 2")
par(mai = c(.6, .35, .5, .1))           # Change plot margins
barplot(myZ, ylim = c(0, 100), main = "Plot 3")
par(mai = c(.6, .2, .5, .1))            # Change plot margins
dotchart(10 - myX, main = "Plot 4")
```

Within each of the layout cells, you can manipulate the margins and other elements of your plots to optimize the presentation. You can skip a cell with the **plot.new()** command. You can also continue to use overlays to achieve more complex effects. The one thing you can't do is use the **mfcol=** or **mfrow=** parameter options; they are incompatible with the **layout()** approach.

CONCLUSION

As I warned you at the beginning of this chapter, the basic management of device controls, plotting parameters, and graphic layouts can be a little bit tedious. It is, however, the foundation for building interesting and informative plots. Once you develop a set of parameters and layouts you generally like for your graphs, you can save that boilerplate code to use over and over again. If you are really committed to it, you can create a new set of defaults for your own work.

Enough with the housekeeping, let's get to the fun stuff. In our last two graphics chapter, we'll focus on the kinds of modifications that will really move us from the simple plots of Chapter 12 to realizing R's potential for the systematic production of fully customized graphics.

CHAPTER **14**

R GRAPHICS III

THE FUN STUFF—TEXT

In this chapter and the next, we finally turn to the more interesting techniques for customizing R graphics. In this chapter, we'll work with all of the various things that you can do with text. And in Chapter 15, we'll turn to the variety of shape elements that can be added to a plot. Our work in this chapter has to begin with an unfortunate detour into fonts. But then, we will be able to work on using and enhancing the several formal text elements, such as legends, axes, and titles, as well as the more informal placement of text anywhere in a figure. We have seen a lot of text already in the figures of this book, but here is where we will really learn to exercise full control over these important graphics elements.

ADDING TEXT

There are three main ways to add text to a plot. The first, and most straightforward, is to add or modify text in the preordained positions: legends, axes, and titles. The second is to utilize text in the same manner as points, that is, to place it systematically on the plot based on x and y data values. The third is the ad hoc placement of text at particular places. These second two are actually the same process, the real distinction being whether you are utilizing data to automate text placement or are adding

Figure 14.1 Adding Text to the Plot

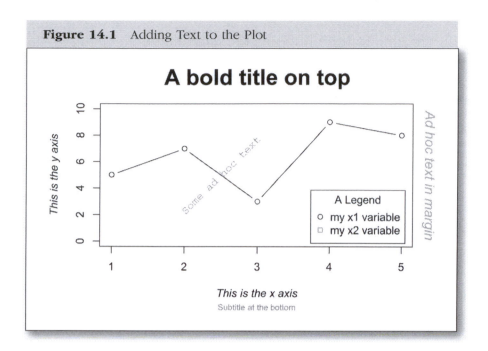

particular text to a particular spot on the plot. To get us started, Figure 14.1 shows the placement of a variety of regular and ad hoc text.

```
myV1 = c(1, 2, 3, 4, 5)              # Set up some temporary data
myV2 = c(5, 7, 3, 9, 8)

plot(myV1, myV2,                     # Plot the data
    ylim = c(0, 10),                 # Set range for y axis
    type = "b",                      # Set line type connecting dots
    main = "A bold title on top",    # Add a title at the top
    font.main = 2,                   # Bold for  main title
    cex.main = 2,                    # Set font size for the main title
    sub = "Subtitle at the bottom",  # Put a subtitle on the bottom
    cex.sub = .75,                   # Set font size for the subtitle
    col.sub = "darkgray",            # Set color for subtitle
    xlab = "This is the x axis",     # Add text for the x axis
    ylab = "This is the y axis",     # Add text for the y axis
    font.lab = 3,                    # Set axis label font to italic
    col.lab = "black")               # Set color for axis labels
```

```
# A legend
legend("bottomright",                   # Location of legend
   inset = .025,                        # Distance from edge of plot region
   legend = c("my x1 variable",         # Legend Text
     "my x2 variable"),
   col = c("black", "darkgray"),        # Legend Element Colors
   pch = c(1, 22),                      # Legend Element Styles
   title = "A Legend")                  # Legend title

# Some ad hoc text
text(x = 2.5, y = 5,                    # Add some ad hoc text at x=2 y=5
   labels = "Some ad hoc text",         # The text to add
   srt = 45,                            # Rotate 90 degrees
   family = "mono",                     # Use mono-spaced font
   col = "darkgray")                    # Set color to dark green

# Ad hoc text in margin
par(usr = c(0, 1, 0, 1))               # Set usr parameters to 0,1 space
text(x = 1.05, y = .5,                  # Place text just outside right border
   labels = "Ad hoc text in margin",    # Text to use
   xpd = TRUE,                          # Allow text outside of border
   font = 3,                            # Italic font
   cex = 1.25,                          # Font size to 1.25
   srt = 270,                           # Rotate string 270 degrees
   col = gray(.75))                     # Set color to gray .75
```

I know all this does look fun, but before we get too far along with the text commands, we've got to spend a little time thinking about fonts.

○ Setting up a Font

Fonts. Let me just say that if you really aren't all that into fonts this would be a good section to skip. You will go through the rest of your life in blissful ignorance and be a happier person for it. The unpleasant reality is that R doesn't deal with fonts very well.[1] It isn't entirely R's fault, as fonts

---

1. The extrafont and Cairo packages can help with this. See Appendix C.

are complicated by the idiosyncrasies of different output devices. Since you've come with me this far, we'll look at a few ways to make it a little less painful.

The Built-In Fonts

The first and easiest approach is to simply work with the basic built-in fonts and leave it at that. There are three built-in font mappings: a sans-serif font (the default), a serif font, and a mono-spaced font. Each of these, in turn, can be set as plain (the default), **bold**, *italic*, or ***bold italic***.

To choose among the different font faces, use the **family=** parameter, where the choices are **"mono"**, **"serif"**, or **"sans"**. Then, select normal, bold, and so on, with the **font=** parameter, using 1 for plain, **2 for bold**, *3 for italic*, or ***4 for bold italic***. Figure 14.2 shows these options at work. At the risk of getting a little ahead of ourselves here, you can select different **font=** values for the title (**font.main=**), for the axes (**font.axis=**), for the axis labels (**font.lab=**), and for the subtitles (**font.sub=**).

Figure 14.2 Font Families and Styles

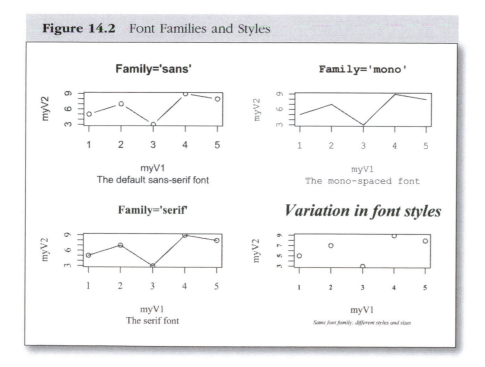

```
par(mfcol = c(2, 2))                  # Set 2x2 grid of plots
plot(myV1, myV2, type = "b",          # A simple plot
  main = "Family = 'sans'",           # A title
  sub = "The default sans-serif font", # A subtitle
  family = "sans")                    # Set font family to sans

plot(myV1, myV2, type = "o",          # A simple plot
  main = "Family = 'serif'",          # A title
  sub = "The serif font",             # A sub-title
  family = "serif")                   # Set font family to serif

plot(myV1, myV2, type = "l",          # A simple plot
  main = "Family = 'mono'",           # A title
  sub = "The mono-spaced font",       # A sub-title
  family = "mono")                    # Set font family to mono

plot(myV1, myV2, type = "p",          # A simple plot
  main = "Variation in font styles",  # A title
  sub = "Same font family, different styles and sizes",
  family = "serif",                   # Set font family to serif
  font.main = 4, cex.main = 1.75,     # Title in larger bold italic
  font.axis = 2, cex.axis = .75,      # Axis fonts small but bold
  font.sub = 3, cex.sub = .6,         # Subtitle fonts in italic & larger
  font.lab = 1, cex.lab = 1)          # Axis labels plain & default size
```

The final plot of Figure 14.2 shows the use of different font styles and sizes in a single plot. You cannot select different font families for these different elements within a single **plot()** command. If you want to go there, the easiest approach is to overlay these other elements in their own **title()** commands. You can see an example of this approach in Figure 14.5. In just a moment, we'll also look at getting into editing the Rdevga file to achieve that result.

Another quick approach to nab a few more font varieties is to use the PDF device as discussed in Chapter 13. While this adds a few nice fonts to the repertoire, you do have to be careful about using the same code to output to other devices with different font mappings. Usually in that case, R will just pretend to have no clue what you are talking about and will output everything in the default sans-serif font.

Device dependency, alas, is the reality of the current R font world. If you move beyond the default serif, mono, and sans fonts, you will have to deal with device dependency. That is, your plot will look different if you run it on different devices. This can even be a problem with the basic fonts inasmuch as the Mac, Linux, and Windows environments use slightly different fonts for their defaults.

The Font-Mapping Approach

Once you accept that your code is likely to be device dependent, you'll have a lot more options. In the Apple Mac world, using the Cairo device output can get you access to a plethora of installed fonts. The Windows world, as so often, isn't quite as straightforward.[2] But one reasonably easy way to get to the other available fonts is to temporarily map the built-in fonts to other fonts. You can see the current windows mappings with the **windowsFonts()** command. Here it is in action:

```
> windowsFonts()                        # Show windows font mappings
$serif
[1] "TT Times New Roman"

$sans
[1] "TT Arial"

$mono
[1] "TT Courier New"
```

The trick is that you can also use this command to remap any of these fonts. In Figure 14.3, we'll switch the sans-serif font to the much maligned Comic Sans font and the serif font to the preposterous Blackadder ITC font.

```
par(mfcol = c(2, 1))                    # Set up 2 plots vertically
windowsFonts(                           # Reassign the sans font
```

---

2. The Cairo package can add this functionality to Windows computers. See Appendix C.

```
   sans = "TT Comic Sans MS")          #    to Comic Sans
plot(myV1, myV2, type = "b",           # A simple plot
   main = "Some Comic Sans Action!",   # A Title
   family = "sans")                    # Font family for plot

windowsFonts(                          # Reassign the serif font
   serif = "TT Blackadder ITC")        #    to Blackadder
plot(myV1, myV2, type = "b",           # A simple plot
   main =
      "Please don't use this font!",   # A title for the plot
   family = "serif")                   # Font family for plot

windowsFonts(sans = "TT Arial")        # Reset these fonts back to defaults
windowsFonts(serif = "TT Times New Roman")
```

Figure 14.3   Changing Fonts With `windowsFonts()`

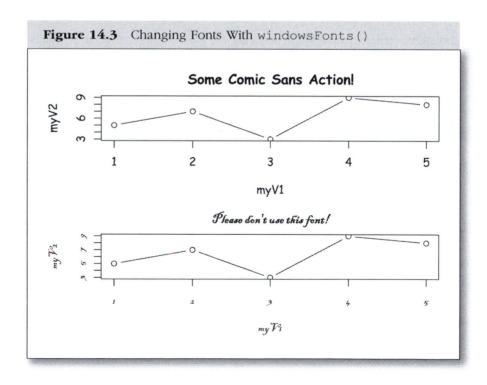

The Rdevga Approach to Font Mapping

Finally, a somewhat ugly work-around for Windows is that you can add font families into R's DNA by editing the Rdevga file.[3] Find the Rdevga file in R's "etc" directory, and then following the simple pattern you'll see there, add your desired font family to the end of the list. Restart R. You access these fonts (here's, the ugly part) by using one of the **font=** options and referencing the line number (not counting the blank lines and comments). So not only is this not reproducible code for other people's computers; it cannot even be understood without heavy commenting or reference to the specific custom Rdevga file. The one bit of compensation for this approach is that you can mix fonts in a single **plot()** statement, as in Figure 14.4.[4]

Figure 14.4 The Rdevga Method Under Windows

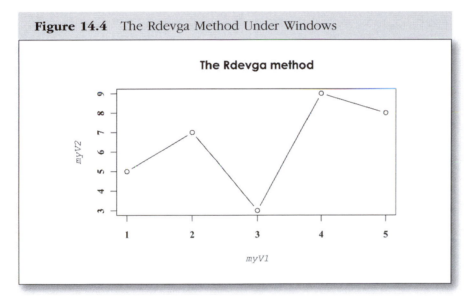

Note: Directly addressing the Rdevga font table allows you to add additional fonts and to mix fonts in a single **plot()** statement.

---

3. Remember to make a backup copy first, and also note my mention of the extra-font package and the Cairo package as other approaches to this issue.

4. If you have a set of signature fonts that you use all the time, you could set up variables to map those font line numbers, for example, **Century.Gothic. Bold = 15**. Then, your code could read something sensible like **font.main = Century.Gothic.Bold**. That won't solve the reproducibility issue, but at least it makes the code more interpretable.

```
plot(myV1, myV2, type = "b",          # A simple plot
   main = "The Rdevga method",         # A Title
   font.main = 15,                     # This should be Century Gothic bold
   font.lab = 12,                      # This should be Courier italic
   font.axis = 7)                      # This should be Times bold
```

For this example, I have added a line to the Rdevga file setting up Century Gothic bold as a font. That line is the 15th line in the Rdevga file (not including blank lines and comments), so we reference it as number 15. Courier italic and Times bold were already in the Rdevga file on lines 12 and 7, respectively.

Font Size and Rotation

Once you have the font families and styles you are looking for, you can adjust the size, color, and rotation of fonts. The font size is set with the **cex=** option. When the **cex** setting is used in a **plot()** statement, it includes an indicator for the element that it applies to, as in the code for Figure 14.1. The size of the font for the main title will be set with **cex.main=**, the subtitle with **cex.sub=**, and so on.

The **cex=** setting sets the size of fonts (and some other objects) relative to the default size for the device or the size you set when you set up the device. If, for example, you are outputting a PNG file and set the font size to 14pt, then the **cex=** setting will be relative to that 14pt font size: 0.5 will be 7pt, 1.5 will be 21pt, 2 will be 28pt, and so on.

Text color is set with the **col=** option. We'll look at that in much more detail in Chapter 15. For now, it will suffice to work with a few color names that are enclosed in quotation marks. (There are actually 657 of these, the complete list of which can be displayed with the **colors()** command.)

Text can be rotated in two different ways. Text strings are normally rotated with the string rotation option, **srt=**. The argument for this is a number between 0 and 360, representing the degrees of counterclockwise rotation. Rotation of the axis-label text works with the **las=** option. **las** takes on a value between 0 and 3. **las = 0** puts the labels parallel to the axis (the default), **las = 1** forces the labels to be horizontal, **las = 2** puts the labels perpendicular to the axis, and **las = 3** makes the labels vertical.

Individual letters can sometimes be rotated with the **crt=** option. As with string rotation (**srt=**), this is measured in degrees of rotation. This setting is a little more context specific. It works with some devices but not others, and the R help warns that it may not work in increments of other than 90 degrees.

You can see variations in font size, color, and rotation at work in Figure 14.1, as well as in many of the other plots in this chapter.

Now that we have a handle on some of the intricacies of fonts, we can really turn to putting words down on the page. We'll start with the more formal text categories—titles, legends, and axes—and then will look at placing ad hoc text elements.

TITLES AND SUBTITLES

Titles and subtitles can be either added from within the **plot()** command or called separately with the **title()** function. It's pretty simple. Use **main = "my Title"** for the title at the top of the plot and **sub = "my Subtitle"** for the subtitle at the bottom of the plot. You can also use a character variable instead of putting the text in quotation marks.

```
myTitle = "My Nice Title"              # Create a txt variable with title
plot(myX, myY, main = myTitle)         # Plot using txt variable title
```

As discussed in the section on fonts, choose between normal, bold, italic, and bold italic font styles with **font.main=** and **font.sub=**. The values 1, 2, 3, and 4 select among those options, respectively. The font sizes are controlled with **cex.main=** and **cex.sub=**. The **cex=** option is relative to the default size. So 1 is the default size, 0.5 is half the default size, and 2 is twice the default size, and so on. **adj=** places the title at the left (0), center (.5), or right (1) of the plot. **adj=** cannot distinguish between titles, subtitles, and labels. If you want to have different values for those different elements, you'll need to use separate **title()** commands, as shown in Figure 14.5.

Figure 14.5 Titles and Subtitles

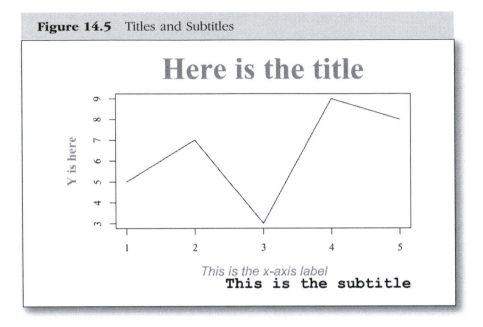

```
plot(myV1, myV2, type = "l",          # A simple plot
    main = "Here is the title",        # The main title
    family = "serif",                  # Use serif family font
    font.main = 2,                     # Set title font to bold
    cex.main = 3,                      # Set title font size to double
    col.main = "darkgray",             # Set title to dark gray
    xlab = NA, ylab = NA)              # Supress axis labels
title(                                 # Put subtitle on plot
    sub = "This is the subtitle",      # A subtitle
    adj = 1,                           # Put it on right side
    family = "mono",                   # Use mono-spaced font
    font.sub = 2,                      # Use bold for subtitle
    cex.sub = 1.5,                     # Subtitle font size = 1.5
    col.sub = "black")                 # Subtitle color

title(                                 # Put X-axis label on plot
    xlab = "This is the x-axis label", # X-axis label text
    family = "sans",                   # Use sans-serif font
    font.lab = 3,                      # Use italic for x axis label
    cex.lab = 1.25,                    # X-axis label font size
    col.lab = "darkgray")              # X-axis label color
```

```
title(                            # Put Y-axis label on plot
    ylab = "y is here",           # Y-axis label text
    family = "serif",             # Use serif font
    font.lab = 2,                 # Use bold for y axis label
    cex.lab = 1.25,               # Y-axis font size = 1.25
    col.lab = "darkgray",         # Y-axis label color
    las = 2)
```

While **main=** and **sub=** are pretty straightforward, you do not have to live with the constraints of the title and subtitle processes. As we discussed at the beginning of the chapter, you can also just use the **text()** command to place your title or subtitle text with even more flexibility.

There is also an **mtext()** command, which can also be used for placing text in the margins. **mtext()** places text by identifying the side of the plot and the number of lines into the margin. I'm not a big fan of **mtext()**, since it doesn't allow for rotation and the same thing can be accomplished with the regular **text()** command by using relative coordinates and allowing text to be written outside the plot area. Set **par(usr = c(0, 1, 0, 1))** and then use the **xpd = TRUE** option in the **text()** command. See Figure 14.1 for an example of this (the text in the right-side margin).

CREATING A LEGEND

Many plots will require a legend to be clear. You could do this entirely with shape and text elements, but that would be exceedingly tedious. Fortunately, R is set up to do this relatively painlessly while giving you reasonable control over the details.

The **legend()** command is issued after the plot is created. It has three essential arguments. The first locates your legend with the shorthand **"top"**, **"bottom"**, **"topleft"**, **"topright"**, **"bottomleft"**, **"bottomright"**, and **"center"** options. The second is the fill colors, line types, or symbol styles to match the plot elements (e.g., **fill = c("red", "blue")**, **lty = c(1, 2)**, or **pch = c(16, 22)**). If you use **fill=**, R creates little boxes filled with the appropriate colors. If you use **lty=**, you'll get short samples of the specified types of lines. If you use **pch=**, you will get copies of the specified symbols (the **pt.cex=** option changes the size of the point symbols). The third argument is the text you want for each element (**legend = c("myVar1", "myVar2")**). As you can see in the following examples, the fill and text or line-type arguments are vectors with one value for each element you wish to identify in your plot.

As you will have no doubt already come to expect, there are many additional parameters of control for a legend. **help(legend)** will get you the full list. Here are a few of the most useful.

If you place your legend with one of the keywords (**"top"**, **"bottom"**, **"topleft"**, **"topright"**, **"bottomleft"**, **"bottomright"**, or **"center"**), you can specify some distance from the edge of the plot region with the **inset=** option. The inset distance is based on a percentage of the plot region, so **inset =.05** will place the legend with 5% of the plot region as a margin between the legend box and the edge of the plot (see Legend 1 in Figure 14.6).

While the legend box can be automatically created with just one point, you can also provide two points to define the upper-left and lower-right corners of the legend box using **x=** and **y=**. If, for example, your *x*-axis values are years from 1900 to 2000, and your *y*-axis goes from 0 to 100, then **x = c(1900, 1950)**, **y = c(20, 0)** would put a legend box starting in the lower-left-hand corner and covering half the width of the plot. You can use **locator()** to help figure out the right coordinates for positioning your legend.

Sometimes it is easier to think about the coordinates relative to the plot area. This can be a helpful approach when you are mass-producing plots with different coordinate systems. I also find this approach a little easier for placing a legend box at consistent distances from the top and side borders. You place a legend relative to the plot area by changing the **usr=** parameter, as discussed in Chapter 13, to the default **c(0, 1, 0, 1)** coordinate system: **par(usr = c(0, 1, 0, 1))**.

xjust= and **yjust=** determine where the legend box is placed relative to a set of single **x=**, **y=** coordinates. For **xjust=**, 0 is left justified, 1 is right justified, and 0.5 is centered. For **yjust=**, 0 is bottom justified, 1 is top justified, and 0.5 is centered.

box.lty= allows you to change the style for the box around the legend. **box.lwd=** and **box.col=** allow changing the width and color of the box border (see Legend 3 in Figure 14.6). **bg=** changes the color of the background in the legend box. **bty="n"** will suppress the box altogether.

title= adds a title to your legend box. As usual, you can use **cex=** to change the size of the text. On the other hand, you cannot change the title font style or size independently of the other text in the legend box. This can be an irritation. A work-around is to do the same legend twice: once with the title set the way you want it and once with the other elements set their way. You'll need to do the title first and set the undesired elements to the background color in order to leave them out. You can see an example of this approach in Legend 3 in Figure 14.6. Getting too adventuresome in this regard can lead to troubles with R's fitting the legend box correctly. You can either leave the legend box off or turn it off and replace it with a custom-fitted box using the **rect()** command.

If you are working with a lot of elements in the legend, you might want to use the **ncol=** argument to set the legend up with multiple columns. The **horiz = T** option can be used to set the elements up horizontally rather than vertically (see Legend 2 in Figure 14.6).

When you use combinations of lines and symbols for your plot elements, use the **merge = TRUE** option to tell R to combine points and line types in the legend (see Legend 4 in Figure 14.6).

Figure 14.6   Some Legend Options

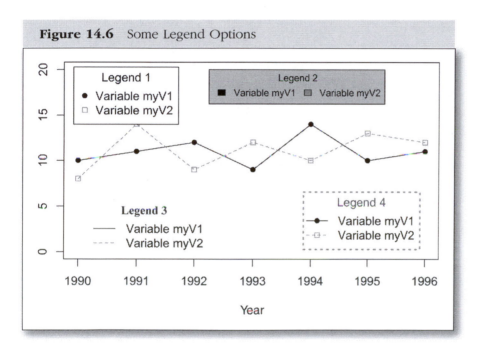

```
# Set up some data
year = 1990:1996                    # Create a series of years
myV1 = c(10, 11, 12, 9, 14, 10, 11)  # Create some values for myV1
myV2 = c(8, 14, 9, 12, 10, 13, 12)   # Create some values for myV2

# Create a simple plot
plot(year, myV1,                    # Plot myV1 against year
    ylim = c(0, 20),                # Set y axis scale
    ylab = NA,                      # Turn off y axis label
```

```
    type = "o",                        # Set as line plot with points
    lty = 1,                           # Solid line
    pch = 16)                          # Point style

points(year, myV2,                     # Add myV2 to plot
    type = "o",                        # Set type as line with points
    col = "darkgray",                  # Set color to red
    lty = 2,                           # Dashed line
    pch = 22)                          # Use square box for point style

# Legend 1
legend("topleft",                      # Location of legend
    inset = .025,                      # Distance from edge of plot region
    legend = c("Variable myV1",        # Legend Text
      "Variable myV2"),
    col = c("black", "darkgray"),      # Legend Element Colors
    pch = c(16, 22),                   # Legend Element Styles
    title = "Legend 1")                # Legend title

# Legend 2
legend(x = 1992.25, y = 20,            # Location of legend on x & y scale
    legend = c("Variable myV1",        # Legend Text
      "Variable myV2"),
    cex = .8,                          # Text size set to .8
    fill = c("black", "darkgray"),     # Legend Element Colors
    title = "Legend 2",                # Legend Title
    horiz = T,                         # Set legend horizontally
    bg = "light gray")                 # Set color for legend background

# Set up percentage coordinates system for legend
my.usr = par("usr")                    # Save current coordinate units
par(usr = c(0, 1, 0, 1))               # Set coordinate space to 0,1 scales

# Legend 3 Bold Title
par(font = 2, family = "serif")        # Set bold serif font
legend(x = .05, y = .3,                # Legend location in percent units
    yjust = 1,                         # Put legend below y value
```

```
  legend = c("Variable myV1",        # Legend Text
    "Variable myV2"),
  lty = c(1, 2),                      # line types for legend elements
  col = c("black", "darkgray"),       # Legend Element Colors
  title = "Legend 3",                 # Legend title
  title.col = gray(.2),               # Legend title color
  text.col = "white",                 # Set text color to be invisible
  bty = "n")                          # No box around legend

par(font = 1, family = "sans")        # Return default font to normal sans

# Legend 3
legend(x = .05, y = .3,               # Legend location in percent units
  yjust = 1,                          # Put legend below y value
  legend = c("Variable myV1",         # Legend Text
    "Variable myV2"),
  lty = c(1, 2),                      # line types for legend elements
  col = c("black", "darkgray"),       # Legend Element Colors
  title = NA,                         # Legend title turned off
  bty = "n")                          # No box around legend

# Legend 4
legend(x = .95, y = .05,              # Legend location in percent units
  xjust = 1,                          # Left justify legend box
  yjust = 0,                          # Bottom justify legend box
  legend = c("Variable myV1",         # Legend Text
    "Variable myV2"),
  lty = c(1, 2),                      # Line type for legend elements
  col = c("black", "darkgray"),       # Legend Element Colors
  pch = c(16, 22),                    # Symbol styles for legend elements
  merge = TRUE,                       # Merge line/symbol legend elements
  title = "Legend 4",                 # Legend Title
  title.col = gray(.4),               # Legend title color
  box.lty = 9,                        # Legend box line type
  box.lwd = 2,                        # Legend box line width
  box.col = "darkgray")               # Legend box color
```

If you want to place your legend outside the plot area, you'll need to use the **xpd = TRUE** option. This can be set either in a **par()** statement or just within the **legend()** function. In either case, it tells R that it is okay to draw things outside the plot area. Be sure that you set the margins large enough to hold the legend. Place the legend outside the plot area by simply extrapolating the desired coordinates from the plot scale. Figure 14.7 provides a couple of examples.

Figure 14.7   Legends Outside the Box

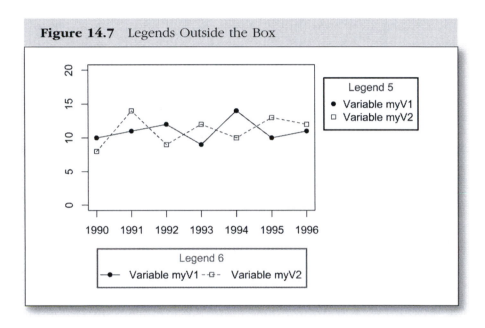

```
year = 1990:1996                    # Create a series of years
myV1 = c(10, 11, 12, 9, 14, 10, 11) # Create some values for myV1
myV2 = c(8, 14, 9, 12, 10, 13, 12)  # Create some values for myV2

# Create a simple plot

par(mai = c(1.5, 1, .25, 2))        # Right margin space for legend

plot(year, myV1,                    # Plot myV1 against year
    ylim = c(0, 20),                # Set y axis scale
    ylab = NA,                      # Turn off y axis label
```

```
   type = "o",                        # Set as line plot with points
   lty = 1,                           # Solid line
   pch = 16)                          # Point style
points(year, myV2,                    # Add myV2 to plot
   type = "o",                        # Set type as line with points
   col = gray(.2),                    # Set color
   lty = 2,                           # Dashed line
   pch = 22)                          # Use square box for point style

# Legend outside the plot on right

legend(x = 1996.5, y = 15,            # Location of legend
   xpd = TRUE,                        # Allow drawing outside plot area
   xjust = 0,                         # Left justify legend box on x
   yjust = .5,                        # Center legend box on y
   legend = c("Variable myV1",        # Legend Text
     "Variable myV2"),
   col = c("black", gray(.2)),        # Legend Element Colors
   pch = c(16, 22),                   # Legend Element Styles
   title = "Legend 5",                # Legend Title
   title.col = gray(.2),              # Legend title color
   box.lty = 1,                       # Legend box line type
   box.lwd = 2)                       # Legend box line width

# Legend outside the plot on bottom
legend(x = 1993, y = -6.5,            # Location of legend
   xpd = TRUE,                        # Allow drawing outside plot area
   xjust = .5,                        # Center legend box on x
   yjust = 1,                         # Top justify legend box on y
   horiz = TRUE,                      # Set legend horizontally
   legend = c("Variable myV1",        # Legend Text
     "Variable myV2"),
   lty = c(1, 2),                     # Line type for legend elements
   col = c("black", gray(.2)),        # Legend Element Colors
   pch = c(16, 22),                   # Symbol styles for legend elements
   merge = TRUE,                      # Merge line & symbol for legend
```

```
title = "Legend 6",                  # Legend Title
title.col = gray(.4),                # Legend title color
box.lty = 1,                         # Legend box line type
box.lwd = 2,                         # Legend box line width
box.col = gray(.4))                  # Legend box color
```

○ SIMPLE AXES AND AXIS LABELS

As with titles and subtitles, simple axis labels can be set up from within the main **plot()** command. The **xlab = "my X axis label"** and **ylab = "my Y axis label"** options set up the axis labels. The default, if these are not included, is to just use the variable names. **cex.lab=**, **font.lab=**, and **col.lab=** work just as with the titles to set font size, style, and color for the axis labels.

xlim= and **ylim=** are used to set the range for the *x*- and *y*-axes. If you don't specify these values, R will make its own choices, which usually looks something like a range from the smallest to the largest value you have provided. **xlim=** and **ylim=** both need a vector of two values: the minimum and the maximum. If, for example, you want the *x*-axis to run from 0 to 100, then use **xlim = c(0, 100)**.

You can also set up log scale axes from within the **plot()** command. **log = "x"** makes the *x*-axis logarithmic; **log = "y"**, the *y*-axis; and **log = "xy"**, both. If you need help with this, you'll find it under **help(plot.default)**.

Working on the axes from within the **plot()** command constrains you to keep the formatting of the *x* and *y* labels the same. If you want to make them different or break out in other creative ways, you'll have to set them up outside the **plot()** command. You can turn off the default axis labels with **xlab = NA** or **ylab = NA**. If the axis labels are the only issue, those can be handled with the **title()** command, as shown in Figure 14.5.

If your aspirations for axis aesthetics are more adventuresome, you'll need to move to the real axis process, which builds the axes independently as an add-on outside the **plot()** command.

BUILDING MORE COMPLEX AXES

If more fine-grained control of the axes is required, they will need to be built after the plot is set up. The first step for this is to turn off the default axes with the **xaxt = "n"** and/or **yaxt = "n"** options in the **plot()** function. You can turn both axes off with the **axes = FALSE** option, although for some reason this also turns off the box around the plot area.

The main axis-building command is **axis()**. The three critical options are **side=**, **at=**, and **labels=**. The **side=** option tells R on which side of the plot to put the axis: 1 is for the *x*-axis, 2 is for the *y* axis, 3 goes on top, and 4 goes on the right. **at=** is a vector of values where the tick marks should go, and **labels=** is the vector of text used to label the tick marks.

Usually, you'll have a matched set of vectors, one holding the values for positioning tick marks and the other an equal number of character variables to label those tick marks. If your tick mark labels are the same as the values, then you don't need to do anything beyond the **at=** option. R will automatically add the values corresponding with the tick marks.

Figure 14.8 is an example with several modifications, including adding a custom numeric axis at the bottom and using the built-in **LETTERS** vector to put an alphabetical axis on top. The bottom *x*-axis includes minor tick marks, which we'll cover in just a moment.

```
myV1 = c(1, 3, 4, 7, 9)              # Set up some x values
myV2 = c(4, 6, 5, 3, 7)              # Set up some y values

plot(myV1, myV2,                     # Plot myV1 and myV2
   xaxt = "n", yaxt = "n",           # Supress axes
   xlim = c(0, 10))                  # Set x range

axis(side = 1,                       # X axis
   at = c(seq(0, 10, by = 2)))       # tick marks every 2

axis(side = 1,                       # X axis minor tick marks
   at = c(seq(1, 9, by = 2)),        # Set on odd numbers
```

```
   labels = NA,               # No labels for minor tick marks
   tcl = -.25)                # Shorten minor tick marks

axis(side = 3,                # Put another axis on top
   at = c(0:10),              # Ticks at 0-10
   labels = LETTERS[1:11])    # Use alphabet labels

axis(side = 2,                # Add Y axis
   at = c(3:7),               # Tick marks from 3-7 by 1
   las = 1,                   # Rotate labels to perpendicular
   lwd = 0,                   # Turn off axis line
   lwd.ticks = 2,             # Set tick width to 2
   col.ticks = gray(.3))      # Set tick color
```

Figure 14.8   Custom Axes

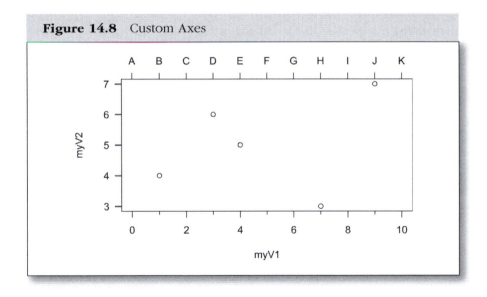

The location of the axis, itself, can be adjusted in two ways: (1) by the number of lines set into the plot or the plot margin or (2) by using the scale values from the plot itself for the positioning. The **line=** option sets the number of lines into the margin (positive values) or into the plot area (negative values) for drawing the axis. The **pos=** option does the same thing but uses the value scale from the plot. With **pos=**, the effect of negative and positive values depend on the plot scale. If the plot starts at the origin **(0,0)**, then negative values will move into the margin. But if, for example, the plot starts at 50 (e.g., **xlim = c(50, 100))**, then **pos = 45** will put the *y*-axis into the left margin by five units.

More complicated scales can be built up by overlaying multiple-axes commands. Figure 14.9 shows this for the *y*-axis (adding minor tick marks) and also shows some of the other positioning and text effects.

Figure 14.9 More Axis Effects

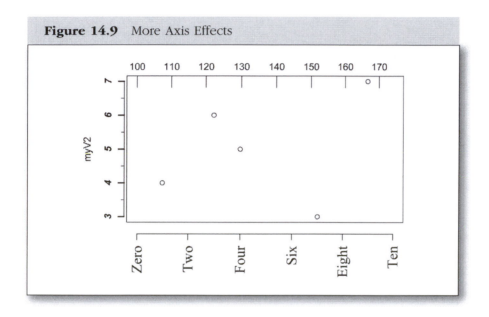

```
plot(myV1, myV2,                      # Plot myV1 and myV2
    xaxt = "n", yaxt="n",             # Suppress axes
    xlim = c(0, 10),                  # Set x range
    xlab = NA)                        # Turn off X label

axis(side = 1,                        # Set up new X axis
    at = c(seq(0, 10, by = 2)),       # Tick marks trom 0-10 by 2
    labels = c("Zero", "Two", "Four", # Labels for tick marks
               "Six", "Eight", "Ten"),
```

```
   family = "serif",                    # Set font
   cex.axis = 1.5,                      # Increase font size by 50%
   las = 2,                             # Make labels perpendicular to axis
   line = 1)                            # Put axis 1 line into the margin

axis(side = 2,                          # Set up new Y axis
   at = c(3:7),                         # Set tick marks from 3-7 by 1
   font = 4,                            # Set font to bold italic
   lwd.ticks = 2,                       # Set major tick line width at 2
   pos = -.5)                           # Set axis at -.5 on X scale

axis(side = 2,                          # Overlay minor tick marks on Y axis
   at = c(3.5:6.5),                     # Put them on the .5 marks
   labels = NA,                         # No labels
   tcl = -.25,                          # Set length of tick marks
   pos = -.5)                           # Set position of axis

axis(side = 3,                          # Add another axis on top of plot
   at = c(seq(0, 10, by = 1.35)),       # Set another scale
   labels = c(seq(100, 170, by = 10)),  # Add labels
   padj = 1,                            # Adjust labels downward
   tcl = 1)                             # Put long tick marks into plot area
```

You may notice that by default the axes don't meet at the (0,0) origin. This is R's way of trying to pretty things up with about 4% overage at each end of the axis. If you need the axes to start exactly at 0 (or the limits you specify with the **xlim=** and **ylim=** options), use the **xaxs="i"** and/or **yaxs="i"** options.

Tick Marks

Tick marks are a central element of any axis scheme. R provides complete control over tick marks, but it takes a little bit of preplanning. The default tick marks are drawn at the same places as the placement of the axis labels, indicated with the **at=** option. The width, length, and color of those tick marks can be controlled with **tcl=** for the tick length, **lwd=** for the tick mark width, and **col.tick=** for the tick color.

tcl= sets the tick length. Positive **tcl=** values put tick marks into the plot area, while negative values put them outside the plot area. Use **lwd. ticks=** to adjust the line width of the tick marks and just **lwd=** to adjust the width of the axis line itself. If you set **lwd = 0** or **lwd.tick = 0**, R will suppress the printing of the axis line or the tick marks, respectively. **col.tick=** uses all the standard color options, which we'll consider in greater length in Chapter 15.

Figure 14.10 Major and Minor Tick Marks

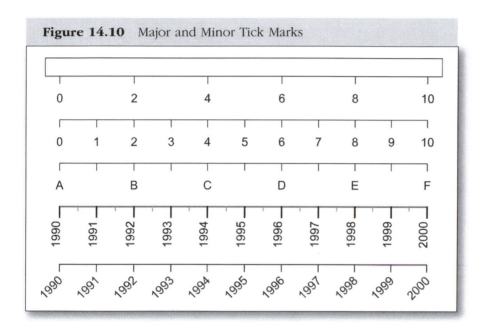

As we've seen in these examples, minor tick marks take a little more work.[5] Minor tick marks use all the same control options and are added by overlaying a second **axis()** command and suppressing its labels (**labels = NA**). Figure 14.10 shows all these approaches in action.

```
par(mai = c(3.5, .25, .25, .25))        # Set margin sizes in inches

plot(myV1, myV2, type = "n",            # Setup w/no points & default x axis
     xlab = NA,                         # Turn off x axis label
     ylab = NA,                         # Turn off y axis label
```

5. Along with many other nice things, the Hmisc package has a function for adding minor tick marks (**minor.tick()**).

```
    yaxt = "n",                      # Turn off y axis
    xlim = c(0, 10))                 # Set x axis range

axis(side = 1,                       # New x axis
    at = c(0:10),                    # Ticks at 0-10
    line = 3)                        # Move axis down to 3rd line

axis(side = 1,                       # New x axis
    at = c(seq(0, 10, by = 2)),      # Major ticks at 0-10 by 2
    labels = LETTERS[1:6],           # A-F as labels
    line = 6)                        # Put axis on 6th line

axis(side = 1,                       # New x axis
    at = c(seq(1, 10, by = 2)),      # Minor ticks at 1-10 by 2
    labels = NA,                     # Turn off labels for minor ticks
    line = 6)                        # Overlay axis on 6th line

axis(side = 1,                       # New x axis
    at = c(0:10),                    # Major ticks at 0-10
    labels = c(1990:2000),           # Use years for labels
    las = 2,                         # Rotate labels to be perpendicular
    col = gray(.5),                  # Set main axis line to med gray
    tcl = -.75,                      # Major tick length .75 below line
    col.tick = "black",              # Make major ticks black
    lwd = 2,                         # Make major ticks longer
    line = 9)                        # Put axis on 9th line below plot

axis(side = 1,                       # Add overlay axis for minor ticks
    at = c(seq(.5, 10, by = 1)),     # Minor ticks at every .5
    labels = NA,                     # No labels for minor ticks
    tcl = -.3,                       # Minor ticks length .3 below line
    lwd = 0,                         # No main axis line for overlay
    lwd.ticks = 1.25,                # Set minor tick width to 1.25
    col.tick = "darkgray",           # Color for minor tick marks
    line = 9)                        # Overlay axis on 9th line
```

```
axis(side = 1,                              # New x axis
   at = c(0:10),                            # Major ticks at 0 - 10
   labels = NA,                             # Turn off labels
   tcl = -.5,                               # Major tick length .5 below line
   lwd = 1.25,                              # Make major ticks thicker
   line = 13)                               # Put axis on 13th line

text(x = seq(0.3, 10.3, 1),                 # x values for axis labels
   y = -46,                                 # y value for axis labels
   xpd = TRUE,                              # Allow writing outside plot area
   labels = as.character(c(1990:2000)),     # Years as text labels
   pos = 2,                                 # Left align labels
   srt = 45)                                # Rotate strings 45 degrees
```

Axis labels cannot be rotated with the string rotate option (**srt=**), so the bottom axis in Figure 14.10 combines an **axis()** command to set up the tick marks and then a **text()** command to place the year labels. In this case, the years are just string variables that increment by 1. When we need to have an axis that is keyed to a date or time variable (see Chapter 9), we need to be a little more careful.

Axes With Dates or Times

Dates, as you may have anticipated, make things a bit trickier. The thing about dates in axes is that they have to be spaced according to the time dimension rather than a simple order dimension. And we need to worry about all those formatting options for how dates are displayed. Fortunately, the discussion of dates in Chapter 9 gets us most of what we need to manage this.

The key here is telling R that you are working with dates and passing the necessary information about the date formats. Once R knows that dates are in the mix, it will make some pretty good guesses about setting things up. Figure 14.11 is a serviceable example of R's proficiency in this area.

Figure 14.11   A Simple Date Variable Plot

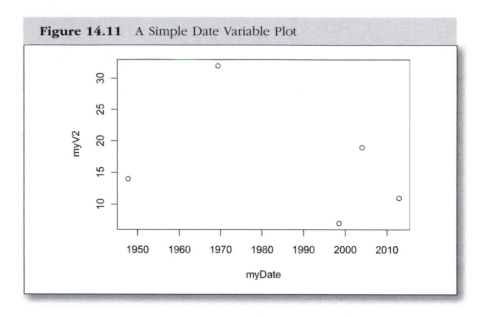

```
dFormat = "%m/%d/%Y"                     # Set up a date format
myDate = as.Date(c("10/12/1947",         # Set up a date variable
   "5/14/1969", "7/2/1998", "1/3/2004",  #   with several dates
   "11/24/2012"), dFormat)               #   using the format above
myV2 = c(14, 32, 7, 19, 11)              # Another simple variable

plot(myDate, myV2)                       # Basic plot with defaults
```

If, as is often the case, "pretty good" isn't good enough, you'll need to set up a custom axis. In Figure 14.12, we turn off the default axis, then provide a new axis based on a sequence of dates. The relevant function is now either **axis.Date()** or **axis.POSIXct()**, depending on which date format you are using (see Chapter 9). In Figure 14.12, I have used standard American dates (month/day/year) so have to provide the format information. If you are using the default (year/month/day), you can just provide the dates alone. Just for the practice, we'll also add some minor tick marks, a vertical line, and some text that is placed using the time scale of the x-axis. Here, the labels are simply years. To generate other sequences, return to the discussion at the beginning of Chapter 9.

Figure 14.12 A Customized Time Axis

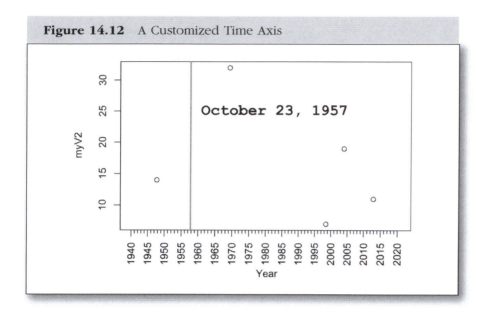

```
plot(myDate, myV2,                      # Customized plot
  xlim =                                # Set X axis range
    c(as.Date("1/1/1940", dFormat),     # Starting date
    as.Date("12/31/2020", dFormat)),    # Ending date
  xaxt = "n",                           # Turn off X axis
  xlab = "Year")                        # Set X axis label

axis.Date(side = 1,                     # Set up new X axis w/ major tick marks
  at = seq.Date(                        # Create a sequence of dates
    as.Date("1/1/1940", dFormat),       # Starting point for sequence
    as.Date("12/31/2020", dFormat),     # Ending point for sequence
    by = "5 years"),                    # Increment value for sequence
  labels = seq(1940, 2020, by = 5),     # Labels for major tick marks
  las = 2)                              # Rotate labels perpendicular

axis.Date(side = 1,                     # Overlay X axis w/ minor tick marks
  at = seq.Date(                        # Create a sequence of dates
    as.Date("1/1/1940", dFormat),       # Starting point for sequence
    as.Date("12/31/2020", dFormat),     # Ending point for sequence
```

```
    by = "year"),               # Increment value for sequence
  labels = NA,                  # Turn off labels
  tcl = -.25)                   # Set length at .25 below axis

abline(                         # Add a line
  v = as.Date("10/23/1957", dFormat), # Vertical placement on 10/23/1957
  col = "darkgray",             # Set color
  lwd = 2)                      # Line width at 2

text(x = as.Date("1/1/1959", dFormat), # Label for the line - X coordinate
  y = 25,                       # Y coordinate
  pos = 4,                      # Put text to right of coordinates
  label = "October 23, 1957",   # Text for label
  cex = 1.5,                    # Set font size 50% bigger
  family = "mono",              # Set font style
  font = 2)                     # Bold font
```

Really, not so bad, was it?

Before leaving this topic, here is a quick review of some of the most useful axis options that can work within the **par()**, **plot()**, or **axis()** commands. In each case, I have included the default value for the option in parentheses at the end.

cex.axis= *Font size for axis notations:* This is set relative to the default font size. Note that you can use the normal font control parameters, such as **crt=** for font rotation. (1)

cex.lab= *Font size for the axis labels:* Again, this is set relative to the default font size. (1)

col.axis= *Axis color:* See the discussion on setting colors in Chapter 15. (black)

col.lab= *Axis labels color* (black)

las= *The orientation of the labels relative to the axis:* 0—parallel to axis, 1—horizontal, 2—perpendicular to axis, and 3—vertical (0)

AD HOC TEXT

Finally, we set all constraint aside and move to the techniques for placing text just anywhere we want. The mostly straightforward key to this process is the **text()** command. This approach is so useful that I've already snuck it in several places, including Figures 5.4, 13.1, 13.3, 13.4, and 14.1. If you want to look ahead for additional examples, you can skip to Figure 15.2, 15.8, 15.9, 15.13, or 15.14.

The primary key for the **text()** command is simply providing R with the coordinates where you want the text placed. As demonstrated in Figure 5.4, these coordinates can come directly from your data. The actual text to place on the plot is provided by the **labels=** argument. Size (**cex=**), color (**col=**), rotation (**srt=**), and font style (**family=** and **font=**) are controlled in the same manner as in the discussion of fonts at the beginning of this chapter. These options can also be set to vectors so that each label in a set is controlled independently.

Two additional **text()** options that can be helpful in placing text are **adj=** and **pos=**. **adj=** indicates where the text should be placed relative to the given x, y coordinates. It uses a vector of two values, the first for the horizontal (x) dimension and the second for the vertical (y) dimension. The values for **adj=** should be between 0 and 1, where 0 puts the text to the right of or above the coordinates, 1 puts it to the left or below (which, I'll admit, seems backward to me), and 0.5 centers the text.

pos= is a simplified version of **adj=**. As shown in Figure 14.13, it can only take values of 1, 2, 3, or 4, indicating that the text should be below, to the left of, above, or to the right of the given x, y coordinates, respectively. The use of **pos=** overrides any values of **adj=**.

The **labels=** argument provides the text to actually place on the plot. It can be either a character variable (or a vector of character variables) or an expression for incorporating equations and mathematical symbols. To do an expression, you have to encase it in the **expression()** function and then use the plotmath facility to access the necessary symbol and layout elements. You can see how to access these symbols, which allow the building of quite extensive equations, from **help(plotmath)**.[6] Combining plotmath and variable values requires the use of the **bquote()** function.

---

6. If you use **demo(plotmath)**, R will generate a series of plots showing the different equation elements in use. Use the enter key to page through the successive plots.

Figure 14.13   The Ad Hoc Placement of Text

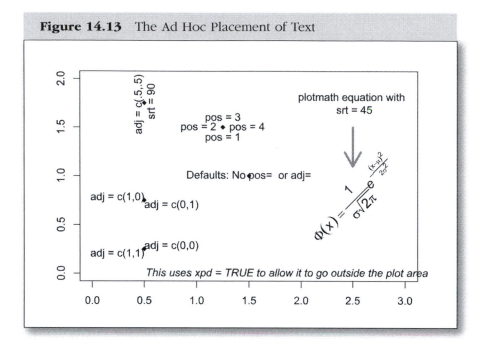

The simple instruction for doing this is to build your expression using plotmath and then encase any variables that you want evaluated within parentheses with a preceding period: **.(myVariable)**.[7] The use of plotmath and **bquote()** is also demonstrated in Figure 15.9.

If you need your text to extend beyond the internal plot boundaries, just set the **xpd=** option to **TRUE**.

```
plot(x = 1.25, y = 1.5,          # Start plot with first point
    xlim = c(0, 3),              # Set x range of plot
    ylim = c(0, 2),              # Set y range of plot
    pch = 18,                    # Diamond shaped plotting symbol
```

---

7. The more complex and more accurate explanation is that **bquote()** manipulates the environment in which an expression is evaluated.

```r
  xlab = NA,                          # Turn off x axis label
  ylab = NA)                          # Turn off y axis label

points(1.5, 1, pch = 18)             # Add diamond-shaped point
text(1.5, 1,                          # Add text at same position
  labels = "Defaults: No pos= or adj=")

# Using the adj= option
points(.5, .25, pch = 18)            Add diamond-shaped point
text(.5, .25,                         # Add text at same point
  labels = "adj = c(1, 1)",           # Text to add
  adj = c(1, 1))                      # Adjust position to lower left

text(.5, .25,                         # Add more text at same point
  labels = "adj = c(0, 0)",           # Text to add
  adj = c(0, 0))                      # Adjust position to upper right

points(.5, .75, pch = 18)            # Add diamond-shaped point
text(.5, .75,                         # Add text at same point
  labels = "adj = c(1, 0)",           # Text to add
  adj = c(1, 0))                      # Adjust position to lower right

text(.5, .75,                         # Add text at same point
  labels = "adj = c(0, 1)",           # Text to add
  adj = c(0, 1))                      # Adjust position to upper left

points(.5, 1.75, pch = 18)           # Add diamond-shaped point
text(.5, 1.75,                        # Add text at same point
  labels = "adj = c(.5, .5) \n srt = 90",
  srt = 90,                           # Rotate text 90 degrees
  adj = c(.5, .5))                    # Adjust position to center text
                                      #   (note this is also the default)

# Using the pos= option
points(1.25, 1.5, pch = 18)          # Add diamond-shaped point
text(1.25, 1.5,                       # Add text at same point
  labels = "pos = 1",                 # Text to add
  pos = 1)                            # Set to bottom centered (1)
```

```
text(1.25, 1.5,                         # Add text at same point
  labels = "pos = 2",                   # Text to add
  pos = 2)                              # Set position to left (2)

text(1.25, 1.5,                         # Add text at same point
  labels = "pos = 3",                   # Text to add
  pos = 3)                              # Set position to top centered (3)

text(1.25, 1.5,                         # Add text at same point
  labels = "pos = 4",                   # Text to add
  pos = 4)                              # Set position to right (4)

# Using xpd= to go outside the plot area
text(.55, 0,                            # Add text at bottom of plot
  labels = "This uses xpd=TRUE to allow it to go outside the plot area",
  pos = 4,                              # Place text to right of point
  xpd = TRUE,                           # Set xpd=TRUE to allow
  font = 3)                             # Set font to italic

# plotmath expression
text(2.5, .75,                          # Add an expression w/plotmath
  labels = expression(Phi(italic(x))    # Build the expression
    = over(1, sigma * sqrt(2 * pi)) *
    italic(e)^ -over((x - mu)^2, 2 * sigma^2)),
  srt = 45,                             # Set at 45 degree angle
  cex = 1.25)                           # Increase size to 1.25

text(2.5, 1.75,                         # Add text for expression detail
  labels = "plotmath equation with \n srt = 45")

arrows(x0 = 2.5, x1 = 2.5,              # Add an arrow
  y0 = 1.5, y1 = 1.1,                   # y coordinates for arrow
  lwd = 3.5,                            # Set linewidth to 3.5
  col = "darkgray")                     # Set color to dark gray
```

And that should allow you to do almost anything with text that your heart might desire. In combination with the coordinates systems we learned in Chapter 13, text is easily placed anywhere in a figure. Building the more specific structures, such as legends and axes, is a little more tricky. But the same core principles are at work in all the text operations.

Moving beyond text, we are now ready for the final approach to customization, which is the use of customized shape elements: the lines, shapes, and images that give us full control over R's graphic output.

CHAPTER **15**

R GRAPHICS IV

THE FUN STUFF—SHAPES

In addition to the joy of text, the other class of R graphics modifications are the custom shapes: the lines, symbols, polygons, and even images that can be placed on your plots either in specific ad hoc ways or in ways that are systematically determined by your data. As I'm sure you have come to expect by now, R gives you complete control over all of these elements. And once you have learned these techniques, these basic shapes can be combined such that the only limits to what you can put onto and into a graphic will come from the extent of your imagination, and maybe a little bit from your underlying artistic capabilities. We'll start by looking at the use of color.

◌ DOING COLORS

Just as we had to go through fonts before we could do much with text, we have to get through colors before we do too much with points, symbols, and shapes. Colors, happily, for our purposes are much more straightforward. On the other hand, as you may have noticed, this book is in black and white, which will make our discussion of colors a little awkward. You'll need to use your imagination a bit.[1]

---

1. You can find slightly more dramatic color versions of some of the plots at http://www.sagepub.com/gaubatz.

Colors are mostly set through the wide variety of **col** options. Here are the major color options that can be set either in the **par()** command or under the auspices of the various element commands:

col= is used whenever the element to which it applies is unambiguous. So within a **text()** or **box()** command, for example, it can only apply to one possible element. Where the element might be ambiguous, the more specific color instructions are used.

col.lab= sets the color of the axis labels.

col.main= sets the color of the main plot title.

col.axis= sets the color of the axis line.

col.sub= sets the color of the subtitle.

col.tick= sets the color of the axis tick marks.

bg= sets the color for the whole plot. There actually isn't a regular option to do the color for just the plot area within the axes. That requires the extra step of setting up a rectangle with the coordinates of the plot area. (You can see this demonstrated in Figure 15.1.)

Specifying Colors

Colors are indicated either with RGB values or with a set of standard character labels. RGB values are six-digit-long hexadecimal numbers that specify the mix of red, blue, and green to create any color. The first two digits indicate the intensity of red, the second two the intensity of green, and the last two the intensity of blue. Unless you are an artist or savant, that is probably not so useful. More helpful are the seemingly hundreds of Internet sites that provide color-hex code translations. Just search for "hex color table," and you'll find all kinds of resources for identifying colors by the RGB hex code.

The standard character labels are an easier way to specify basic colors. These labels cover 657 different colors, running from "aliceblue" to "yellowgreen." There are four shades of "chartreuse" and 99 shades of gray for those of you who are into that. You can display the complete list with the command **colors()**.

```
 [9]  "aquamarine1"      "aquamarine2"      "aquamarine3"      "aquamarine4"
[13]  "azure"            "azure1"           "azure2"           "azure3"
[17]  "azure4"           "beige"            "bisque"           "bisque1"
[21]  "bisque2"          "bisque3"          "bisque4"          "black"
[25]  "blanchedalmond"   "blue"             "blue1"            "blue2"
[29]  "blue3"            "blue4"            "blueviolet"       "brown"
[33]  "brown1"           "brown2"           "brown3"           "brown4"
[37]  "burlywood"        "burlywood1"       "burlywood2"       "burlywood3"
[41]  "burlywood4"       "cadetblue"        "cadetblue1"       "cadetblue2"
[45]  "cadetblue3"       "cadetblue4"       "chartreuse"       "chartreuse1"

...

[617] "steelblue2"       "steelblue3"       "steelblue4"       "tan"
[621] "tan1"             "tan2"             "tan3"             "tan4"
[625] "thistle"          "thistle1"         "thistle2"         "thistle3"
[629] "thistle4"         "tomato"           "tomato1"          "tomato2"
[633] "tomato3"          "tomato4"          "turquoise"        "turquoise1"
[637] "turquoise2"       "turquoise3"       "turquoise4"       "violet"
[641] "violetred"        "violetred1"       "violetred2"       "violetred3"
[645] "violetred4"       "wheat"            "wheat1"           "wheat2"
[649] "wheat3"           "wheat4"           "whitesmoke"       "yellow"
[653] "yellow1"          "yellow2"          "yellow3"          "yellow4"
[657] "yellowgreen"
```

You can create groups of ordered colors for filling graphics using the **rainbow()**, **topo.colors()**, **terrain.colors()**, or **cm.colors()** commands. In each case, you provide the number of colors you want in the palette, and then R gives you what it thinks are a good selection of distinct colors.

For shades of gray, use the **gray()** command. This works a little differently than the other color palettes in that the input is a number between 0 (black) and 1 (white) that indicates how dark the shade should be. Conveniently enough, this can be spelled either **gray()** or **grey()**. You can use **gray.colors(n)** to generate a palette of *n* shades of gray.

Figure 15.1 attempts, somewhat pathetically in this black-and-white book, to demonstrate the use of the **rainbow()** color palette. **rainbow(8)** generates a palette of eight colors spanning the rainbow spectrum. These color values are then assigned systematically to the points in the plot according to the vector set up to correspond to the *y* values in the data. The argument for the **col=** option is a created vector with numbers 1 to 8, indicating which of the eight colors from the palette to use.

Figure 15.1 Using Colors

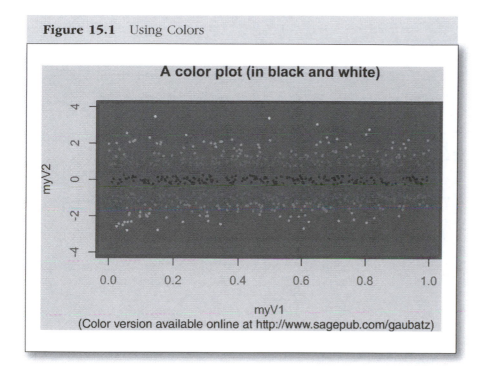

A color plot (in black and white)

(Color version available online at http://www.sagepub.com/gaubatz)

```
myV1 = seq(0, 1, by = .001)              # Set up some x values
myV2 = rnorm(myV1)                       # Y from random normal dist

# Here we will create a vector of integer values sorting myV2 which ranges
# between -4 and +4 into 8 values between 1 and 8. We'll then use these
# to select colors from a palette of 8 colors

myV2colors = abs(round(2 * myV2, 0)) + 1
```

```
par(bg = gray(.9))                       # Set plot background to light gray
plot(myV1, myV2, type = "n",             # Setup plot without points
   ylim = c(-4, 4),                      # Set y range
   main =                                # Set main title and subtitle
     "A color plot (in black and white)",
   sub = "(Color version available online at http://www.sagepub.com/gaubatz)",
   col.lab = "red",                      # Color for axis labels
   col.axis = "blue",                    # Color for axis and ticks
   col.main = "darkblue")                # Color for main title

rect(                                    # A rectangle w/plot area coords
   par()$usr[1],                         # left x value at usr[1]
   par()$usr[3],                         # Right x value at usr[3]
   par()$usr[2],                         # Bottom y value at usr[2]
   par()$usr[4],                         # Top y value at usr[4]
   col = gray(.5),                       # Set rect color to medium gray
   lwd = 8,                              # Border with line width 8
   border = "red")                       # Set border color to red

myPalette = rainbow(8)                   # Create a palette of 8 colors

points(myV1, myV2,                       # Add points to plot
   pch = 16,                             # Use solid circle
   cex = .5,                             # Set the points at half size
   col = myPalette[myV2colors])          # Set color based on myV2 value
```

Colors and Transparency

You can generate semitransparent colors with hex codes by adding two more digits so that the first six digits determine the color and the last two determine the degree of transparency. The first six digits are the same as indicated by **colors()**. The last two digits are called the Alpha Channel and run from 00 (fully transparent) to FF (fully opaque) (see Figure 15.2).[2] Alas, transparent colors are not supported on all output devices, so they may not work in all situations.

---

2. This is the hexadecimal scale. It runs 0,1,2,3,4,5,6,7,8,9,A,B,C,D,E,F for each digit. So 00 is the lowest value and FF the highest.

`Col = "#FF000050"` is a high-transparency red.

`Col = "#C0D9AFD0"` is a barely transparent lichen green.

Figure 15.2   Transparency

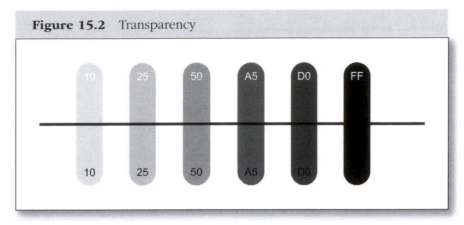

Note: The hexadecimal values running from 00 to FF determine the opacity of the color.

```
par(mar = c(0, 0, 0, 0))              # Set all margins to 0
plot.new()                            # New plot

abline(h = .5,                        # Add a horizontal line at .5
   lwd = 4)                           # Set line width to 4

segments(                             # Segments w/degrees of transparency
   x0 = seq(.1, .9, by = .15),        # The first x values for the lines
   y0 = .1,                           # The first y values for the lines
   x1 = seq(.1, .9, by = .15),        # The second x values
   y1 = .9,                           # The second y values
   col = c("#00000010", "#00000025",  # Black w/increasing opacity
      "#00000050", "#000000A5",
      "#000000D0", "#000000FF"),
   lwd = 40)                          # Line width = 40

text(                                 # Black labels for degree of opacity
   x = seq(.1, .9, by = .15),         # x values
   y = .1,                            # y value
   labels =                           # Text to show alpha channel values
   c("10", "25", "50", "A5", "D0", "FF"))
```

```
text(                                      # White labels for degree of opacity
   x = seq(.1,.9, by = .15),               # x values
   y = .9,                                  # y value
   col = "white",                           # Set color to white
   labels =                                 # Text to show alpha channel values
       c("10", "25", "50", "A5", "D0", "FF"))
```

All of the color palette functions we looked at in the previous section (**rainbow()**, **gray.colors()**, **topo.colors()**, **terrain.colors()**, **cm.colors()**) can also take an **alpha=** option, which sets the transparency level for that set of colors (set the value between 0 and 1, where 0 is fully transparent and 1 is opaque).

Now that we have done all the background work and have tackled the basic color issues, we can finally turn to adding points, lines, shapes, and images to a plot.

Ó CUSTOM POINTS

The points of a graph can be modified in three places: (1) you can change the default parameters through the **par()** statement, you can modify them within the **plot()** function, or you can add customized points after the plot has already been set up. You can also add multiple layers of points. Most of the basic principles are the same however you do it.

If you are going to customize the points after the plot has been set up, you'll need to turn off the points in the **plot()** statement itself. To create axes with no points, use the option **type = "n"** in the **plot()** statement. You are now set to add custom points with the **points()** function.

The **points()** function works a lot like the basic scatterplot process. You give it the *x* and *y* coordinates for each point and then tell it what you would like the points to look like. There are a number of choices for preset point shapes, which are accessed with the **pch=** option. Figure 15.3 shows the 25 built-in point shapes.

In addition to these symbols, you can use any single letter or number as a symbol. Just set **pch=** to the number or symbol. **pch = "g"** will plot

Figure 15.3 pch Symbols

0 =	□	13 =	⊠
1 =	○	14 =	☑
2 =	△	15 =	■
3 =	+	16 =	●
4 =	×	17 =	▲
5 =	◇	18 =	◆
6 =	▽	19 =	●
7 =	⊠	20 =	•
8 =	✳	21 =	○
9 =	⊕	22 =	□
10 =	⊕	23 =	◇
11 =	⧓	24 =	△
12 =	⊞	25 =	▽

Note: **cex=** is set at 1.5 to increase the size of the symbols by 50%.

gs, **pch = "&"** will plot ampersands. **pch = "3"** will plot threes. You can also provide a vector of different symbols and have R plot those. Figure 15.4 shows how this works.

```
plot(x = c(1:4), y = c(2, 4, 3, 4),     # Plot some x & y values
     pch = c("g", "&", "3", "H"),       # Assign alphanumerics to each point
     cex = 2,                           # Scale symbols to double size
     xlim = c(0, 5), ylim = c(0, 5),    # Set range of plot
     xlab = "X", ylab = "Y")            # Set axis labels
```

Figure 15.4   Plotting Text Symbols

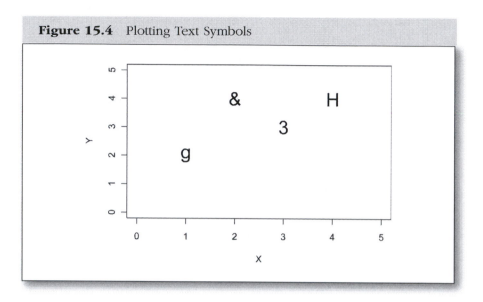

This only works for single letters or numbers. If, as would be perfectly reasonable, you want to plot whole words, you'll need to use the `text()` command, as discussed at the end of Chapter 14.

Another frequently useful modification to points is the `jitter()` function. If your data points are piling up on top of each other so that you can't see how many occurrences there are in any one place, jittering can move things around just a little bit so that you can get a better sense of the density. The main argument in the `jitter()` function is just the name of the variable you want to adjust. There are two other arguments that affect the amount of jitter, but R usually does this pretty well, so you probably won't need those.

Connecting the Dots

Points can be connected with lines by using the `type=` option. Here, I'm afraid, you again have to remember rather arbitrary letter codes for the types of connectors. `type = "p"` is just points, `type = "l"` is just lines, `type = "b"` is lines and points, `type = "s"` does stair steps, `type = "h"` is for vertical lines, and `type = "n"` suppresses the points altogether. Figure 15.5 shows each of these in action.[3]

---

3. The rather repetitive code for the six plots in Figure 15.5 can be found at http://www.sagepub.com/gaubatz.

Figure 15.5 Point Connector Types

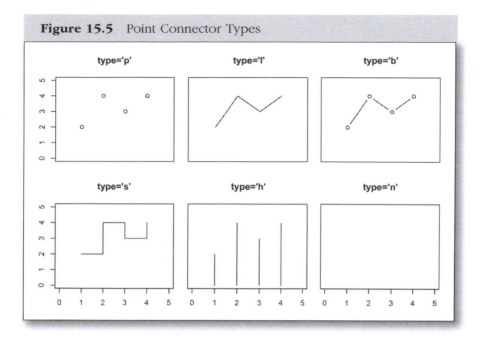

The connecting lines can be modified with all of the expected kinds of attributes, which we'll cover when we look at lines more generally in just a moment.

Plotting With **symbols()**

Another useful approach to plotting symbols is to use the **symbols()** command. This does circles, squares, rectangles, stars, thermometers, and box plots with characteristics that can be derived from your data set (e.g., the radius of the circle). So, for example, you can use *x* and *y* coordinates to locate the symbol, and then use a *z* value to determine the size of the symbol. The *z* values are assigned with the option for the kind of symbol. The Help menu gives the number of dimensions required for the different kinds of symbols. For example, the **circles=** option requires only one dimension for the radius of each circle. **rectangles=** requires a matrix with two columns, the first for the rectangle widths and the second for heights. The **symbols()** command sets up its own plot, unless you set the **add=** option to **TRUE**, in which case it adds the symbols to an already open plot. Figure 15.6 plots some circles and rectangles using the **symbols()** approach.

Figure 15.6 Symbols() Plots

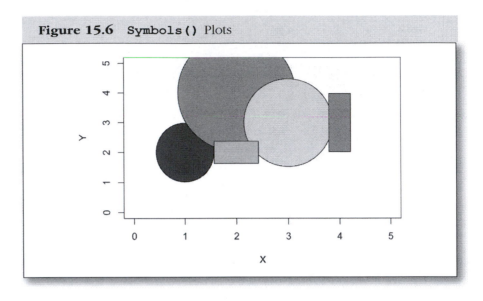

```
symbols(x = c(1:3), y = c(2, 4, 3),      # Set up some X and Y values
    circles = c(1, 2, 1.5),              # Circle radii
    bg = gray.colors(3),                 # Circle colors from gray palette
    xlim = c(0, 5), ylim = c(0, 5),      # Set range of plot
    xlab = "X", ylab = "Y")              # Set axis labels

myRect = rbind(c(1.5, .75),              # Set widths for 2 rectangles
    c(.75, 2))                           # Set heights for 2 rectangles

symbols(x = c(2, 4), y = c(2, 3),        # 2nd symbol plot X & Y coords
    add = TRUE,                          # Overlay on previous plot
    rectangles = myRect,                 # Add rectangles
    bg = c("lightgray", "darkgray"))     # Rectangle colors
```

ADDING LINES

There are two main commands for adding lines to a plot. The first, **lines()**, uses end points to define a line or a set of lines. The second, **abline()**, works with either a linear equation (i.e., $y = mx + b$) or for placing simple horizontal or vertical lines. We'll also look at three more specialized line commands: **segments()**, **arrows()**, and **grid()**.

Basic Lines

If you want to add lines connecting points or to place arbitrary lines on the plot, then **lines()** is the approach to use. The main driver for this command is the list of *x* and *y* values to connect. If you are putting lines between data points, you just run this like the **points()** function. For example, to put a line between coordinates (1,10) and (2,20), you would use **lines(x = c(1, 2), y = c(10, 20))**.

The two main controls over lines are the line type and the line width. **lty=** does the type of line. The usual things are possible here. **lty = 0** is no line, and **lty = 1** is a solid line. The higher numbers start various dashed or dotted line patterns. You can also specify the line type with a character string, as shown in Figure 15.7 (e.g., **lty = "dashed"**). If that isn't enough for you, it's actually possible to customize lines. Likewise, there are a set of more esoteric line controls that govern the ends of lines and how they are joined up. When you are ready for these, you are ready to tackle **help(par)**.

Figure 15.7 Line Types

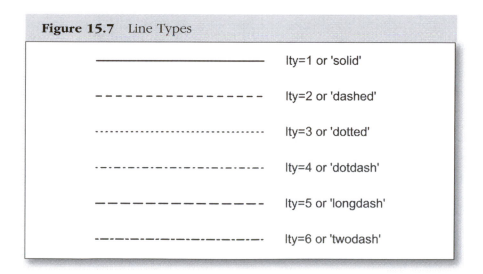

Line width is controlled with the **lwd=** option. The default is 1, and everything else is a multiple (or fraction) thereof.

To add horizontal or vertical lines, use **abline()** with the **h=** or **v=** options. **h=** gives the *y* values at which to place a horizontal line. **v=** gives the *x* values at which to place a vertical line. You can use either a single value to place one line or a vector to place a set of lines.

You can also use a regression model object to define the line (see Appendix B). If you have done a regression model and given it a name, you can plot the resulting line directly with the **reg=** option (see the code for line 5 in Figure 15.8).

As in Figure 15.6, the R default is for the lines to be constrained to the plot area. If you want to draw outside the box, you need to set the **xpd** parameter to **TRUE**. You can see this at work for line 4 in Figure 15.8.

Figure 15.8   Miscellaneous Lines Added Willy-Nilly to a Plot

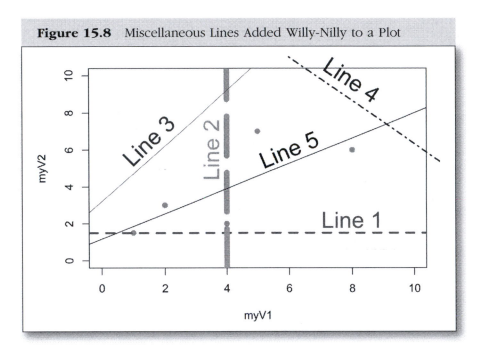

```
myV1 = c(1, 2, 4, 5, 8)                  # Some data to work with
myV2 = c(1.5, 3, 2, 7, 6)

plot(myV1, myV2,                         # A simple default scatterplot
   pch = 19, col = "darkgray",           # Solid point markers in darkgray
   xlim = c(0, 10), ylim = c(0, 10))     # Set range for x & y axes

# Line 1 - a horizontal dashed line
abline(h = 1.5,                          # Add a horizontal line at y = 1.5

   lwd = 3,                              # Give it a width of 3
```

```
  lty = 2,                          # Dash it all
  col = gray(.4))                   # Make it medium gray

text(x = 8, y = 2.2,               # Add label for line 1
  label = "Line 1",                # Label text
  cex = 2,                         # Set size to 2
  col = gray(.4))                  # Set color to gray .4

# Line 2 - a vertical line with long dashes
abline(v = 4,                      # Add a vertical line at x = 4
  lwd = 8,                         # Give it a width of 8
  lty = "longdash",               # Use long dashes
  col = gray(.7))                  # Make it light gray

text(x = 3.5, y = 6,               # Add label for line 2
  label = "Line 2",                # Label text
  cex = 2,                         # Set size to 2
  srt = 90,                        # Rotate text to vertical
  col = gray(.7))                  # Set color to light gray

# Line 3 - abline using coefficients
abline(a = 3.2,                    # Add a line w/ intercept = 3.2
  b = 1.5,                         #   and slope = 1.5
  lwd = .5,                        # Give it a width of .5
  col = gray(.2))                  # Make it dark gray

text(x = 1.5, y = 6.5,             # Add label for line 3
  label = "Line 3",                # Label text
  cex = 2,                         # Set size to 2
  srt = 44,                        # Rotate text
  col = gray(.2))                  # Set color to dark gray

# Line 4 - Line segment
lines(x = c(6, 12),                # x values for line segment
  y = c(11, 4),                    # y values for line segment
  lty = 4,                         # Dot-dash pattern
  col = gray(.1),                  # Make it dark gray
  lwd = 2,                         # Set line width at 2
  xpd = TRUE)                      # Allow outside plot area
```

```
text(x = 8, y = 9.75,            # Add label for line 4
  label = "Line 4",              # Label text
  cex = 2,                       # Set size to 2
  srt = -34,                     # Rotate text
  col = gray(.1),                # Set color to dark gray
  xpd = TRUE)                    # Allow to extend beyond plot

# Line 5 - A regression line
myReg = lm(myV2 ~ myV1)          # A simple regression model

abline(reg = myReg,              # Use reg model to define line
  col = "black")                 # Set color

text(x = 6, y = 6,               # Add label for line 5
  label = "Line 5",              # Label text
  cex = 2,                       # Set size to 2
  srt = 23,                      # Rotate text
  col = "black")                 # Set color
```

Figure 15.9 Line Segments

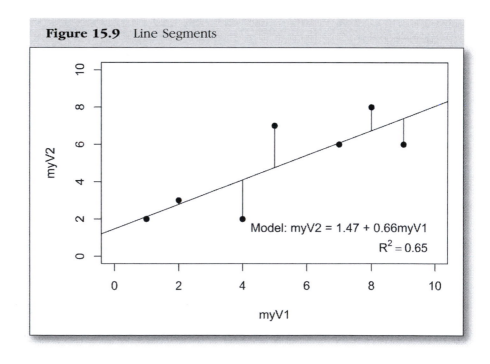

Line Segments

While the ability to add ad hoc lines willy-nilly to a plot is terrific, the real power of R graphics comes from systematic and data-driven modifications. Figure 15.9 utilizes the **segments()** function to systematically add line segments showing the errors in a regression model plot. It uses vectors extracted from the linear model function, **lm()**, to define end points for the line segments. Following up on our discussion of the **text()** function at the end of Chapter 14, note also how this figure does some slightly more exotic work with text, using the **bquote()** function to include the superscript for the R^2 label.

```
myV1 = c(1, 2, 4, 5, 7, 8, 9)          # Some data to work with
myV2 = c(2, 3, 2, 7, 6, 8, 6)

myReg = lm(myV2 ~ myV1)                 # A quick regression model

plot(myV1, myV2,                        # The scatterplot
   pch = 19,                            # Solid point markers
   xlim = c(0, 10), ylim = c(0, 10))    # Set range for x & y axes

abline(reg = myReg)                     # Use reg model to define line

segments(x0 = myV1, x1 = myV1,          # Add line segments from observed
   y0 = myV2, y1 = myReg$fitted.values) #   to fitted values

# Add model equation text to plot
# First paste together the model text
myModel = paste(                        # Paste together reg model as text
   "Model: ",
   names(myReg$model)[1],               # Get dependent variable
   " = ",
   round(myReg$coefficients[1], 2),     # Get y intercept coefficient
   " + ",
   round(myReg$coefficients[2], 2),     # Get slope coefficient
   names(myReg$model)[2],               # Get independent variable
   sep = "")                            # No space between paste elements
```

```
text(x = 10, y = 1.5,                # Add model to plot
   label = myModel,                  # The model as text
   pos = 2)                          # Right side alignment

# Get the R-squared value from the summary function
myR2 = round(summary(myReg)$r.squared, 2)

# Add the R-squared value to the plot
text(x = 10, y = .5,                 # Add R-squared value to plot
   label = bquote(R^2 == .(myR2)),   # Use bquote to paste elements
   pos = 2)                          # Right side alignment
```

Arrows

Another helpful line function is the **arrows()** command. This works just like **lines()** but includes an arrow head. In addition to the normal line format options, the **code=** option sets whether the arrowhead is drawn at the start of the line (**code = 1**), at the end of the line (**code = 2**), or on both ends (**code = 3**). As you can see from **help(arrows)**, you can also change the length and angle of the arrowhead lines.

If, like me, you sometimes like to use a solid arrowhead, you are out of luck with basic R. Take heart, however, as this limitation, along with my faint memories of trigonometry and vector algebra, affords an opportunity to draw on all that is good and noble in R to develop our own solid arrowhead function. The beauty of it is that once it is set up, you or anyone else can copy and paste it to use anywhere.

```
myArrow = function(x0, y0, x1, y1,   # Set up arrow function ------------+
   L = .25,                          # Default arrowhead length          |
   angle = 30,                       # Default angle of arrowhead        |
   code = 2,                         # Default arrowhead at x1,y1        |
   col = par("fg"),                  # Default color                     |
   ljoin = par("ljoin"),             # Default line joint style (0)      |
   lty = par("lty"),                 # Default line type                 |
   lwd = par("lwd"),                 # Default line width                |
   xpd = FALSE){                     # Default stay within plot area     |
```

```
                                    # Start function code           |
                                                                    |
    if(code == 1){                  # Reverse arrow direction        |
      tmp = x1; x1 = x0; x0 = tmp   # Switch x values                |
    }                               #                               |
    if(code == 1){                  #                               |
      tmp = y1; y1 = y0; y0 = tmp   # Switch y values                |
    }                               #                               |
#                                                                   |
#                                                                   |
# We need to control for the aspect ratio or for different x,y scales |
#   in setting up the arrow heads. We'll do that by translating the  |
#   usr parameter setting from the original x,y units to units based |
#   on the plot dimensions measured in inches. This will allow us to |
#   adjust the angles to account for different x and y scales. Note, |
#   however, that rescaling the plot after it is drawn will distort  |
#   the arrowheads.                                                  |
#                                                                   |
    X0 = (x0 - par()$usr[1])/(par()$usr[2] - par()$usr[1]) * par()$fin[1]
    Y0 = (y0 - par()$usr[3])/(par()$usr[4] - par()$usr[3]) * par()$fin[2]
    X1 = (x1 - par()$usr[1])/(par()$usr[2] - par()$usr[1]) * par()$fin[1]
    Y1 = (y1 - par()$usr[3])/(par()$usr[4] - par()$usr[3]) * par()$fin[2]
#                                                                   |
    oldusr = par("usr")             # Save original usr settings     |
    par(usr = c(0, par("fin")[1],   # Set up new usr settings based  |
               0, par("fin")[2]))   #   on plot dimensions in inches |
#                                                                   |
    t = angle * pi/180              # Convert angle degrees to radians |
    slope = (Y1 - Y0)/(X1 - X0)     # Calculate slope of line        |
    S = atan(slope)                 # Slope angle in radians          |
                                    #                               |
    M = ifelse(X1 < X0, -1, 1)      # Set a marker for X1 < X0        |
                                    # Set length of vector XA         |
    XA = sqrt((X1 - X0)^2 + (Y1 - Y0)^2)              #             |
#                                                                   |
```

```
# Get arrowhead vertices from rotated vectors                              |
    XC = X0 + M * ((XA - L) * cos(S) + L * tan(t) * sin(S))          #  |
    YC = Y0 + M * ((XA - L) * sin(S) - L * tan(t) * cos(S))          #  |
    XB = X0 + M * ((XA - L) * cos(S) - L * tan(t) * sin(S))          #  |
    YB = Y0 + M * ((XA - L) * sin(S) + L * tan(t) * cos(S))          #  |
#                           |                                              |
# Draw arrow line stopping at beginning of the arrowhead                  |
    lines(x = c(X0, X1 - M * L * cos(S)),                            #  |
       y = c(Y0, Y1 - M * L * sin(S)),                               #  |
       lty = lty, lwd = lwd,            # Apply line format options       |
       col = col, xpd = xpd,            #                                 |
       ljoin = ljoin)                   #                                 |
    polygon(x = c(X1, XB, XC),          # Draw arrow head                 |
       y = c(Y1, YB, YC),               #   at vertices                   |
       col = col,                       # Apply format options            |
       border = col,                    #                                 |
       xpd = xpd)                       #                                 |
    par(usr = oldusr)                   # Reset to original usr settings  |
}                                       # End of myArrow function ------------+
```

Figure 15.10   Plotting Arrows

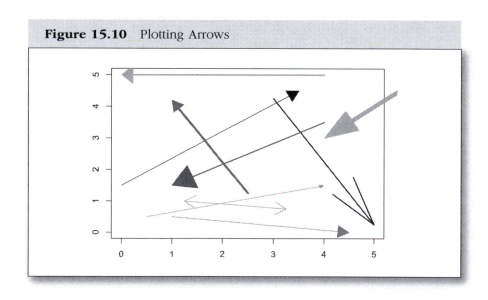

Figure 15.10 shows a variety of arrows, both R's native arrows and our spiff new solid arrows, in action.

```
plot(x = 0, y = 0, type = "n",      # Set up a blank plot
   xlim = c(0, 5), ylim = c(0, 5),   # Define x and y range
   xlab = "", ylab = "")            # Turn off axis labels

# Diverse arrows
arrows(x0 = 3, y0 = 4.25, x1 = 5, y1 = .25,
   length = 1, angle = 15, lwd = 2)
arrows(x0 = 1.25, y0 = 1, x1 = 3.25, y1 = .75,
   col = "darkgray", code = 3)
myArrow(x0 = 0, y0 = 1.5, x1 = 3.5, y1 = 4.5,
   col = "black")
myArrow(x0 = 1, y0 = .5, x1 = 4.5, y1 = 0,
   col = gray(.6))
myArrow(x0 = 4, y0 = 3.5, x1 = 1, y1 = 1.5, L = .5,
   col = gray(.4), lwd = 2)
myArrow(x0 = 2.5, y0 = 1.25, x1 = 1, y1 = 4.2,
   col = gray(.5), lwd = 4)
myArrow(x0 = 6, y0 = 5, x1 = 4, y1 = 3,
   col = "gray", lwd = 8, angle = 20, L = .75, xpd = T)
myArrow(x0 = 0, y0 = 5, x1 = 4, y1 = 5,
   col = "gray", lwd = 3, angle = 40, code = 1)
myArrow(x0 = .5, y0 = .5, x1 = 4, y1 = 1.5,
   col = "darkgray", lwd = 1, angle = 20, L = .1)
```

Grid Lines

Finally, it is often helpful to include grid lines to facilitate the identification of individual points. This, not surprisingly, is done with the grid() function. The main parameters for grid() are the number of vertical and horizontal partitions (nx= and ny=) and the usual options to describe the line type (lty=), color (col=), and width (lwd=).

The two central challenges with grid lines are, first, getting the number of partitions correct to ensure that the lines are coordinated with the axis tick marks. The second problem is that the little bit of extra space R provides on the axis line is included in the area that the grid lines partition. This means that unless you turn this feature off, they are almost certain to be misaligned with the axes. One simple fix for both of these problems is to leave **nx=** and **ny=** off, in which case, R automatically aligns the grid marks with the tick marks. If this happens to coincide with where you want your grid lines, then you are in great shape. Otherwise, you'll probably want to turn off the about 4% overage that R adds to the axes: Use the **xaxs = "i"** and **yaxs = "i"** options discussed in Chapter 14.

Figure 15.11 uses the **layout()** method to show three different approaches to grid lines. In the first plot, across the top, the vertical lines are turned off, and the *y*-axis is controlled with the **yaxs = "i"** option to be sure that the horizontal lines are properly aligned. The second plot, at the bottom left, sets up the grid with the empty **grid()** command, and thus shows the default settings. In that case, you can see that R automatically aligns the grid with the tick marks. The third case sets up a grid out to the edges of an empty plot. Instead of the default light gray dashed lines, it sets up solid black lines.

```
layout(matrix(c(1, 1, 2, 3),         # Set layout of 3 plots
    ncol = 2,                        #   organized as 2 columns
    byrow = T))                      #   and filled by row.

par(mai = c(.5, .5, .5, .25))        # Set the margin sizes

plot(0:10, pch = 19,                 # Plot 1 w/solid dots
    main = "Horizontal Lines",       # Title for plot 1
    xlab = NA, ylab = NA,            # Turn off axis labels
    yaxs = "i")                      # Eliminate y axis overage

grid(nx = NA,                        # Create a grid w/o verticals
    ny = 5,                          #   and 5 horizontal partitions
    lty = 1,                         # Set line type to solid
    lwd = 2,                         # Set line width to 2
    col = "gray")                    # Set color

points(0:10, pch = 19)               # Redo points on top of grid

plot(0:10, pch = 19,                 # Plot 2 w/solid dots
    main = "Default Grid",           # Title for plot 2
    xlab = NA, ylab = NA)            # Turn off axis labels
```

```
grid()                               # Add default grid on tick marks

par(mai = c(0, 0, 0, 0))             # Set margins to zero

plot(0:10, type = "n", yaxt = "n")   # Create an empty plot
grid(nx = 10, ny = 10,               # Add gridlines
  lty = 1,                           # Use solid lines
  col = "black")                     # Set color to black

par(usr = c(0, 1, 0, 1))             # Use usr par
text(.5, .55,                        # Add text at center
  labels = "An empty grid",          # Text to add
  cex = 2)                           # Set text size at 2
```

Figure 15.11   Grid Lines

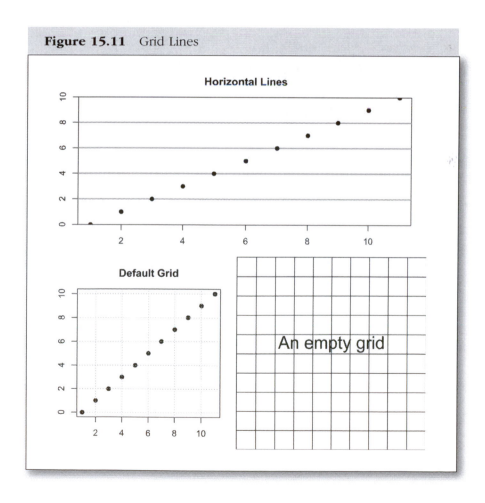

If you need more fine-grained control over setting up a grid, you can always use the **abline()** approach. This gives you more complete control over exactly where each vertical or horizontal line appears and how each line is formatted.

○ SHAPES

We have already seen how to do some basic shapes with the **symbols()** function. We can get more control over single shapes with the **polygon()** command. The basics of polygon drawing are pretty simple. *x* and *y* vectors contain the coordinates for the vertices (corners) of the polygon. The main options are about how you fill the polygons in. **border=** determines the color of the border. The usual kind of line type and width options (**lty=** and **lwd=**) determine the character of the border line. **col=** fills the shape with whatever color you choose.

It gets only slightly more complex if you want to use line shading instead of a solid fill color. **density=** sets the density of the shading lines in lines per inch. **angle=** sets the angle of the shading lines in degrees, going counterclockwise from the origin (i.e., starting at 3 o'clock on the clock face). The color of the shading lines is set by **col=** whenever the **density=** option has a positive value. Otherwise, **col=** does the fill color. You can't do both a fill color and shading lines in the

Figure 15.12   Filled Polygons

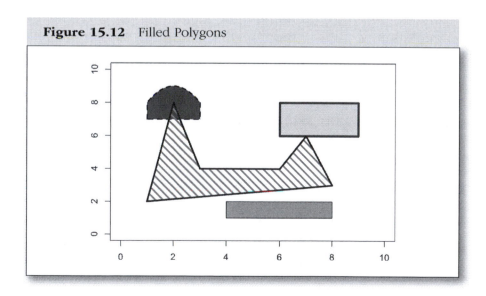

same command. For that effect, just repeat the **polygon()** command, first with the color fill and then with the shading lines. Likewise, if you use shading lines, the **lwd=** setting sets the width for both the border and the shading lines. If you want those to differ, you'll need to overlay two polygons with the different values (Figure 15.12).

```
# Some demonstration polygons

M   yX1 = c(1, 2, 3, 6, 7, 8)          # Set coordinates to work with
myY1 = c(2, 8, 4, 4, 6, 3)
myX2 = seq(1, 3, by = .001)
myY2 = 9 - (2 - myX2)^2
myX2 = c(1, myX2, 3)
myY2 = c(7, myY2, 7)

plot(x = 0, y = 0, type = "n",         # Set up a blank plot
   xlim = c(0, 10), ylim = c(0, 10),   # Define x and y range
   xlab = "", ylab = "")               # Turn off axis labels

polygon(x = c(4, 4, 8, 8),             # Set x & y values for rectangle
   y = c(1, 2, 2, 1),
   col = gray(.7))                     # Fill color

polygon(x = c(6, 6, 9, 9),             # Set x & y values for rectangle
   y = c(6, 8, 8, 6),
   border = gray(.2),                  # Add a dark gray border
   lwd = 4,                            # Line width 4 for border
   col = gray(.9))                     # Light gray fill for rectangle

polygon(myX2, myY2,                    # A polygon using preset points
   lwd = 2, lty = 2, border = "black", # Dashed border with line width 2
   col = gray(.3))                     # Fill color

polygon(myX1, myY1,                    # A polygon with preset points
   border = gray(.1),                  # Border color
   lwd = 3,                            # Border & shading width = 3
   density = 10,                       # Shading density = 10 lines/inch
   angle = 135,                        # Shading line angle = 135 degrees
   col = gray(.6))                     # Color of shading lines
```

The polygon shapes can be quite complex. Figure 15.13 uses the coordinates for the state of California extracted from a Google Earth .kml file.[4]

Figure 15.13   California Polygon

Data source: Google maps kml file, https://www.google.com/fusiontables/DataSou rce?docid=1mcFVaoy0cB0BREspeFhkPDzEhzpqS60yosAkpI0.

```
> CAshape = read.csv(
+    file = "http://www.sagepub.com/gaubatz/data/calif-coords.csv",
     Header = FALSE)

>

> summary(CAshape)                        # Show range of coordinates
        V1                   V2
  Min.   :-124.4    Min.   :32.54
  1st Qu.:-122.3    1st Qu.:33.78
```

---

4. The calif-coords.csv file contains two columns, one with the *x* values and one with the *y* values. When these are read it creates a matrix (CAshape) with the two default variables V1, and V2.

```
Median :-120.0    Median :35.31

Mean    :-119.0    Mean    :36.10

3rd Qu.:-114.6    3rd Qu.:38.08

Max.    :-114.1    Max.    :42.00

> plot(x = 0, y = 0, type = "n",     # Set empty plot

+    xlim = c(-125, -113),           # X range

+    ylim = c(32, 43),               # Y range

+    axes = FALSE,                   # Turn off axes

+    xlab = NA, ylab = NA)           # Turn off labels

> polygon(x = CAshape$V1,            # x, y values from CA coordinates

+    y = CAshape$V2,

+    col = gray(.8))                 # Fill color

> text(x = -117, y = 39.5,           # Position label

+    label = "California",           # Label text

+    cex = 2.5)                      # Set size to 2.5
```

Figure 15.14 shows the use of polygons to fill in a normal curve. It is a little more functional than Figure 15.12, but it is also bit more complex, as you will see in the following code, which is set up to allow for easy modifications to the test values.

Figure 15.14 Normal Curve Drawing

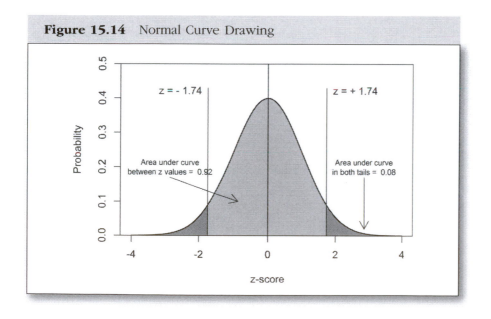

```r
options(scipen = 6)                     # Stop sci notation if <6 dec places

# Provided Values
mean1 = 3.35                            # First sample mean
mean2 = 3.09                            # Second sample mean
sd1 = 1.24                              # First sample std deviation
sd2 = 1.21                              # Second sample std deviation
n1 = 142                                # First sample size
n2 = 126                                # Second sample size

# Calculated Values

seBlend = sqrt(sd1^2/n1 + sd2^2/n2)     # Blended std. error
dMeans = max(mean1, mean2) -            # Calculate difference in means
  min(mean1, mean2)
z = (dMeans)/seBlend                    # Calculate t score
rangeZ = ceiling(abs(z)) + 2            # Set range for x values
rangeZ = ifelse(rangeZ < 4, 4, rangeZ) # Set minimum range of +/- 4

# Hypothesis test results
p = 2 * (1 - pnorm(z))                  # p value for 2-sided z-test
ptext = round(p, 2)                     # Version of p for annotation
OneMinusP = round(1 - p, 2)            # Version of 1 - p for annotation

# Graphing values
X1 = seq(-rangeZ, rangeZ, by = .001)    # Set up sequence of x values
Y1 = dnorm(X1)                          # Set up t curve values for each x
X2 = X1                                 # Second x to use for filling curve
Y2 = Y1                                 # Second y to use for filling curve
cd = data.frame(X1, Y1, X2, Y2)         # Join in data frame

# Plot components
plot(cd$X1, cd$Y1,                      # Plot normal distribution
  type = "l", lwd = 2,                  # Line plot with linewidth = 2
  ylim = c(0, .5),                      # Set range for y axis
  xlab = "z-score",                     # Add x axis label
  ylab = "Probability",                 # Add y axis label
  yaxs = "i")                           # Eliminate y axis overage

abline(h = 0)                           # Horizontal boundary line at y = 0
```

```
lines(x = c(z, z), y = c(0, .43))      # Add short vertical line at z
lines(x = c(-z, -z), y = c(0, .43))    # Add short vertical line at -z

# Set up borders of shaded regions
xz1 = which(
   cd$X1 == max(cd$X1[cd$X1 < z]))     # Find x just to left of z
cd$Y2[xz1] = 0                          # Set y for that x to 0
cd$X2[xz1] = cd$X2[xz1 - 1]            # Shift max x over for vertical line
xz2 = which(
   cd$X1 == min(cd$X1[cd$X1 > -z]))    # Find x just to right of -z
cd$Y2[xz2] = 0                          # Set y for that x to 0
cd$X2[xz2] = cd$X2[xz2 + 1]            # Shift max x over for vertical line

xz3 = which(
   cd$X1 == min(cd$X1[cd$X1 > z]))     # Find x just to right of z
cd$Y2[xz3] = 0                          # Set y for that x to 0
cd$X2[xz3] = cd$X2[xz3 + 1]            # Shift max x over for vertical line

xz4 = which(
   cd$X1 == max(cd$X1[cd$X1 < -z]))    # Find x just to left of -z
cd$Y2[xz4] = 0                          # Set y for that x to 0
cd$X2[xz4] = cd$X2[xz4 - 1]            # Shift max x over for vertical line

# Do shading
polygon(cd$X2[cd$X1 < z & cd$X1 > -z], # Fill for center region
   cd$Y2[cd$X1 < z & cd$X1 > -z],
   col = "light gray")                  # Set color

polygon(                                # Fill for left tail
   cd$X2[cd$X1 < -z],
   cd$Y2[cd$X1 < -z],
   col = "darkgray")                    # Set color

polygon(                                # Fill for right tail
   cd$X2[cd$X1 > z],
   cd$Y2[cd$X1 > z],
   col = "darkgray")                    # Set color

abline(v = 0)                           # Vertical line at x = 0
```

```r
# Add labels
text(x = z, y = .42, pos = 4,           # Add label showing z-score 1
   labels = paste("z = +", round(z, 2)))

text(x = -z, y = .42, pos = 2,          # Add label showing z-score 2
   labels = paste("z = -", round(z, 2)))

label1 = paste(                         # Annotation for area under curve
   "Area under curve\nbetween z values = ",
   OneMinusP)

label2 = paste(                         # Annotation for area in tails
   "Area under curve\nin both tails = ",
   ptext)

text(x = -rangeZ/1.4, y = .2,           # Add label for main pr region
   labels = label1,                     # Use text created above
   cex = .75)                           # Font size

arrows(x0 = -rangeZ/1.4, x1 = -z/2,     # Arrow from text to main pr region
   y0 = .17, y1 = .1,
   length = .15)                        # Set arrowhead size

text(x = rangeZ/1.4, y = .2,            # Add label for tails
   labels = label2,                     # Use label created above
   cex = .75)                           # Set text size

arrows(x0 = z + (rangeZ - z)/2,         # Add arrow from text to tails label
   y0 = .17,
   y1 = .02,
   length = .15)
```

◌ INCORPORATING IMAGES INTO PLOTS

It is possible to add images to your plots, but this requires the use of an additional package to translate other image formats to simple raster images. Some cautions are warranted, as this is an area that is somewhat device dependent. The R wizards don't yet have this working seamlessly across the different platforms (they're working on it). At this point, you are probably okay if you can avoid transparency or rotating the images. If you need transparency, the most likely working approach is to output the plot as a PDF and then extract the picture from the PDF (there are many web tutorials on how to do this). PDFs can be a nice approach in any case, because they are reasonably device independent. We'll demonstrate one of each here to show the difference with transparent images.

A raster image is just a matrix of color codes. We'll use the png package to import some PNG images as custom symbols in the raster format (Urbanek, 2013).[5] With these PNG images, I remove the alpha channel (doing so is only necessary to avoid a bucket-load of warnings) and then add the images to a chart. Note that you have to give the left, right, top, and bottom coordinates for each placement of the images. This means that you'll need to know the aspect ratio of the images you are working with. In Figure 15.15, I show a PNG plot drawing on data from Google's n-gram project to show the recent rise in the frequency of cat and kitten references relative to skull references in the Google collection of scanned English-language texts.[6]

Figure 15.15   Raster Images: Skulls Versus Kittens

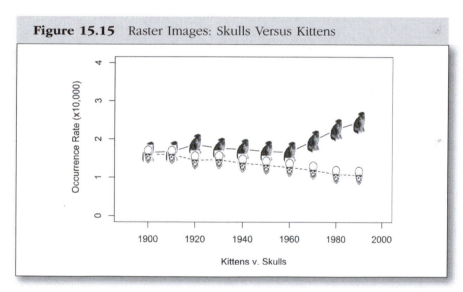

Sources: Data from Google ngrams project, https://books.google.com/ngrams; Kitten photo by Nicolas Esposito, untitled (http://www.fotopedia.com/items/picasaweb-5039223067638365090), used under CC BY 3.0 (http://creativecommons.org/licenses/by/3.0/).

---

5. Skull image is public domain from http://pixabay.com/en/head-skull-bones-weapons-skeleton-43605/ with modifications by KTG. Kitten is an image by Nicolas Esposito (Creative Commons attribution license) from http://www.fotopedia.com/items/picasaweb-5039223067638365090 with modifications by KTG.

6. The code for the PDF version is in the online R code file at http://www.sagepub.com/gaubatz.

```r
library("png")                          # Load the png library
                                        # Then read kitten & skull images
kittenPNG = readPNG("illustrations/kitten-BW.png")
skullPNG = readPNG("illustrations/skull.png")

skull = skullPNG[,,-4]                  # remove alpha channel
kitten = kittenPNG[,,-4]                # remove alpha channel

skull2 = as.raster(skull)               # Convert skull to raster
kitten2 = as.raster(kitten)             # Convert kitten to raster


# Some Data from Google ngrams showing average occurance of skull/s
# and kittens/cats averaged by decade. Decade/skulls/kittens
d0 = c(1900, 1.60, 1.65)
d1 = c(1910, 1.59, 1.67)
d2 = c(1920, 1.45, 1.86)
d3 = c(1930, 1.46, 1.76)
d4 = c(1940, 1.37, 1.73)
d5 = c(1950, 1.32, 1.68)
d6 = c(1960, 1.26, 1.66)
d7 = c(1970, 1.19, 1.96)
d8 = c(1980, 1.08, 2.26)
d9 = c(1990, 1.06, 2.45)

kdata = rbind(d0, d1, d2, d3, d4, d5, d6, d7, d8, d9)
kdata = data.frame(kdata)               # Combine into data frame
row.names(kdata) = kdata$V1             # Set years as row names
colnames(kdata)=                        # Set up column names
  c("Decade", "Skulls", "Kittens")

                                        # Create a png output file
png(filename = "illustrations/fig-15-15-images-plot.png",
  units = "in",                         # Set measurements in inches
  res = 1200,                           # Set resolution at 1200dpi
  width = 6,                            # Width at 6 inches
  height = 4)                           # Height at 4 inches

par(mar = c(4.2, 4, 1, 1))             # Set margin widths in lines

plot(x = kdata$Decade,                  # Set up background plot
  y = kdata$Kittens,
```

```
    xlim = c(1890, 2000),          # Set x range

    ylim = c(0, 4),                # Set y range

    xlab = "Kittens v. Skulls",    # Create X axis label

    ylab = "Occurence Rate (x10,000)",  # Create Y axis label

    type = "l")                    # Use lines without points

points(x = kdata$Decade,          # Add skull points

    y = kdata$Skulls,

    type = "l",                    # Connect with lines

    lty = 2)                       # Use dashed line

rasterImage(image = kitten2,       # Add kitten images

    xleft = kdata$Decade - 3,

    xright = kdata$Decade + 3,      # Left & right x values for kittens

    ybottom = kdata$Kittens - .3,

    ytop = kdata$Kittens + .3)      # Top & bottom y values for kittens

rasterImage(image = skull2,        # Add skull images

    xleft = kdata$Decade - 2,

    xright = kdata$Decade + 2,      # Left & right x values for skulls

    ybottom = kdata$Skulls - .25,

    ytop = kdata$Skulls + .25)      # Top & bottom y values for skulls

dev.off()                          # Ouput png file
```

The unhappy intersection of skulls and kitties in Figure 15.15 can be improved with transparency. Figure 15.16 allows for transparent images by outputting the plot as a PDF file and then extracting the image.

This brings us to the end of this summary of R graphics. Although it may seem a little incongruous coming immediately after a *USA Today*–style plot of kittens and skulls, a short sermon on aesthetics is an appropriate benediction as we wind up our time together.

A FINAL WORD ABOUT AESTHETICS

Although I have in no ways aspired to provide a complete overview of statistical graphing in this short discussion, no responsible discussion of

Figure 15.16   PDF Approach to Skulls and Kitties

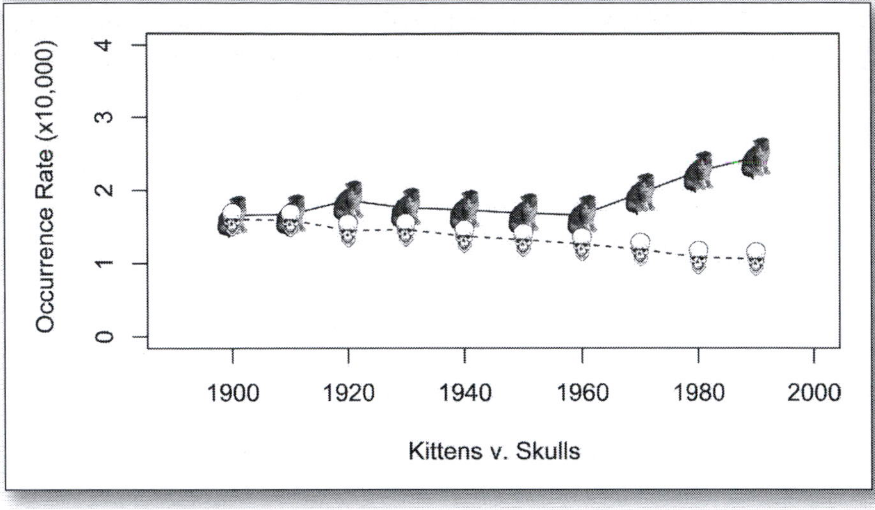

Sources: Data from Google ngrams project, https://books.google.com/ngrams; Kitten photo by Nicolas Esposito, untitled (http://www.fotopedia.com/items/pica saweb-5039223067638365090), used under CC BY 3.0 (http://creativecommons.org/ licenses/by/3.0/).

Note: This plot was done as a PDF (which allows for transparency). The plot image was then extracted from the PDF file and converted to a PNG file using Photoshop.

quantitative visualization should be allowed to pass without a word about the design elements. Just as having a sharpened pencil doesn't automatically make one an artist, having even considerable technical facility with R's powerful graphics engine doesn't automatically give one the aesthetic and design sense required to really produce stunning visualizations. If you have been blessed with that sense, I salute you. For the rest of us, it will be important to be exposed to high-quality graphics and to bind ourselves to some simple rules that can help us steer past the siren call of excessive ornamentation. If allowed only one word for both of these correctives, that would have to be "Tufte." Edward Tufte is the reigning guru of graphic design for quantitative analysis. His landmark book, *The Visual Display of Quantitative Information* (2001), is the essential guide in this field. You can get an introduction to his (admittedly sometimes overbearing) principles of design at http://www.tufte .com. The central Tufte principle is simplicity and maximizing the ratio of information to ink. A key to implementing this philosophy in the age of quick computer graphics is to remember that just because you can doesn't mean you should. The gratuitous use of three-dimensional elements, silly fonts, and cutesy clip art must especially be avoided. To its great credit, R is less prone to this clutter than the canned graphics produced by Excel and other such programs.

One final word that must bear these same cautions is that although almost everything you could want to do to a plot can be accomplished through R, once you have saved a plot in a standard format you can further modify it with almost any graphics editing or drawing program.[7] This adds a lot of flexibility but must be used judiciously as that flexibility comes at a significant cost in replicability.

---

7. For this purpose, SVG files are particularly useful, since the individual elements can be modified with an appropriate editor like the open source software Inkscape. Alas, SVG files aren't yet acceptable for Microsoft programs. If that is your working environment, then once modified in Inkscape or the like, you'll need to save them in another format, such as PNG or EPS.

CHAPTER 16

FROM HERE TO WHERE?

Having reached, at last, the end of the *Survivor's Guide*, you should have a pretty good grasp of the basic elements of R. You are now well prepared to tackle a very wide range of tasks using R for data management and graphics. The bad news is that there is still much more that you can learn. That starts, of course, with all the statistics that are the real purpose of R. There remains an important difference between knowing how to make R do something and understanding the statistical concepts themselves. Still, facility with a statistics program like R is necessary, even if not sufficient. The good news is that the skills we've gained here are highly transferable for working through the extraordinary variety of statistical procedures provided by R. Even as you begin exploring some of the more distant reaches in the world of R add-on packages, you will already have most of the R skills necessary for successful navigation.

Familiarity with the basic logic and procedures of R should equip you well for working through this additional material on an as-needed basis. By now, you should be pretty comfortable with accessing and interpreting R's native help pages. You should also be able to formulate appropriate web searches for specific help as you wade into the very large world of online R Help and move onto the narrowly focused resources for the more specialized tasks you may wish to undertake.

Chief among these more specialized resources are the vast array of R packages. In this book, I have worked through R with relatively minimal reliance on R packages. If you are going to go much further with R, you will soon find yourself relying on a number of R packages. I provide a very brief discussion and guide to some of the most popular packages in Appendix C.

Inevitably, the bottom-up nature of R package creation means that they don't all work the same way, but the basic structure is always there: a set of commands/functions with appropriate options and arguments to engage in specialized tasks. Every mature package has a set of help pages or a vignette setting out its functions and their arguments. Your understanding of the underlying logic of R and, critically, of the basic R object types will allow you to follow these explanations and make effective use of the power of R packages.

Of course, beyond the basic data management and manipulation functions, your abilities may still be limited by the rapid ascension of R packages into the stratosphere of statistical arcana. The ability to manage data sets, conduct some basic statistical analysis, and produce informative and effective graphics can carry you a long way in the modern information-based workplace. But the reality is that we do live in a world of increasingly sophisticated data analytics. In that world, the cutting edge is moving rapidly outward with the advent of computational statistics, which is exactly where R excels. You will have to decide how far you need to, or want to, pursue these technical capabilities, balancing against the likely need to acquire and maintain some areas of substantive expertise as well.

As you push forward, another area of skills to work on is the integration of R into a workflow process. While R works fine as a stand-alone program for statistical computing, the master R wizards have developed and utilize a range of tools to integrate R into the process of communicating analytic results. Three tools to which you might pay particular attention are Sweave/knitr, R Markdown, and shiny. Sweave is an R package that allows you to integrate R code into LaTeX documents so that report writing and data analysis are kept in sync (Leisch, 2002). knitr is a newer variant of Sweave and brings together several other utilities for R/LaTeX integration. In both cases, when your analysis is revised or your data are updated, the associated LaTeX documents change automatically. R Markdown, which comes from the makers of RStudio, works similar magic for web content. In contrast to LaTeX, which is a complex and rich language for document formatting, the Markdown philosophy is aimed at a minimalist framework of text styles and markup language for document creation. Finally, shiny, which also comes from the RStudio team, facilitates the creation of interactive R graphics on web pages.[1] I'm sorry to say that there are fewer tools for integrating R into document production for the large majority of users who rely on Microsoft Word. As the R world continues its rapid expansion, I expect that to come along at some point.

---

1. http://www.rstudio.com/shiny/.

If you aspire to a high level of R wizardry, you will want to subscribe to the R-bloggers list (http://www.r-bloggers.com). There are a lot of exceptionally creative and capable people out there pushing the R frontier and generously sharing their insights and methods. The R-bloggers website integrates their work into one place. You can read it online or subscribe to receive updates by e-mail. This will give you a daily dose of what is going on in the R world. In addition to being regularly astonished by the level of expertise and the expansive knowledge of R's internal idiosyncrasies, you will discover, incrementally, a vast range of relevant and valuable R knowledge.

The real bottom line is that, like so many other things, you learn R by doing R. Work on interesting projects. Do your coding carefully and in ways in which you can learn from it and reuse it. Try to spend a little extra time learning to do things more efficiently and elegantly to get past the tendency to fall back on the more unsophisticated brute-force approaches you may already have in your tool box. In this way, little by little, you will come to appreciate that you are really much more than an R survivor. You are in possession of a functional set of critical skills for the data work of the 21st century.

Appendix A

Installing R and Related Programs

Installing R is very straightforward. There are some ways to customize an R setup that range from the pretty simple to the quite complex; but for most users, this part of getting into R should be relatively painless. In this appendix, I will review the installation of R and then suggest a few small tweaks and a couple of helper programs that might make your R life a little easier. As straightforward as it all is, I should warn you that R is constantly being updated, and the new packages and auxiliary programs that are always coming online can introduce new wrinkles for the process.

Installing R Plain and Simple

The starting point is the World Wide Web headquarters for the R Project for Statistical Computing: http://www.r-project.org (R Core Team, 2013). From there, you will easily navigate to the Comprehensive R Archive Network (CRAN) under the Download section on the left menu. This will give you a wide range of repositories from which to download R. Navigate to one near you, and click on it. Then, choose your operating system (Linux, MacOS, or Windows), and click on that choice.

You'll now see before you several options to learn more about R: the installation FAQ (Frequently Asked Questions) and various things about news and changes for the latest version. If you are anxious to learn what's new in R, you can go to the Changes page to get the latest. You can find out, for example, that in Version 2.6 "the Lea malloc is now used by regex.c, src/extra/pcre and src/extra/xdr," which I'm sure will come as a great relief!

For Windows, you need to click on the latest setup program for R, which will have a name like R-3.0.1-win.exe. You will then have the option to save this file, and the computer will ask you where you want to do so. It doesn't really matter too much where you download it; just be sure you remember where you put it (the Downloads or temp folders are obvious candidates). When you run this executable file, it will let you set up the real R directory under "C:\\program files\R" or wherever else you ultimately want R to take up residence. This is about a 50 megabyte download, so if you are downloading from a dial-up modem in Naamche Bazaar, you'll want to step out for a spot of yak-butter tea while you are waiting.

Once you have downloaded the executable, you can just double-click on it to install R. Pretty easy. Then you'll face a set of installation questions of modestly increasing difficulty.

1. *The installation language:* I recommend choosing one in which you are reasonably fluent.

2. *The installation folder:* R will suggest "C:\Program Files\R\R-3.0.1", or the like. The last folder there indicates the R version number.

3. *The components to install:* You can do them all, which is the default, but if you have any space limits, you really only need either the 64-bit or the 32-bit version. Most reasonably new computers are going to use the 64-bit version. If you do install both, you will have the irritation of having shortcuts installed for both on the desktop. Just delete the 32-bit shortcut. If, as recommended below, you are using RStudio to access R, you can delete both shortcuts.

4. *Start-up options:* The defaults are fine. If you want to customize, here are the things you can do:

   a. *MDI Versus SDI:* The issue here is whether you want R to run in one big window or in separate windows—that is, a graphics window, a console window, a help window, and so on. The former is the MDI (multiple-document interface) option, and the latter, separate windows, is the SDI (single-document interface) option. If you have a multiple-monitor setup, you may want to go for SDI so that you can open different windows on the different monitors. If you use RStudio, this won't make any difference because it is set up for just one large window.

   b. *Help style:* HTML Help will open in your web browser and use the usual browser interface.

   c. *Internet access—standard or internet2:* Unless you know you are on a high-speed internet connection, just go with the standard.

5. *Start menu folder:* Where will you look for R on your Start menu? The default is a new Start menu folder named "R."

6. *Set up where you want your icons—on the desktop or the quick launch bar, both, or neither:* This screen also associates RData files with R and saves the version number in the registry. Leave both of those checked.

That's it. You are off and running!

R EXTRAS

Actually, you are probably off at a slow walk, at best. Indeed, your first experiences with R may be more akin to a slow drag across hot coals. But that is what this book is for. In the meantime, there are a few more ways to make it a little less painful at the start.

As you might hope and imagine, there are a number of people working on user-friendly graphical user interfaces for R. Frankly, most of them are still somewhat disappointing. They are mostly in various states of underdevelopment that often require more user intervention than most R neophytes will be able to muster. They also have the tendency to just put off learning the basic R commands that are the key to unlocking the real power of R.

Instead of a graphical point-and-click helper, it is better to look for what is called "an integrated development environment." These are programs that are centered on an editor to help you write code and more interactively run your R scripts. My strongest recommendation for beginners at this moment is to use the RStudio interface. This is a very nicely integrated R development environment. It gives you a text editor in which to write your code and allows you to send commands directly from the text editor to R. It also keeps a running list of your current R objects and has a nice facility for managing graphics output and the R Help windows. It is available in Mac, Windows, and Linux flavors.[1]

_____

1. My own preference for programming is the Tinn-R editor, which I find a little nicer for spacing and indenting issues and for the color-coded parenthesis matching. JGR is another nice integrated development environment, which in my view has a superior object browser and R Help interface but a somewhat weaker code editor. There are several other available editors that have sometimes quite passionate adherents. People who write code all day every day often gravitate toward the ESS version of Emacs, which is exceedingly powerful once you have memorized a few hundred of its 2,000 commands.

You can download RStudio from http://www.rstudio.org. Run the setup wizard, answer a few simple questions, and you are ready to go. If R is already installed on your computer, it will get itself connected. You then just start RStudio to open up R. There is now an editor window, from which you can send highlighted groups of commands to R either by clicking on the Send button at the top right or by hitting Ctrl-Enter. You can run the whole command file with Ctrl-Shift-r.

Start-Up Configuration for R

If you want to change the default configuration for R, you can do so in several places. My recommendation is to focus on the file Rprofile.site, which you'll find in R's "etc" directory. There is also a start-up file called just "Rprofile" in the library\base\R directory. I would just leave that one alone. You can open the RProfile.site file with a text editor, including RStudio, and set any options or add any commands that you want to run every time you use R (you'll want to make a backup before you mess too much with Rprofile.site).[2]

You might, for example, have some specialized functions or standardized graphics formats that you always want to have available. You can just put these in Rprofile.site, and they will run every time you start R.

At the beginning, you should probably just run with R in its default configuration for a while. Get a sense of what irritates you, and then you can see if those issues can be addressed through Rprofile.site. For the purposes of understanding how customization works, here are a couple of examples of changes that you might want to consider.

As you'll see when you get into Chapter 4, R's default behavior is to change character data into factors rather than character strings when you use either the **`data.frame()`** or the **`read.table()`** function. Personally, I find that annoying and troublesome. If you do too and want to change it, you can include **`options(stringsAsFactors = F)`** in the Rprofile.site file. Be careful about the capitalization with that.

Scientific notation is a wonderful thing for studying atomic weights or the number of angels dancing on the head of a pin. For many fields, it is less necessary. You can tell R to be more judicious about scientific notation with the **`scipen=`** option. This is a number that tells R how many digits of

---

2. With Windows, you'll likely need to right click to choose the option to open your editor as an administrator in order to modify the Rprofile.site file.

precision are required before switching to scientific notation. I think 3 or 4 is a nice value. Just add **options(scipen = 4)** in your Rprofile.site file.

In my field in the social sciences, numeric precision is another sore point. It is never appropriate to talk about seven-digit precision when the data are coming from the United Nations. If you share my allergy to excessive precision in regression and other outputs, you can change the number of digits to display from the default of 7 down to 4 with the **options(digits = 4)** entry in your Rprofile.site file.

Adding these options to the Rprofile.site file makes them the defaults. You can always temporarily change any of these options just by issuing the same command with the new values from within your R session. That is sometimes a better approach since changing the defaults can reduce replicability. Changing how scientific notation displays shouldn't cause too much trouble. But there could be problems, for example, if you have **stringsAsFactors=** set to **FALSE** and you share your data and code with someone who is running R with the factory setting of **stringsAsFactors = T**.

R PACKAGES

Because the add-on R packages are something of a moving target, I have largely avoided them in this book. Nonetheless, as you get into R, you will start to find packages that are helpful or even necessary for your particular needs. A significant part of the power of R comes from the large number of add-on packages that users have developed for specialized analyses. You will start to discover these when you move into more esoteric statistical work. But there are also a number of packages that add to R's more basic capabilities and that are more widely used. I will discuss some of the more general and popular packages in Appendix C. Here, I just want to focus on the package installation process.

Downloading and installing packages is made relatively painless with the RStudio interface. The Packages menu in the lower-right window gives you the list of packages available on your computer and shows which are installed. You can load or unload packages simply by clicking the box next to them. You can download more packages with the Install Packages button at the top left of the Packages window.

As you might expect, the RStudio menu option is really just issuing a set of R commands to manage packages. Packages are managed through a two-step process: downloading them and then loading them into R. You can get a list of the regular R packages that are already available on your computer with the empty **library()** command. If it isn't already downloaded, you'll need to download the package with the **install.packages()** command. If you issue **install.packages()** without anything in the parentheses, it will take you to one of the R software repositories (CRAN mirrors) and show you a list of the thousands of packages that are available. Search through these, and then click on the desired package. It will be automatically downloaded onto your computer. If you already know the name of the package you want to install, you can just include it in the **install.packages("PackageName")** command. Many packages depend on other packages. When this is the case, the dependencies will also be downloaded or installed at the same time.

Once a package is on your computer, you can load it into your R session with the **library(PackageName)** function. Installing the packages is easy. Using them is sometimes harder and will require you to explore the additional help that comes with the package. An overview of the available help topics can be had from the R HTML Help facility. Click on Packages and then the package name.

It usually isn't necessary, but when you are through with it, you can detach a package with the **detach("package:PackageName")** function. You can use these commands directly in your R script if you want to ensure replicability.

```
install.packages("PackageName")
library(PackageName)
   .
   .
   .
detach(package:PackageName)
```

If you want to completely remove a package, you can do so with the **remove.packages("PackageName")** command.

To access the help pages for the functions available in a specific package, you can either go through the main help portal (**help.start()**) or directly open the help pages for the package with **help(package = PackageName)**. Packages often come with some additional help in a PDF document called a "vignette." You can see the vignettes available on your computer with the blank **vignette()** command. Better yet, use the

browseVignettes() command to open a webpage with links to the vignettes on your computer. Specific vignettes can also be opened with the **vignette("PackageName")** command.

If, like me, you are one of those poor souls who sometimes have to labor in an environment with restrictions on administrative rights on the computer, you'll need to take a few more steps. The problem here is that by default R wants to install the packages into the program files directory where R itself is installed, which is blocked for nonadministrators. You can get around this by creating a directory for your packages somewhere where you do have write permission. The **.libPaths()** function will give you a list of the paths where R searches for libraries. To add a new path to this list, while also retaining the current list, you can use the command **.libPaths(c(.libPaths(), "myDirectory"))**. Note that in specifying your new directory path you have to use forward slashes / rather than back slashes \.

UPDATING R

R is constantly under development, and new versions seem to come out a couple of times an hour. It's always tempting to upload the latest, assuming it will have fixed the many little irritations you have encountered when R didn't seem to understand what you were trying to do. In fact, these upgrades usually fix obscure bugs in obscure corners of the program. My recommendation is that if R is basically working for you, avoid the temptation to upgrade too often. When you do have to do so, it is a good idea to uninstall the old version before upgrading.

Whenever you update R, you will also want to update your packages using the **update.packages()** command to be sure that you have the latest versions. You can also get this from the Packages menu in RStudio.

RUNNING R AND RSTUDIO FROM A USB KEY

You can run R and RStudio from a USB key. Don't use the default options for the R installation, because you'll want to tell R not to set up a Start menu folder or a desktop icon and not to write anything to the Registry.

For RStudio, you'll need to install it on anther computer and then just copy over the RStudio directory to the USB key. The executable RStudio program file can then be found in the bin folder. You can create a shortcut on the USB key to get to it more efficiently.

APPENDIX B

STATISTICAL COMMANDS

Reasonably enough, most books on R have a dozen or so chapters on statistical procedures and a single chapter on getting R to behave. This book, which is meant to complement those, takes the opposite approach. My argument has been that working with R, managing your data, and producing effective visualizations are central to quantitative analysis, but these go largely untaught in most statistics classes. This book has been about those areas rather than about statistics per se. Nonetheless, all this stuff isn't worth much if you can't do some statistics once you get the data under control. To that end, I offer here a brief summary of the central commands that might be helpful for the kind of statistics you are most likely to encounter in an introductory class. These procedures, especially the descriptive statistics, can also be very helpful for getting an overview of your data and for assessing their integrity.

In demonstrating these basic commands, we'll draw on data from the datasets package, which is loaded by default when you start R. You can get a list of these data sets with the command **data()**. A more detailed set of descriptions is available through **help(package = datasets)**.[1] These data sets are useful for illustration, but they bypass the critical skills of finding and managing data relevant to your own substantive interests. They also tend to be about rather obscure phenomena. For example, let's start with a data set evaluating the effects of vitamin C on the growth of guinea pig teeth (Bliss, 1952). You can see what is in a data set with the **str(DatasetName)** command.

---

1. Details about each data set can be accessed directly with **help(DataSetName)**.

408

```
> str(ToothGrowth)
'data.frame':    60 obs. of  3 variables:
 $ len : num   4.2 11.5 7.3 5.8 6.4 10 11.2 11.2 5.2 7 ...
 $ supp: Factor w/2 levels "OJ","VC": 2 2 2 2 2 2 2 2 2 2 ...
 $ dose: num   0.5 0.5 0.5 0.5 0.5 0.5 0.5 0.5 0.5 0.5 ...
```

The data set has two numeric and one factor variable. We can learn from **help(ToothGrowth)** that the variable *len* is the length of the teeth. The *supp* variable is a factor indicating whether the vitamin C was given in orange juice or as ascorbic acid. The second numeric variable, *dose*, is the dose size. To make this data set a little easier to work with without my examples getting too cumbersome, I'm going to rename it "TG." The **dim()** command tells us that there are 60 rows (observations) and three columns (variables). I'm also going to add a character (as opposed to factor) version of the *supp* variable, so that we can see the effects of our different operations on that.

```
> TG = ToothGrowth                      # Shorten data set name

> TG$supp2 = as.character(TG$supp)      # Add character version of supp

> dim(TG)                               # Show data frame dimensions
[1] 60   4
```

UNIVARIATE DESCRIPTIVE STATISTICS

The first thing you are likely to learn in any statistics course is the descriptive statistics that give us an overview of a data set. R has many ways to do this, starting with the **summary()** function. **summary()** is a great example of the object-oriented nature of R. It provides different results that adjust automatically to what you give it. If you give it a single numeric variable, **summary(myVariable)**, it will give you the minimum, mean, median, and maximum (as well as the first and third quintiles). Give it a factor, and it will return the frequency count for each possible value of the factor. Give it a matrix or a data frame, **summary(myDataframe)**, and it will return those statistics for all of the variables, distinguishing between factors and numeric variables. As we'll see later, **summary()** is also used to provide the results from specific statistical models and other things as well.

```
> summary(TG$len)                     # Summary of a numeric variable
 Min.  1st Qu.  Median    Mean  3rd Qu.    Max.
 4.20    13.08   19.25   18.81    25.28   33.90

> summary(TG$supp)                    # Summary of a factor variable
OJ VC
30 30

> summary(TG)                         # Get summary of all TG variables
      len             supp          dose              supp2
 Min.   : 4.20   OJ:30    Min.    :0.500   Length:60
 1st Qu.:13.07   VC:30    1st Qu.:0.500   Class :character
 Median :19.25            Median :1.000   Mode  :character
 Mean   :18.81            Mean    :1.167
 3rd Qu.:25.27            3rd Qu.:2.000
 Max.   :33.90            Max.    :2.000
```

These descriptive statistics can also be invoked individually for each variable with the **mean()**, **median()**, **min()**, and **max()** commands.[2] You can also access standard deviation and variance with the **sd()** and **var()** commands, respectively.

```
> mean(TG$len)                        # Mean of numeric variable
[1] 18.81333
> median(TG$len)                      # Median of numeric variable
[1] 19.25
```

---

2. Sums and means can be created by the column for a matrix or a whole data frame with the **colSums()** or **colMeans()** commands, respectively. Remember the **apply()** functions as another approach to applying a specific function over a whole data frame at once (Chapter 7).

```
> min(TG$len)                    # Minimum of numeric variable
[1] 4.2
> max(TG$len)                    # Maximum of numeric variable
[1] 33.9
> sd(TG$len)                     # Std Deviation of numeric variable
[1] 7.649315
> var(TG$len)                    # Variance of numeric variable
[1] 58.51202
```

Note that standard deviation and variance are the sample (denominator = $n - 1$) rather than the population (denominator = N) statistics. If you want the population statistic, you will need to calculate it yourself.[3] (Sorry, think of it as a character-building experience.)

```
> popvar = sum((TG$len - mean(TG$len))^2/length(TG$len))
> popsd = sqrt(popvar)                  # Population standard deviation
> print.table(c("Sample variance: ",   # Here is printing with labels
+    round(var(TG$len), 2),
+    "Population variance: ",
+    round(popvar, 2)))

[1] Sample variance:  58.51    Population variance:  57.54

> print(c(sd(TG$len), popsd))           # Straight print without labels
[1] 7.649315 7.585303
```

For each of these descriptive functions, you have to be careful about missing values. If your data have missing values, you need to include the **na.rm = T** option to tell R to skip the missing values.

```
> TG$len[11] = NA                # Put in a missing value
> mean(TG$len)                   # If we take the mean we get NA
[1] NA
```

---

3. This will be a little more complicated if there are missing values. I've included that approach in the R code on the book's website (http://www.sagepub.com/gaubatz).

```
> mean(TG$len, na.rm = T)                    # This will do it for us
[1] 18.85254

> median(TG$len, na.rm = T)                  # Likewise for these other values
[1] 19.7
> max(TG$len, na.rm = T)
[1] 33.9
> min(TG$len, na.rm = T)
[1] 4.2
```

Interestingly, the **summary()** approach doesn't have the same problem with missing values. **summary()** also has the advantage of telling you how many missing values there are.

On the other hand, the **summary()** function does not include the standard deviation, so you will have to do that on your own. The **sd()** command (for standard deviation) only works on a single variable at a time, so you'll need to use an **apply()** function to apply it to a whole data frame. You can get all the standard deviations for a data frame with the **sapply()** function.

```
> sapply(TG, sd, na.rm = T)                  # Apply std dev to data frame
      len       supp       dose      supp2
7.6493152 0.5042195 0.6288722         NA
Warning message:
In var(if (is.vector(x)) x else as.double(x), na.rm = na.rm):
  NAs introduced by coercion
```

The **sd()** function doesn't like trying to work on character data, so it produces NA for the supp2 character variable, as well as that rather cryptic and unhelpful warning. Notice, however, that R was willing to provide a standard deviation for the factor version of the variable (supp). As discussed in Chapter 3, that is because R thinks about factors as the vector of index numbers, so you have to be careful about this. Remember also that **na.rm = T** is required if you have any missing values in your data frame.

It might be natural to think that a program as powerful as R would give you the mode of a distribution. In this, you are destined for bitter disappointment. Calculating the mode, it turns out, is more complicated than you might think. There are extensive debates about things such as using kernel density approaches for handling this, but as a neophyte, you will not find this too terribly helpful.[4] Here is a quick way to count the number of times each value of a numeric variable appears and then sort the variable in decreasing order by that count. The mode will then be the first value.

```
> mode(TG$len)                         # Object TYPE-not mode stat!

[1] "numeric"

> sort(sapply(split(TG$len, as.factor(TG$len)), length), decreasing = T)
 26.4 14.5 16.5   9.7    10 11.2 15.2 17.3 21.5 23.3 23.6 ...
    4    3    3     2     2    2    2    2    2    2    2 ...
```

To find the mode, we start by changing our numeric variable to a factor. Then, we count the number of times each value appears. Finally, we sort by that count in decreasing order to see the mode.

1. **as.factor()** *turns the numeric variable into a factor.*

2. **split()** *breaks the variable into individual vectors by the values of the factor.*

3. **length()** *counts how long each of the resulting vectors is.*

4. **sapply()** *applies the length function to each of those vectors.*

5. **sort()** *sorts the resulting lengths from the longest to the shortest* (**decreasing = TRUE**).

Another oddly missing first-semester statistics class function is the standard error. Standard errors can be simply calculated as the standard deviation divided by the square root of n. Here's how to do it, first without and then with missing values.

```
> # 1. Calculate standard error (no missing values in data set)
```

---

4. As we saw in Chapter 3, there is a **mode()** command in R, but that just tells you about the object storage mode.

```
> std.error = sd(TG$len)/sqrt(length(TG$len))

> std.error                          # Display standard error
[1] 0.9875223

> # Calculate standard error (missing values in data set)
> TG$len[5] = NA                     # Switch one value to missing

> std.error = sd(TG$len, na.rm = T)/sqrt(length(!is.na(TG$len)))

> std.error                          # Display standard error
[1] 0.9731314
```

These examples should serve as a reminder for why a broader set of R skills is necessary even to do relatively simple descriptive statistics.

Univariate Data Visualization

For the broader purpose of seeing the distribution of a variable, the R plotting facility is quite useful. **hist(myVariable)** gives you the quick distribution by quartiles. As shown in Chapters 13, 14, and 15, there are all manner of ways to fancy this up, but for now, you can just add a second variable indicating the number of breaks you want to use to divide up the data: **hist(myVariable, breaks = 10)**. If you don't provide the number of breaks, R uses its own algorithm to figure out a reasonable set of divisions. Even if you do provide the number of breaks, R takes that merely as a suggestion and will look for a number close to yours that also allows effective divisions.[5] Figure B.1 shows these default outputs.

```
par(mfrow = c(1, 2),              # Set for multiple plots
   mai = c(.85, .85, .25, .25))   # Set margins
hist(TG$len)                      # Default histogram: numeric var
hist(TG$len, breaks = 4)          # Histogram w/about 4 breaks
```

5. For example, if all of your data are whole numbers between 1 and 3 and you ask for five breaks, R is going to stick with just three bins. If you want to insist that R divide it up in different ways, you'll need to switch to **barplot()** as discussed in Chapter 12.

Figure B.1 Univariate Visualization

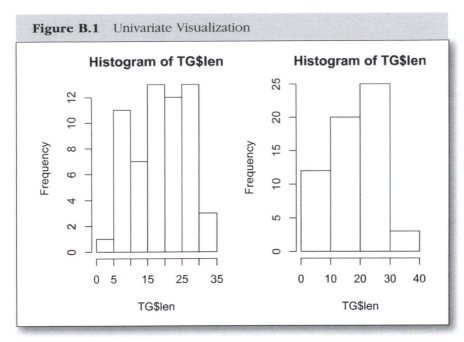

Data source: Built in R dataset on guinea pig tooth growth. Original source is C.I. Bliss, *The Statistics of Bioassay*, 1952. http://stat.ethz.ch/R-manual/R-devel/library/datasets/html/ToothGrowth.html.

Note: Both of these plots are simple default histograms. The plot on the right adds a parameter for the number of breaks to try to control the number of bins.

Histograms for factors can be produced with the **plot()** command, as shown in the first plot of Figure B.2. Here again, object orientation comes to the fore. The **plot()** command recognizes when its input is a factor and responds accordingly with a bar chart of the counts of the factor levels.

```
par(mfrow = c(1, 2),          # Set for multiple plots
  mai = c(.5, .5, .25, .25))  # Set margins
plot(TG$supp)                 # For factors just use plot()
boxplot(TG$len)               # Doesn't get any easier than this
```

In this example, we produce a simple default histogram for a factor, using the **plot()** *command. We also create a simple default box-and-whisker plot with the* **boxplot()** *command. In both cases, axes, titles, labels, colors, and the like can be extensively adjusted, as discussed in Chapters 14 and 15. See* **help(boxplot)** *for the specific box plot parameter options.*

Figure B.2   Factor Histograms and Box Plots

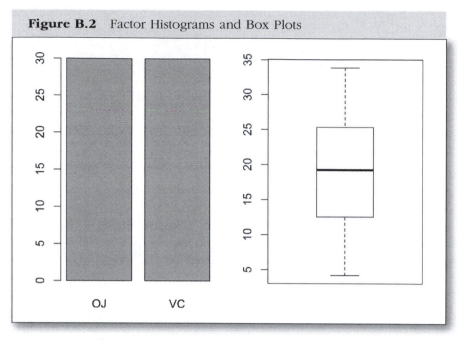

Data source: Built in R dataset on guinea pig tooth growth. Original source is C. I. Bliss, *The Statistics of Bioassay,* 1952, http://stat.ethz.ch/R-manual/R-devel/library/datasets/html/ToothGrowth.html.

Box plots can also provide a quick sense of a distribution. The **boxplot(myVariable)** command does the trick here. The second plot in Figure B.2 is the bare-bones version of a univariate box plot. The box shows the range for the middle 50% of the observations (the interquartile range). The darker horizontal line is the median, while the top and bottom lines show the farthest point that is still within 1.5 times the interquartile range. Any observations outside that region are potential outliers and are plotted as individual points.

As discussed extensively in Chapters 13 to 15, there are many options for customizing these plots to get them just how you want them.

BIVARIATE DESCRIPTIVES: MEASURES OF ASSOCIATION

Moving right along from single-variate descriptive statistics to multivariate measures of association, there are again several elementary R tools to be familiar with.

A basic correlation matrix can be produced with the **cor()** command. The default method is the Pearson correlation, which should serve your purposes. You can choose the Spearman or Kendall correlation if you are so inclined.[6]

cor() can't deal with nonnumeric data, so you'll need to remove the nonnumeric columns before using the function. If, for example, you have nonnumeric data in variables (columns) 1 and 4: **cor(myData[,-c(1, 4)])**, then more universally, you can use the somewhat ungainly **cor(myData[sapply(myData, is.numeric)])**.[7]

Presuming that by now your curiosity about guinea pig teeth has been largely satisfied, let's turn to the trees data set, which looks at the relationship between the girth, height, and volume of 31 black cherry trees (Ryan, Joiner, & Ryan, 1976). For the purpose of illustration, we'll just use the first 26 cases, and we'll add a character ID variable and a factor variable. Here is the basic data set with our modest modifications:

```
> str(trees)                          # Show structure of trees data
'data.frame':   31 obs. of  3 variables:
$ Girth : num  8.3 8.6 8.8 10.5 10.7 10.8 11 11 11.1 11.2 ...
$ Height: num  70 65 63 72 81 83 66 75 80 75 ...
$ Volume: num  10.3 10.3 10.2 16.4 18.8 19.7 15.6 18.2 22.6 19.9 ...

> myTrees = trees[1:26,]              # Use the first 26 observations

> myTrees$treeID = LETTERS            # Add a letter ID for each obs

> myTrees$even =                      # Add a factor variable for even
+   as.factor(c("even", "odd"))       #    and odd observations

> summary(myTrees)                    # Summary of new trees data

      Girth            Height         Volume          treeID          even
 Min.   : 8.30   Min.   :63.00   Min.   :10.20   Length:26       even:13
 1st Qu.:11.00   1st Qu.:71.25   1st Qu.:18.88   Class :character   odd :13
```

```
Median :11.55    Median :75.00    Median :21.80    Mode   :character
Mean   :12.26    Mean   :74.88    Mean   :24.68
3rd Qu.:13.78    3rd Qu.:79.75    3rd Qu.:30.62
Max.   :17.30    Max.   :86.00    Max.   :55.40
```

Now we can do the correlations, limited to the numeric variables. First, we'll be specific about excluding the character and factor variables. Then, we'll take the more generic approach, using R to filter the nonnumeric data.

```
> sapply(myTrees, is.numeric)          # Show which variables are numeric

Girth Height Volume treeID    even
 TRUE   TRUE   TRUE  FALSE   FALSE

> cor(myTrees[,-c(4, 5)])              # Correlation matrix for vars 1-3
           Girth    Height    Volume
Girth  1.0000000 0.3341642 0.9435812
Height 0.3341642 1.0000000 0.4655385
Volume 0.9435812 0.4655385 1.0000000

                                       # Generic numeric filter
> cor(myTrees[sapply(myTrees, is.numeric)])
           Girth    Height    Volume
Girth  1.0000000 0.3341642 0.9435812
Height 0.3341642 1.0000000 0.4655385
Volume 0.9435812 0.4655385 1.0000000
```

If, as is likely, you don't need accuracy out to six digits, you can enclose the **cor()** command within the **round()** function to make the printout a little easier to read: **round(cor(myData), 2)**.

Again, you have to be careful about missing values. There are several choices for how to handle them with the **use=** option. If you have missing values in your data set (and these days, who doesn't?), you'll probably want the **use = "pairwise.complete.obs"** option. That will give you the correlation for each pair of variables using the maximum number of observations available for that pair. The main alternatives are the default **use = "everything"**, which will give you an NA for any pair of observations that contains *any* missing values, and **use = "complete.obs"**, which will only use those observations that have no missing values for *any* of the variables. In the following example, we'll add some missing variables and then redo the correlations.

```
> myTrees$Girth[14] = NA              # Add some missing values
> myTrees$Height[3] = NA
> myTrees$Volume[21] = NA

> cor(myTrees[-c(4, 5)])             # Cor() chokes on missing values
        Girth Height Volume
Girth       1     NA     NA
Height     NA      1     NA
Volume     NA     NA      1

> cor(myTrees[-c(4, 5)],             # Trying to use every obs produces
+   use = "everything")             #   NA if either var has an NA
        Girth Height Volume
Girth       1     NA     NA
Height     NA      1     NA
Volume     NA     NA      1

> cor(myTrees[-c(4, 5)],             # complete.obs uses only those
+   use = "complete.obs")           #   observations that have no NA's
           Girth    Height    Volume
Girth  1.0000000 0.2274795 0.9374096
Height 0.2274795 1.0000000 0.3894619
Volume 0.9374096 0.3894619 1.0000000

> cor(myTrees[-c(4, 5)],             # Pairwise uses obs that are
+   use = "pairwise.complete.obs")  #   complete for each pair
           Girth    Height    Volume
Girth  1.0000000 0.2369017 0.9424047
Height 0.2369017 1.0000000 0.3949826
Volume 0.9424047 0.3949826 1.0000000
```

A bivariate plot is probably the first destination for getting a visual sense of a bivariate relationship. The **plot(myX, myY)** command produces a simple two-way scatterplot (Figure B.3). The regression line can be added by following that command with **abline(lm(myY ~ myX))**. As discussed in Chapter 15, if you want to make that line red, just add the **col=** option: **abline(lm(myY ~ myX), col = "red")**.

Figure B.3   Bivariate Scatterplot

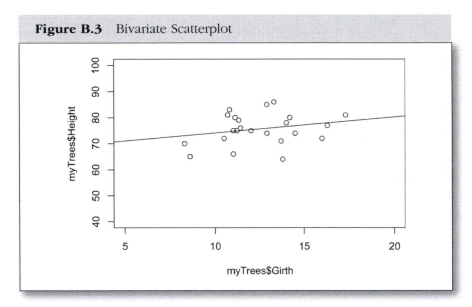

Data source: Built in R dataset on black cherry tree growth. Original source is T. A. Ryan, B. L. Joiner, and B. F. Ryan, *The Minitab Student Handbook*, Duxbury Press, 1976, http://stat.ethz.ch/R-manual/R-devel/library/datasets/html/trees.html.

```
plot(myTrees$Girth, myTrees$Height,      # Default 2-variable scatter plot
   xlim = c(5, 20), ylim = c(40, 100))  # Set axis lengths
abline(                                  # Add 2 variable regression line
   lm(myTrees$Height ~ myTrees$Girth))
```

Probably everyone's favorite quick view of associations is the plots produced by the **pairs()** command (Figure B.4). This creates a very nice matrix of bivariate plots of all the variables in a data frame. On the other hand, if you have too many variables, it will be a mess, so you'll want to select just some of the variables to appear in the **pairs()** parentheses. Again, Chapter 12 goes into more detail, and Chapters 14 and 15 shows some of the many ways to customize this display.

```
pairs(myTrees[-c(4, 5)])          # Pairs to produce bivariate plots
```

Figure B.4 A Pairs Plot

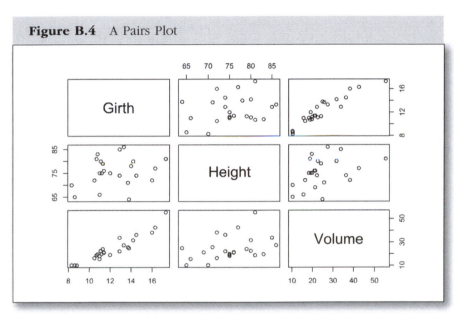

Data source: Built in R dataset on black cherry tree growth. Original source is T. A. Ryan, B. L. Joiner, and B. F. Ryan, *The Minitab Student Handbook*, Duxbury Press, 1976, http://stat.ethz.ch/R-manual/R-devel/library/datasets/html/trees.html.

HYPOTHESIS TESTING

If you are taking a first statistics course, you will likely be called on to do a basic hypothesis test. R facilitates this process in a number of different ways. The most basic is a *t* test, which is accessed with the **t.test(myVar1,**

myVar2) command.[8] For this demonstration, we'll fetch some data from the Internet. This is a set of data from the World Bank combined with information from the United Nations listing for the states that were early signers and adopters of the 1997 Kyoto Protocol, which sought to put some limits on carbon dioxide (CO_2) output.[9] The data and a codebook can be downloaded from the book website at http://www.sagepub.com/gaubatz.

```
edata = read.delim("http://www.sagepub.com/gaubatz/data/Appendix2Data.txt",
   colClasses =                     # Set column storage modes
      c("character", rep(NA, 8)),   #   1st col char, R chooses rest
   header = TRUE,                   # Use column headers for var names
   row.names = 1)                   # Use first column for obs names
edata$Kyoto = as.logical(edata$Kyoto) # Make signatory status logical obj
```

Our central interest is in the change in CO_2 output between 1998 and 2009. There are two significant outliers in this data set, Equatorial Guinea and the Turks and Caicos Islands. This is not the place for a digression into the philosophy of removing outliers, so suffice it to say that I've removed them from the data set.

```
> print(edata[which(abs(edata$dCO2) > 2.5), c("Kyoto", "dCO2")], digits = 2)
                          Kyoto    dCO2
Equatorial Guinea             0    22.7
Turks and Caicos Islands      0     4.9
> # Drop outliers
> edata2 = edata[which(abs(edata$dCO2) < 2.5),]
```

---

8. There is no z test in the base R package. You can get a **z.test()** command from the TeachingDemos package. It works just like the t test. Alternatively, you can easily calculate a z score ((observed mean − hypothesized mean)/(standard error)) and then use the **pnorm()** function to get the probability under the normal curve to the left of the z score. See the code for Figure 7.1.

9. The early signers were those states that signed the Protocol in 1998 and 1999. The United States is not included as a signer, since it never ratified the agreements. Canada is included, even though it withdrew from the Kyoto Accords in 2012.

This selects the countries with dCO2 values with an absolute value less than 2.5 (a 250% change up or down since 1998). Alas, it also shows how even seemingly simple tasks can sometimes take somewhat more complex R code.

We'll start by looking at the change in CO_2 output between 1998 and 2009, asking whether the mean change is different between the signatory and nonsignatory states. Before doing a *t* test, it is a good idea to check whether the variances are plausibly equal. This can be accomplished with the **var.test()** command, which computes the *F* statistic for the ratio of the variances for the two samples.

```
> edata$Kyoto = as.logical(edata$Kyoto)  # Make signatory status logical obj

> var.test(                              # Check variances to be sure
+    edata2$dCO2[edata2$Kyoto],          #   t-test is appropriate
+    edata2$dCO2[!edata2$Kyoto])         # This generates an F-statistic.

        F test to compare two variances

data:  edata2$dCO2[edata2$Kyoto] and edata2$dCO2[!edata2$Kyoto]
F = 0.6162, num df = 76, denom df = 109, p-value = 0.02575
alternative hypothesis: true ratio of variances is not equal to 1
95 percent confidence interval:
0.4092916 0.9422620
sample estimates:
ratio of variances
        0.6161645

>

> kCO2 = t.test(                         # Construct t-test to compare mean
+    edata2$dCO2[edata2$Kyoto],          #   change in CO2 output between
+    edata2$dCO2[!edata2$Kyoto])         #   signatories/non-signatories.
> kCO2                                   # Print results

        Welch Two Sample t-test
data:  edata2$dCO2[edata2$Kyoto] and edata2$dCO2[!edata2$Kyoto]
t = -1.6752, df = 182.521, p-value = 0.09561
alternative hypothesis: true difference in means is not equal to 0
95 percent confidence interval:
-0.24229571  0.01978168
```

```
sample estimates:

mean of x mean of y

0.1234593 0.2347164

> summary(kCO2)                                # Show elements in the t-test

          Length  Class    Mode
statistic  1      -none-  numeric
parameter  1      -none-  numeric
p.value    1      -none-  numeric
conf.int   2      -none-  numeric
estimate   2      -none-  numeric
null.value 1      -none-  numeric
alternative 1     -none-  character
method     1      -none-  character
data.name  1      -none-  character

> kCO2$statistic                               # Print just the t-statistic
         t
-1.675194

> kCO2$p.value                                 # Print just the p-value
[1] 0.09560852
```

We see here that the early Kyoto signatory states have had a change in CO_2 per capita that is about half that of the other states (0.12 vs. 0.23). Nonetheless, this difference does not meet the conventional .05 standard for statistical significance ($t = -1.7$, p value = .096).

In this model, we gave the test a name (kCO2). This allows us to recall the test or any of its elements. The results of the **t.test()** are contained in a list. The example then shows how in this context the **summary()** command shows the elements in the list that result from the **t.test()**. The t statistic alone is recalled with **kCO2$statistic**. Alternatively, if we weren't interested in retaining the results, we could have used the **t.test()** command alone to get the results immediately.

 ## CROSS-TABULATION

Another tool for bivariate analysis of two variables with categorical values is cross-tabulation. This test looks at how skewed the distribution of observations is in a table and asks how likely that degree of skewness is under the null hypothesis that there is no relationship between the row and column variables. The **xtabs()** command will do this for us. **xtabs()** uses a little different construction, with the **formula=** option set to the two dimensions of the table—denoted with a leading tilde (~) and connected with a plus sign (+). In the following example, I'll use the same data set about the Kyoto Protocol. In this case, we look at states with relatively good scores on a World Bank measure of "voice and accountability" (WBVA) in governance, that is, those governments that are considered more accountable to their citizens and provide more opportunities for citizens to express their views and preferences. We'll ask whether those states were any more likely to be early signers of the Kyoto Protocol than states that score relatively poorly on the WBVA metric.

```
> edata2$VA98 =                        # Create a dichotomous measure of
+    ifelse(edata2$WBVA98 > 0, T, F)   #    voice and accountability
> dkxtab = xtabs(                      # Crosstab 1998 VA and Kyoto
+    formula = ~ edata2$VA98 + edata2$Kyoto)
> dkxtab                               # Display cell values
              edata2$Kyoto
edata2$VA98 FALSE TRUE
       FALSE    73   23
        TRUE    30   54
> summary(dkxtab)                      # Display crosstab results (chi-square)
Call: xtabs(formula = ~edata2$VA98 + edata2$Kyoto)
Number of cases in table: 180
Number of factors: 2
Test for independence of all factors:
        Chisq = 29.764, df = 1, p-value = 4.879e-08
```

In this case, we can see that more open governments appear to have been more likely to sign up early for Kyoto ($\chi^2 < .0001$). In combination with our t test, which was about behavior in the period following the Kyoto Protocol signing, this is suggestive that the signing may have been more related to government openness than to attitudes about CO_2 output.

If you are working directly with a contingency table (i.e., you already have the frequency counts that go in each cell of a two-dimensional table), then you can just use the **chisq.test()** function. The principal argument passed to this function is the matrix with your cell values. In the example below, we re-create the crosstab analysis conducted above, but this time starting with the 2 × 2 contingency table. The **xtabs()** function we used earlier does not do continuity correction (i.e., adding or subtracting 0.5 to each cell to compensate for the step change in counts), while the default for **chisq.test()** is to do continuity correction. I have turned continuity correction off to allow for direct comparison of the results for the two examples.

```
> VAK = table(                  # Get table showing frequencies
+    edata2$VA98,               #    for high/low V & A and
+    edata2$Kyoto)              #    Kyoto signature status
> VAKtest = chisq.test(VAK,     # Chi-square test for matrix
+    correct = FALSE)           # Turn off continuity correction
> VAKtest                       # Display results

        Pearson's Chi-squared test

data:  VAK
X-squared = 29.7643, df = 1, p-value = 4.879e-08

> VAKtest$expected              # Show expected cell values matrix

           FALSE      TRUE
  FALSE 54.93333  41.06667
  TRUE  48.06667  35.93333
```

6 ANALYSIS OF VARIANCE

The analysis of variance (ANOVA) is a relatively generic method with many variations. This, not surprisingly, leads to some complexities. But in the context of an early statistics class, this methodology would most likely be used to do intergroup comparisons. The central logic of ANOVA is the comparison of the variation within each group with the variation between the two groups. If there is about as much variation within each group as between the groups, we can discount the possibility that there is a statistically significant difference between the groups.

We saw earlier that there wasn't a statistically significant difference between early Kyoto Protocol signers and nonsigners in terms of the subsequent change in their CO_2 output. We can ask the same question about economic growth. In this case, the economic growth variable (EG) measures the total change in gross domestic product (GDP) per capita over the same period from 1998 to 2009. If the variation between the signatories and nonsignatories looks a lot like the variation within the groups, then we would suspect that the early Kyoto Protocol signatories haven't been significantly penalized in terms of subsequent economic growth.

Before doing an ANOVA, we probably would want to look at the respective means. This can be done with the **tapply()** function to apply the mean function to the economic growth variable partitioned by Kyoto Protocol signatory status. There are missing values in the data, so we have to include the **na.rm = TRUE** parameter.[10]

```
> tapply(edata2$EG,          # Tapply mean() to Econ Growth
+    edata2$Kyoto,            # Partition data by Kyoto
+    FUN = mean,              # Apply mean()
+    na.rm = T)               # Remove missing observations
     FALSE        TRUE
  1.370871  1.259976
```

The **anova()** function can do the ANOVA analysis for us, although it is set up for comparing linear models, which adds a small additional step in the analysis. The **aov()** function does it a little more directly. One difference between the two approaches is that the results of the **aov()** function are displayed with a **summary()** function, while the results of the **anova()** function are displayed directly. At the end of the day, they both require about the same effort.

```
> myAOV = aov(EG ~ Kyoto, data = edata2) # ANOVA w/aov()
> summary(myAOV)                          # Display results
            Df  Sum Sq  Mean Sq  F value  Pr(>F)
Kyoto        1    0.54   0.5356    0.368   0.545
```

---

10. **tapply()** is discussed in Chapter 7.

```
Residuals   176 256.26  1.4560

10 observations deleted due to missingness

> myAnova = anova(              # ANOVA w/anova()
+   lm(edata2$EG ~ edata2$Kyoto))   #  analyzing a linear model
> myAnova                       # Display results
Analysis of Variance Table

Response: edata2$EG
                 Df  Sum Sq Mean Sq F value Pr(>F)
edata2$Kyoto     1    0.536 0.53557  0.3678  0.545
Residuals      176 256.258 1.45601
```

As you can see, both approaches produce the same results. In this data set, there is no statistically significant difference between the group of early Kyoto signatories and other states in terms of their subsequent economic growth ($F = 0.37$, $p = .55$).

A box plot is the traditional way to visualize an ANOVA analysis.[11] You can see worked-out examples of box plots in Figures 12.7 to 12.9. Figure B.5 shows a box plot for our current ANOVA.

```
boxplot(EG ~ Kyoto, data = edata2)     # Produce boxplot
points(1 + jitter(as.integer(edata2$Kyoto)), edata2$EG)
```

LINEAR REGRESSION

The core of any introductory statistics class is likely to be linear regression. Basic linear regression is very easy with R. The `lm()` command gets you started. This creates a linear model. To really take advantage of it, you need to give it a name so that you can recall and work with the results. The basic format for the material that goes in the command is a modeling statement built with the dependent variable followed by a tilde (~), and then a list of the independent variables connected by plus signs: `lm(depVar ~ indVar1 + indVar2 + indVar3)`.

11. The granova package provides some interesting and more sophisticated visualization tools for ANOVA analysis.

Figure B.5   A Box Plot

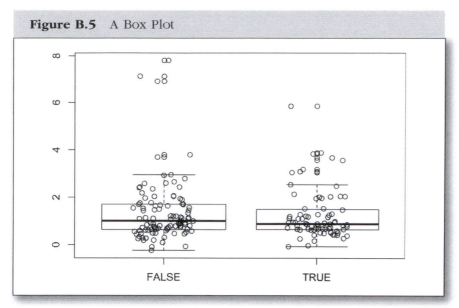

Data sources: Kyoto signatory status from UN, http://unfccc.int/kyoto_protocol/
status_of_ratification/items/2613.php; and GDP growth data from World Bank,
http://data.worldbank.org/indicator/NY.GDP.PCAP.CD.

Note: This box plot shows the difference in the distributions of economic growth
between 1998 and 2009 for those states that were not early Kyoto Protocol signatories and those that were. The economic growth variable is overlaid with jittering so
that it is easier to see the distributions (see Chapter 15).

In the following example, we'll use another World Bank development
indicator as our dependent variable. WBQR is a World Bank measure of the
quality of government regulation. It is an attempt to get at the business environment, with a particular focus on freedom from corruption and the ease of
starting and running businesses. Here, we'll just look at how that metric
relates to national wealth (GDP per capita) and the WBVA. It makes conceptual sense to use the natural logarithm of GDP, since we would expect a
bigger effect from a $1,000 increase in per capita GDP for countries with a
GDP per capita of $4,000 than in countries with a GDP per capita of $50,000.
Before running the regression model, we should check on the correlation
between our independent variables, since it is more than plausible that government accountability and GDP could be strongly related.

```
> cor(edata2$WBVA, log(edata2$GDPc),    # Check correlations
+   use = "pairwise.complete.obs")      # Use all complete observations
[1] 0.6198632
```

As expected, there is a relatively high correlation (.62) between the independent variables. This will inflate the standard errors and weaken the *t* tests. How big an issue that is depends on whether our purpose is more focused on assessing the individual coefficient effects or on the overall model fit. With that noted, we'll go ahead with building the regression model. We give the regression model a name, and then the results are stored as a list, which you can access with the **summary()** functions.

```
> myModel = lm(              # Set up a linear model with
+    edata2$WBRQ ~           #   quality of regulation as a
+      edata2$WBVA +         #   function of Voice/Accountability
+       log(edata2$GDPc))    #   and the log of GDP per capita
> summary(myModel)           # Show model results

Call:
lm(formula = edata2$WBRQ ~ edata2$WBVA + log(edata2$GDPc))

Residuals:
     Min       1Q    Median       3Q       Max
-1.66688 -0.25352   0.07719   0.33231   1.20302

Coefficients:
                   Estimate Std. Error t value Pr(>|t|)
(Intercept)        -2.61972    0.27677  -9.465  < 2e-16 ***
edata2$WBVA         0.43830    0.05021   8.730 2.38e-15 ***
log(edata2$GDPc)    0.30880    0.03182   9.706  < 2e-16 ***
---
Signif. codes:  0 '***' 0.001 '** ' 0.01 '*' 0.05 '.' 0.1 ' ' 1

Residual standard error: 0.4946 on 169 degrees of freedom
  (16 observations deleted due to missingness)
Multiple R-squared:  0.7258,    Adjusted R-squared:  0.7225
F-statistic: 223.7 on 2 and 169 DF,  p-value: < 2.2e-16
```

Not surprisingly, these phenomena are closely related. The overall model fit is measured with the adjusted R^2 of .72. About 72% of the variation in the quality of regulation is associated with the variation in the voice and accountability and national wealth. The voice and accountability and the quality of regulation are measured on the same 5-point scale, so we can see from the coefficient of .44 that when voice and accountability goes up by 1 point the quality of regulation goes up by a little less than 0.5 points. This effect is statistically significant with a p value well below .0001. Of course, as always in these analyses, these associations cannot by themselves prove causality.

There are whole books' worth of other things that can be done with regression modeling. Those books are out there, so here are just some things to look for.

If you plot your model output, **plot(myModel)**, you'll get a set of diagnostic plots, started off with the very important scatterplot of errors against fitted values. If you are using RStudio, you will want to include the **ask=F** option. This allows R to produce all four of the diagnostic plots without waiting for input from you. You can cycle through them using the forward and back arrows on RStudio's plot window.

You can get a complete list of all the available model elements with **attributes(myModel)**. Most important, you can access the regression residuals with **myModel$residuals** or with **residuals(myModel)**. **rstandard(myModel)** produces the standardized residuals from a regression model. Use **hist(myModel$residuals)** for a quick view of the distribution of the residuals. **qqline(myModel$residuals)** will generate the residuals quantile-quantile (QQ) plot, which is used to assess how well the data satisfy the normal distribution assumptions of traditional least squares regression. Predicted values are available either from **myModel$fitted.values** or **predict(myModel)**. **plot(myModel)** creates a nice set of diagnostic plots, including the residuals QQ plot (hit Enter to cycle between them). **step(myModel)** reworks your model using stepwise regression.

As discussed at the end of Chapter 11, you need to be careful about the role of missing values in your regression analysis. The regression tool automatically uses **na.omit()** to limit the analysis to those observations that have no missing values. Use the **na.action = na.exclude** option if you want **predict()** or **residuals()** to pad out the unused observations with NAs. Note that this doesn't change **myModel$residuals** or **myModel$fitted.values**.

ls.diag(myModel) generates several helpful diagnostic tools, including standardized residuals, a correlation matrix, and the standard errors of the coefficients, among others. The most straightforward way to access them is by saving the diagnostic output to a new name and then calling the subelements of that. Again, **attributes()** will help you work those particular names out.

```
> myDiag = ls.diag(myModel)               # set up model diagnostics
> attributes(myDiag)
$names
[1] "std.dev"    "hat"      "std.res"    "stud.res"    "cooks"    "dfits"
[7] "correlation" "std.err"  "cov.scaled"  "cov.unscaled"

> round(myDiag$correlation,2)             # Show correlation matrix
                   (Intercept) edata2$WBVA log(edata2$GDPc)
(Intercept)              1.00        0.61            -0.99
edata2$WBVA              0.61        1.00            -0.62
log(edata2$GDPc)        -0.99       -0.62             1.00
```

By necessity, this has only been a very brief review of the statistical power of R. Of course, statistics is what R does best, and it is best learned in the context of a statistics class and an R-based statistics book. Once you have learned your way around the basics of R and start getting used to the nature of the R Help facility, the huge set of other statistical procedures available as add-ons for R should be reasonably manageable. Finally, it is to R packages that we turn next. We covered the basic installation, care, and feeding of R packages in Appendix A. In Appendix C, we'll briefly touch on some of the more commonly used packages.

APPENDIX C

R PACKAGES

The discussion of R packages has been limited in this book.[1] This is mostly because the packages are a moving target, and once you get a handle on the R fundamentals, the packages are relatively straightforward to manage. At the moment in which I am typing these words, there are 4,970 R packages available. By the time you read this, I expect there will be many more.[2]

A lot of the power of R comes from the wide variety of packages developed for implementing or enhancing specialized statistical processes. These will be of great use when you get to that point. In the meantime, there are some packages worth mentioning as more important for the kinds of basic R usage and data management that we have covered in this book.

We'll start with some packages that help in data management, then turn to some graphics helpers, and end with a few other miscellaneous utilities.

DATA MANAGEMENT PACKAGES

Hadley Wickham is one of those certified R geniuses who has produced several of the most widely used packages on the planet. Two of his most popular data management packages are **plyr** and **reshape2**. **plyr** enhances the process of subsetting data sets and then applying other functions systematically across the subsets.[3] **reshape2** is used for managing data

---

1. I discussed the installation and management of packages in Appendix A.

2. You can get a complete list from the cran.r-project.org website.

3. See the website at plyr.had.co.nz. There is also a new version called dplyr that works more efficiently on data frames.

transformations that involve aggregation and transposition. The basic concept is to use the **melt()** function to disaggregate a data set and then the **cast()** function to rebuild it into the form you are looking for.

There are several great packages for working with missing data. **mi** and **mice** are packages for doing imputations to fill in for missing data. **VIM** is another package for imputation; it also includes a stand-alone graphical user interface and is particularly nice for missing-data visualizations.

As discussed in Chapter 9, if you are working with time-series data, you will likely need the **tseries** package. Other prominent packages in this area include **timeSeries**, which has more functions for financial data analysis, and **zoo**, which helps with irregularly spaced time series. **chron** is a package that tries to simplify working with dates and times. The R archive (CRAN) maintains a summary page on the many other time-series packages at cran.r-project.org/web/views/TimeSeries.html.

foreign is a critical package for translating to and from other file types. If you've got to get some data into or out of SPSS, STATA, SAS, and the like, this is what you'll need. As we saw in Chapter 8, **RCurl** can be very helpful for importing web data. As you get further into web scraping, you'll probably also find the **XML** package useful.

When you are ready to use SQL (Structured Query Language) database queries, you'll likely want to turn to the **RODBC** package. **SQLite**, **RMySQL**, and **sqldf** are other packages that can also help with connecting R to SQL database operations.

○ Graphics Packages

ggplot2, which also emerged from the mind of Hadley Wickham, is increasingly popular as an alternative approach to R graphics. It is built on the eminently sensible notion that there should be a generic graphics grammar defining plot elements (hence the name "ggplot").[4]

lattice is another alternative graphics system.[5] It is based on the Trellis graphics system developed for S, working from the visualization concepts popularized in Cleveland's book *Visualizing Data* (1993). It is particularly popular for graphics using subsetted data (Sarkar, 2008).

Geographic information sciences (GIS) is a rapidly growing area of data visualization and analysis. GIS started with a focus on geographic mapping but has expanded to a wide range of spatial phenomena. There

---

4. See http://ggplot2.org/.

5. See http://lattice.r-forge.r-project.org/.

are a lot of things going on here, but the central packages for managing geo-spatial data include **sp**, **maps**, and **maptools**.[6]

shape is a nice package that gives you more control over plotting various shapes, including ellipses, circles, cylinders, and the like. **png** is a package for reading in PNG files. As we saw at the end of Chapter 15, you'll need this package if you are interested in the judicious and aesthetically careful incorporation of images in your plots. **jpeg** and **tiff** are similar packages for JPG and TIFF files, respectively. **Cairo** is already the default graphics device on Macs. On PCs, you'll need this package to access Cairo devices and, particularly, to output SVG files.

MISCELLANEOUS PACKAGES

Hmisc is a package filled with a wide-ranging set of very useful utilities contributed by R-meister Frank Harrell Jr. from the biostatistics department at Vanderbilt University. It would require another chapter or two to go over all the different things **Hmisc** does. It can help with doing graphics, imputing missing values, making nicer tables, working with string variables, and a host of other things.[7]

texreg can produce publication-quality multiple-model comparison tables. **texreg** outputs to LaTeX or HTML. The HTML version can be leveraged for use in Microsoft Word or other word processor documents. Other packages that also produce nice model tables include **hwriter**, **xtable**, **memisc**, and **stargazer**. If you use LaTeX for text processing, you will also want to explore **knitr** and **Sweave**, which allow for interaction between R and LaTeX output. But if you do LaTeX, you probably already know that and much more.

Needless to say, this is but a tiny fraction of the corpus of R packages. If there is anything else you want to do, simply do a web search of it along with the words "R" and "package", and you will likely find that someone else has had a similar hankering and has already built the package to handle it.

---

6. I have provided some examples of using R for map data online at http://www.sagepub.com/gaubatz.

7. See http://biostat.mc.vanderbilt.edu/wiki/Main/Hmisc.

APPENDIX D

SOME STYLE GUIDELINES

Donald Knuth, in his seminal article on "literate programming," famously advanced the position that programming code has to be focused on human readers rather than on computers.

> Let us change our traditional attitude to the construction of programs: Instead of imagining that our main task is to instruct a *computer* what to do, let us concentrate rather on explaining to *human beings* what we want a computer to do. (Knuth, 1984, p. 97)

Writing your R programs with an appropriate and consistent style is more than just a matter of programming convention. A clean and effective programming style can help you, or others, see much more clearly what you are doing and can help avoid errors. R is relatively insensitive to program layout. For example, it sees the following two bits of code as equivalent, even though it is clearly easier for mere humans to make sense of the second.

```
# Example 1 - No white space and no comments

myVariable = c(1, 4, 6, 7, 9, 13, 15, 52, 62, 78)
popvar = sum((myVariable - mean(myVariable))^2/length(myVariable)); popsd =
sqrt(popvar); print.table(c("Variance: sample -", round(var(myVariable), 2),
"population -", round(popvar, 2)));print(c(sd(myVariable), popsd))
```

```
# Example 2 - White space & comments

# Create some data
myVariable = c(1, 4, 6, 7, 9, 13, 15, 52, 62, 78)

# Calculate population variance
popvar = sum((myVariable - mean(myVariable))^2/length(myVariable))

# Calculate population standard deviation
popsd = sqrt(popvar)

# Print results with labels
print.table(c("Variance: sample -",
    round(var(myVariable), 2),
    "population -",
    round(popvar, 2)))

# Print results without labels
print(c(sd(myVariable), popsd))
```

This is not the place for a comprehensive review of good programming practices. Programming style is an area of many strongly held personal preferences and, hence, of some surprisingly heated controversies. But it is worth discussing a few style elements that can be helpfully applied to R programming. There are other, more comprehensive R style guides out there—most famously, the style guide for R used internally at Google (2013).

MODULARITY AND PROGRAM STRUCTURE

As much as possible, you should break your program into manageable chunks with comments to make it clear what each chunk is doing. This approach is helpful both because it makes it easier to see what the program is doing and to track down bugs. Modularity also gives you discrete pieces that may be helpful for building other projects.

The overarching structure of the program should flow from top to bottom. Jumps to distant subroutines or functions should be minimized. Where such jumps are necessary, they should be clearly marked. Functions and subroutines that are referenced from a variety of places in your program should be grouped together in a marked-off section, probably either at the beginning or at the end.

The challenge in making a program modular is keeping straight what variables are defined within a given section and which ones have come from outside. These kinds of elements can be indicated in your comments and in a header for a given section.

ARGUMENT IDENTIFICATION

As discussed in Chapter 1, R has the uncanny ability to recognize the arguments passed to functions simply by their position. You can write `plot(myV1, myV2, "b")` because R knows that the first argument to the plot statement is the x values, the second is the y values, and the third is the plot type. R is clever this way, but you and others may not share this deep knowledge of argument order. Apart from a handful of obvious ones, it is probably better to use the specific argument labels: `plot(myV1, myV2, "b")` works fine for R, but `plot(myV1, myV2, type = "b")` will make it easier for you, or any other human beings who happen by, to understand what you were trying to do.

COMMENTS

As I have emphasized at several points, comments are critical for making the structure and functioning of your program code clear. This is important both for allowing others to understand what you have done and for helping you remember how and why you have done what you have. Making your intentions clear in the comments can also help you, and others, spot errors where your code does not agree with your intentions.

Excessive commenting is not considered good programming style. Good coding should speak for itself. This is an appropriate perspective for the world of professional programmers. The vast majority of R users are not professional programmers. They have a research focus somewhere else, and R is a tool for helping in that research.

Another common commenting rule is that comments should explain why you are doing something and not just repeat what you are doing. This, again, is fine advice for programmers who are fluent in the language. But for neophytes, communicating what you are trying to do can be as important as why you are doing it. As you become more fluent, you will need fewer comments. But others who come after you may still benefit from more copious annotation.

My recommendation is that if you are confident that you are going to become an R maven and are not going to need to share your code with anyone who has not attained a similar rank, then you can be parsimonious with your comments. For the rest of us, it's pretty much the more comments the better. R doesn't care how many comments you put in (it ignores them all).

There is also a strong principle that comments should not break up commands and functions. As you have seen, I do this throughout this book, breaking up functions across several lines and providing comments for each element of a function. This starts as a pedagogical tool. But I'll confess to doing this in my own coding as well. I find such heavy commenting useful because R statements can contain many options and can get quite complex. A more moderate version of this rule might be that your comments should be clearly distinct from your code. The decisive principle is to focus on readability.

As with all writing, knowing your audience is important. If your code will be read by people with a shaky handle on R, you need to provide more commentary. I will confess that I often forget some of the intricacies of R as fast as I learn them. For most of my R code, my audience is my future self, who I expect to return to a project a year and a half later having forgotten what I was trying to do and how I was trying to do it. Well-annotated R code can save you considerable grief when 5 years from now some graduate student or external reviewer has the temerity to ask you how you arrived at some important result.

Good comments are particularly important in collaborative work. Here again, they have to be targeted toward the least fluent team member. The team may well include an R expert and a subject matter expert, but clear and copious comments are more likely to help the subject matter expert catch slippage between intentions and implementation.

Finally, across all disciplines, there is an increasing emphasis on documentation and reproducibility of results. When your code is going to be shared with a broad audience, it behooves you to be sure that it is as accessible as possible.

WHITE SPACE

The judicious use of white space can make your project and its structure much clearer. R is indifferent to the number of blank spaces and line returns you include in a project (except for spaces inside quotation marks). So there is no reason not to use blank spaces and blank lines to help identify the structure of your project.

In the first place, you should use some blank lines to clearly demarcate the sections of a project. Readers should be able to see the discrete parts of your project. You can also use comment-based separators to help with this demarcation, but even then, some blank lines help the eye see the structure more clearly.

```
# Examples of section demarcation:

# ================================================

# ----------------< Function One >----------------
```

Indentation is equally important for providing a clear visual picture of the structure of your program. Use spaces to indent different elements and show nesting and program flow. Most important, when a single command flows over onto a new line, the continued material should be indented. RStudio automatically adds indention (frankly, not always in a helpful way).[1] Likewise, appropriate indentation can help identify where complex nested commands end. I mostly use nested double-space indentation. This makes the code a little more compact, which is a virtue given my tendency toward excessive commenting and the placement of comments on the same line as the code. A common and effective alternative is to indent continuing lines to align with and highlight the parenthetical structure of your code. These two alternatives are shown here:

```
# Double space indentation
myData = read.delim("myDataFile.txt",
  headers = TRUE,
  colClasses = c("character", "logical,
    "logical", "numeric", "factor",
    "character", "numeric", "Date")
  na.strings = "N/A")
```

---

1. RStudio tries to figure out your program structure to help with some indentation. If RStudio's indentation is acting up, it is probably because you have an unmatched parenthesis, brace, bracket, or quotation mark somewhere earlier.

```
# Parenthetical alignment indentation
myData = read.delim("myDataFile.txt",
                       headers = TRUE,
                       colClasses = c("character", "logical, "logical",
                                        "numeric", "factor", "character",
                                        "numeric", "Date")
                       na.strings = "N/A")
```

There is a surprisingly vigorous debate among programmers as to whether indentation should be done with spaces or with tabs. I'm somewhat partial to spaces because they keep your indentation scheme independent of the editor settings. Others prefer tabs because they are not independent of the editor settings. This allows the indentation scheme to change to meet the preferences of different coders. You can do whatever works best for you. Just be aware that you may be in for criticism from partisans on the other side.

PLACEMENT OF PARENTHESES AND BRACES

The appropriate placement of parentheses and the like is similarly contested. The important thing is to make your code more readable and to make unmatched parentheses less likely. For complex statements that appear within parentheses, brackets, or braces, the opening parenthesis, bracket, or brace should be placed on the same line as the statement. Some programming languages demarcate the end of the complex statement by placing the closing parenthesis or brace on its own line after the included elements. I would recommend doing this for curly braces, especially when they are closing a function. It probably isn't necessary for regular parentheses, unless you have a consistent problem with leaving the closing parenthesis off.

```
myFunction = function(x, y, z){        # Open w/ curly bracket on same line
   print("This function doesn't do anything")
}                                        # End w/ curly bracket on own line
```

Naming Conventions

Effective names can help make your program much clearer. In olden times, computer memory was expensive, and variable names were often limited to eight characters; many papers were published with statistical results reported using short and cryptic variable names like MGFTY or SMLPOPT. R, happily, is very flexible about long and compound variable names, as long as you don't get the capitalization wrong. The trade-off here is between long variable names and more unwieldy program text. So "*x*" and "*y*" can keep the written program very efficient when they are sufficiently clear. More often, it is worth taking a little extra space to make sure the variable name provides some useful clues as to what the variable is about. The bigger trade-off is with data frame names, since these can get tedious and unwieldy if you aren't attaching the data frame.

```
MyOverlyLongName.df$myVariable1 + MyOverlyLongName.df$myVariable2
```

Since there should be a limited number of data frames in your project, and their meaning should be relatively clear, the best approach is probably to err on the side of very short data frame names and longer and more meaningful variable names.

There are a number of different approaches to using variable names to help keep track of object types or other hierarchical dimensions. However you choose to use capitalization and periods (but not spaces or dashes) to help structure variable names, the important thing is to try to be reasonably consistent.

```
CalculateDeflatedValues.function
myDataframe.df
ThePriceOfGasInTunisia
GasPrice.lagged
```

R allows underscores in variable names: **this_is_my_variable**. Personally, I am unenthusiastic about this approach as it extends the length of the name, it disappears if anything is underlined, and people often read past them, so they can easily get lost.

The important thing is to be consistent and to pay attention to R's rules about case sensitivity and prohibited characters, while trying to provide the reader with as much information as possible about what is happening in your program.

THE BOTTOM LINE: CLARITY AND REPLICABILITY

An appropriate ending point for the final pages of this book is to emphasize the two overarching principles that should guide your coding style: clarity and replicability. Clarity means making sure that it is as easy as possible for others to understand what you are trying to make your R code do. Replicability, which depends to a significant extent on clarity, is about making sure that others can reproduce your results. To this end, it is important that, as much as possible, your data handling is done within R and in a systematic rather than in an ad hoc manner. Making it clear where the data have come from and what form they came in will contribute greatly to replicability.

While, admittedly, clarity is not necessarily one of R's native strengths, replicability most assuredly is. The struggle to accomplish clarity, then, is perhaps the more important of these virtues. Where there is clarity, replicability will follow.

REFERENCES

Allison, P. D. (2001). *Missing data*. Thousand Oaks, CA: Sage.

Cleveland, W. S. (1993). *Visualizing data*. Summit, NJ: Hobart Press.

Crawley, M. J. (2002). *Statistical computing: An introduction to data analysis using S-Plus*. Chichester, England: Wiley.

Forta, B. (2004). *Sam's teach yourself regular expressions in 10 minutes*. Indianapolis, IN: Sams.

Friedl, J. E. F. (2006). *Mastering regular expressions* (3rd ed.). Sebastopol, CA: O'Reilly Media.

Google. (2013). *Google's R style guide* [Online]. Retrieved from http://google-style guide.googlecode.com/svn/trunk/Rguide.xml

Kernighan, B. W., & Plauger, P. J. (1974). *The elements of programming style*. New York, NY: McGraw-Hill.

Knuth, D. E. (1984). Literate programming. *The Computer Journal, 27*(2), 97–111.

Leisch, F. (2002). Sweave: Dynamic generation of statistical reports using literate data analysis. In W. Härdle & B. Rönz (Eds.), *Compstat 2002: Proceedings in computational statistics* (pp. 575–580). Heidelberg, Germany: Physica-Verlag.

R Core Team. (2013). R: A language and environment for statistical computing. [Computer software] Vienna, Austria: R Foundation for Statistical Computing. Retrieved from http://www.R-project.org/

Ripley, B., & R Core Team. (2013). *R data import/export guide*. Retrieved from http://cran.r-project.org/doc/manuals/R-data.html

Robbins, N. B. (2004). *Creating more effective graphs*. Hoboken, NJ: Wiley.

RStudio. (2013). RStudio: Integrated development environment for R [Computer software]. Boston, MA: RStudio. Retrieved from http://www.rstudio.org/

Sarkar, D. (2008). *Lattice: Multivariate data visualization with R*. New York, NY: Springer.

Tufte, E. (2001). *The visual display of quantitative information* (2nd ed.). New Haven, CT: Graphics Press.

Urbanek, S. (2013). png: Read and write PNG images (R package version 0.1-5). Retrieved from http://CRAN.R-project.org/package=png

Urbanek, S., & Horner, J. H. (2012). Cairo: R graphics device using Cairo graphics library for creating high-quality bitmap (PNG, JPEG, TIFF), vector (PDF, SVG, PostScript) and display (X11 and Win32) output (R package version 1.5-2) [Computer software]. Retrieved from http://CRAN.R-project.org/package=Cairo

Watt, A. (2005). *Beginning regular expressions*. Indianapolis, IN: Wrox.

Data Sources

Bliss, C. I. (1952). *The statistics of bioassay*. New York, NY: Academic Press. (R internal data set "ToothGrowth")

Freedom House. (2013). *Freedom in the world*. Retrieved from http://www.freedom house.org/reports

Google. (2013). *Google Ngram data*. Retrieved from books.google.com/ngrams

Marshall, M. G., Gurr, T. R., & Jaggers, K. (2013). *Polity IV project* (Center for Systemic Peace). Retrieved from http://www.systemicpeace.org

Ryan, T. A., Joiner, B. L., & Ryan, B. F. (1976). *The Minitab Student handbook*. North Scituate, MA: Duxbury Press. (R internal data set "trees")

Stockholm International Peace Research Institute. (2013). *Military spending dataset*. Retrieved from http://www.sipri.org/research/armaments/milex

Transparency International. (2013). *The Corruption Perceptions Index*. Retrieved from http://www.transparency.org

World Bank. (2013). *World development indicators* (World Bank Open Data Project). Retrieved from http://data.worldbank.org

Main Index

Index of R Commands and Expressions

$SAGE research**methods**

The essential online tool for researchers from the world's leading methods publisher

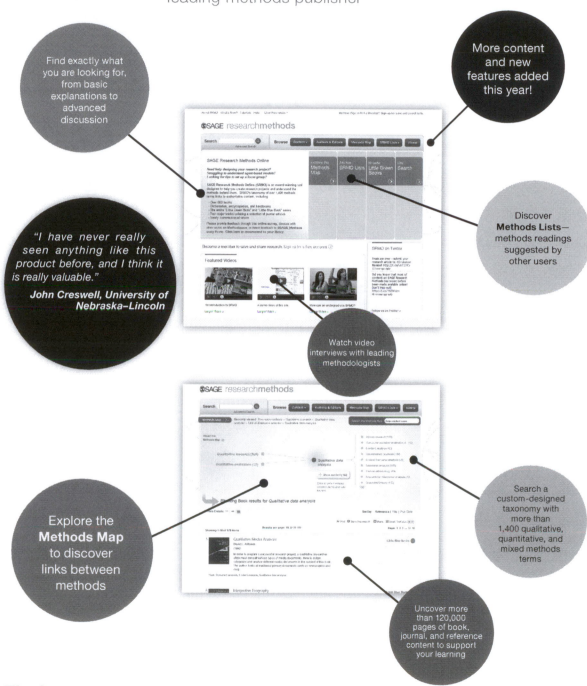

Find exactly what you are looking for, from basic explanations to advanced discussion

More content and new features added this year!

Discover **Methods Lists**— methods readings suggested by other users

"I have never really seen anything like this product before, and I think it is really valuable."

John Creswell, University of Nebraska–Lincoln

Watch video interviews with leading methodologists

Explore the **Methods Map** to discover links between methods

Search a custom-designed taxonomy with more than 1,400 qualitative, quantitative, and mixed methods terms

Uncover more than 120,000 pages of book, journal, and reference content to support your learning

Find out more at
www.sageresearchmethods.com

Made in the USA
Columbia, SC
21 January 2021